DEDICATION

This book is dedicated to Scotland's Regional and Island Councils 1975 -1996
for making so much of it happen.

COMMUNITY EDUCATION: THE MAKING OF AN EMPOWERING PROFESSION

Charlie McConnell has worked in community education since the early 1970's, in a community school, in action research and as a trainer in further and higher education. From the mid 1980s he worked across Britain on policy and practice development and from 1989-1993 on european programmes for the Community Development Foundation, working with the Council of Europe and OECD. In 1993 he returned to Scotland as Chief Executive of the Scottish Community Education Council. He is the author and editor of several books on community education and development.

Acknowledgements

The Scottish Community Education Council gratefully acknowledges The Scottish Office, Scottish and National Institutes of Adult and Continuing Education, Aberdeen University Press, Mainstream Publishing, Northern College, Strathclyde Regional Council, University of Nottingham, Penguin Books, Polygon, Routledge and Kegan Paul, Open University Press, British Comparative and International Education Society, Scottish Standing Conference of Voluntary Youth Organisations, Community Development Foundation, Principal Community Education Officers, Central Regional Council and Convention of Scottish Local Authorities. Crown copyright is reproduced with the permission of the Controller of HMSO.

COMMUNITY EDUCATION
THE MAKING OF AN EMPOWERING PROFESSION

CONTENTS

FOREWORD

KENNETH ALEXANDER

One way of approaching this excellent collection of material on the development of community education over the twenty one years since the publication of *The Challenge of Change* would be to ask is it coming of age when already past its sell-by date, or is the best still to come? Although I have not been able to read all of the contents I am reassured by clear signs that the concept of community education has survived (partly as a result of an exciting evolutionary process). It is also clear, however, that the delivery of the service is judged to have fallen short of what supporters feel should have been achieved, and this volume is particularly valuable in the suggestions for further development which are proposed.

One particularly encouraging feature is the wealth of attention and creative thought reflected in the thirty two chapters. When the committee which produced *The Challenge of Change* began its task there was no equivalent wealth of material we could turn to. Although I have recently suggested that so much has changed over the last twenty one years that it is time for a new official review of community education, this volume provides evidence that a dynamic process of review has been taking place, partly originating from national and local government, partly from non governmental bodies and partly from individual professionals. That is a useful reminder that a healthy sector within education is capable of performing the valuable function of self-review, from which much can be learned and on which progress can be built.

I doubt whether any member of the Committee which authored *The Challenge of Change* would be surprised that there has been a continuing debate about the linking of informal adult education with youth and community work. Our terms of reference were limited to informal adult education, and as Charlie McConnell writes in his stimulating editorial introduction our report recommended a merger without any detailed comment on "the state of the art or the potentialities of youth and community work". To have attempted this, without the authority to conduct a thorough examination of these services, was not possible, and I was surprised at the time that there was no direct challenge to our recommendation on the grounds that its foundations were unsound. Our motivation was to widen participation in informal education, but moving into the territories of others was a bold, and perhaps dangerous, suggestion. It is very encouraging to read that, although practice falls short of intent in some instances, there has been success in the objective of widening participation.

Such success has to be qualified by the concern that the educational element in the service can suffer as the price of achieving wider participation. On this, so much depends upon the casts of mind of the administrators and professionals in the service, which in turn depends on the education and training required for entry to it, and the purposes which politicians see as most desirable. I would argue strongly against rebuilding the fences which we recommended should be brought down, and urge that greater emphasis be placed on achieving the educational objectives.

On the perceived conflict within educational philosophy between emphasis on the individual and the group (family, community etc.) our report recognised that the success of all education depended on the response of individual minds, but that individual minds could benefit from collaboration with others and from developing a problem-solving approach to shared situations. For the origins of this approach, take David Hume's approach to how the reasoning of an individual is affected by the attitudes of a particular society and John Dewey's ... "the individual who is to be educated is a social individual, and the society is an organic union of individuals. If we eliminate the social factor ... we are left with only an abstraction; if we eliminate the individual ... we are left only with an inert and lifeless mass".

The extent to which community education should have links with further education, and how formal these links should be, is important and is given attention in this book. The new structure of local government provides an opportunity to re-think this relationship. As always in such cases the fears are that mergers can strengthen the position of some interests at the expense of others, fears which are accentuated in periods of financial cut-backs. It would be unfortunate if such new arrangements, with their potential for further widening of participation, were to founder because of the now largely discredited distinction between informal and vocational education. A dividing line seen by some within education as sharp and definitive is incorporeal to most students and to many employers. I doubt, too, whether there is any pedagogical theory or philosophy which would justify such a distinction. I believe it is in the interests of informal and community education to be within the expansive framework of education, and be financed as such. The healthy development of community education owes much to the approaches adopted by the local authorities established in 1975 on the basis of the Wheatley Report, and it is realistic to expect that this will continue when the new authorities take over in 1996.

Given such changes, the remarkable developments in community education over the last twenty-one years, and the opportunities now presented by the new technologies, it would be timely to have another *official* in depth examination of the roles of community education, its structure of provision and the sources of finance now appropriate. Change is dynamic and new challenges deserve the attention of fresh minds enriched by the experience of the many new facets of community education.

It is natural that I should be pleased at the idea of a publication timed to coincide with the twenty-first anniversary of *The Challenge of Change*, and even more pleasing when the book itself should be of such very high quality. I hope that other readers find it as thought-provoking as I have done, and that the concept and practice of community education is further developed with the help readers will derive from this excellent book.

COMMUNITY EDUCATION
THE MAKING OF AN EMPOWERING PROFESSION

PREFACE

Over the past twenty-one years, community educators have become established in Scotland alongside their more recognised cousins – school teachers and college lecturers. Using contemporary texts, this book traces the emergence of this occupation since the publication of the Alexander Report *'The Challenge of Change'* (which proposed the creation of Community Education Services by local authorities) and of the establishment of the authorities who made that proposal a reality, the Regional and Island Councils, in 1975. The book is aimed at a Scottish and a wider UK and international audience. In recent years educators south of the border and overseas have become increasingly interested in the Scottish model.

This volume embraces the period from 1975 to 1996. Texts have been selected from lists recommended by a panel of twelve readers, practitioners and trainers of community educators. Choices were made on the basis of policy, research and practice theory significance. All have been previously published and thus in the public domain and all are about Scotland. The final selection lay with the Editor on the basis of those recommen-dations.

The starting points for the book grew out of a belief that the Scottish experience was indeed significant and pacesetting. In no other part of the UK or Europe has the emergence of community education been so sustained or recognised. Our belief was that we wished to make available to a wider audience, as well as to the profession itself and those training to enter it, some of the influential texts that have shaped that profession and through them a greater awareness of the debates and choices made and an understanding of why it is as it is. This has a contemporary importance at a time when a further round of local government re-organisation in Scotland will test just how well rooted that provision is.

A second stimulus was that not merely were some of these texts now out of print, but that surprisingly this body of Scottish material was not being given sufficient attention in the very training institutions responsible for training professional community educators. Reading lists are dominated by non-Scottish material. This is not an argument for ethnocentricity or exclusivity, (Scottish community education has long been influenced by both English and non-UK writing), but rather to assert that there is a rich source of published material born of a Scottish experience and that this body of knowledge should be passed on. This experience is important not simply because Scotland has a separate education tradition from other parts of the UK, but because it highlights the more sustained role that local government has played through support for community development. There is an important lesson here for those concerned with tackling the needs of disadvantaged communities and with building an empowered learning society capable of addressing the challenges of the new millenium.

This is the story then of the part, albeit limited, that educators can play within local communities in empowering people, young and old, to deal with and to determine change. It is a story about the relationships between the state and the citizen and of the role of a state funded and encouraged occupation that has established a place not only within local government education services, but across other services and sectors. The rhetoric at least of community involvement, participation and empowerment is now part of the fabric of political consensus in Scotland and it is the community education profession that has developed many of the techniques that make this rhetoric a reality.

The selected texts fall into four types:

-   The first are national (ie Scottish) policy publications emanating from the Scottish Office, from national agencies and associations (governmental and non-governmental).

-   The second are regional (ie local authority) inspired or commissioned publications describing local government-led policies and strategies.

-   The third are research and evaluation studies examining different aspects of community education policy and practice.

-   The fourth are more polemical, reflective texts, including critiques of policy and practice and arguments for alternative methods and approaches.

The selected texts are not primarily case studies of particular community education programmes, issues or client groups, unless they were considered to illustrate a significant model that has had wider impact. Other volumes of Scottish case studies do exist and an extensive bibliography of these is currently being drawn together by the Scottish Community Eduction Council.

The texts do of course vary in style. Some are clearly more 'promotional' than analytical. The sources for the texts have been books, research and working party reports and journal articles. Other than the need to select extracts from what in some cases were quite lengthy publications, the original text stands. That said, for presentational purposes we have adopted a consistent design style.

There are many I should wish to thank for assisting with the production of the book. First and foremost the authors of the various texts. I am especially indebted to the selection panel of Ted Millburn, Colin Kirkwood, Chris Pilley, Ken McCulloch, Elizabeth Bryan, Alex Downie, Tom Schuller, Gerri Kirkwood, Ian Martin, Mae Shaw, Laurie Bidwell and Pat McMenamin and for additional advice from Duncan Kirkpatrick, Rowena Arshad, Vernon Galloway, Lyn Tett, David Wiseman and Rory McLeod. Thanks also to Carol Swan, Julie Wilson, Allan Hall, Maureen Quinn and Matthew Johnson for typing, designing and proof reading the text and to Natasha McConnell for support throughout. Finally I should wish to thank all those politicians, advisers, trainers, managers and fieldworkers in community education who have done so much to create a profession and public service of which we can be proud.

Charlie McConnell
March 1996

COMMUNITY EDUCATION – THE MAKING OF AN EMPOWERING PROFESSION

EDITORIAL INTRODUCTION BY CHARLIE McCONNELL

If I say that I am an educator, I suspect with some confidence that the image that has come to your mind is that of a teacher in a school, or a lecturer in a college. When we think of educators we immediately think of the setting in which they work. Indeed the prefix school or college describes the context for learning. From the age of five to sixteen children and young people attend school. For the teacher trained to work in that setting there is a captive audience albeit at times reluctant. They attend an institution which has classrooms and the learning, the curriculum and teaching styles are determined by the nature of the setting and the relationship between teacher and young person, however much these may have changed in recent years. The traditional model of education was that it was in schools that we were prepared for adult life. If you wanted to enter into more skilled occupations and if you were able to achieve at school and go into higher education, the years in an institutional learning setting, the college or university, would increase. This image of education, that you go to an institution to learn, to be 'schooled', is still the dominant one. The Scots are very proud of their education system and by that they mean schools, colleges and universities.

All of us have learning needs throughout our lives. These may be personal, social, economic, indeed political. A democratic and socially just society should enable all of its citizens to develop their various talents and interests to the full. Any society, democratic or not, in this competitive world cannot afford to have large parts of its population unproductive, dependent or unable to change to meet new challenges in the labour market. Certainly for Scotland although it has an impressive record of higher education achievement compared with many other countries within the OECD, its participation rates in continuing education are amongst the lowest. It has been argued that one reason why our economic competitiveness has lagged behind that of other countries is because of an inadequate investment in education and consequently lower participation rates.[1]

Whether we need to learn new skills in order to get a job, to be more discerning consumers, to care for the environment or for our health, it is now recognised that the education system must reach out, encouraging and engaging people *throughout life* into learning. Whatever the agenda, education for a healthy economy, for democracy, for problem solving or for physical, social or cultural regeneration, the system needs to be more relevant and more accessible.

It was a recognition of this imperative in the 1970's across the countries of the OECD, that led to the notion of lifelong learning and in more recent years in Scotland to the concept of the Learning Society. But there also emerged a realisation that it was not possible simply to attract people back into learning based on the assumption of compulsory attendance within institutions. Schools, colleges and universities will probably always demand the largest proportion of any country's education budget. But there is ample evidence to show that such institutions have to date failed large numbers of people within Scottish society.

Knowledge is power. It is not the only source of power. The contrasting adage that it is not what you know, but who you know is also a very real truth. If you have wealth and good contacts your relative empowerment is considerably greater. But the majority of people do not inherit large amounts of wealth. So although, in the great order of things, education can only be one factor in the more equitable distribution of power it is for so many going to be one of the few keys available to realise greater equality of opportunity. Whilst the integument of power is in part composed of deference and ignorance, education can empower through assisting people to be more confident, knowledgeable and skilled. Education can be an enormously liberating experience. It also serves the functional purpose within any society of training people for certain economic and social roles. A spectrum of these imperatives underpins all education and training systems. Whether the agenda be an equal opportunities or utilitarian one, whether it be to enable people to be less dependent upon welfare, to harness new technology or to tackle unemployment, the message is still the same. The system needs to reach out in a much more relevant and accessible way.

It is indeed true that if you think education is expensive try ignorance, but nonetheless there will always be limits to and competing demands upon public expenditure. So although there has been a recognition of a need to reach out to non-participants since the early seventies, to attract people back into purposive learning, there has also been an inertia within a system that continues to tie up 99% of public expenditure on education within formal school, college and university settings and upon educators trained to work in institutions. There are exceptions of course. One is the concept of open learning exemplified by the Open University. The other of equal significance is community education. Both began from the same concern: how to open up access to learning opportunities. The former aims to do this by way of technology, the latter by way of employing outreach specialists to work *within* local communities.

THE CHALLENGE OF CHANGE

This is the story of how a new occupation of educationalists emerged in Scotland from the mid 1970's, set with the challenge of engaging with people to develop a range of learning opportunities to meet their personal, social, economic and political needs. It is the story of how building upon the techniques of informal adult education, community work and youth work a new educational modus operandi was forged. This educational occupation we call community education. We have in Scotland in the mid 1990's over 1,500 trained and practising community educators employed by local authorities (primarily in education departments but also with significant numbers in social work, neighbourhood, community and leisure services) and other agencies notably the non governmental voluntary sector. They in turn support tens of thousands of part-time and voluntary sessional staff. They are educationalists. Indeed they undertake a three year degree or post graduate qualification to be trained as educationalists. They are skilled at helping people to learn. Their setting is neither primarily a school nor a college, though they certainly utilise such resources, it is outreach into the community, into the neighbourhood and the workplace, into the rural village, the peripheral housing scheme, the inner city and for a few into the middle class suburbs. Under 1% of total educational expenditure in Scotland goes on community education. The average community educator works within a community of several thousand people with a smaller ratio in designated disadvantaged communities. Their task to engage with people *within* that community identifying needs and motivating and enthusing individuals and groups to acquire new knowledge, skills and confidence, promoting learning that is enjoyable, relevant, accessible and empowering to the participating learners.

But if this is primarily a story of community education in Scotland and of the making of an empowering profession, a significant sub text is a story of people power. It is a celebration of the incredible achievements of people, young and old – of individual and community action and learning. This is no better demonstrated than in the first of the texts selected – *People Power* by Tony Gibson. Gibson in the mid 1970's was piloting his Planning for Real technique, a method now adopted by community educators, community architects and progressive planners across the U.K. I first met him along with Ralph Ibbott, a community worker and Danny Keegan a local volunteer youth leader, at this time. This short case study is not atypical of many community-led initiatives, here around youth work and crime prevention, that have mushroomed across Scotland from Gibshill to Craigmillar.[2] They remind us so clearly that the communities into which community educators intervene are neither passive, nor apathetic. They may be communities within which there is a poverty of expectations and of income and wealth, but certainly not a poverty of ideas, co-operative values and practical self-help.

Today in the mid 1990's community education has become a profession. Community education is recognised by central Government as a part of its lifelong learning strategy. Community education methods have proved to be highly cost effective ways of

— Supporting young people and adults to return to education and training throughout life, with community based guidance and provision, particularly for those who are disadvantaged.

— Supporting young people and adults in improving their communities, increasing self-help and voluntary community action in tackling problems.

— Enhancing the ability of central and local government and other agencies to listen to the needs and concerns of local people and the consumers of services.

— Assisting government and other agencies to raise awareness of issues through public education campaigns such as crime prevention, drugs awareness and environmental action.

— Stimulating the effective involvement of local people in personal, social, cultural, economic and political development, helping people to participate actively in determining change.

But even with the imprimatur of support from Government, from Shadow Ministers, the Convention of Scottish Local Authorities, the Association of Directors of Education and a host of other interests, its provision by the new local authorities is being questioned. The reasons for this vary. It has been argued by some that it is a non statutory service and thus not the responsibility of local government, although central Government and COSLA have clearly stated that this is not the case; others have argued that it is expensive, yet no single case has been demonstrated to show that the public investment in community education is anything but cost effective; others have argued that an integrated community education profession has damaged its constituent parts – adult education, community work and youth work, yet staffing and performance levels in all three activities have never been greater; others have argued that it is little more than a duplication of the leisure service, yet it is easy to demonstrate a significantly different locus of need and provision; still others have argued that it has failed to impact upon mainstream formal education or that it would benefit from moving outwith the local authority services, merging with for example the incorporated colleges of further education, continuing a pattern that has existed on the boundaries of the profession's development over the past twenty years. Such questions pose the severest challenge yet to this still young profession.

Community educators and those who support community education need to be able to explain clearly what they do, why it is worth public investment, what would be the effect if it did not exist and why it has never been more urgent for community eduction to be embraced and expanded by those concerned with widening not merely educational and training opportunities and tackling educational disadvantage but also broader social, economic and political development. These are not new questions. Twenty one years ago when Scottish local government was last being re-organised, these questions and similar concerns about Scotland's economic competitiveness and well-being were high on the political agenda. Revisiting those debates and reminding ourselves of the decisions taken then and subsequently, we can begin to make more informed decisions over the future of community education, where challenges to change are welcomed because they build upon best practice and a commitment to make that practice even better.

1975 was a watershed year for education and for local government in Scotland. In April of that year the new local authority system was formally put into place establishing the Regional and Island councils as education authorities. In addition it saw the publication of the Government's report *The Challenge of Change* chaired by Kenneth Alexander, which recommended the setting up of the Community Education Services in Scotland. Whilst community education had its origins prior to 1975 the Alexander Report gave public policy recognition to the term, by recommending to central and local government the merging of the former adult education, youth and community work services under a new title – community education and, by placing community education within a lifelong learning paradigm.

The Alexander Report and the new local authority system were products of a high degree of consensus on public policy and administration. Both the Commission which had led to local government reform and the Alexander Committee were established prior to the incoming Conservative Government in the summer of 1970. And, whilst it was the Conservative Government that enacted the Local Government (Scotland) Act in 1973, the intention behind it, devolution of power to local authorities on the one hand and the creation of bigger cost effective units on the other, had broad political support. Devolution was at the top of the political agenda in Scotland with the surge in support for the Scottish National Party committed to independence. But if there was a political imperative to support the devolution of power there was also an economic one. One word perhaps sums this up – oil. The oil crisis of 1973 exposed the vulnerability of Britain's post imperial economy in the very year it entered the European Economic Community. The oil crisis led to an upward spiralling of inflation that both cost the Conservatives the general election and put enormous pressures on public expenditure upon the in-coming Labour government. In a Scottish context oil was also to have a political significance in that its discovery in the North Sea was seen to herald enormous potential for the economic and social regeneration of the country. But inflation and concerns about the cost of public expenditure need also to be set against the continuation of considerable deprivation across large parts of urban and rural Scotland and growing political pressure for initiatives that would promote greater participatory democracy and equality of opportunity.

It is in the second of the selected texts that we get a clear statement of the commitment to public participation and equality of opportunity behind the Labour Government's support for community education in 1975. Robert Hughes was at that time the Under-Secretary of State for Scotland. He was addressing the annual conference of the newly formed Community Education Service Association. At the time of his speech the main recommendations of the Alexander Committee although not published were widely known. The significance of the paper is that it gives us an insight into the Government's thinking at this time on the challenges ahead. There seem to have been two broad themes. First was that local communities should be given greater encouragement to participate in shaping social and economic development, with educational opportunities being made more widely available within the community as a means of encouraging both individual and community development. Second was a strong commitment to the principle of equality of opportunity. Here the priority was to tackle educational disadvantage, to right the wrongs of the past.

From the outset then, the Government was quite clear that community education should contribute towards the building of a participatory democracy and the promotion of equality of opportunity through positive action towards the disadvantaged. But there were two other challenges. One rationale behind the integration of adult education with youth and community work was that this was seen as a cost-effective way of bringing together related disciplines that could more effectively engage non-participants. The creation of a new Community Education Service was seen not merely as an administrative reorganisation but as a practical way of creating larger integrated units with an enhanced capacity to effect change.

Hughes makes a statement that has echoed down the years since *"at times of economic difficulty such as the present every service has an obligation to look closely at its objectives and at the use it makes of existing resources"* From the very early days whilst it was recognised that community education required highly professional and competent community educators, other people and resources would also need to be mobilised. The Community Education Services were unlikely to be injected with additional amounts of public expenditure to meet the challenges identified.

The Alexander Report is acknowledged by the community education profession as a milestone in its development. The continuing influence of that Report over a period of 21 years reflects the achievable nature of many of its recommendations. Even in the mid 1990's the Report reads with great relevance. It is often forgotten that the Alexander Committee was in fact established to investigate the future of informal adult education in Scotland and neither youth nor community work. Indeed herein lies its major weakness, there is barely any reference at all to the concerns, the state of the art or the potentialities of youth and community work. Here was a committee of adult education interests setting the pace for the creation of a new education service involving two other traditions that it could be argued were as much on the boundaries of social work as they were of education.

The Committee took as its starting point a concern that informal education could no longer be justified as a marginal enterprise serving the interests of a relatively small proportion of the population. What was needed was a co-ordinated approach in order to have the capacity to widen participation. We see from the chapter selected from the Report a range of proposals for the kinds of provision that, they argued, would assist in the realisation of this objective. An agenda is set including general targets as to particular groups within the community with whom community education work should be prioritised, issues which community education should tackle and agencies with whom they should collaborate. The Report only briefly touches on methodology but argues that the bringing together of the these services provided opportunities for innovation and the cross fertilisation of approaches, one approach highlighted being community development.

The Alexander Report in making these recommendations was challenging Government, voluntary and statutory providers and practitioners to change. Implicit in the Report was a criticism that practice at that time was, albeit unintentionally, delivering provision to those who needed it least. Provision was cosy and far too traditional. What was needed was a new style of educational intervention, capable of reaching far larger numbers of people within the community. To this end a second working party was established chaired by Elizabeth Carnegy to examine professional education and training for community educators. Their Report, published in 1977, detailed the knowledge and skills required of community educators and made recommendations as to future professional education and training provision, calling for the establishment of an all graduate profession and a new central body to recognise and validate training courses.

Developments in the emergence of a new community education practice did not await the deliberations of national working parties. The integration of adult education, youth and community work recommended by the Alexander Report was already beginning to take place prior to publication of Alexander and local government reorganisation. With reorganisation the majority of the new Regional and Island authorities established Community Education Services, with staff taking on new job titles as Community Education Workers and new areas of responsibility. The employers then, particularly in the local authority sector, were from the outset as much the architects of community education in practice as the members of national committees.

Chief amongst these was Strathclyde Regional Council. Strathclyde was the largest of the new authorities, including within its boundaries half of the population of Scotland. Reorganisation had brought new ideas concerning policy priorities and the management of services. From the outset Strathclyde made a political commitment to tackle multiple deprivation and corporately to promote community development. Within community development they identified four main objectives. The promotion of community networks, the encouragement of self-help, the identification and stimulation of local leadership, and the provision of 'effective and sympathetic' resources and services to meet a community's needs. For Strathclyde all of its new departments had a role to play in the promotion of community development. But three services in particular were identified as having a lead role – education, social work and the police.

It was to review the respective roles of these services that a senior officer/member group was established chaired by Councillor Tony Worthington. The Worthington Report and Strathclyde's community development and anti-deprivation strategies are of great significance in the development of community education. They both set community education within a wider community development and anti-deprivation strategy and emphasised that in implementing such a strategy it was essential for the education and social work departments, both of which employed professionally trained community education workers, to collaborate in supporting community empowerment. From an employer's perspective the Report examined respective roles and made a broad range of recommendations concerning appropriate methods, training and structures at local community and regional level. The Worthington Report had considerable influence upon policy makers, managers and practitioners not only in Strathclyde. Across the central belt from the late 70's many of its approaches and recommendations began to permeate policy and practice.

One of the main recommendations in the Alexander Report was that a national Council for Community Education should be established to advise the Secretary of State and the statutory and voluntary providers on all matters relating to community education. An independent national resource centre, the Scottish Community Education Centre, (previously the Board for Information on Youth and Community Service) already existed with funding support from central government and local authorities. In 1979 the Government responded to Alexander by establishing the Scottish Council for Community Education with a small secretariat serviced from the Scottish Office. The Council and the Scottish Community Education Centre would within three years merge to form the Scottish Community Education Council.

The Scottish Council for Community Education came into being at time of political change in central government. Whereas Alexander had been the product of what in retrospect is now seen as a period of post war consensus in social policy between 1945 and the mid 1970's, the latter 70's had seen a breakdown in that consensus as Britain's economy faltered with growing unemployment, public expenditure constraints and the victory of the New Right fundamentally opposed to both Keynesian economic policy and Beveridgean social policy. Community education in Scotland as envisaged by Alexander was in many respects the product of a social democratic ethos. Whilst 1979 did not bring an abrupt end to that ethos in Scotland, it was quite apparent that central Government's agenda was to change. There would still be an emphasis upon people participation but now the language was of individualism, consumer power, enterprise and self-help. Equality of opportunity was to be given a much lower profile.

For a period there was a fear that the very word 'community' (as with the word 'society') was anathema, overtones of socialism at a time when an ideology of individualism was very much to the fore. Yet beneath the rhetoric there was a remarkable continuity of Scottish Office support for community education. But what sort of community education?

One of the few publications from the Scottish Council for Community Education was its *Discussion Paper Number One*. As well as reproducing that paper in full we have also selected a critique by Ian Martin published a few months later. We see in these two papers the ideological debate developing within community education between the policy establishment and practitioners and trainers. The SCCE paper picks up from the Alexander and Carnegy Reports and presents some initial ideas on its views on the concept and direction of community education. There is a heavy emphasis upon individualism and the primacy of the individual learner throughout the paper. Community education is viewed not as the title of a particular service but as a process, an approach to helping individuals to learn. The Council argued that community education in Scotland should be seen as a label identifying the Scottish brand of lifelong education, but noted, with some concern, that the synthesis of adult education, youth and community work seemed not to have yet led to any marked change in practice on the ground.

Ian Martin's critique entitled *Signposts to Nowhere* questioned the supposed consensual view of community education adopted by the Council. He was highly critical of the polarisation within the paper with its emphasis upon a working definition of community education that focused only upon meeting the learning needs of individuals. He argued that collective forms of learning are both feasible and necessary and saw here a fundamental ideological divide which he says explained the Council's individual inadequacy model of educational disadvantage. This was the 'crunch where the cosy consensus begins to break down'. For Martin the real cause of educational disadvantage was structural inequality. Community education therefore had to prioritise rather than offering a free market, first come, first served consumer service, with those with consumer 'power' able to exploit the opportunities presented.

Community education needs to have a 'redistributional' intention and by this he does not argue for it to become a compensatory service, but a new type of radical practice drawing upon the analysis and methodology of such writers as Paulo Freire. Martin sets five basic principles as underlying his model of community education. First is that community education should be opening up access to opportunities. Second there must be space for innovation in responding to local priorities and needs identified *with* local people rather than being caught in a routinised provision. Third he calls for a move away from traditional methods. Fourth he urges community educators to challenge professional demarcation lines and in particular to question the professional monopoly of teaching. And finally he calls for community educators to combine education with problem solving, relating interventions to the real problems in people's lives and working with local people to do something about them.

THE BOUNDARIES OF CHANGE

Already in the latter 1970's debates about contrasting ideologies and practice were occurring within community education in Scotland. Community education is not axiomatically radical. Although the origins of modern community work can be traced to the community action movement of the late 1960's, much youth work provision was of a very traditional nature and with few exceptions adult education had not concerned itself directly with social action in ways that had occurred for example in the Liverpool Education Priority Area (EPA) and Community Development Project (CDP). A progressive Trainers' Forum was established in 1979 and Scottish publications urging a more social action oriented practice rooted in a structural analysis of inequality and disadvantage were permeating professional training. This was not surprising. This period was bringing mass unemployment and poverty back to Scotland with fears that the Government's strategy for 'training' the unemployed through the Manpower Services Commission might incorporate community education – the chair of the Manpower Services Commission and the Scottish Community Education Council being the same person – Elizabeth Carnegy. The Government itself was perceived by many as the major causal factor in the increase in unemployment and deprivation. It certainly was leading the drive for a reduction in public expenditure at the very time when the personal, social and economic needs of the disadvantaged were increasing.

Alongside this debate it is important to recall that much local government in Scotland throughout this period remained firmly in the hands of the Labour Party, vociferously opposed to many of the national economic and social policies of central government. The Worthington Report for Strathclyde Region, for example, in endorsing the Association of Community Workers' publication *Knowledge And Skills In Community Work* was encouraging staff to develop programmes around the concerns and agendas set by local communities. It was placing community education within a positive discrimination and wider social strategy to combat multiple deprivation. Indeed the politicians leading this drive tended to be almost as critical of the local authority management in community education in blocking more innovative interventions in areas of multiple deprivation as they were of any central government intentions. As we entered the 1980's it was local government along with some of the more innovative grassroots voluntary organisations in large part funded through the Urban Programme, that were setting the pace for the next phase in community education. Whilst the trainers of community educators at the four Scottish colleges of education – Jordanhill, Moray House, Dundee and Aberdeen and at Edinburgh University were embracing such models of community education practice in part as a response to criticism from the local authority employers. Dundee College of Education was the first training institution in Scotland to introduce a named community education course, encompassing adult education, community work and youth work, in 1979.

One significant area of locally led innovation was the development of community schools. Unlike England where the development of community education and community schools has been closely linked, the Alexander Report had not acknowledged a community education practice theory emerging from a schools context in Scotland. The U.K. Education Priority Areas programme had placed community schools more centrally onto the educational agenda. Whilst there had been an EPA pilot project in Dundee,[3] the report of that action research initiative had come out as not particularly sympathetic to the community school concept. But in Grampian and Lothian Regions the community school idea gained local political support. As the paper by John Nisbet, Leo Hendry, Chris Stewart and Joyce Watt entitled *Towards Community Education* notes if community education was to develop in a period of economic stringency it made financial sense to combine it with the resources contained within the existing school system and to open these resources up for wider community use. But the proponents of the community school concept were concerned to go far further than just the more cost effective use of buildings. They wanted to bridge the gap between school teachers and community educators to provide more effective learning opportunities for the local community.

This study evaluated the first generation of community schools in Grampian Region. A number of findings were significant. The first concerned the contrasting philosophies of education which were identified as existing between teachers and community educators. If community education was to be implemented in a way that brought the school and the community more closely together then the philosophical starting points of the two educational professions needed to find some common ground. There was a considerable lack of understanding between teachers and community educators of each other's philosophy and therefore approach. In trying to track what was the source of this misunderstanding there was criticism of the colleges of education where both groups of professionals were trained but where there was little contact between them on the training programmes.[4]

A second area of innovation at this time was with the interface with further education. The Strone and Maukinhill Informal Education Project (SMIEP) in Greenock was the first documented example of a community based adult learning project in Scotland involving a further education college. The significance of this project was that it sought to mobilise the resources of a college and to combine community work and adult education techniques. From an initial experiment in taking college classes out into a working class community, it moved on to negotiating a wide range of learning programmes linked to both personal and social action concerns. The SMIEP initiative was significant at the time. It clearly demonstrated that such an approach could dramatically break through barriers to adult learning. It set the important precedent in Strathclyde for subsidised assistance within designated Areas of Priority Treatment ie deprivation. And significantly it was community controlled. The project was also well documented, with an action research and evaluation input from the Local Government Unit in Paisley. The action research approach pioneered in Scotland with the Dundee EPA and Paisley CPD (Community Development Project) from the early days indicated a concern by funders and practitioners to assess the impact of community education. It was also a convenient way of stalling mainline investment. The SMIEP paper does however highlight the important role that further education colleges made and continue to make to community education in Scotland – a role which in later years has led to the more ambitious concept of community colleges.[5]

The Scottish Institute of Adult Continuing Education was also concerned with the interface issue. It was at that time the principle national membership body of adult education practitioners. Its membership came from both the formal and the informal adult education side. In 1981 the Association concerned with continuing cuts in public expenditure published a manifesto entitled the *Right to Learn*. The Association wanted to keep the development of an open and comprehensive system of post school education incorporating both the formal and informal sectors high on the agenda. They argued that there was a need for much closer collaboration, indeed integration, between these two sectors.

In calling for a comprehensive strategy for post school education encompassing both the vocational and non vocational, the formal and informal, the Institute argued that these distinctions were inappropriate, even unhelpful. The selected extract begins by classifying six different types of adult education provision to which both formal and community based adult education provision contributed. It lists examples of lifelong learning ranging from the Open University through adult basic education, to women's education, outreach projects in the community and partnerships with broadcasters. They briefly mapped the range and variety of provision in both formal and community based adult education at this time and noted, with concern, that except where special funding had been secured, for example, through the Urban Programme or Manpower Services Commission, adult educationalists on the ground were having difficulty coping with the increased needs and demands.

The Institute called for new policies. It argued that the Alexander Report had not received sufficient attention from either the Labour or Conservative Governments. They noted that the call by Alexander for the appointment of an additional 200 professional staff to work in this field had not been adequately addressed by the merger with youth and community work. Their main recommendation however was that the distinction between the formal and community education sectors should be dropped and that these sectors should work collaboratively in the promotion of learning programmes for adults. For the Institute then Alexander had not gone far enough, indeed by linking informal adult education with youth and community work rather than further education, it had gone in the wrong direction.

The issue of boundaries came increasingly to the fore in the early 1980's. As community education was becoming a more established local authority service, and the approach better known if not as a term being adopted by the voluntary sector, arguments as to what constituted community education and what lay within the informal education sector began to shift. We have already seen the dialogue (or rather the lack of it) emerging between teachers and community educators. Although the Scottish Institute of Adult Continuing Education did not address the relationship between college lecturers and community educators, it is implicit in their campaign that they wished to see much more integrated working if the education system was going to involve what it called the 'excluded majority of people'.

The relationship between community education and social work also merits examination. Following the 1968 Social Work (Scotland) Act, Social Work departments had begun to recruit community workers. Social work training was adopting community work methods alongside case work and group work[6]. Community work was a young quasi profession however and many of its practitioners sought neither incorporation within social work nor community education. In practice a large majority of community workers recruited by Social Work departments undertook their initial professional training through the youth and community work and later community education route. And those responsible for community work training within community education courses also drew upon social work practice theory. The Trainers' Forum, referred to earlier, included trainers from both the social work and community education sides.

One social work initiative in particular had an influence upon community education training at this time. This was the concept of the fieldwork training unit. The first fieldwork training unit to focus upon community work training was established in the Gorbals in Glasgow managed by the Crossroads Youth and Community Association. It provided placement opportunities for students from both social work and community education courses. Crossroads has another significant place in the history of community education in Scotland. It was here that the practitioners sought to develop a method of intervention with youth and community groups based around the writings of Saul Alinsky from the United States. Here was a model of issue based problem solving learning that was radical and linked to social action. The starting point was poor housing and dampness and related issues of health. Together these were to prove powerful motivating forces for community participation and empowerment. The paper by Barbara Holmes and Richard Bryant describes the campaign, the learning and empowerment that resulted and the process through the words of community participants and professional community workers. It was recognised at the time as an inspiring example of community based learning through collective action.

The voluntary sector at this time was increasingly supporting community work and employing community education trained staff. The Scottish Council of Voluntary Organisations (SCVO), the umbrella body for the sector, under Director Ros Flockhart and Assistant Director Willie Roe was making an important contribution to practice through its own development programme, through support for local Councils of Voluntary Service (which they termed community development agencies) and through establishing initiatives such as the Tenant Participation Advisory Service (TPAS), a training and information resource for tenants' associations. Local CVS's were sponsoring innovative voluntary sector community work projects such as the Tenants and Workers' Information Network (TWIN) in Edinburgh and community work student units in Edinburgh and Aberdeen. The Home Office sponsored Community Projects Foundation, (formerly the Young Volunteer Force Foundation and later renamed the Community Development Foundation), was active in Scotland from the mid 1970's funding local demonstration projects in Fife, Strathclyde, Tayside and Lothian. Whilst in the Highlands and Islands, the Highlands and Islands Development Board (HIDB) under the chairmanship of Kenneth Alexander was supporting community enterprises, combining community work expertise with local economic development.

The late 1970's early '80's was a period of considerable activity on the publications front in community education. The Scottish Community Education Centre publishers of SCAN newspaper launched the new *Community Education* magazine. There was a short-lived magazine entitled *Scottish Radical Education* edited by community educators and trainers based in Dundee and Lothian. Strathclyde practitioners published a series of case studies on community development. The voluntary sector notably the Workers' Educational Association, the Scottish Council of Voluntary Organisations and the Standing Conference of Voluntary Youth Organisations were publishing practical handbooks. Scottish practitioners were publishing through the Routledge ACW series, the Community Development Journal and the Scottish Journals of Youth and Community Work and Adult and Continuing Education.

On the research front, Paisley College of Technology was the base for the Scottish Local Government Unit headed up by Councillor Ronald Young one of the leading architects of Strathclyde Region's community development strategy. The LGU was publishing research papers throughout the late 70's and early 80's on community development, community education, community councils, community health and community enterprise and running training courses for elected members and officers. The paper by Ronald Young is significant not simply because of its content on Social Strategy. The author was a highly influential politician committed to both corporate management and support for local community action. Young along with Tony Worthington and Rev Geoff Shaw, the first Convenor of Strathclyde Region and a former Minister in the Gorbals, were strong proponents of community development. The subsequent direction of community education and community development would have been very different had it not been for the political support from the likes of Shaw, Young and Worthington in Strathclyde and others such as George Foulkes in Lothian in those early years.

TRAINING FOR CHANGE

In 1982 Dundee College of Education published the first of two books on community and continuing education. The first was entitled *Community Education and Community Development* edited by Laurie Bidwell and myself and containing papers on policy and practice from the period from across Scotland. It was the first published book of Scottish community education case studies. The paper selected reviews the debate at that time around definitions and methods. This was a period of reflection on the first half a dozen years of post Alexander and local government reorganisation. It was a period of innovation and of experimentation due in large part to access to short-term Urban Programme funding in designated areas of need. Mainstream local authority Community Education Services were for some (including the Editors of the book) seen as too conventional. There was a growing criticism that the well intentioned reports and name changes of the 1970's had been a case of old wine in new bottles, a change in rhetoric rather than a change in practice. One particular concern was that too many community educators still failed to get out of their centres into local communities. We echoed Worthington's arguments that by linking community education to community development and social action community educators would be able to focus upon disadvantaged communities, to engage participants in an educational process that could be both empowering and focused upon the real life concerns and problems in their lives. This was not a description of the majority of practice at that time.

Community education was at this time young, over ambitious, seeking to prove its value, to mark out its terrain and to gel together its constituent parts. One of the areas where there was a common agenda between the three strands was in a shared commitment to extending participation. As the Alexander Report had noted both youth workers and community workers did this by working in less formal ways. Adult educators brought to the mix more structured educational methods.

One reason why community development approaches were receiving a higher profile was because the reduction in public expenditure was working its way through into the local government system. The local state was being pushed from being service provider to enabler. The concept of consumer empowerment in the public sector took off in the 1980's with central Government support for tenant participation in housing management and for parent participation in the management of schools. Community development at a time of economic stringency seemed increasingly appealing. This is perhaps over cynical. For many of the proponents of community development saw in it a framework for community education linking community based learning with social action and problem solving and a way of empowering people to have a say over determining the conditions which affected their lives. Tony Worthington sums up what at the time was perhaps the most coherent political and economic rationale for why local government should back this approach. If in cost benefit terms the gains were enormous and the outlay small surely we could not afford to ignore this message, particularly if by animating local communities they could become better educated, healthier, safer places to live.[7]

A growing concern with issues of youth unemployment, drugs, delinquency and the race riots experienced in parts of England, led Strathclyde to establish another officer/member working group which published its report *Working with Young People* in 1984. Again this working group was dissatisfied with much of the traditional youth work provision within the Region. Indeed they went further to argue that education departments alone did not have the ability to tackle the growing problems facing young people. They concluded that youth work should take on a community development approach as part of a multi-agency area based strategy. The working group stressed the importance of community involvement and participation by young people through local youth fora and they set as priorities the need for work with young people at risk, work with girls and young women, rural youth work and collaborative links between the statutory and voluntary sectors. Finally the report raised doubts that a generic community educator responsible for informal adult education, community work and youth work could effectively focus upon the needs of young people. Whilst committed to the notion of an integrated Community Education Service, they recommended that area teams be established within which there should be specialists in youth development work.

The argument for specialisms within community education was also made by the proponents of a relatively new area of work with adults in the community – adult basic education. Adult basic education (ABE) had grown out of the adult literacy media campaign of the mid 70's. It was eventually to form part of the Community Education Service. As we see from the paper published by the Scottish Adult Basic Education Unit, from the early days it had developed innovative methods of reaching non-participants and engaging them in adult learning. Almost by definition these learners were some of the most disadvantaged lacking essential literacy and numeracy skills. Clearly lack of literacy and numeracy interacted with personal, social and economic difficulties for many adults (estimates of at least 200,000 at that time in Scotland). The techniques developed for working in this area were far more intensive, often involving a one to one relationship with the learner. By the early 1980's there were some 230 full-time adult basic education workers across Scotland along with 4,000 volunteers helping nearly 18,000 students. As well as new techniques of outreach and guidance a whole range of learning and tutoring materials were developed. One key long term outcome of the campaign was the building of close links between community educators and the mass media.

Adult basic education has played a significant role in shaping community education. The high profile media campaign highlighting this issue and the failures of the formal education system led to the employment of specialists in this work. Of all the areas of growth in community education at this time, it was in ABE that additional personnel were employed. Paradoxically the rapid employment of full time staff necessitated recruitment of many people not trained in community education. Although the colleges of education had now adapted to the post Carnegy model of training for community education they did not provide training opportunities for work with this target group of learners. Very often it was teachers who were recruited into such posts. Indeed not until the mid 1980's with the Scottish Adult Basic Education Unit now forming part of the Scottish Community Education Council and regional Community Education Services taking over responsibility for this function did the colleges respond to employer demand by introducing training as well as placement opportunities in this specialism.

The Scottish Community Education Council by merging the former Council, Centre and SABEU was by the mid '80's not simply an important national resource agency for practitioners, combining as it did in part, the functions of several agencies south of the border, but itself a pace-setter. Ralph Wilson, SCEC's first Director, outlines the work of the Council, one of its key roles being to advise the Secretary of State and Scottish Education Department on all matters relating to community education. There has never been an equivalent agency with this role in any other part of the U.K. or E.U. SCEC was certainly comparatively well resourced and able to initiate national community education campaigns, raising issues and encouraging local action. One of the most significant of these being *Young Scot*, led by Marc Liddle SCEC's Assistant Director, a survival guide for all school leavers and subsequently a model adopted in other parts of the U.K. and across Europe.

Community education in Scotland was now heading towards its 10th anniversary. A new language (some would say jargon) had been adopted by the profession – the language of lifelong learning, community development, positive discrimination and equal opportunity. The professional training of community educators had undergone a comprehensive review and was now delivering the post Carnegy generation of practitioners. But at the very time when community education was beginning to establish a profile in Scotland there were concerns that it could not deliver all that it claimed, not least from within the profession itself. Individual and community needs had grown enormously with a concomitant increase in workloads and there were just not enough community educators to do the job. The concept of the generic all purpose community educator had never been intended by the Alexander Report, but the reality on the ground was that responsibility for informal adult education, community work and youth work was now contained within the job description of a single post-holder. Was this a case of trying to put three pints into a one pint pot? There were certainly voices within each of the three areas calling for a greater recognition of specialisms whilst at the same time supporting a common core of values, principles and processes. Clearly many of the employers were having doubts. Not only were the regional Community Education Services appointing specialist workers and giving community educators within an area team a specific remit but the proliferation of more narrowly focused posts e.g. through the Urban Programme, as well as the demands of voluntary sector and other local authority employers of professionally trained community educators (now the destination of the majority of graduates) necessitated a further look at professional training.

The Scottish Community Education Council appointed one of its members, Geoffrey Drought, to head up a second working party on community education training. I was a member of this working party. Their Report *Training for Change* was published in 1984. It traced developments since the Alexander and Carnegey reports concluding that the picture of community education was one of a rapidly expanding field of practice in which from the three traditional roots a wide variety of new areas, specialist settings and client groups was emerging. That field of practice was considerably broader than that of the local authority Community Education Services yet should be classified as community education. This changing pattern of employment had implications for training. The working party examined what the worker in the community did and concluded that whilst the process of intervention was common to all community educators the settings varied enormously. Therefore all prospective community educators required common training in the process *and* opportunities for specialisms at qualifying level to enable them to acquire knowledge and skills related to a specific setting or arena of work.

What was required was a core and options model of training with flexibility in terms of access routes and accreditation of prior learning and experience. Three training routes were identified. The first was for a person who was already trained in a specific area such as health, who wished to practice that specialism in a community context. The second was for someone probably directly out of school at 18 who wished to become a full-time graduate community educator. The third was for a person probably without Highers or in some cases any school leaving qualifications who, having developed experience in for example youth work or as a community activist, wished to achieve a full professional community education qualification. Extensive consultations with the field also led the working party to conclude that employers should have greater say over professional training, that supervised fieldwork practice should be given a greater emphasis on training programmes and that training should be modularised within a national system of credit accumulation and transfer.

THE MEASURING OF CHANGE

But what was actually going on in practice amongst the local government Community Education Services at this time? In 1984 David Alexander, Tom Leach and Tim Steward from Edinburgh University published *A Study of Policy, Organisation and Provision in*

Community Education and Leisure and Recreation in Three Scottish Regions – Tayside, Central and Fife. This was the first comprehensive evaluative research examining the development of policy, organisation and provision post Alexander. It was concerned to examine the range, nature, quality, balance and purpose of the programmes offered and to study the nature and patterns of participation. The extracts selected are primarily those relating to the Community Education Services, but throughout what is a very substantial research report, reference is made to areas of similarity in practice and the interface between the Community Education Services and the Leisure and Recreation Services. They concluded that at that time a great deal of what might be termed the curriculum content of community education was built around leisure as opposed to broader social, economic or political needs of young people and adults. Issue based and more cognitive educational work had not developed significantly and they noted that on the ground community educators particularly from a youth work tradition were having difficulties in integrating educational skills into their practice.

The study described in some detail the organisational arrangements and policies in the three regions. In all three there was a mismatch between a policy commitment towards targeting disadvantaged non-participants and practice. There were tensions between a continuing legacy, perhaps baggage, of responsibility for the management of community centres and the new policies and patterns of training which were focusing upon outreach work within the community. They concluded that the existing structures and programmes within these services were not capable of providing effective access to the disadvantaged sections of society. This was not because the community educators were either complacent or lacked a commitment to outreach development work, but because they were hampered by a lack of defined priorities and inappropriate allocation of resources and management support. This was a significant finding. Was there indeed a mismatch between the new community education rhetoric and what was being delivered on the ground? Had the hopes for community education and the agenda of issues for it to address been too great?

Colin Kirkwood in a paper entitled *Key Texts in Community Education* commenting on this period, although not published until the end of the decade as part of a book entitled *Vulgar Eloquence*, argued that one of the key problems lay with the very concept of generic community education as a single process and profession. His underlying concern was that there had been an underestimation of the 'cultural' differences between youth and community work and adult education. These were, he argued different worlds with fairly negative views of each other. They had different training traditions, the former through colleges of education with an emphasis upon the acquisition of practical skills and the latter through the universities where there was more of a theoretical approach. It was certainly true that the majority of the senior management in the new local authority Community Education Services came from a youth work background and other than in adult basic education there had not been a new injection of posts for adult education work, merely an added responsibility for youth and community work trained staff to take on this role.

Youth and community work had to a certain extent also been a misnomer. It was primarily a youth service with the word 'community' tagged onto it. Although community development ideas had been permeating youth work practice since the late 60's there were

Scottish practitioners who sought to engage only in community work and had little interest in youth work and vice versa. There was now a growing practice theory of community work quite distinct from youth work, influenced especially by the writings of Henderson and Thomas and the Community Development Projects (CDP).[8] Community work had also greatly influenced the policies of local authorities such as Strathclyde, the reports on community education training and the training providers far in excess of its proportion in terms of practice on the ground. Quite simply the proponents of community work were better organised and more sophisticated at articulating their approach.[9] Certainly as we shall see later the first published Guidelines for qualifying training published by the national council for the validation and endorsement of community education training in 1990 took as its philosophical starting point a set of principles drawn neither from adult education nor youth work but from community work.[10]

By the mid 1980's community education could demonstrate that *at its best* it had significantly broken through the barriers of non-participation. The question was no longer how can we engage non participants, particularly from disadvantaged communities, but would government invest in community education to make it happen? But there were still clearly differing schools of thought as to whether as a profession it should be generic or should allow for specialist interventions. As we have seen there was an increasing call for community education practice to allow for specialist interventions directed by the needs of particular groups, for example those with literacy problems or minority ethnic or language communities, by the settings, for example whether in rural or inner city contexts, or by the issues, for example posts concerned with health education, environmental education or community arts. The core with options model of training was providing undergraduate community educators with at least a taster of more specialised work. There was also a growing investment in specialist staff development programmes by both the local authority and voluntary sector employers and in in-service courses run by the colleges.

A parallel concern reflected in the literature at this time was whether community education was genuinely educational. Jean Barr working with the Workers' Educational Association (WEA) was one of several writers who argued that rigorous adult learning seemed less visible within community based programmes particularly those adopting a community development approach. The WEA had a long tradition of work with trade unions, workplace education and latterly led the field in Scotland in Women's Studies courses particularly in Aberdeen. The official statistics did indicate a decline in participation in traditional adult education classes, largely caused by fee increases, but was the huge expansion in alternative community based programmes most of which were free and targeted within APT's (Areas of Priority Treatment) actually educational? In particular did the new forms of community education for the disadvantaged sell people short in terms of cognitive content? Barr argued that much of it did.

Following Alexander and Worthington and influenced by such writers as Tom Lovett and by such projects as the Strone and Maukinhill Informal Education Project, the application of the community development approach had become more widespread. Ted Milburn writing in 1987 argued that community education programmes utilising this approach had led to a considerable increase in participation in adult learning. Milburn's paper was concerned to counter the criticism that non didactic issue based educational provision was not sufficiently cognitive. Community based provision might be second chance learning, it certainly wasn't second best. The starting point for this approach was rooted in issues and needs identified with local people, with the 'curriculum' negotiated between the educator and the learning group. Certainly this approach was attracting considerable numbers of previously non participating adults. And once the barriers had been broken community educators then quite appropriately assisted participants to progress through more structured education programmes in further education colleges or even universities. This, Milburn argued, was the key part that community education could pay in a broad strategy for education and training for the post 16 age group. He describes one such strategy where schools, FE colleges, the careers service and the Community Education Service had come together to identify educational needs, to plan provision and to pool together the strengths of informal and formal education.

One particular example of community based adult learning at this time, tried to bridge education and social action approaches. The Adult Learning Project (ALP) developed as a systematic attempt to implement Paulo Freire's methods in Scotland. Freire had been an influence upon community education since his publications were translated and made more widely available in Scotland in the mid 1970's. By the 1980's they were amongst the standard titles for under-graduate community education student essays. But his methodology had never been all that easy to understand and what the Adult Learning Project achieved was not only the adaptation of this methodology to a Scottish context but also the dissemination of this in a more accessible language. ALP was not without its critics. It was an intensive model of community based adult learning. It was also relatively well financed with a staffing ratio more generous than one would usually find within a local authority community education team serving a similar population area. Although influential, the project has not been replicated across Scotland, but it is a clear demonstration that community based programmes could be issued based, cognitive and rigorous.

Although community based education programmes were attracting more participants it was difficult to measure the educational outcomes. In formal education this is more straightforward. At its crudest the measurement is the passing of a qualification. As the eighties ended community educators came under increasing pressure to measure the benefits of their work. In 1991 Leo Hendry, Ian Craik et al published the findings of a study entitled *Measuring the Benefits of Youth Work*. They concluded that at that time there was indeed little systematic measurement, being undertaken. This research looked at participants in youth clubs and youth organisations. It was argued by community educators that young people grow through youth organisations towards more independent living in the adult world. Thus youth work could be seen as an important part of the development of young people enabling them as adults to make independent decisions. Although Hendry and Craik could find evidence that participation in such activities had developed self confidence, social skills and wider horizons there was no evidence to assess whether the benefits of this participation could be traced into adult life. The findings of this study indicated however that the young people did by and large relate very well to the more informal styles adopted by youth workers. But and here was a significant point, the majority of the face-to-face workers were not qualified community educators but part time and voluntary youth leaders. The professionally trained community educator due to an increasing workload was less likely to be the person actually delivering the supposed informal education programme. If there was a purposive youth work curriculum it had to be said it was difficult to find.

Concern about youth work curriculum had led the Standing Conference of Voluntary Youth Organisations to set up a working group in 1989 to identify what was meant by youth work curriculum and to produce one. Their starting point was that it was important to distinguish between youth work as an educational intervention and youth provision. The latter being simply the provision of services and facilities for young people after school. For SSCVYO a community education approach to youth work was always educational. It should place learning as a central goal. Indeed SSCVYO went as far as to argue that youth activities that do not involve purposive education are not youth work. This is highly significant for here we see an attempt to place clear water between what SSCVYO call youth work i.e. educational work and youth provision through the Leisure and Recreation Services. The report was endorsed by the Convention of Scottish Local Authorities and positively welcomed by the Scottish Office Education Department. It had clear implications for the training not only of professional community educators but also of part time and voluntary youth leaders who as Hendry and Craik had demonstrated were highly unlikely to have been trained to practice in this way.

If those in adult education and youth work were concerned to demonstrate that albeit informal and community based what was actually going on was educational, could this be demonstrated by the third arm of community education, community work? The paper by Richard Bryant and Barbara Holmes clearly shows that the participants involved in that particular community action campaign had become empowered. They had learned about the political system, they had developed political skills, organising skills, presentational skills, and certainly a lesson in the realities of power. But it is difficult to find many Scottish publications about community work which have focused upon it as a educational intervention.[11] In 1991 the Community Development Foundation published a book entitled *Practising Community Development*[12] by Alan Barr which examined what community workers did in the social work department of Strathclyde Region. As has been stated already the majority of those community workers were professionally trained community educators. Although this book was significant in terms of evaluating what community workers actually did rather than what they said they did, it did not explicitly examine the educational outcomes of that intervention. By the early 1990's probably 20% of local authority sector qualified community educators were employed by social work departments as community workers or eg I.T. (Intermediate Treatment) youth workers, an indication of the value of community education approaches to other sectors, but also of the influence of the positive cross fertilisation of praxis between social development and education in Scotland.

In 1992 the Principal Community Education Officers (PCEO) of the Local Authority Community Education Services published the third in the series of three pamphlets. The previous two had looked at adult education and youth work. By the early 1990's the title community work was in fact being dropped by many local authority Community Education

Services and in its place we see to describe both the third arm and an approach underlying the other two the term community development. It is difficult to trace exactly why and when community work as a title began to be dropped by the education services. One reason may well have been because of various regional council reviews which tried to draw a greater distinction between what Social Work and Education Department community workers did. The Scottish Office Education Department increasingly used the term community development from this period. This was probably more a case of a loose use of the jargon in community education than it was an intention to drop community work from community education or to de-politicise it. Nor could it be said that community development was somehow a more acceptable term than community work. After all the CDP's had in the eyes of some in both local and central government placed the language of community development beyond the pale.

Although the Principal Community Education Officers' publication does at times confuse the two terms, it is nonetheless a significant document in that for the first time there was agreement, or perhaps one might say an aspiration, across all of the senior managers within the local authority Community Education Services that the community development approach and working around issues of inequality, disadvantage and marginalisation and of seeking to empower such communities be high on the agenda. A model endorsed in the PCEO report was one developed by the Community Education Service in Lothian Region. The report examines the practical implications for a local authority using a community development approach and the blocks that might undermine its effectiveness. The PCEO's concluded that community development was a significant approach, although "not necessarily applicable to all community education work … .it cannot be!".

In 1993 the SOED Research and Intelligence Unit commissioned a major research study on community education and community development. The research sought to examine how effective different kinds of educational input have been in (a) allowing members of the community to gain additional skills, and in (b) contributing to the achievement of the objectives of the community development programme itself. (The report of this research, *Learning for Change*, carried out by Alan Barr, Robert Hamilton and Rod Purcell of the newly formed Scottish Community Development Centre is to be published in spring 1996). This research contains a number of significant findings. On the basis of an in-depth analysis of seventeen community education case studies from across Scotland from Ross and Cromarty to Wigtown and from the statutory and voluntary sectors there is clear evidence that community work interventions do demonstrate a strong commitment to informal training with either an emphasis on skills or on knowledge, embracing eg: committee work, supporting participants to engage more effectively in democratic decision making processes, assertiveness training and negotiation skills.

The research describes examples where the community education practitioners supported learning through issue based problem solving around locally identified concerns "resulting in the formulation of collective action strategies". In all but one of the projects evaluated there is clear evidence of personal empowerment gains amongst participants and in all a strengthening of 'community networks' ie: mutual support. The researchers have also identified outcomes concerned with the development of knowledge and skills which can be collectively deployed to effect change on behalf of a community – what they call 'the aggregate organisational product of the learning process', in twelve of the case studies. The researchers do conclude however that opportunities for this latter type of practice seem to be more available within the voluntary sector than the statutory Community Education Services:

> "The evidence of the seventeen case studies provides some interesting insights into the merits of these community work sponsors. The consideration of educational inputs as variables suggest that the most effective educational contributions to the process are not necessarily provided by the most frequent host – Community Education Services. However, it should be noted that the majority of the workers, whatever the organisational context of practice, were drawn from community education training backgrounds. The evidence is that community education workers are able to offer a very competent community work service, but their employers need to ask whether they are necessarily deployed in the organisational settings most conducive to making the best use of their evident skills".

Community development as we have seen, has not been without its critics, particularly those like Colin Kirkwood and Jean Barr who whilst recognising its ability to 'multiply' i.e. to wider participation have queried its educational effectiveness once the participants were engaged. It has of course not been the only method used for reaching non-participants. The lessons from the adult basic education movement have also demonstrated the enormous power in influencing the 'demand side' of the lifelong learning equation by combining adult learning with the mass media. This has been amply demonstrated in Scotland with the launch of *Adult Learners' Week* in 1992, co-ordinated by SCEC.

However the evidence suggests that mobilising the power of the mass media,whether in marketing learning or an education campaign such as the *Young Scot* work on drugs awareness, does not in itself generate cognitive learning or lead to behavioural change. It is perhaps more accurate to say that the lessons from the community education experience are that a combination of approaches is more likely to be effective in terms of engaging and empowering both individuals and groups. Once young people and adults are engaged, it is appropriate to utilise didactic teaching methods as well as for example group work techniques. Good community educators need to be able to apply a range of appropriate methods and certainly through youth and adult guidance to be able to link participants with other educators as part of the broader strategy referred to by Milburn. This was a key lesson echoed by such national Scottish Office Education Department initiatives as the Scottish Wider Access Programme, the Adult Education Guidance Initiative in Scotland and in the HMI reports on *Youth Work in Scotland* and on *The Education of Adults in Scotland*[13].

In 1990 practitioners and trainers linked to the three colleges of education, Moray House, Jordanhill and Northern College launched the journal of Contemporary Community Education Practice Theory *Concept,* edited by Mae Shaw. The journal was established to provide a critical forum for practitioners to reflect upon their practice. Two developments in community education in the early 1990's in particular led to heated debate. Both were related and essentially to do with what it was community educators actually did and how to measure the outcomes of their intervention. These were the debates around Competences and Performance Indicators. Over fifteen years community education had been synthesising community development and other educational methods. What was emerging was a new hybrid of competences, in effect a distinct educational occupation. The community educator of the 1990's was a different animal from the informal adult educator, the community worker, or the youth worker prior to 1975 i.e. more than the sum of its parts.

In 1990 the Minister of Education, Michael Forsyth, finally approved the setting up of a national body for the validation and endorsement of community education training, CeVe (Community Education Validation and Endorsement), as a committee of SCEC. It was thirteen years since the Carnegy Report and six since *Training for Change* had called for such a national body. Of all the national professional training initiatives CeVe has created a national profile of what community education is and what community educators should be trained to do. Its first *Guidelines for Qualifying Training* published in 1991 presented a definition, subsequently adopted across Scotland, a statement of values and principles underpinning practice and following a 'functional analysis' of what community educators do, a competence based framework for training. Significantly the first Guidelines (these were subsequently reviewed and revised in 1995 with an extract of the revised Guidelines being selected) were heavily influenced by community development values. Only following extensive consultations during 1994 was a balance re-emphasising a wider range of educational methods and techniques finally put at the core of training, at last reconciling the protagonists of the 1980's. By the 1990's three colleges of education (two now Universities) and one employment-based apprenticeship route, the Linked Work and Training Trust, validated by Glasgow University, were providing degree level training programmes in community education endorsed by CeVe.

Tony Jeffs and Mark Smith writing in *Concept*[14] in 1993 saw the introduction of a competence model, led primarily by local authority employers, (CeVe being an employer led body chaired respectively between 1990 and 1996 by three senior community education managers, Fraser Patrick, Alan Blackie and Stewart Murdoch), as 'a testament to the power of functionalism' and the 'pseudo commercial language of markets, investments and products'. Their critique that a competence approach was over-mechanistic has some validity. But the community education profession was sensitive to this and has drawn upon that which is useful from the competence model but also shaped it and re-interpreted it in a way which does stress the integration of knowledge, skills and values, with the competent community educator being encouraged *"to think, to act and to critically reflect upon practice"*.

The importance of promoting good management and staff development in community education goes back well into the 1980's if not earlier. Building upon the CeVe definition, in 1993 HMI published the first *Performance Indicators for the Community Education Services*. This was the outcome of a collaborative exercise between HMI, the Association of Directors of Education (ADES) and PCEO's. P.I.'s are a way of evaluating practice, of measuring how the community educator is performing. As can be seen from the extract, from what was a weighty document, one of the aims of the P.I. scheme was to make it possible to collate local authority statistics *"nationally to give a much needed Scottish picture of community education"*. They focus upon qualitative as well as quantitative indicators with a recognition that the context in which community education takes place was also a key variable. As it stands the current scheme is over complex and requires to be simplified. But what is certainly now central to Government's agenda is for community education agencies to more clearly demonstrate the outcome and efforts of their intervention. An agenda that is now broadly welcomed by the profession. The gathering of statistics as comparative data will be used to inform resource and financial planning decisions in community education as they are in other sectors of education. Whilst community educators have to date successfully argued against "the numbers game" as a crude measure of engaging participants in community based learning, it is a measure of sorts and one that is used by the Government as part of national education and training target setting. There is suspicion of the scheme as evidenced by articles in *Concept*, but with the support of local authority managers the measurement of outcomes is now central to the management agenda.

The key measures of the success of a community education intervention should of course be that which gave birth to it in the first place, the widening of participation particularly by the disadvantaged and the empowerment of participants in terms of an increase in knowledge, skills, confidence and the ability to influence change. As John Nisbet and Joyce Watt's research study entitled *Educational Disadvantage in Scotland* demonstrates, community education for all its limitations has achieved much in both rural and urban areas particularly when forming part of a wider collaborative social strategy involving schools, further and high education and other agencies. But as the paper concludes, emphasis upon certificates and qualifications as *the* measures of success, has narrowed the empowerment agenda, relegating community education's adult education role and focus upon the disadvantaged, to an access function and to an agenda dominated by vocational education and training. This is an important agenda, but as community educators and others argue, it should not be the only one.

The first published outcome of the PI's exercise, the Scottish Office Education and Industry Department's Bulletin of 1994-95 Community Education Statistics (to be published in April 1996) confirms that around 13% of the population now regularly participate in local authority Community Education Service projects in an average week, encompassing around half a million individual participants and 30,000 youth and community groups. Of these there is currently a 50:50 split between children and young people and adults (the latter category encompassing both adult education and community work projects). Statistics are not currently available for the voluntary sector or non education service local authority sectors. This is a significant increase in participation over the estimated 4% of adult participants identified by the Alexander Report in 1975, and the near 6% total youth and adult participants in Community Education Service programmes identified by John Horobin for the Scottish Council for Community Education for the year 1979.[15] Its significance is all the greater as a far higher proportion of participants now come from disadvantaged areas and groups, the result of social strategy targetting policies by the Regional authorities.

CHANGING CHALLENGES

In 1994/95 we found ourselves returning again to local government re-organisation in Scotland. The publication of the White Paper on local government re-organisation in 1993, with the scenario of unitary local authorities and the inference that Community Education and Leisure and Recreation Services might be brought together led to an immediate mobilisation of community education interests under a joint *Value for People* campaign co-ordinated by the Scottish Community Education Council. This campaign brought SCEC, ADES, PCEO's, SACES (Scottish Association of Community Education Staff) and the main voluntary sector providers together in a common strategy to retain community education as an integral part of an education service, comprising adult education, community work and youth work. A public relations prospectus entitled *Value for People* was published which explained what community education was about, its three functions and its underlying commitment to community development. Parliament, Government and Opposition were lobbied, and key supporting statements made in the House of Commons from all sides.[16] With the election of the Shadow councillors to the new authorities all received briefing packs and were targeted in a national media campaign. Two practical and I believe in the long term significant outcomes of the campaign were the agreement by COSLA (Convention of Scottish Local Authorities), at the request of SCEC, to set up its first ever community education working party and by the Scottish Education Department to publish Guidance to the new Councils that would state clearly the statutory obligations the new Councils were under.

Both Education and Leisure and Recreation Service interests during the passage of the bill adopted a somewhat defensive, perhaps predatory position. From the community education sector this was not because they did not greatly value closer cross sector co-operation at corporate and local level with Leisure and Recreation professionals. It was clear that former Regional and District Council services would be integrated in some way and that any duplication of resources would have to be addressed. But the concern was (a) to ensure that decision-makers had an informed briefing as to what community education was, in particular that it *was* an educational intervention and (b) to argue that whatever new structures were created they be built upon community needs.

The clearest exposition of how the two services might relate is outlined in the paper by Douglas Sinclair presented to a 1994 HMI conference. Sinclair was at that time Chief Executive of Central Regional Council and in 1995 became General Secretary of COSLA. He urged the two services to rise above the 'battleground' of professional self interest and for elected members and senior management to examine the needs of local communities within an holistic framework and to put the *"local back into local government through an extensive scheme of decentralisation"*. Both the *COSLA Report* and the *SOED Guidance* (6/95) echo this approach, with the latter also outlining the functions of community education which central Government regards as *'essential'*, regardless of organisational arrangements.

At the time of writing, the detail of the new organisational configurations is still unclear. Certainly the two services are in many of the new Councils being placed together, either within a broader Education or Community Services Department, with in the latter case community education being transferred in whole or part outwith the Education Service. Two positive signals seem to be that the majority of authorities are retaining the post Alexander framework of adult education, community work and youth work and where community education has been transferred and linked with aspects of Leisure and Recreation, it is being located with a Community Services or in one case Neighbourhood Services Department, an indication that neither service is being envisaged as taking over the other. At the end of the day much will depend upon the quality of political and managerial leadership. The learning needs of individuals and groups, of course, go on.

If much of the past two years has been taken up with raising the public profile, community education has continued to plough new ground in the campaign for building an active, participative and learning society. Through such initiatives as *Adult Learners' Week* a joint education/media campaign co-ordinated by SCEC, the profile of community education is now much better established in Scotland than in any other part of the UK. There is now a growing popular awareness of what community educators do. It is significant that of all the education sectors in Scotland community education, the smallest, has secured the central role in promoting the 1996 *European Year of Lifelong Learning*. The community education sector now provides one of the most comprehensive european information services on education and training programmes in Scotland – *Eurodesk*. For many years Scottish community educators have often been at the forefront in the UK in organising educational exchanges across Europe, in influencing pan european policy through both the Council of Europe and European Union, and in securing european funding. As the competences of the European Union have grown in recent years, so too have the concerns of community educators that Europe is a tier of government over which the individual citizen has limited power.[17]

The final paper, entitled *Scotland the Learning Society,* was published in 1995. It was the outcome of a SCEC working party chaired by Fraser Patrick, Assistant Director of Education, Tayside Region. This paper maps out the elements of what a new Scotland could look like, a Scotland that is not only a democratic country, with a strong culture, society and economy, but one that values learning and is willing to invest in it. *Scotland the Learning Society* is an outline, a route map perhaps, rather than a blueprint. It challenges, as community educators have at best always done, all the key institutions and centres of power to join together in building a new Scotland. We still have far to go in even getting close to overcoming the blockages to change. The revised Scottish Education and Training Targets launched by the Secretary of State in December 1995 are slowly beginning to acknowledge the scale of this challenge. What is for sure is that the part community educators have played in breaking down the barriers to learning and redefining the very nature of education has been significant and will be of critical value in the years to come.

In the short term there is an agenda that community educators will need to address and that is one of sustaining the developments of the last 21 years. Unlike the situation south of the border, Scotland has established integrated local authority Community Education Services. In most cases they have been large enough to provide a support structure for staff such as staff development, specialist resource and information services as well as a career ladder with senior posts at Principal Officer level and increasingly within the Directorate.

Community education in Scotland has thereby had an organisational and administrative identity within the local government system. This is not to say that much innovative and important practice has not been able to take place within other parts of the local authority system or from a college, school or voluntary sector base. But there have been difficulties for community educators located in short term funded posts. e.g. through the Urban Programme or within agencies for whom community education is not their main raison d'être. (The exceptions have been in Strathclyde and Fife where a large number of community work staff located in Social Work has allowed for the development of a similar support structure.)

The disaggregation of services with local government reorganisation into smaller units (affecting the urban areas of Scotland), is almost certainly likely to have a negative effect upon of provision. We are already seeing the demise of certain specialist services such as outdoor education. However there are examples of cross authority initiatives such as ACT (A Consortium of Training), which currently provides training support for community educators across several local authorities in the south of Scotland, and which will probably continue. There is a very real apprehension that we may be witnessing a haemorrhaging of the service in different parts of the country over the next year or two. That said, as the CoSLA report identifies, there are opportunities with new configurations of service delivery and multi-disciplinary working within a unitary local authority. The legislative requirements upon local authorities to implement decentralisation schemes can, as Douglas Sinclair's paper highlights, provide a more central role for staff with community education skills. It was to address this new challenge that in January 1996 the Scottish Community Education Council established its *Community Government* Service and published guidance and best practice on decentralisation and community empowerment.[18]

Across Scotland we have in positions within the new local authority system, in education departments, but also in chief executive units, community services, neighbourhood services and social work, senior managers who have been community educators. Many councillors have been involved in adult education, community work and youth work as professionals or volunteer activists such as Merv Rolf in Dundee, Keith Geddes in Edinburgh, Corrie McChord in Stirling and Val McIver in Highland Council. This is an enormous deposit of expertise and support which could bode well for the future.

Community education, of course, is no longer new. The 'young turks' of the mid 1970's are now in their 40's and 50's. The young people involved in the 1970's youth projects are parents in their mid 30's. A generation of Scots who participated in community education have often found their lives profoundly changed by the experience. The Scotland of the latter 1990's is a very different place from that identified by the Alexander committee. Whilst it is difficult to pinpoint the unique contributions that community educators have made towards changing social and political culture, the evidence does seem to suggest that those who have become active within their community as young people or as adults are more informed, less deferential and more confident to tackle and address change. Once people have been empowered in this way the route to equal opportunity and more participative forms of democracy begin to seem a bit more achievable.

To a certain extent it matters not one jot to the consumer, the learner, whether the educators who are working with them at local level are employed by an education department, a community services department or a further education college. What does matter is that the community educators be professional and that the quality of the learning experience is high. As is clear from some of the latter papers in this Reader both local authorities and central government have been anxious to ensure quality control. Local authorities such as Lothian and Grampian Regions have developed impressive quality assurance systems for community education. The work of Her Majesty's Inspectorate on performance indicators, as well as its periodic inspection reviews and development work, has been a significant factor in promoting best practice. The Scottish Office circular 6/95 will be the template by which HMI inspect all of the new education authorities, irrespective of whether community education is located within an education department. But cuts at central government level in the numbers of Inspectors is placing severe pressures upon this monitoring role. The proposal to end the national Specific Grant Scheme for in-service training for community educators, will also probably mean a loss of staff development investment in a number of local councils.

I have no doubt whatsoever that much of the impressive work of community education across the sectors over the 21 years, has been because there has been an increase in investment in the employment of professionally trained staff. Schools and colleges cannot operate without professional teachers and lecturers. Nor can community education. The role of the trained volunteer and the part time sessional worker is critical and a central feature in the provision of community education, but at its heart lies the full time professionally trained community educator. For some of the new councils we could be seeing a reduction in professional support with one community educator now working to a patch of 20,000 people or even more. Let us recall that they are responsible within such an area for organising youth work, community work and adult education either as a specialist or generalist. It is hardly surprising that many needs are never going to be met. For the voluntary sector too there still remains a need to ensure that full time staff are professionally trained. At the present time the voluntary sector lags significantly behind the statutory services in the employment of professionally trained staff although this need has been recognised as evidenced by the growing demand for CeVe endorsement. In general full time community education staff in the local authority sector are professionally qualified but are frequently over-stretched and in need of continuing professional development, not least at middle and senior management level. A particular cause for concern remains the need for investment in the training of part-time and voluntary staff, who as we have seen are central to the delivery of face-to-face work in local communities.

The weakness of the present legislation underpinning community education places its provision in a vulnerable situation, as has been manifested in some English local authorities with a similar statutory base. It was for this reason that the *Value for People* coalition campaigned during the passage of the Local Government (Scotland) Bill to strengthen the legal base. The Government has argued that this is not necessary, but community educators are not reassured by this statement and further pressure will be required over the next period to influence the law makers to introduce new legislation perhaps along the lines of the sufficiency requirements in Northern Ireland.

Strengthening the legal base for community education, as well as advocating for other legal changes and incentives to support participation in lifelong learning and to end policies that inhibit participation, must form part of Scotland's learning society agenda. There is also a case for changes in public administration within central government. The merger of the Scottish Office Education and Industry Departments has been broadly welcomed by the community education field, although there is a concern that this may lead to a narrow vocational emphasis and a further reduction in support for liberal education and active citizenship.

For educators, particularly educators committed to the principle of people empowerment, the democratic deficit in Scotland and the continuation of structural deprivation and social exclusion continue to focus attention upon the need for further political, social and economic reform. Community educators may work at a local level but they and the young people and adult groups with whom they work, are often well aware that the causes of many of the problems that affect individuals and communities lie outwith the local area.

With a heritage that draws upon such writers as Saul Alinsky, community educators require to be proficient in campaigning. In February 1996 the Scottish Community Education Council in association with the Advisory Scottish Council for Education and Training Targets and the Royal Society of Arts launched a *Scottish Campaign for Learning*. This is a five year campaign intended to bring together educationalists from both formal and informal education with people from the media and marketing. It will seek to profile the importance of learning in the same way that environmentalists during the 1980's successfully placed the environment not only onto the political, but also the personal agenda.

The Opinion Polls suggest that education is likely to be one of the key areas of debate in the lead up to the General Election. We now have a clearer picture of what an active, participative, learning society could look like and what is required to build such a society. Community education is an important part of that vision.

REFERENCES

1.   NIACE 1994 Research quoted in *Scotland as a Learning Society; Myth, Reality and Challenge*. SCEC 1995

2.   See for example Helen Crummy, *Let the People Sing!* Argyll 1992

3.   See the EPA *Report on the Scottish Action Research Project. A Scottish Study* edited by Charles Morrison, Joyce Watt and Terence Lee HMSO 1973

4.   Interestingly this criticism still exists. See *Community Education and Schools*. SCEC 1995

5.   For a recent review of community colleges in Scotland see *Open All Hours?* SCEC 1995.

6.   See the *Teaching of Community Work*. CCETSW paper 8 1974.

7.   Tony Worthington. *Why Local Government should encourage community development*. Community Development Journal Vol 17 No 2 1982.

8.   See for example Henderson P and Thomas D *Skills in Neighbourhood Work*. London Allen and Unwin 1980 and publications from the CDP Information and Intelligence Unit. The Scottish CDP was in Paisley.

9.   It is difficult to assess this, but my not objective feeling at the time was that community work advocates, particularly within the training agencies and on the SCEC *Training for Change* working party were more assertive.

10.   The Gulbenkian Report. *Community Work and Social Change* Longmans 1968.

11.   See Charlie McConnell. *The Community Worker as Politiciser of the Deprived*. Paisley 1977. Chapter 3 has a theoretical chapter on community work as a political education process.

12.   Alan Barr. *Practising Community Development: Experience in Strathclyde*, Community Development Foundation 1991.

13.   See *Paving the Way*. AEGIS SOED 1994. *Youth Work in Scotland* HMI HMSO 1991. *The Education of Adults in Scotland* HMI HMSO 1992.

14.   Tony Jeffs and Mark Smith. *A Question of Competence*. Concept Vol 3 No. 1 1993.

15.   John Horobin *Community Education Statistics* Scottish Council for Community Education 1980.

16.   See the *Local Government Reform Pack* prepared by the Scottish Association of Community Education Staff, published by Northern College in 1994 and *SCAN Briefing*, published by the Scottish Community Education Council for a blow by blow account of the campaign.

17.   For information on *Eurodesk* contact the Scottish Community Education Council's offices in Edinburgh, Rosebery House, 9 Haymarket Terrace, Edinburgh EH12 5EZ. Tel: 0131 313 2488; or Brussels, Egmont House, 15 B-1050, Brussels. Tel: 00 322 512 6155. For coverage on Europe and the 'democratic deficit' see Charlie McConnell and Marilyn Taylor eds *Community Development: The European Dimension* C.D.J. Oxford University Press 1991.

18.   Mike Martin *Decentralisation and Community Empowerment*. SCEC 1995

TONY GIBSON
PEOPLE POWER

PENGUIN BOOKS 1979 Ch.4

Gibshill is an overcrowded estate to the east of Greenock, high on a bare hill overlooking the Clyde shipyards, isolated from shops and other services by two low railway bridges, so low that the fire engines have to go the long way round to get to a fire. In 1972 it had nine hundred dwellings, for the most part concentrated in tenement flats, built on meagre Council budgets during the pre-war depression years, and neglected by successive corporations ever since.

This neglect, plus some of the worst unemployment figures in Britain, made people bloody-minded. The record for vandalism was such that one senior police officer used to say that all the vandalism in the United Kingdom started there, and spread as the local authority moved families out to other living areas. There was increasing resistance by Greenock Councillors to the idea of rehousing such families elsewhere. They quoted the 1969 recommendations of the authority's Planning Officer that there should be no major redevelopment of the area since this would 'merely result in the redistribution of the "problems" throughout the town'.

Gradually the area had become a ghetto where it was assumed that 'problem families' and 'delinquent youth' were concentrated. The place lived down to its reputation. There were frequent muggings, burglaries, looting and malicious damage to parked cars. The Gibshill label seemed to attract hostile treatment. Young job applicants reckoned that their chances vanished once the prospective employer saw on the application form where they came from. Relations with the police were bad. Residents were convinced that innocent youngsters were often 'lifted' for offences that others had committed. 'The Panda man' was a bogey to frighten children with. The tenement walls were scrawled with slogans attacking the local police by name.

In the spring of 1972 it would have been difficult to find any area more completely alienated from the rest of the community, more thoroughly stigmatised by the local authorities, or more completely demoralised about its own competence and character. Four and a half years later, in the autumn of 1976, Gibshill acquired a new reputation. At a time when elsewhere in the country the crime rates for teenagers and young children have been on the increase, a September 1976 police report showed that crimes and offences by Gibshill youngsters had been *halved*. There had been a 47 per cent reduction in the number of children reported, and a 56.6 per cent reduction in referrals, compared with the same nine-month period in 1975. The report said that the credit for this

> '... continuing and sustained process ... must be given mainly to the Gibshill community, since it is the people in that community who have brought this situation about, assisted by and supported in their efforts by the Local Authority and the officers of the Strathclyde Police.'

HOW DID IT HAPPEN?

First, there had been a bureaucratic reshuffle. In 1969 the Labour opposition persuaded the Liberal majority on the Greenock Council to encourage changes that brought the heads of the Council departments closer together. Working with the Chief Officer they began to plan a concentrated attack on the needs of each area. The plan remained on the shelf until May 1972, when the second big change occurred: Labour won power in the local elections. The new Council majority was committed to 'major' redevelopment but not at all sure whether any of it should take place in Gibshill. Many Councillors were inclined to argue that the place was such a write-off that any attempt, at redevelopment would be good money thrown after bad.

The third new factor was the Tenants' Association. It originated early in 1972 in the spurt of activity generated by the run-up to the local elections. It replaced a long-established local Residents' Association which had very little support, and even less influence in local affairs. The new Association was an almost despairing effort to obtain some say for Gibshill in its own future. Its first big decision was that every available member of the Association should go to the Council chamber for the crucial meeting, in June 1972, on the redevelopment proposals. To everyone's surprise sixty-eight members turned up. They had to listen to 'insults to the Gibshill people spoken by some of the Councillors', but they stuck it out; and their silent presence probably tipped the balance. The decision to redevelop Gibshill, as a priority commitment, went through.

The minority argument (that it would be wasted effort) might well have been justified had it not been for the fourth element in the situation: the youth. The Tenants' Association meetings were well attended by adults, but in its early days many local youngsters showed their feelings about the generation gap by stoning the TA hut as the members came out. Most adults regarded this as typical juvenile behaviour, and left it angrily at that. One member of the Association did not. Danny Keenan was then in his early fifties, an ex-bus driver and shop steward with a heart condition and troubled with asthma. He had no qualifications in youth work, no special experience, and his formal education had been cut short at thirteen and a half, when he had to go out to work to help support his family; but he decided that something should be attempted which would give youngsters a stake of their own.

At this time the only official provision for youth was a club in the church hall, run twice a week on very traditional lines by a policeman paid as a part-time youth leader by the local Education Authority. Attenders tended to be ' goodies ' and they and the premises were frequently stoned by the 'baddies' outside (who eventually set fire to the place). With some difficulty Danny Keenan persuaded his Association to allow him the use of their hut for a kids' disco. He managed to borrow a tape-recorder and a radiogram, and to persuade one or two teenagers to help him. In no time at all they had sixty to seventy 10-12-year-olds – ex baddies as well as ex-goodies – all mixed together and no trouble to speak of.

This was the situation, early in 1973, when the Council took the initiative, in response to the TA's turn-out at the Council meeting, and called a meeting of residents. At this the key officials in the Chief Officer's team unfolded their redevelopment plan for Gibshill. Their plan. For though there had been a few minor leaks, there had been no previous consultation. This time 150 residents turned up. They heard out the Council's plans, and then began to comment on them from the floor.

They said that they didn't want the pub that had been planned: it would be better to have licensed club premises, under the tenants' control, free of commercial pressure to push hard drinking. They wanted the chemist's shop kept as a local resource, instead of being absorbed into a shopping complex outside the area because that would be too far away for elderly people. They had more to say on the type of shops that were needed, and on modernising the houses and flats.

Some senior officials had come reluctantly to the meeting, expecting either an apathetic turn-out, or a barrage of complaints. They began to admit to themselves that the tenants' suggestions were shrewd and relevant. Others who had been more optimistic found their hopes exceeded. Overnight the idea of 'joint consultation' began to make sense. But the structure they set up took some of the steam out of the operation. The inter departmental Technical Co-ordinating Committee of officials was linked up with 'the Subcommittee' – a liaison group of tenants with a newly appointed neighbourhood worker, and the community development officer. It embarked on a long series of discussions. Meanwhile the plans began to be implemented. There were some minor revisions to meet the tenants' earliest suggestions, but the tenants themselves found it harder and harder to influence official priorities, or to keep track of the costing revisions. The officials blamed inflation: the tenants said ' the monies have been whittled away' because of bad planning. But they couldn't get close enough to prove it.

The work proceeded. Existing houses were modernised, some new houses built, the first phase of the landscaping completed, all more or less according to plan – the officials' plan. Towards the end of 1976 one of the instigators of the whole consultation exercise, Ronald Young, now a Regional Councillor, took stock of what he called 'the planning process:'

> *"in local government terms the progress has been considerable but a weakness throughout has been the failure of tenants to be supplied with or themselves to collect, basic information to permit them to chase progress – let alone anything more ambitious ...*
>
> *With one exception, the architects and quantity surveyors particularly could not establish a proper client relationship with the representatives of the neighbourhood ... no real dialogue took place ... the reasonable aspirations of tenants were quickly translated by professionals into expensive schemes which were beyond the willingness (or ability) of the political system to supply.*
>
> *The programme was tightly controlled by the professionals who in no way changed their traditional operational behaviour and assumptions."*

On the official side, then (given the setbacks of the three-day week and the Government cuts), modest progress in meeting deadlines. On the community side, initial enthusiasm that gradually drained away as it became apparent that the officials were going their own way, regardless. With one crucial exception.

The 'exception' can be traced back to the tenants' consultation meeting convened by the Council officials in January 1973. At the back of the hall stood a bunch of the toughest of the older teenagers. When the meeting was formally ended they button-holed the Director of Social Work and asked him 'What's for us?' He handed them straight over to the newly appointed neighbourhood worker, Ralph Ibbott, who put the question back to them: Will you tell us what you want ?

Yes, they would, but there must be time and a place provided to do it properly. He stepped across the floor, then and there, to the Tenants' Association Chairperson and got her, possibly before she quite realised what was happening, to offer these notorious knife-carrying youngsters the use of the Association's hut in a few days' time. The group turned up on schedule, met Ralph Ibbott and Danny Keenan (whose work with the 10-12-year-olds had first caught their fancy) and told them what was what.

They wanted a coffee bar meeting-place and facilities to organise football and table tennis. And most of all they wanted something done about the behaviour of the police. They backed their criticisms with a long string of detailed allegations.

Adults at the previous meeting had already suggested replacing the panda car patrols by 'beat ' policemen, and setting up a police office within the area as a liaison point. Ralph Ibbott and Danny Keenan got hold of the Chief Constable, and the Superintendent in charge of 'community involvement', and persuaded them to meet some of the Tenants' Association members and thrash the whole thing out. As a direct result the panda patrols were reduced in favour of policemen who were allowed to volunteer for the beat, and who began to establish better relations, with adults as well as with youngsters.

The 16-17-year-olds became further involved in the work being done by Danny Keenan (now working full time; with his pay provided by a charitable Trust). Some of those who were out of work joined him in helping to repaint the TA hut. More joined in with him in operating the 10-12s disco (now running four nights a week, with a noticeable drop in police 'liftings' for juvenile offences).

In July 1973 the 17-year-olds helped to organise a very successful holiday trip for thirty-six 10-14s. In August, sixteen of the toughest 15-16-year-olds turned up and explained that they wanted to have a camp for themselves. They went into a huddle then and there and produced their own 'rules for the camp' (unasked and before even the tents had been obtained). They returned from a very successful, and relatively law-abiding camp to become the founder-members of the youth group which now began to form in order to build a youth hut.

The hut project had the advantage of a steady improvement in everyone's morale. Children were getting into trouble less often. The community was beginning to think well of the teenagers. The teenagers began to feel better about themselves. The authorities became much more helpful.

A derelict contractor's hut was obtained via the Police Superintendent. The Council Amenities Committee provided cement, bricks, extra timber, paint, and electric fittings. Brick foundations were laid by six kids from a List D (Approved) school, two of them locals, supervised by their instructor. The contractor working on the estate modernisation scheme contributed plumbing materials and allowed two trainee plumbers to work on the scheme in the firm's time. During a strike at the local Chrysler works one of the strikers, who was a skilled joiner, helped supervise the carpentry. Intensive work by the youth group got the hut installation completed and occupied in under three months.

Early in 1974 the 'traditional' youth club, that had been run in the church hall, folded. The new group, now thriving in its own hut, applied to the education department for permission to take over. At first the authority was very doubtful. After all Danny Keenan was not 'qualified' as a youth worker. But negotiations were eventually successful; a new, and greatly expanded club was opened, catering for the whole of the 10-16 age group, with the 17-year-olds helping Danny to run it.

At this point the 'community' strand in the Gibshill story begins to tangle with the 'planning process' mentioned earlier. The professionals, particularly the architects, had their own clear ideas about how Gibshill should look when finished. There would be a splendid new social centre, catering for both adults and youngsters, which would bring the whole life of the community into focus (and look rather well, from a distance – say half-way across the river) as the key feature in the whole design.

The Tenants' Association did not see it that way. They figured, correctly, that the scale first proposed by the planners would price the centre right out of any practical scheme for the immediate future. So their first step was to back those on the District Council who wanted a less expensive scheme (£200,000 instead of £550,000). Their next proposal was even more distasteful to the architects. The TA had recently lost their own premises through a freak electrical fire; they were sharing the teenagers' hut with them. But the Association put its own interest aside. The needs of the youth must come first. They wanted the youth section of the centre separated from the rest of the premises, so that it could (a) have its own open space surrounding it, and (b) be constructed first, without waiting for the remainder of the centre to be completed.

The 'Subcommittee' (the liaison group of tenants set up by the Council's Technical Co-ordinating Committee) was now the arena in which tenants and planners locked horns over the new centre. The tenants won their point and got the youth centre detached, having gained the support of the Social Work Department. But during 1975 as the building work on the youth centre proceeded, they suddenly found themselves with a fresh set of administrators to educate.

The new Region of Strathclyde had lurched on to the scene, sending officials flying in all directions. There was now a newcomer at the head of the Department of Leisure and

Recreation whose first step was to announce his plans for the staffing of the new centre with people who should be 'properly qualified'.

The first reaction of the Tenants' Association was to assert their right to share in making these new appointments. It was agreed that they should be represented on the Selection Board. But the more they thought about the situation the less they liked it. Even supposing that Danny Keenan were to apply for one of the jobs, and be selected – what kind of set-up would result? Who really would be running the show? After nine months of negotiations, and with the centre almost completed, the Tenants' Association worked its way through to the final and entirely logical decision, and forced its acceptance, very reluctant, on the authorities: the new youth centre should be run by, as well as for, the community it served. The Council's Leisure and Recreation Committee appointed and paid the caretaker and the cleaners. But the management became the responsibility of the Tenants' Association.

In April 1976 the youth hall opened, with Danny Keenan in charge, helped by a dozen other TA members, plus a loose-knit 'working committee' of upwards of twenty 14-17-year-olds who ran the juniors. The Association arranged to rent the premises from the Council with funds obtained by charging door money (5p to juniors, 10p to seniors). The centre operates seven nights a week, and caters for around 400 youngsters. There is no formal constitution. Membership secures cheaper rates for certain items, but local youngsters who are not members can use the place too, if they behave.

'Behaviour problems' are rare inside the centre, and becoming more rare outside it. The drop in the crime rate reported by the police has been maintained in 1977. By the end of 1976 vandalism had almost ceased; anyone could walk around the area after dark, unmolested; whereas five years earlier you wouldn't park a car at night and expect to see it intact the next morning.

Gibshill has roughly the same number of residents to draw on as the Winstanley Tenants' Association. It lacked Winstanley's strong tradition of mutual help; and it started out with a much worse reputation. But it seems to have caught up; and in some respects come further. It had the advantage of an incoming Labour majority on the Council which had sharpened its principles and clarified some of its objectives while in opposition. The new Council encouraged a few enlightened Council officials to collaborate with each other, and to recognise that the community had something of its own to contribute. But few, apart perhaps from Councillor Ronald Young, had bargained for the strength of purpose the community has shown.

Local people discovered their strength at the Council meeting when sixty-eight TA members by their mere presence seemed to tip the balance in Gibshill's favour. But the really convincing evidence of what could be done was provided by Danny Keenan and his gradually increasing band of teenage collaborators. They convinced first themselves, and then others, by what they did, rather than what they said about it.

When the TA took part in joint consultation meetings with the planners, although their initial advice was good, their influence in the long run was small. When they decided to shift the argument about the social centre to their own ground, their own experience began to count. They could act, and therefore speak, with conviction. They could demonstrate, to themselves as well as to others, not merely what should be done but their own capacity to do it.

The Gibshill story so far is a piece of self-revelation by members of the community, which is slowly being recognised by officialdom. Local people discovered that in certain important respects they knew better, and could do better, than the professionals; and that this was because they cared more.

For many authorities this is still a dubious assumption. They know the sheer size of the problems they are up against. They cannot see how anyone else can expect to achieve more than they are achieving already. For people to take things into their own hands seems impertinent, as well as ill-advised.

ROBERT HUGHES
COMMUNITY EDUCATION WITHIN THE CONTEXT OF REORGANISATION OF LOCAL GOVERNMENT

SCOTTISH JOURNAL OF YOUTH AND COMMUNITY WORK
THE BOARD FOR INFORMATION ON YOUTH & COMMUNITY SERVICE 1975

The theme of my remarks emphasises the important point reached in the life of Scotland and of the Youth and Community Service. This raises two immediate questions: What do we mean by community education? What will be the effect of local government reorganisation?

Let me begin by examining the second question. The philosophy behind the Local Government (Scotland) Act 1973 is to devolve more power on local authorities. On the one hand, we will have bigger local government units. New Departments including Departments of Recreation will bring different services together. I am aware of the deep concern in Youth and Community Service that the new Departments of Recreation might assume some of the responsibilities of the present education authorities for providing facilities for leisure and recreation. Even at present, of course, local authorities other than education authorities have powers to provide these facilities. The power to provide facilities has never been the sole preserve of education committees. I do not think however that there would be much benefit in using this occasion to deal in detail with local authority organisation. I would prefer to look more positively at the future role of your service though I hope to touch on the question of relations between education and other services later.

One of the new features of the Local Government Act is the provision which has been made for greater involvement by the community through community councils, and school and college councils. Greater public participation is something which the Government has encouraged in all aspects of living: industry, planning, housing. It follows that local communities should be given greater encouragement to participate in the running of educational establishments. This is not something new for people who have been engaged in the Youth and Community Service. Voluntary commitment and participation is something which other services strive for, but which this Service can almost take for granted. It is accepted without question that over 50,000 people, the vast majority of them volunteers, should give up their time to encourage young people and adults to develop their skills and enrich the quality of their own lives and that of the communities in which they live. It is accepted without question that the Youth and Community Service should encourage the users of centres to become closely involved in the management and running of the facilities. Voluntary participation is a basic tenet of the Service, and over the years the Service has developed an expertise in encouraging and developing voluntary commitment for the good of the community as a whole. This gives it a unique contribution to make in the future. No change in our institutions of Government, local or national, can be free of controversy or be free of doubt, but local government reorganisation does offer exciting opportunities for people in every community in Scotland to become more involved in Government in all its aspects.

I think we all accept the desirability of greater public participation, but how much of this is a kind of ritual part of speech? How can community education help to promote participation and what do we mean by 'community education'? In its widest sense it can embrace all forms of education, be it formal education, school education or whatever. In its more limited sense it may mean nothing more that the job being done now by the Youth and Community Service. My own impression, however, is that the Association has adopted the term 'community education' for two reasons. First, the Association is conscious of the task to be done in making education opportunities more widely available in the community as a means of encouraging people to develop their own interests and talents and to enrich the quality of life in the communities in which they live. Secondly, I think it represents an invitation from the professional workers in the Youth and Community Service to other educationalists involved in this type of activity, particularly to adult educationalists, for closer co-operation in meeting this educational challenge.

It is an open secret that the Alexander Committee will recommend closer integration of Adult Education and Youth and Community Service. Professor Alexander himself speaking at this Conference last year, made this clear. Already, however, education authorities have been moving in the direction of an integrated Youth and Community Service and Adult Education Service, frequently under the name of 'Community Education Service'. I believe this closer integration is both inevitable and desirable. But it cannot merely be an administrative exercise within the departments of national or local government. Purely administrative integration can lead perhaps to undesirable comparisons and professional conflict which are sterile and can only be to the disadvantage of those for whom the service is intended, namely the individual in the community. Nor can it be a takeover by one service or the other. The coming together must be based on recognition by all of the common aims of the two services and the task to be done. I believe that the aim of this conference is above all to help and define that task, not as something which is the province of a Youth and Community Service, or of statutory authorities as opposed to voluntary organisations, but as something in which all concerned with every aspect of informal further education, have a contribution to make. Voluntary youth organisations, voluntary adult organisations, professional youth and community workers and adult educationalists each have a part to play.

We have seen that the reorganisation of local government presents a new challenge and fresh opportunities for community involvement in all aspects of government. Basically, this means the involvement of people in improving and developing their own skills and improving the quality of life in the communities in which they live. We only have to look around to see the vast changes taking place in Scotland. There are problems of social and urban deprivation on the one hand and of providing adequate social infra-structure in the neglected older areas of our cities; and on the other hand problems arising in the expanding areas of the North East, and of course new problems in our modern estates. In this latter case it may be the same problems in a different form, but we are all conscious of the pressures which living in a highly mechanised society puts on the ordinary man and woman. It is not for me to give you a programme of community education on which the Youth and

Community Service and Adult Education Service might work together. Such a programme would depend on local circumstances. But it is clear to me that the Youth and Community Service has a continuing educational role in helping communities and I should like to look at some aspects of the work to be done.

There is the principle which lies at the heart of the Government's social policy – the principle of equality of opportunity. You may have noticed that the Queen's Speech at the opening of this Parliament contained a reference to the Government's commitment to legislate to make equal opportunities available to women and men in a whole range of services, from employment to education. In education our policy of comprehensive schooling is firmly based on our belief that there should be equal opportunity for all. But as we try to improve opportunities in school we must try to ensure that opportunities for continuing education are available to all members of the community. Young people who are encouraged to develop interests in school should be given a chance to develop these interests further outside school. People who have never had the opportunity to develop their interests can and should be encouraged to realise their potential.

I have mentioned economic and social change. One of the most obvious results of the changes taking place in our society is the increased leisure time which people have at their disposal. An immense amount of work has been done by education authorities, adult education bodies, such as the WEA and voluntary youth organisations, to make more and more opportunities available for leisure education. But is it enough to make opportunities available and hope that people will use them? Some people do not know about the opportunities and other do not feel that they are suitable for them.

Now that the service is better staffed than formerly we should be thinking more of going out into the community, discussing with people what they feel their needs to be and helping them to decide for themselves how to satisfy these needs. We should not allow the provision of facilities to distract the education service from the underlying educational problem – how to get people involved, first in developing their own personal resources, and then in harnessing these to the needs of the community.

Every community offers a multitude of opportunities for self expression. But since we are looking this evening specifically at community education in the context of local government reorganisation let me mention two examples – school and college councils and community councils. I have already referred to the intention behind the local Government (Scotland) Act to balance the bigger local government units with bodies capable of offering local people a direct say in the running of community affairs. If these councils are to succeed there can be no question of a particular service taking them over. But that is not to say that community education has no part to play in helping the councils to be successful. There is a need to inform the public of the democratic right to participate in these councils. But a Community Education Service if it is to help prepare young people, parents, every member of the community to contribute towards improving the quality of life in the community, must take educational opportunity into the community.

It would be foolish to suppose that we can successfully promote education in the community without making contact with people in their homes and as they go about their daily business. One educational problem which perhaps brings this out more than any other is the problem of illiteracy and semi-literacy among the adult population. This is a complex problem. Its precise scale is not known, but is has been suggested that there may be as many as two million adult illiterates in the UK. We in the Government have been considering what steps might be taken to help education authorities and voluntary organisations to tackle this problem in the immediate future. The problem goes much wider than teaching people to read and write, and this is where co-operation between youth and community workers, adult educationalists and other volunteers is so necessary. There are difficulties of making contact with people who cannot read conventional adverts or write asking for help. There are psychological difficulties as well as problems of communication, for there is a great deal of social stigma attached to a basic handicap or deprivations like illiteracy. It is a problem which a Community Education Service closely in touch with a community's need could contribute greatly towards resolving. Literacy problems are only some of those on which community education could make an impact. Others you know well: the social problems of young people; consumer education; environmental education and many more.

The task is immense and will require more resources. But at times of economic difficulty such as the present every service has an obligation to look closely at its objectives and at the use it makes of existing resources including those of other services. I would like briefly, therefore, to develop some aspects of the use of resources. First, the use that is made of physical facilities. Second, the need for co-operation among professional workers; and third the role of the voluntary bodies and individual volunteers.

I referred earlier to the responsibilities of various local government departments for providing community facilities in the widest sense – community centres, swimming pools, arts centres, libraries, etc. The provisions in the Local Government Act which give concurrent responsibilities for the provision of community facilities could, let us face it, lead to disputes over demarcation of responsibilities. The question may be asked, "Who should provide community services", the Regional education department or the District recreation department? It would be a pity indeed if a legislative provision designed for maximum flexibility and co-operation were to lead to inter-service jealousy. Local authorities must recognise that community facilities are what they say they are – facilities for the people in the community. It may be for a particular service to provide certain types of facilities but if they are not available to the community as a whole the exercise is futile. (e.g. when school swimming pools are provided for other than school use, sometimes this is only for organised clubs. I do not want to digress too much but I sometimes feel in leisure activities we are becoming too organised.)

The views of the Government on the use of schools by the community are well known. I am well pleased with the evidence I have seen of school facilities being widely used by clubs and voluntary groups, but I am convinced that more can still be done.

It would not, however, be consistent with the theme of my remarks if I over-emphasised the importance of buildings. Buildings, no matter how many or how costly, are only a means to an end – and they are not the only means. This brings me to my second point. Professional staff are, if used properly, our most valuable resource not only because of their own skills but also because they themselves can mobilise resources, including the professional staff from other services. The formal education, recreation, social work and community education services must work closely together to provide a widely-based service. They will have to rely heavily on voluntary effort to assist them. Indeed community education might measure its success in proportion to the voluntary effort which it generates, since the whole raison d'être of the service should be the development of the individual. Ideally, every person in the community is a voluntary resource working for the good of the community. We are far from that situation.

We must ask ourselves to what extent this is the result of rapid changes in society and a lack of awareness among ordinary people that they can change things. How far are people aware that they can improve the quality of their own lives? How far are they aware of the contribution which they as individuals can make to the quality of the communities in which they live? I have mentioned the use of physical resources to meet the aims of community education. But what about human resources? Ordinary people in the community have much to offer if they can only be made aware of the needs of the community and, above all, of the opportunities of developing and improving life in the community! It is the community itself which must surely be the main resource of a Community Education Service.

I have talked about a possible way ahead for the Youth and Community Service working closely with adult education towards common aims. It would be imprudent not to recognise that there will be human problems to overcome before a common programme can be worked out and put into practice. Close co-operation means recognition of things which people have in common rather than the differences. The development of professional qualifications leads so often to too much weight being given to differences: differences of status, of qualification, or professional orientation. As professionals in the Education Service you have an essential contribution to make to community education and community development. Only if this is made in full co-operation on equal terms with other educationists and professionals outside the education service can the community as a whole derive full advantage from what local government reorganisation offers for participation by individuals in the community. I have spoken about the need to make these opportunities as widely available as possible. I hope that the Youth and Community Service in contributing to community education and participation will recognise these aims and do all it can to promote them.

ALEXANDER REPORT
THE CHALLENGE OF CHANGE

HMSO 1975 pp 25-58

AIMS OF ADULT EDUCATION

General Considerations

If the concept of education as a life-long process is to be given reality the education of adults must be accepted as an essential component of national policy designed to deal with the pressures of change and to improve the quality of life. The view of adult education as a marginal enterprise serving the interests of a relatively small proportion of the population can no longer be justified.

Learning is a basic characteristic of life and man can learn as a result of every experience he undergoes. Education is a more organised or structured form of learning, by no means always associated with an institution. Continuing education, of which adult education is a part, is thus a series of learning experiences organised, structured or deliberately created by the learner or by others. It therefore covers a wide range of situations such as some forms of industrial and vocational training and retraining, the voluntary continuation of studies begun in initial education, activities undertaken for recreational purposes, the pursuit of knowledge and skills to further the aims of specific organisations, and individual study. The impact of newspapers and the broadcasting media or the activities of pressure groups and propaganda cannot be overlooked. Often the form of continuing education is highly specific to particular groups as in the case of sports clubs and political organisations. The educational service for adults must take account of other available educational opportunities and make provision which, taken together with these other opportunities, is comprehensive and relevant and is responsive to the needs not only of individuals but of the community and of society itself.

Distinctions between different aspects or fields of education are necessary for administrative purposes but it has to be recognised that they are often imprecise and arbitrary. Adult education for example merges imperceptibly with formal education in schools, colleges and universities and with the informal activities of youth clubs, community centres and voluntary organisations. Distinctions made for administrative purposes can create barriers which impede the development of education as a life-long process. Various recent developments in initial education are removing traditional barriers and should help to foster a more widespread recognition of the continuity of education.

With the very wide connotation given to education the question of values assumes greater importance. So long as education was equated with teaching and restricted to specific institutions the aims and objectives of the process, though much argued over in detail, tended to be fairly uniform and to reflect the dominant values, of the society which controlled it. Society is now less certain about the values it should uphold and tolerates a wide range. Individual freedom to question the value of established practices and institutions and to propose new forms is part of our democratic heritage. To maintain this freedom, resources should not be put at the disposal only of those who conform but ought reasonably to be made available to all for explicit educational purposes. The motive of those who provide education need not necessarily be identified with the motives of those for whom it is provided.

We have used the term 'need' on several occasions and feel that it requires some definition. The term is a confusing one; we use it to indicate the gap between the present state of an individual and the more desirable one to which he aspires. This concept can be applied to a community or to society as a whole. Needs in this sense are derived from an individual's way of life and his environment. He cannot always clearly recognise them nor can they be simply identified by external observation. Their identification emerges as a result of a process of interaction involving those thought to be in need and those able to provide for its satisfaction. Nor must it be assumed that the assessment of need is a once-and-for-all matter. It must be a continuing process and in regard to adult education is an essential one if provision is to be relevant.

SPECIFIC AIMS

In an attempt to define a clear role for adult education we have taken into account such factors as the growing technological basis of our society, the dehumanising aspect of many kinds of work and the impact of the mass media, all of which tend to erode individuality and paradoxically to increase a sense of isolation and alienation. There is therefore a growing need for opportunities which enable individuals to develop their capacities for a full and rich personal and social life and for educational provision to be directed at reducing to the minimum impediments to this development. Therefore we see the reaffirmation of individuality as the first aim of adult education.

Further the increasing range and sophistication of the products of modern technology, the sheer scale of its institutions and the complexities of modern bureaucratic processes make it more essential than ever to ensure that people have the necessary skill and knowledge to use to the full the resources of society. The effective use of the resources of society is a second aim.

In a society that encourages freedom of association and stresses the rights of the individual it is inevitable that groups of people will emerge whose common interests, problems or characteristics may be regarded, in some cases only initially, as those of a minority. Sometimes their attitudes will differ only in degree from that of the community at large; an organisation like Shelter, for example, highlights society's general if less active concern about housing conditions. Occasionally minority groups will have beliefs that differ more radically from those of contemporary society, as those of trades unions once did. In either case acceptance of the very existence of such dissenting groups entitles us to describe our society as pluralist and to consider ourselves as living in a free community in which individuals have the right to unite with like-minded people and give expression to their opinions. This right to form groups, along with the right of opposition to and criticism of the government of the day and other forms of authority, is fundamental to a pluralist society. Such groups have a right to seek a share of the resources available for adult education whenever the purpose can reasonably be regarded as educational. To foster the pluralist society is a third aim.

The final aim we have identified is education for change itself. Many individuals wish to play a more active part in shaping their own physical and social environment. They seek opportunities to participate in the making of decisions that affect the facilities, amenities and organisations on which the quality of life very much depends, The institutions of society are undergoing continuous transformation and, while on some occasions these changes are willed by the individuals and groups most affected, on other occasions these individuals and groups are the reluctant victims. In both cases new ways of acting and new ways of learning must be developed.

We now make proposals for the kind of provision that will assist in the realisation of these several aims.

REAFFIRMATION OF INDIVIDUALITY

Recreation

Each day many thousands of adults involve themselves in recreational activities. They may join a group or class for one of the many forms of physical recreation, a choral group or a music ensemble, a painting class or a class in ceramics, a class in conversational French or in dog obedience, a class in sewing, woodwork, literature, philosophy or one of a hundred others. Their motives in joining are many and varied—to acquire a new skill, to enjoy new activities, to keep abreast of social, political or cultural development, or simply to meet people. Over the country as a whole an impressive variety of activities appears to be provided. Local provision is limited however and is not always equally available to all. We are in no doubt that involvement in the kind of activities instanced here can add new dimensions to life. Providing bodies must ensure that provision is made at appropriate times and in appropriate places so that all members of the community from the most disadvantaged to the most gifted have access to these opportunities for self-fulfilment.

The Family

The family has always made important contributions to the education of the young and to social well-being generally and it is a matter of concern that its capacity to make these contributions may be reduced by the increasing stresses and strains placed upon it by social change and technological advance. Good parenthood requires an understanding of the physical, mental, emotional and social development of children and an awareness of the relative contributions of home and school to the child's education. Furthermore the creation of a home has financial and managerial as well as emotional aspects. Preparation for the responsibilities of parenthood starts in the school but opportunities for learning about these responsibilities and how to discharge them must continue to be provided until well into adult life. Already there is a demand for provision aimed at improving the quality of the family home, the quality of family life and the quality of the relations between and among members of the family. These demands will undoubtedly increase and provision must therefore be made more widely available to all sections of the community. Activities and a programme directed at the family as a whole can contribute a great deal and should be further developed.

In almost all families there comes a time when the roles of parent and child are all but reversed. While the elderly parent is an individual in his own right and should be encouraged to participate in whatever educational facilities are provided we see no reason why the grown-up child should not be assisted to understand the problems of the elderly.

The Elderly

Advances in medical and welfare services have had significant effects on the age structure of the population. An increasing proportion of the population is aged 60 or over. Many elderly people are active and are capable of using to the full whatever educational facilities are available to the community as a whole and should be encouraged to do so. Nevertheless the elderly retired person often has particular problems concerning, for example, health, change of status and the amount of leisure and so requires provision of a particular kind. Pre-retirement courses and retirement courses have developed over the last few years and we hope that this development will continue.

The Disadvantaged

Over the last decade or so attention to those at a disadvantage in our society has shown that their plight is due to a variety of social, economic, educational and personal deficiencies which, because they tend to be handed down from one generation to the next, are to a large extent self-perpetuating. Education alone cannot break this 'cycle of deprivation' but it has a role to play in altering the attitudes of adults caught up in it. Without an alteration in these attitudes the effects of any change in the physical environment might be nullified. This is an area of work where a co-ordinated approach involving housing, social work and health departments as well as education is clearly called for. It is also an area of work of high priority where costs will be relatively high and results slow to materialise.

The Handicapped

In our society there are some who differ from the majority in that they are affected by mental or physical handicap. The precise nature and extent of the handicap varies considerably as do the social and educational needs of the individuals concerned. Much is done to meet the educational needs of the handicapped who are still of school age but investigations carried out on our behalf show that little or nothing is being done to meet the special educational needs of the mentally or physically handicapped adult. Those who are able to do so are expected, rightly in our view, to take advantage of conventional adult education provision; those who cannot however are largely disregarded. Clearly this is an area of need which requires special attention.

Remedial Education

It is disappointing that in spite of the increasing length of schooling there is still a significant number of adults whose basic educational and social skills are inadequate. This inadequacy makes it difficult for them to secure and retain employment compatible with their true ability, reduces their effectiveness as citizens and prevents them from exploiting to the full the opportunities of life. Facilities for remedial education, wider in content than those available in primary or secondary education, must be provided in post-school education in settings and with methods that take full account of the insecurity experienced by the adults concerned.

EFFECTIVE USE OF RESOURCES

Consumer Education

The major thrust of our economy is directed towards the production of consumer goods. Though many of these goods reach a high level of sophistication they are aimed at the ordinary man or woman. Competition to sell products results in high pressure salesmanship where the essential qualities of the product are hidden behind verbiage and hyperbole. The very size and impersonality of retail outlets make it difficult for consumers to be discriminating in their purchasing and difficult for them to register complaints. The rights of the consumer are being more widely recognised but protective legislation can be only partially effective in a situation where astute commercial brains are continuously looking for methods of increasing sales. Although there has been substantial provision of classes on decimalisation and Value Added Tax and specialised provision by voluntary organisations such as the Electrical Association for Women with their courses in the use of electricity, education for the consumer is an area which has been relatively neglected. Consumer education must concern itself with how to use, how to choose, how to distinguish fact from opinion, how to seek redress and how to bring pressure to bear on producers in the interests of the consumer.

Large and growing numbers of people now buy articles on credit with very little idea of what the facility of credit is costing them. Many are quite unaware of how the rents of their houses are calculated, of the difference between rent and rates, of the comparative returns they get in satisfaction from the proportion of income which they spend on food, clothes, rent, rates, entertainment, holidays and so on. The complexities of the welfare state and the rights and obligations it brings are often little understood by those who should most benefit from it. Involvement in even the most minor way with officialdom can create acute feelings of uncertainty and anxiety among large sections of the population. We have recorded evidence that this is a vast area of unsatisfied educational need and we commend this to the attention of the providers of adult education.

Health Education

The demands of society place on the individual a considerable stress both of a physical and of a mental nature and his ability to respond to them is greatly dependent on his state of health; yet it is only in pre-retirement or retirement courses that health education features prominently. There is need for educational provision directed at creating a more positive attitude to good health and a more sensitive understanding of physical and mental health. Provision of this kind should be extended to the various groups in the community with common health problems or hazards. Perhaps an even greater need is to ensure that all members of the community are fully informed about the interrelation of health, diet, work, exercise and the environment in which they live. Any programme of health education should concern itself with the prevention of accidents and with the dangers of smoking, alcohol and drugs. Probably more than any other this area of education of adults requires co-ordination of effort, involving as it does different departments of local and central government as well as many voluntary organisations. Agencies of adult education generally must contribute more widely than in the past to the provision of opportunities leading to personal and community action to maximise the use of the available resources for the promotion of good health in all its physical, psychological and social manifestations.

FOSTERING THE PLURALIST SOCIETY

Industrial Relations

The quality of industrial relations affects the lives and livelihoods of everyone. Human relations at work and collective bargaining form an area of activity which has not been backed by an educational provision adequate to prepare people for their involvement in it. This has been particularly true of the employee side of industrial relations with trades unions depending for most of their administrative skill and leadership at local level on the voluntary activity of branch officials and shop stewards. On the management side too there are still serious gaps in the educational provision for supervisors, foremen and those at higher levels of management who are directly involved in industrial relations, in many cases without an adequate understanding of the problems involved and the skills required to resolve them. This may be a deficiency in vocational rather than adult education and for that reason outwith our terms of reference. However this is an area in which we find it difficult clearly to draw such a distinction and we consider it appropriate for us to stress that there is a strong case for expanded provision of education for trade unionists, supervisors and management in the skills required in industrial relations.

Immigrants and Foreign Workers

The educational needs of immigrants and foreign workers are of two kinds: those relating to their parent culture and those concerned with their assimilation into the Scottish culture. There is little evidence in the public sector of any provision aimed specifically at maintaining the cultural life of the immigrant, yet if education is to meet the needs of all this is a very easily identifiable area of need. A number of bodies such as the Institut Francais d'Ecosse exist to further the interests of their own nationals and others attracted to their culture. Generally they demand a relatively high educational standard. The influx of greater numbers of foreign workers as a result of our membership of the European Economic Community or of the attractions of the oil industry will probably increase the demands for this kind of provision. Education for assimilation—and we prefer this term to integration—is provided readily for the children of immigrants. A knowledge of English is clearly a pre-requisite to assimilation but little evidence was given to us to suggest that much in the way of provision of this kind is being made at present for adult immigrants. A few classes in 'English as a second language' were provided in some urban areas but these catered for only a few specific groups of non-English-speaking adults and did not elicit much response; one voluntary agency was developing a home-visiting scheme to teach English to immigrant Asian women. There is an obvious and urgent need for investigation into the particular educational needs of adult immigrants of all kinds and for appropriate provision to meet them.

Members of Voluntary Groups

Our society has a great variety of organised voluntary groups, social, educational, sporting, religious or political in purpose, through which many adults find learning opportunities. Some of them may be entirely local in their operations and connections; others may as a result of affiliation or for other reasons have regional or national interests. Some receive assistance or advice from national bodies such as the Scottish Sports Council, the Scottish Arts Council, the Scottish Community Drama Association and the Association of Arts Centres in Scotland. The educational role performed by many of them, whether they are purely local or have national connections, is such as to bring them within what we have termed community education and consequently within the concern of the education authorities. These authorities already recognise the contribution voluntary groups make to a comprehensive education service and in a variety of ways help many of them to be effective. We wish to record our view that it is desirable that the help given to them should be extended still more widely.

EDUCATION FOR CHANGE

Community Development

The process by which those who live in a community (defined in either geographical or social terms) are helped or encouraged to act together in tackling the problems which affect their lives has come to be called community development. Implicit in this process is the assumption that having been helped to solve one problem those involved will be sufficiently motivated and will have acquired sufficient skills to tackle other problems. The educational character of community development is therefore readily recognised and the youth and community service has long been involved in the process. Much less obvious is the precise role that the adult educationist should play in it. Involvement in community development calls into question traditional didactic approaches and emphasis on classes and class numbers; but it provides new opportunities for reaching large sections of the population hitherto untouched by adult education. Elsewhere in this report we refer to the need to place greater emphasis on the adult educationist's role of stimulating and promoting interest in adult education activities. The French aptly describe what we have in mind as 'animation'. Experiments along these lines undertaken by the Department of Educational Studies of the University of Edinburgh in the new town of Livingston have met with some success but have also highlighted the problems and difficulties involved. Adult education should participate increasingly in community development and much more experimentation is needed.

Social and Political Education

We received little evidence relating directly to social and political education. At one time subjects which were held to have a bearing on national and international affairs—civics, political science, current affairs, international relations – figured prominently in educational programmes. Although these subjects have declined in popularity there has been an expansion of provision related to specific civic functions – children's panels, lay magistrates, the professional social worker and the volunteer – or to more specific areas of public concern – 'Caring for People', 'Drugs and the Community', 'Roots of Crime'. This kind of provision reflects a desire on the part of many people to involve and inform themselves about particular social issues. The WEA, trades unions and more recently some universities have undertaken programmes of trade union education. The Community Councils provided for in the Local Government (Scotland) Act 1973 ought to give many more people an opportunity to participate in their own local affairs. Provision in this area of adult education is still relatively meagre; there is some evidence that certain educational agencies are prepared to deal with controversial issues of public concern but in general not nearly enough is being done. Educational providers have here an opportunity and a responsibility to make real the concept of the participating democracy.

Development and the Environment

Urbanisation and industrial expansion impose hidden costs on the community. Greater demand for land can deny to sections of the community the amenity which they have enjoyed for years; exploitation of natural resources at local, national and global levels can affect present and future generations; pollution and the disposal of waste are problems that face both the ordinary householder and the industrial giant. Education has a responsibility to ensure that these hidden costs are made more widely known and more thoroughly understood. People who are directly concerned in any issue involving the environment need help to acquire the skills and the expertise required to present their case effectively. The complex industrial developments affecting Scotland at the present time will intensify the need for this kind of provision.

Bridging the Educational Gap

Major developments in educational policy, such as the raising of the school leaving age and advances in methods and practices in school education, can have the effect of widening the educational gap between the new generation which benefits directly from them and older people whose full-time schooling took place before they were introduced. At present those over the age of 40 who left school at the statutory leaving age have had a year's less schooling than those under 40, who left school after the age had been raised to 15. There will soon be a further group of adults who will have had full-time education up to 16. The education of the older generation was designed by and for a society which differed in many ways from that of today. It was less than adequate by present day standards and in some respects narrower than that received by younger people. In our view, therefore, major advance in school education should be accompanied by measures to help encourage older people to widen their education correspondingly. So far such measures as have been taken have been quite inadequate, and 'second chance' and continuing educational opportunities at all levels must be much more generally available At the level of higher education the Open University has demonstrated the truth of the adage that it is never too late to learn.

Professional Groups

Opportunities to enable individuals to acquire new or additional professional or technical qualifications and for others to master new concepts and practices in their professions have been provided for many years in institutions of further and higher education. Of recent years many professional and quasi-professional bodies have been looking to adult education agencies also to make this kind of provision. A number of university extra mural departments such as Glasgow are already providing refresher courses for professional groups. This growing awareness of the interest in continuing education for the professions will make increasing demands on adult education.

Understanding Science and Technology

Our world is a complex one in which the relationships between science and technology and the various social and cultural activities of man must be widely understood and discussed. Without informed discussion and policies based upon such discussion more and more people will feel that they are recipients, even victims, of the consequences of change rather than members of a society which wills and controls the changes which are taking place. Adult education can make an important contribution towards avoiding such alienation. One of the most important of its roles should be the interpretation of science and its associated technologies to the non-scientist. Everyone is affected by scientific and technological developments yet few are able to make balanced judgements on the industrial and social implications of scientific discoveries and technological developments. In order to do so the non-scientist should learn something of the language of science and, even more importantly, appreciate the nature of scientific method and thought. Scientific developments will provide a main source of intellectual excitement in the coming decades. The opening up of this field to the wider public outside the universities, research establishments and other laboratories will become increasingly desirable and valued. This process of distilling and transmitting the essentials of scientific development deserves the attention of mature scientists of high calibre who are willing to forego the esoteric language of their specialisms and to relate science and technology to social philosophy and the arts. This is therefore an area in which the universities can make a particularly valuable contribution.

ATTRACTING AND MOTIVATING STUDENTS

The kind of provision outlined above indicates what we mean by a comprehensive educational service for adults. Merely to provide classes or courses directed at meeting the kinds of needs identified however is not enough. Participation in adult education is still very much a minority interest but for providers to place the blame for this situation on the 'apathy' of the people they are seeking to serve 'is not only to congratulate oneself and criticise others – it is also to declare that there is no reason to look any further for explanations'. This quotation is from the Interim Report of the Department of Educational Studies, University of Edinburgh, on 'A Study of the Role of Adult Education and the University of its Potential Contribution to the Community in Edinburgh and South-East Scotland' commissioned by the Committee. The report continues, 'Our research shows that further and more helpful explanations are readily available and that people's apathy towards what is at present offered in adult education must mean that they would accept activities which were educational if they were presented in a different way'.

The perennial question for adult education is what compels adults to learn, for learning is work and sometimes hard work. The motives may be as numerous as the students attending—a sense of educational inadequacy, intellectual curiosity, vocational interest, a desire for companionship or simply to escape from the home. The apparent triviality of some of them should not be allowed to obscure the fact that they are very real to the individuals concerned. The extent to which these motives are satisfied during the early periods of attendance at classes will often determine the student's future attendance; but those which bring a person to the activity in the first place may not be strong enough to keep him there, much less cause him to continue to learn. There is now sufficient evidence to show that adults will be more highly motivated to learn if emphasis is placed on the applied rather than on the theoretical, if content is related to the performance of everyday tasks and obligations and if the methods used take into account their accumulated experience of life. Any statement of the aims of adult education such as we have just completed will be of little avail unless adults can be encouraged to pursue them.

COUNSELLING

To capitalise on motivation, to maintain interest and to extend the horizons of the increasing number of adults we expect to respond to a revitalised service will demand a closer personal support of each adult student by the educationalist. The counselling role already developing within the guidance system during the phase of initial education requires to be extended more effectively within adult education. Basically this will mean ensuring not only that opportunities for adult learning exist but that these opportunities are recognised and that people are assisted to choose the course or activity most relevant to their individual needs.

COMMUNITY EDUCATION

At the beginning of this report, when defining terms, we said that 'Social, cultural, recreational and educational activities for adults are so interrelated that any attempt to distinguish between them or to deal with one without regard to the others would be undesirable even if it were possible'; and we adopted the term 'community education' to describe the wide spectrum of educational opportunities which these activities sponsored by a variety of statutory and voluntary agencies made available. It is our view that the aims we have proposed for adult education are practicable and achievable only if adult education is fostered and developed as an element of community education—an element which, while having characteristics and requirements specific to it, shares with the other elements common aims requiring for their accomplishment the collective resources and expertise of all the elements.

The spectrum is so wide that all the parts cannot be linked in one organisation and in some cases special arrangements will have to be made for co-operation and collaboration. This may for example be the most practicable way of dealing with the overlapping interests of education departments and the departments of leisure and recreation now emerging as a result of the Local Government (Scotland) Act 1973. However, we are convinced that it will be in the best interests of the adult education service, as well as of those it seeks to serve, if it is regarded and operates as part of a community education service which also embraces the youth and community service. Adult education and youth and community service already overlap and interrelate to a considerable extent; but there would be much advantage from still closer collaboration. Sections of the public hitherto virtually untouched by adult education would become more accessible and adult education would acquire valuable, committed allies in the large staff – full-time, part-time and voluntary – in the youth and community service. We have reason to believe too that the benefit would not be one-sided. The infusion of work of a more intellectual kind into the programmes of the youth and community service would we understand be welcomed by many of the workers in that service. Cross-fertilisation of ideas, methods and approaches would be of general benefit as would be the sharing and maximising of the use of resources and facilities. *We therefore recommend that adult education should be regarded as an aspect of community education and should, with the youth and community service, be incorporated into a community education service...*

CARNEGY REPORT
PROFESSIONAL EDUCATION AND TRAINING FOR COMMUNITY EDUCATION

HMSO pp5-7, 23-36 1977

THE NATURE AND AIMS OF COMMUNITY EDUCATION

The Report of the Committee on Adult Education in Scotland – *the Alexander Report* – was specifically mentioned in our remit and is a natural starting point for this account of the Working Party's deliberations and findings. The Alexander Committee did not invent the term community education but gave national currency to it. The term was adopted by that Committee and used in its Report to describe the wide spectrum of educational opportunities which are made available through the social, cultural, recreational and educational activities sponsored by a variety of statutory and voluntary agencies. Because of its remit, the Alexander Committee did not attempt explicitly to describe or define with any precision the nature and aims of community education as a whole. A number of pointers which are helpful to the formulation of a description were, however, provided.

The Alexander Committee clearly envisaged the continuation and wider development within community education of the established provision for adults of "courses with a pronounced intellectual content related to or derived from the various established academic disciplines" and courses related to practical and aesthetic interests and activities. The nomination by the Committee of the Youth and Community Service as the other major element of a Community Education Service carried the implication that community education, like the youth and community service, would be concerned with people of all age-groups. It also strengthened references made elsewhere in the Committee's report to the relevance of community development and the distinctive importance of the contributions by voluntary organisations and groups in this sector of education. Other significant pointers were: the broad connotation which the Committee ascribed to education as a whole and the emphasis it put on the inter-relationship – and in some respects the overlapping – of community education with other aspects or sectors of education; its references to reciprocal relationships between community education and other local authority services, particularly social work and leisure and recreation, and organisations with a close concern for education such as trade unions; its identification of groups in need of special attention; its indication of the importance of tailoring provision to needs and of devoting time and effort to the stimulation of interest and to motivation; and its reminder that community education must, in its organisation and character, be fully responsive to democratic influence.

Working Party's Approach

The task given to the Working Party requires for its performance a general conception of what community education is and might be, a knowledge of the agencies concerned or capable of being concerned with it, and an understanding of the settings in which it can take place and of the methods and approaches characteristic of it. But it is our view that the performance of this task does not require us first to formulate a precise and specific definition of community education; and we doubt the desirability – and even the feasibility – of such a definitive formulation. It is rather the needs and responses of individuals and groups which must primarily determine the nature of community education and the specific aims to be pursued. As these needs and responses change, so should the nature and the specific aims of community education.

Second only to the participants in their influence on the nature and aims of community education are the practitioners – the full-time, the part-time and voluntary community education workers. By their skill in identifying and interpreting needs, in stimulating and motivating action and in creating appropriate learning situations they should be able continuously to develop new opportunities in community education.

We consider the concept of community education to be consistent with current international thinking about education as a whole, as represented for example by the phrases "education permanente", "recurrent education", and continuing education". It reflects a view of education as a process

(a)   which is life-long

(b)   in which the participants should be actively and influentially involved and the traditional stress on teaching outweighed by the emphasis put on learning; and

(c)   in which the needs of participants rather than academic subject divisions or administrative and institutional arrangements should determine the nature and timing of provision.

The distinctive contribution which the concept of community education may be said to bring to these international concepts is its emphasis on the process as one in which the benefits to and the contributions of the individual are matched by those of the groups and communities to which he or she belongs; and one which can be enjoyable as well as beneficial, relaxed as well as rigorous. Community education recognises the educative influences and the educational potentialities inherent in a local community and operating through multifarious groups and agencies, formal and informal, industrial, commercial, religious, social and recreational as well as explicitly educational

We therefore see community education as a constantly evolving process of interaction between the needs of people and the educational resources of the community, a process to which fixed boundaries cannot be set. Nevertheless we believe that the tradition and experience which community education has inherited and the evidence of what is happening now in the field, together with some anticipation of future trends and development, can provide the basis for a working statement of the broad general aims and characteristics of community education sufficient for the identification of the education and training needs of full-time community education workers.

Broad Aims of Community Education

In our view, community education has the following broad general aims:

(a)   to involve people, as private individuals and as members of groups and communities, irrespective of age and circumstances, in the ascertainment and assessment of their needs for opportunities to

      (i)   discover and pursue interests;

      (ii)   acquire and improve knowledge and skills;

      (iii)   recognise their personal identities and aspirations;

      (iv)   develop satisfactory inter-personal relationships;

      (v)   achieve competence in their roles within the family, the community and society as a whole; and

      (vi)   participate in the shaping of their physical and social environment and in the conduct of local and national affairs; and

(b)   to seek to meet these ascertained needs in the most appropriate settings with the co-operation of individuals and groups and by identifying and deploying appropriate educational resources, wherever they may reside...

TYPES OF STAFF, THEIR FUNCTIONS AND PROFESSIONAL NEEDS

By implication, the Alexander Report suggests that the provision of adult education calls for three broad categories of staff, concerned primarily though not exclusively with policy making and administration; organising and stimulating; teaching and discussion. Evidence received by the Working Party and information about developments which have already taken place in the field suggest that community education requires a greater diversity of staff. In seeking to lay the basis for an outline of broad patterns of training, however, it seems desirable to avoid over-fine differentiation and the consequent identification of a plethora of categories of staff. Care can be taken of minor differences within categories e.g. by providing for optional elements in training. We have, therefore, made a deliberate effort to restrict the number of categories by grouping together jobs which, though differently styled, involve to a large extent similar broad functions; and the result has been the identification of the four categories. It must be emphasised, first, that the categories are not watertight since a worker may have functions which appear under several categories; and, second, that we do not regard these categories as representing a hierarchy.

We have had particular regard to the staff required for what may be identifiable as "the Community Education Service". However, as the Alexander Committee recognised, community education functions may be performed within services and agencies outwith the community education service e.g. schools and colleges, social work and leisure and recreation departments, the prison service, industrial bodies, and local and national voluntary organisations whose avowed aims are not primarily educational. These functions may often be performed on a part-time basis but sometimes they will constitute the full-time duties of a specially employed member of staff of the agency or organisation concerned. The training needs of such staff should be kept in mind and account has been taken of this in constructing the following categories.

As our remit required, we have concentrated our attention on staff employed full-time in a professional capacity in community education. We have no doubts about the importance of such staff and of their proper education and training. Yet we are aware that in almost every sector or aspect of community education an essential part is and will continue to be played by a much larger number of voluntary workers and paid part-time staff. We are conscious, too, that the sharp divisions, interest and expertise which exist in many fields between professionals and non-professionals are not and should not be characteristic of community education. In the process of community education, the full-time staff and the voluntary and part-time workers – and, indeed, the "consumers" – are partners whose functions and roles are not immutably fixed and are at times inter-changed, and each of whom should have an opportunity to acquire the professionalism which consists of high quality and standards. Though this and subsequent sections of our report do not purport to deal with the functions and training needs of other than full-time staff, to which we expect attention will in due course be given, we hope that what we have to say will be found to have relevance to them.

CATEGORY I The first category embraces a large number of workers who operate mainly in direct contact with participants or potential participants in community education and who, though employed in a variety of posts, have in common the principal broad functions of stimulation, group work and tutoring. Posts occupied by workers in this category include: in the statutory sector, community and youth centre assistants, school and college-based staff, district youth leaders, area or neighbourhood community workers and tutors; and, in the non-statutory sector, youth leaders, area or neighbourhood community workers and community activists.

The broad functions common to this category of workers embrace a number of more specific functions or responsibilities e.g. the ascertainment of community needs and resources; the organisation and management of programmes; the provision of social education; counselling; the support and training of part-time staff; the supervision of trainee students; and contributing to the development of professional practice and community education policy. In addition to their common functions, each type of post in this category involves one or more special functions or responsibilities, e.g. basic institutional management; linking with school or college staff and curriculum; stimulation and support of community organisations; youth work; teaching; advising on community action.

CATEGORY II Staff in the second category, which is numerically smaller, characteristically operate through Category 1 staff, part-time staff, or community organisations though they also work in direct contact with participants in community education. Their distinctive common functions are organisation, management and tutoring and supervision. Included in this category are workers holding posts in the statutory sector as area community education officers (or deputies), wardens or managers of community or youth centres, heads of adult education institutes or tutor organisers; and in the non-statutory sector as tutor organisers, area community development officers, or wardens or managers of community or youth centres. Besides their functions of organisation, management and tutoring, workers have the major functions that are common to Category 1 staff; and in posts within this category one or more of the following specific functions is emphasised; staff management; support and training; determination of priorities; stimulation and support of voluntary organisations; institutional management; and teaching.

CATEGORY III The third category consists of staff with specialist, advisory or supportive functions which relate to the work of other members or prospective members of staff, full-time or part-time and in some cases to the development or specialised aspects of community education. Workers in this category hold posts in the statutory sector as training officers, subject or activity organisers or advisers, resources and information officers, or research officers; and in the non-statutory sector as training officers, lecturers or tutors in community education (in training institutions), staff tutors, tutor organisers with specialist roles (e.g. in the WEA), or activity organisers or advisers.

Besides the functions of supporting and advising other staff which are common to this category (and which require for their performance an understanding, of varying depth, of the theory and practice of community education), there are functions specific to particular types of posts viz. formulating and implementing plans for training courses; teaching and instructing; promoting development of interest and participation in a subject or activity; supervision including that of students in training; developing the availability and use of resource material and technology; organising the collection, collation, retrieval and distribution of information; stimulating, advising on and conducting research.

CATEGORY IV Workers in the fourth category operate primarily in the areas of organisation, administration and policy, and they carry responsibility for the overall effectiveness of the provision made by their employing authorities or organisations. They hold: in the statutory sector, posts as divisional community education officers (or deputies), regional community education officers (or deputies), and deputy or assistant directors of education (community education); and in the non-statutory sector, posts as regional, divisional or district officers, directors or deputy directors of university extra-mural departments, and chief officers or deputy chief officers of national voluntary organisations.

The principal functions of workers in this category are: developing and formulating policy for community education (or a particular aspect of it); securing, evaluation and reporting on the implementation of policy; advising and servicing committees, establishing and developing co-operation with related services and organisations; securing and managing staff and resources; overseeing staff development and training; and contributing to the development of professional practice.

KNOWLEDGE AND SKILLS REQUIRED BY ALL CATEGORIES

We have sought to identify the knowledge and skills which each of the categories of staff requires. From our study, certain areas of knowledge and skills emerge as necessary parts of the professional equipment of the great majority community education workers in all categories. We refer to these later as "the common core"; and though we list them separately below, we would emphasise that knowledge and skills, theory and practice, should be closely integrated.

Knowledge

Education Theory and Practice, with particular reference to community education.

Psychology of Human Growth and Development in a social context.

Sociological Theories and Concepts, particularly those relating to the nature of communities, organisations and groups.

Social Policy and Administration, including relevant law, safety and insurance requirements, and principles of corporate management.

Community Work.

Group Work.

Political Science, especially in respect of the inter-relationship of social policies and community action.

Growth and significance of leisure.

Skills

Promoting inter-personal relationships; stimulating and supporting individual and group initiatives; use of survey methods; identifying and analysing needs; securing and programming the use of resources; financial management; planning and organising action; counselling; tutoring; supervising, supporting and training staff, part-time and/or full-time; recording and reporting; use of publicity methods.

Workers in certain posts in Category III and in posts in Category IV may not directly or regularly employ all the skills listed but the possession of them will greatly facilitate and often be crucial to satisfactory performance in those posts.

PARTICULAR KNOWLEDGE AND SKILLS

The areas of knowledge and skills identified as peculiar to particular posts within individual categories are as follows:

Category I   –   basic management, administrative and committee procedures
                 –   formal education structures, objectives and procedures
                 –   work with a particular age group
                 –   a particular academic subject or subjects
                 –   community development and welfare rights
                 –   conflict, confrontation and protest;

Category II   –   staff management, support and training
                 –   institutional management and procedures and skills

– aims, structures and procedures of voluntary organisations
– teaching methods and skills;

Category III – planning, organisation and evaluation of training
– training methods and aids
– teaching skills
– specialised knowledge of a subject or skill in an activity
– stimulation or "animation"
– educational technology
– storage and retrieval of information
– preparation of summaries and construction of aids
– research methods and techniques;

Category IV – advanced knowledge of scope and potentialities of community education (or an aspect of it); objectives, structures and practices of related services and agencies; nature and functioning of local and national government, political processes and social policies
– advanced skills in management of staff and resources, corporate management, preparation of analyses and reports, preparation of objectives, plans and programmes.

FUTURE PROFESSIONAL EDUCATION AND TRAINING

Terminology

Our remit required us "to identify and evaluate the various forms which pre-service and in-service professional education and training for a community education service might take". As has been indicated earlier, we have gone somewhat beyond the strict letter of the remit by taking account of the training needs of persons who, though engaged full-time in community education, are not employed by a body within a community education service. We have also chosen to use the terms "initial training" and "further training" in preference to "pre-service training" and "in-service training". "Pre-service" is liable to be misleading since it does not provide for situations where, as with trainees and unqualified workers, the training referred to post-dates a period of full-time service. "Further training" is preferred to "in-service training" because it emphasises the need for continuity and may lessen the risk of over-emphasis on improving the performance of staff in their current rôles to the neglect of the wider development of individual potential which is vital to community education as well as to the satisfaction of staff.

INITIAL TRAINING

General Considerations

Initial training, which we see as leading to professional status as a community education worker, is the most prolonged and systematic period of training most workers are likely to receive. It must therefore seek, by means of appropriate academic studies, to give students a comprehensive understanding of the theory, practice and potentialities of community education and to lay a foundation on which further training and a full career in community education can be based. Initial training must also enable the students to acquire expertise and skill relevant to the posts they are likely to take up on completion of this training. What these posts are and the functions associated with them can be indicated by reference to the categories of staff outlined.

Relationship with Initial Posts

Most new entrants into full-time work can be expected initially to take up posts in Categories I and II, i.e. posts which involve a substantial amount of direct contact with actual or potential participants in community education. Though a number of Category II posts would normally be regarded as requiring some previous full-time experience and probably be graded as promoted posts, circumstances in some areas and organisations, including, for example, staffing complements and size of communities and centres, seem likely to result in continuance of the present practice of appointing new entrants to some such posts.

The majority of appointees to posts in Category III, i.e. specialist, advisory and supportive posts can be expected to be qualified workers with suitable post-qualifying experience. Some new entrants, however, because of previous relevant education, training and/or experience, may be fitted to go direct from initial training into posts in Category III, and it should be possible in the initial training system to make provision for individual potentialities and orientations of this kind. Cases are likely to occur in which persons are recruited direct to certain posts in this category. e.g. resources, information and research posts, on the strength of specialised qualifications acquired by other means, the training they have received elsewhere being regarded as the basic initial training appropriate to their main functions. Such additional training as they require for the posts they hold can be provided as further training. If, however, such persons wish to have a broadly based career in community education they should take a course of appropriate initial training in community education. Consideration should be given to providing means whereby some concessions in respect of relevant previous qualifications and experience could be obtained.

It is expected that persons appointed to posts in Category IV will normally have had substantial and varied experience and further training following qualification from initial training.

It is concluded, therefore, that initial professional training should have particular regard to the functions and responsibilities attaching to posts in Categories I and II but should include provision designed to equip persons already possessing appropriate specialised knowledge and skill for specialist posts in Category III.

Content

We have outlined a body of knowledge and skills which, in our view, community education workers with few exceptions require to possess. That knowledge and those skills, we consider, should be an essential part of initial education and training for community education. Besides this "common core", initial training should also provide a range of optional opportunities for study and practice related to the particular needs of posts in Categories I, II and, to a limited extent, III.

Objective: All-graduate Entry

We have sought to convey our sense of the importance of community education to society and the individual members of it. As we have now shown, the demands which arise form the responsibility and functions given to those taking up full-time professional work in community education are great and varied. It is hardly surprising, therefore, that we consider that, in initial education and training, sights and standards should be set high – as regards intellectual ability as well as practical competence and personal qualities. We are of the view that, as soon as it is feasible, entry to the career of community education worker should be limited to graduates (or their equivalents). We envisage the following means of entry.

(a)   A recognised professional degree course in community education, combining theory and practice, employing flexible study methods, and with flexible entry requirements permitting admission of persons who do not hold normal university entrance qualifications but are otherwise suitable.

(b)   A recognised professional post-graduate certificate or diploma course for graduates (and equivalents) with relevant degrees, the course to combine theory and practice and employ flexible study methods.

(c)   A recognised professional transfer or conversion course for graduates (and equivalents) who have already acquired a qualification in another profession, the course to combine theory and practice and employ flexible study methods.

We appreciate that the achievement of this objective will take some time and the consideration of patterns of initial training which follows relates to this interim period. We believe, however, that much of it has relevance to the longer-term objective.

Possible Systems of Training

Initial education and training can be organised in a number of ways. We outline below six possible systems which we will later evaluate.

A.   *UNITARY OR SINGLE STREAM SYSTEM*

In a Unitary system, all students would be required to undergo a broadly similar course, with limited minority time devoted to optional specialisms. For example, two thirds to three quarters of the course might be devoted to the common core and one quarter to one third to options.

B.   *BINARY OR TWO-STREAM SYSTEM*

This system would provide two distinguishable, though not entirely different, paths into full-time work. One would be oriented towards that end of the community education spectrum which has strong links with formal education i.e. adult education in academic disciplines and school/college-based work, while the other would be oriented towards the informal and community development end of the spectrum. There would be elements common to both, introduced not only to recognise existing areas of over-lap and collaboration but also to provide the basis for future collaborative initiatives. In both cases, some minority time could be devoted to optional specialisms.

C.   MULTI-CHOICE SYSTEM

In this system, there would be a common core for all students, occupying, say, about one third of the training time. For the remaining two thirds, each student would select a specified number from a range of specialised courses or units of study such as:

> the education of adults
>
> work with communities
>
> work with youth
>
> school/college-based work
>
> work with disadvantaged groups
>
> community action
>
> promotion of the arts
>
> sport and recreation
>
> welfare rights
>
> prison-based work
>
> industry-based work

D.   CREDITS SYSTEM WITH COMMON CORE

A development from the Multi-Choice system, the Credits system would involve the organisation of the total course content into numerous self-contained units and the accumulation by each student of a specified number of "credits", each representing either satisfactory completion of one of the units or production of evidence that the content of a unit had been satisfactorily covered in previous education, training or experience. In order to retain the concept of an identifiable common core, certain subjects would be obligatory; but, relative to the Multi-choice system, the obligatory elements would be more limited.

E.   CREDITS SYSTEM WITHOUT COMMON CORE

Unlike D above, this system would contain no obligatory credits and there would therefore be no discrete, identifiable common core. Certain common elements, attitudes and approaches might however be introduced or encouraged by careful construction of the units of study and by the training methods employed.

F.   APPRENTICESHIP SYSTEM

The five systems described above would each provide for some practical work experience; but they all comprise formalised institutional training of a relatively prolonged nature. The sixth system embodies the view that professional expertise can best be acquired on the job and that training through apprenticeship is preferable to institution-centred training. It would involve the attachment of the students, for a period to be determined and in the ratio of perhaps two to one, to experienced workers who would be responsible for guiding and supervising their apprentices in the practical fieldwork which would occupy most of each working week. The remainder of the week would be spent in day-release studies, which could relate closely to the fieldwork on which apprentices were engaged and in private study.

THE SYSTEMS VIS-A-VIS A COMMON CORE

It will be noted that systems A, B, C and D envisage the inclusion of a common core as a compulsory, identifiable part of initial training; that the proportion of time allocated specifically to the common core tends to diminish progressively from system A to system D; and that the common core, as a readily identifiable component, disappears in systems E and F.

EVALUATION OF SYSTEMS

The Unitary system, with its heavy emphasis on the common core, would be most likely to equip students to undertake any one of a range of initial posts with some degree of competence. It would also be helpful in creating a sense of common purpose among full-time workers and in ensuring that all staff had equal opportunity for advancement. On the other hand, individual versatility would be secured at the expense of the diversity of well-founded expertise and skill which community education requires from its full-time workers as a whole. Furthermore, the system would create a need for early specialised further training on a scale that seems very unlikely to be possible.

The Binary system would provide a degree and depth of specialism impossible under a Unitary system and would have the practical advantage of relatively easy and economical development from existing training provision. However, the range of specialisms it would provide would not sufficiently match the diverse needs within community education. More importantly, a Binary system would be likely to reinforce traditional attitudes and practices, to create a permanent division among workers, and to frustrate the emergence of an adequately integrated service and the realisation of hopes engendered by the Alexander Report.

The Multi-Choice system would correspond to the diversity of community education. It would also have advantages in suiting the training to the needs of persons with particular previous education, training and/or experience, and in encouraging training agencies to use field settings and resources, thereby increasing the involvement of fieldworkers in the training of students. On the other hand, a system of this kind might present administrative difficulties. It could well be impracticable for each training agency to offer all specialisms, and there might be difficulty in reaching agreement about where particular specialisms should be provided. The constriction of the common core might also create problems for further training because less could be assumed about the knowledge the students had in common.

The Credits system with Common Core would result in an output of community education workers very diverse in knowledge and skills but with some shared understanding and expertise. It would also have particular merits in relation to persons with certain higher education qualifications and other professional training. There would, however, be problems in equalising credits and in determining equivalencies, e.g. where previous study had been purely theoretical. In the construction of credit units, too, great care would be required to avoid the production of packages of purely academic education unrelated to practical work; and narrow specialisation would have to be prevented by grouping cognate credits and limiting the number of credits which could be taken from any one group.

The advantages of the Apprenticeship system would be the close inter-relationship of theory and practice and the production of workers fully alive to the realities of practical work. There would, however, be great difficulty in ensuring a reasonable uniformity of standards and considerable danger that new entrants might acquire a narrow conceptual basis, a limited understanding of developmental possibilities and a set of ready-made, "hand-me-down" practices and skills. Unless adopted as the sole means of entry, the system would create a sharp dichotomy in the profession.

Four of the six systems outlined above seem to us to have major disabilities in the context of community education. Attractive though it may be in a promising unified, homogenous profession, the Unitary system is ill-matched to the varied needs of community education and would leave to further training an insupportable burden of necessary diversification. The Credits without Common Core system goes to the other extreme, giving little assurance of producing any sense of common purpose and identity or a basis for collaboration among community education workers. We fault the Binary system because it would perpetuate existing divisions and obstruct the change that is desired. As an experiment in training for a particular aspect of community education e.g. community work, the Apprenticeship system may be worth further consideration; but in our view it would in itself be too hazardous a choice for education and training leading to a full professional qualification in community education.

Preferred Systems

The other two systems, the Multi-Choice and the Credits with Common Core, are in our judgement generally suited to the requirements of community education. They seem likely, as does none of the others, to produce a corps of workers with common professional purposes and attitudes and yet deploying as a whole a diversity of individual expertise and specialisation. Not only do we regard each of these systems as superior to the rest in the balance of advantages it offers; we also consider that in combination they could constitute a total pattern of initial education and training within which the varied needs of the diverse types of recruits required in community education could be most readily met. We recognise, however, that it would be difficult at the present time with existing resources to organise a Credit system and we suggest later how some of the difficulties might be overcome.

Variety of Students

The pattern of initial education and training should reflect the diversity and range of community education not only in the content of courses but also in the variety of types of suitable students who can be admitted. To attain this, positive action will be needed throughout the field to recruit students from as varied backgrounds as possible. In terms of arrangements for admission to courses, the salient features of the variety desired are age, educational qualifications, experience and other professional training.

Age of Entry

Recent experience in the youth and community service indicates that young people accepted into training straight from school at about age 18 have in 3 years been prepared to a level which has fitted them to occupy posts in that service. Young teachers and graduates, too, at or about the age of 21 have proved to be suitable recruits, in adult education as well as in youth and community work. It may indeed be argued that, as regards work in the youth sector of community education, entrants not too far removed from their teens have in certain respects advantages over older entrants in that they can more easily relate to young people, especially to the extent that they share or are sympathetic to the culture of the young. Therefore, while acknowledging that maturity cannot be associated with any specific age and that it may be possible to demonstrate that some functions in community education could be competently performed by young people in their late teens, we suggest that the minimum age of entry into initial training should be such as to secure that entry into full-time professional posts in community education does not take place before the age of about 21.

Many posts in community education are suitable for new entrants of mature years. Some indeed which involve work with older people can best be filled by persons who bring to them long and varied experience of life – personal, domestic and occupational. So varied are individuals as well as the needs of community education that we hesitate to suggest a maximum age of entry to initial training. We would only say that a factor which should be taken into account in each case is the likely return in terms of service for the amount of public money expended on training.

Educational Qualifications

At present, the minimum educational qualifications required from persons under 23 years of age seeking entry to courses leading to a qualification in youth and community service (2 Higher and 4 Ordinary Grade passes in the SCE examination) is somewhat below that for entry to a degree course. Our information, however, is that currently the overwhelming majority of the young students admitted have qualifications in excess of the minimum, many considerably in excess. This, together with the reduction in teacher-training places, encourages us to propose that for persons under 23 years of age the minimum educational qualifications for entry to courses leading to a qualification in community education should be those required for entry to a first degree course.

The mature entrants mentioned briefly should not, in our view, be solely persons in possession of standard educational qualifications. Experience as well as the nature of community education, appears to establish the value of admitting to initial training mature persons who, while not possessing the normal educational qualifications for entry to a degree course, bring to training and to their subsequent work in the field an occupational background in industry, business, commerce, agriculture or one of the public services and some practical experience of part-time community work. The sharing of the general occupational background and educational history of the majority of potential participants in community education may be regarded as giving such entrants advantages, e.g. in establishing meaningful contact and communication, over entrants whose preparation for the role of community educators has been a progression from one educational institution to another. A number of such entrants have demonstrated their capacity and competence to go on to high-level organising and administrative posts and it is hoped that the path to promoted posts will remain open to others of similar background. Some mature students on the other hand may wish after training to stay and work in the area (or an area similar to that) in which they have been living and active in community work. Such workers seem to have a particular contribution to make as a result of their strong identification with the residents of a particular community or type of community.

We consider that all candidates capable of achieving a degree in initial training of acceptable duration should be enabled to do so by the introduction of a degree course in community education of the kind described. We would wish therefore to see arrangements made which would ensure that no candidate who was otherwise suitable and was judged to be capable of reaching degree standard would be prevented from training to be a community education worker solely because his or her certificated educational qualifications were below the normal standard for entry to a degree course.

Transfer Related Professions

Because of the acknowledged links and overlaps between community education on the one hand and formal education, social work and leisure and recreation on the other, provision should be made in the pattern of initial training to enable trained teachers, social workers and leisure and recreation staff to transfer to full-time work in community education. (Provision of this kind is currently made for teachers and social workers in the pattern of youth and community work training). The identification of areas of knowledge and skills that are common or generic to these linked professions would help to facilitate the planning of transfer courses.

We hope that, eventually, reciprocal arrangements will be negotiated which will make transfer from as well as to, community education more easily possible in respect of all three of these other professions. But the development of such transfer opportunities as may be achievable at an early date should not be delayed until the agreement of all to co-operate is secured.

Timing of Initial Training

It is desirable to make it possible for initial education and training to be taken at the pre-service stage, after a period of service or concurrently with in-post service. The main provision should, in our view, take the form of courses involving full-time attendance over periods varying from 1 year to 3 or even 4 years, depending on the qualifications students have on entry. These courses would cater for persons at the pre-entry stage, i.e. young people seeking training on or soon after completion of school education and older people transferring as mature students from other professions and occupations; and for "trainees" and most unqualified workers in community education. (In the last few years, education authorities have appointed a number of trainees in youth and community service under arrangements which provide the opportunity for later secondment for full-time training. Currently, there is a total of some 50 trainee posts).

Unqualified Workers

It is recognised, however, that continuous full-time attendance at a course may present insuperable difficulties for some unqualified workers already in post. It is therefore suggested that provision should be made for "sandwich" courses which combine part-time attendance with short periods of full-time study. In such courses it is imperative that local practices and standards are not automatically adopted as the desirable norms and that the standards of achievement in theory and practice required in the full-time courses are maintained.

We regard as of great importance the training and qualification of as many as possible of the unqualified workers currently employed in community education. Financial arrangements other than those of the Students' Allowances Scheme are necessary to enable such workers to undertake full-time training without undue hardship. Currently, the only provision is for the pooling of expenditure incurred by local authorities (a) in releasing their unqualified youth and community service workers for full-time training on full pay, and (b) in enabling voluntary organisations to release their unqualified workers on similar terms. We would urge that this arrangement – or one with similar benefits to the workers – should apply to the training of unqualified community education workers and that authorities should exercise, as we understand they have not done to any extent in the past, their powers to assist voluntary organisations in this respect.

Trainees

Having regard to the criticism that, in pre-service training, relevance to the realities of fieldwork is less easy to establish and recognise than when training is given at a later stage, we have considered the possibility that traineeship might be developed as the sole or major avenue into professional work in community education. We have concluded, however, that although traineeship can be useful preparation for training, the stability and quality of service to the public would inevitably be affected adversely by any significant increase in the number of trainee posts beyond the present total of 50. For adult education and youth and community service combined, the annual intake of students has recently been about 190-200 and the total number in training in a year around 360-380. The task of supervising fieldwork practice for students already imposes a heavy burden on the 500-600 full-time workers engaged at levels of fieldwork appropriate for student placements. If to this burden were added the task of arranging suitable experience and supervising the work of 100 to 200 trainees, the normal duties of fieldworkers in relation to the public would be greatly affected. Account has to be taken, too of the extra costs which trainee entry to the profession involves and the difficulties over professional recognition which can arise.

Suggested Interim Structure

During the period which we hope will be short, before it becomes possible to change to an all-graduate entry to the profession, the following over-all structure of training provision, in our view appropriate to present needs, would begin in a small, easily controllable way the movement towards the eventual objective, and could embrace the two systems – Multi-Choice and Credits with Common Core – which we have preferred.

(a)   Courses leading to a Diploma in Community Education:

(i)   Courses of two years' duration for persons aged 23 and over with relevant experience and either having three Higher Grade passes in Scottish Certificate of Education or giving evidence of equivalent capacity to complete the course satisfactorily;

(ii)   courses of one year's duration for graduates, teachers, social workers and other professional workers whose training has contained substantial elements equivalent to those in training for community education.

(b)   Courses leading to a degree in Community Education:
Courses of three or four years' duration leading to a University or CNAA degree in community education.

On balance, the Multi-Choice system seems to be the more appropriate for courses (a)(i), while the Credits with Common Core system is probably the better suited to courses (a)(ii) and (b).

Control of Credits and Major Options

It is desirable that control should be exercised of the number and types of credits and major options offered, in order to avoid excessive training costs and such narrow specialisation that the employability of students is seriously reduced. Initially, credits and major options might be limited to broad areas such as: – adult education; youth work; community work and community organisation; community development and community action; management; teaching methods and skills; the arts; sport and recreation. The range could subsequently be increased as and when this is seen to be clearly necessary.

Recognition and Validation of Courses

Responsibility for recognising courses of initial education and training as leading to a professional qualification in community education should be entrusted to a central body, which the national council for community education should establish and which should be representative of employing bodies, professional associations, training institutions and "consumers". That central body should produce guidelines indicating the broad requirements for recognition; and within these guidelines a training institution should validate in detail the course it proposed to introduce. Recognition should not be awarded until the central body has satisfied itself as to:

(a)   the need for the proposed course in the light of the availability of already recognised courses and the prevailing opportunities for employment in community education; and

(b)   the structure (duration, organisation of elements, entry qualifications, and availability of resources), content (balance of subjects, provision for practical work, and range of options) and standard (depth of study required, and role of external examiners) of the course.

The decision to grant recognition to any course should be subject to review at regular intervals.

POLICY REVIEW GROUP ON COMMUNITY DEVELOPMENT SERVICES IN STRATHCLYDE

STRATHCLYDE REGIONAL COUNCIL 1978 pp 1-30

THE POLICY REVIEW GROUP AND ITS WORK

The work of the Policy Review Group on Community Development services has it origins in the re-organisation of local government in Scotland. Re-organisation not only implied a new structure but also the need to respond to growing pressure for new and more corporate approaches and procedures in the management of local government affairs.

At the end of the first year of the Regional Council's existence, the implications of re-organisation were discussed by elected members at a seminar which was concerned to obtain members' general reactions to the running of the new council to identify the changes in procedures or organisation which might be required to enable them to fulfil both their 'constituency' and 'committee' roles more fully and more adequately.

Among the issues raised, it was considered to be crucial to establish new machinery to *allow groups of members to review policy* on 'across the board' issues affecting more than one department. The outcome of this concern was a proposal to institute various *"Policy Review Groups:* to examine a number of selected issues involving more than one committee/department and in which either Regional Council policy may have become fragmented or duplication or overlap of service may exist. Accordingly, in November 1976, the Regional Council approved the formation of this Policy Review Group, in order to permit a wide-ranging review by members of those Community Development Services provided by the Regional Council and to enable members to be better informed concerning the delivery of Services at local level.

The Groups formal terms of reference are:

1. To examine the present contribution to community development of:

    (a) Regional departments, in terms of aims and methods;

    (b) voluntary and community organisations and other bodies e.g. District Councils, S.S.H.A., new town development corporations.

2. To examine alternative approaches to community development with particular emphasis on the need to stimulate purposeful community participation.

3. To make recommendations as to the ways in which the Regional Council can further community development.

While membership of the Policy Review Group includes the two largest parties in the Regional Council, the number of members was restricted to ten in line with the recommendations of the Regional Council, and in view of the far-reaching nature of the review envisaged.

In relating the Group's experience in writing this report to the issues which prompted it, we recognise, now more than ever, the need, particularly in times of increasing demands on scarce resources, to examine and question current policies and practices and to try to identify and evolve more effective ways of meeting the needs of communities. We see this not only as an essential element in the management of local government affairs, but also a prime task for the elected member, – an aspect of his or her work too often neglected in the past for various reasons.

Finally, we would wish as a Group to express our sincere thanks and appreciation to all the many members of the Strathclyde community who have helped us to complete this report. These have included many outside organisations such as Universities and Colleges; voluntary bodies; our own Departments of Education, Social Work, Leisure and Recreation, and Strathclyde Police; and our fellow Regional Councillors who completed a questionnaire and discussed many issues with us. Most of all we should like to thank the many active people out in the varied communities of Strathclyde for the help they gave us when we visited them. We have seen the relevance of, and pursued many of the points they have made, and trust our report measures up to their expectations.

THE NATURE OF COMMUNITY WORK

It may well be that some readers of this report are slightly uncertain over the precise meaning of "community development". It is certainly true to say that the authors of the report were, at least to begin with, in a similar situation. It is therefore only appropriate that, in a report devoted to community development services, we should try to explain for others what we understand by the terms *'Community'* and *'Community Development'*.

It would be futile to attempt a precise definition of *community*, since it is a 'catch-all' term used by people for their own varying purposes. However, the term as we understand it frequently incorporates three key elements:

1. A geographical area (which may vary greatly in size depending on the particular aspect of life which is being considered). People live, for different purposes, in multiple communities ascending in size from a close neighbourhood to the national level. In this report, we are generally concerned with the neighbourhood aspects of community.

2. A sense of relationship to other people with shared values, interests and history.

3. A sense of wholeness. Community is used as a total, all embracing term involving all relationships between people including work, religion, family, leisure and so on. It involves all ages and classes of people. Community is about interlocking relationships; community is society in microcosm.

We have found a great deal of unthinking nostalgia for the self-contained urban or rural village. In our opinion, it is virtually impossible to recreate this kind of 'village' community fully (even if this were desirable) because of a number of changes in the pattern of contemporary life. Among the most crucial are:

(a)   The scale and pace of life has greatly increased. This operates in many dimensions – size of firm or school or local authority; the mass media; travel. In addition, most of our needs are now organised from outside the area in which we live.

(b)   Much of life's activity is segmented. For example, recent planning practice has designated large areas for particular specialised purposes such as housing, and thus other aspects of life tend to be excluded. We believe that shared experience and activities give a neighbourhood its social cohesion, and obviously the growth of acquaintanceships depends on how much opportunity there is to meet other people. This, in turn, depends partly on how often they need to meet or inevitably meet or are helped to meet. We found that, in many areas, there is a lack of reasons for people to meet.

(c)   Many of us live where we do for reasons which have nothing to do with a commitment to that area. (For example "it was the only house that the Housing Manager had available" or "it was the only house that we could afford" often determines where we live).

(d)   We now have many incomplete communities without a balanced housing mix or social mix or age mix. This puts an unfair strain on the limited resources of some communities.

The concept of "community development" has its roots in African and Indian rural settings where attempts were made to combine two elements in an approach to an area. First, *participation* by the people themselves with as much self reliance as possible. Second, *the provision of outside technical and expert assistance* in ways which further self-help and initiative.

The contemporary use of community development is difficult to define exactly, especially when it is used by some people to refer to an objective, and by others to refer to a method of working. However, community development, as we understand it, seems to have four persistent threads:

1.   The creation or encouragement of a sense of belonging to an area and the strengthening of community networks so as to ensure effective communication among neighbours. This is necessary for a variety of reasons for example, to provide the necessary informal controls over undesirable behaviour; to care for the weak; to respond effectively to a threat to the community.

2.   The encouragement and stimulation of self help activities. The desirability of this stems from an acknowledgement of the damaging impact which an over-reliance on outside sources can have, and the need to avoid the alienating effects of living in a world over which one has little influence.

3.   The identification and stimulation of local leadership. This we see as particularly important in communities where the population is constantly changing or where self confidence is lacking or has been removed. We believe that it is important to increase the role of local initiative as the stimulant of change, particularly in those areas where there is a lack of faith in solutions imposed from outside.

4.   The need for an effective, respectful and sympathetic response by the authorities in making resources available and in providing services appropriate to the area's needs. These authorities should seek appropriate ways of devolving power to local communities, and of increasing their influence on decisions.

The above represents our perceptions of community development. While the exposition of these has been somewhat brief, we feel it necessary to provide readers with some indication of our understanding of community development in order to provide an overall context for our examination of our present community development services, our findings and conclusions concerning these and our detailed recommendations for the future.

COMMUNITY DEVELOPMENT SERVICES IN STRATHCLYDE

In one sense, every department of the Council has a role to play in community development as we have outlined it in the previous section, and the quality of our response to local communities is crucial to morale in those communities, no matter what kind of service is under discussion. However, in the narrower sense, community development services of a direct nature are provided by three Regional agencies – Education, Social Work and Strathclyde Police. Operating through their Community Education, Community Development and Community Involvement sections respectively, they provide a varied range of services throughout the Region...

Although we do not wish to describe in great detail the range and extent of the various departmental activities, we do feel that a brief look at the aims and objectives underlying the approach of each of the three is appropriate.

In general, the aim of the Community Education Service is the planned and integrated provision of opportunities for "learning through life" and the education to help people become active in civic and political life and more involved in the activities of the community. In more specific terms, the Carnegy Report on *Professional Education and Training for Community Education* has defined Community Education as having the following aims:

1.   To involve people, as private individuals and as members of groups and communities, irrespective of age and circumstances, in the attainment and assessment of their needs for opportunities to:

(a)   discover and pursue interests

(b)   acquire and improve knowledge and skills

(c)   recognise their personal identities and aspirations

(d)   develop satisfactory inter-personal relationships

(e)   achieve competence in their roles within the family, the community and society as a whole

(f)   participate in the shaping of their physical and social environment and in the conduct of local and national affairs

2.   To seek to meet these ascertained needs in the most appropriate settings with the co-operation of individuals in groups and by identifying and deploying appropriate educational resources wherever they may reside.

These aims are carried out first, on an individual level, by helping people to develop existing and latent talents, and secondly by preparing groups of individuals to participate fully in society and increase their scope to predict and control those changes which result from their social and material development. Services provided include services for young people of all ages (e.g. youth centres, youth clubs, summer camps etc.); informal adult education (e.g. classes for young mothers and other special groups within the community, car maintenance and other practical classes); services to the community (e.g. provision of resources, support of community centre councils, pre and post retirement courses, opportunities in the arts, cultural pursuits etc.).

For the Social Work Department, Community Development is seen, particularly in areas of need, as a crucial part of that department's wider and more fundamental role of promoting social welfare. Social Work Departments tend to find themselves, for the most part, dealing with continuous crisis situations, thereby tackling the symptoms rather then the causes of social problems. In pursuing community development strategies, the approach of the Social Work Department is to help community groups tackle problems from within the community, before they reach crisis level – (i.e. a preventative strategy). In their submission to us, the Social Work Department detailed this approach as follows:

"The Social Work Department sees community development as a deliberate intervention in local communities and interest groupings to assist and enable them to:

(a)   come together

(b)   identify needs and interests

(c)   take appropriate action to deal with these

(d)   develop further confidence in their own capacity to achieve these aims.

Essentially community development is a problem-solving process. We are concerned to ensure that the individual citizen is prepared to take responsibility and demonstrate concern for his own and his neighbours' welfare. This is unlikely to happen unless he is encouraged to make his contribution particularly with regard to issues which most closely affect his community and about which he often feels powerless."

As has already been mentioned, one of the main reasons for setting up the Policy Review Group was the fear that the various agencies, while pursuing broadly similar remits, were doing so in an unco-ordinated way. We feel from the above statements that there is ample reason for this apprehension. We have therefore seen it as one of our tasks to look more closely at these two services, in an attempt to find solutions which avoid duplication and offer a reasonable demarcation of responsibilities, while at the same time leaving departments sufficient scope to engage in co-operative activity. Although there are areas of activity which are quite clearly and distinctly the preserve of education (e.g. formal, classroom based learning situations or relationships with bodies such as the Workers

Educational Association and University Extra Mural Departments), there are also large areas of overlap and it is on these areas that this report concentrates. In addition, recent trends in Community Education appear to accentuate the duplication of intentions. For example, there are proposals to make Community Education "area based" rather than "centre based", to stimulate voluntary activity, and to concentrate activities in deprived areas where social work has traditionally taken the lead in community development.

The Police Community Involvement Branch has the responsibility for organising and advising on matters relating to:

> Practical or 'physical' crime prevention;
> Social Crime Prevention; and
> Community Relations

Practical Crime Prevention can be summarised as providing a service to industry, commerce and the general public, covering all methods of security including the following major items.

– Advising the members of the force on crime prevention methods and studying and keeping abreast of preventive techniques and practices.

– Carrying out crime prevention surveys of business premises and other vulnerable properties and advising members of the public on the security of their houses, cars and personal possessions.

– Organising crime prevention at local and regional level and arranging exhibitions of all types designed to focus public attention on specific security weaknesses and the means of rectifying them.

– Arranging and co-ordinating Crime Prevention Panel meetings.

– Inspecting explosive stores and magazines.

– Maintaining good liaison with architects and planners in order that crime prevention advice can be implemented at the earliest planning stage of new buildings and housing estates. Lectures to students of architecture is an important part of this procedure.

– Vandalism is regarded as a special problem and Community Involvement Branch officers pay particular attention to it and in particular to giving guidance on how it can be prevented by good planning and design of buildings and housing estates.

Social Crime Prevention covers a wide range of duties including the following:

– Processing and allocating all reports relating to child offenders and the general supervision of police procedures arising from the Social Work (Scotland) Act 1968.

– Operating the Strathclyde Police Youth Advisory Service. This scheme is essentially a crime prevention measure designed to identify and divert potential and petty offenders at the earliest possible stage.

– Establishing and maintaining liaison with Reporters, Social Workers, local authorities, environmental experts and planners, youth and community workers and others concerned with the problems of juvenile delinquency.

- Organisation of the 'Good Citizen' programme in primary and secondary schools. The programme of talks, films and projects involves area constables and police school liaison officers and is essentially crime prevention in its truest sense and is designed to show a child at an important formative stage the value of a lawful and orderly society.

- A major part of Social Crime Prevention is devoted to arranging and supervising police involvement in special community projects and evaluating their effectiveness in reducing crime and anti–social behaviour. The area constables play a vital role in this work and the Branch is responsible for assisting them in every possible way. It is essential that good lines of communication are established and maintained with tenants associations, ratepayers associations and similar organisations.

- Community Relations can be said to cover many aspects of Social Crime Prevention but the following two aspects are of particular importance in this field.

  - Race relations is happily not a major problem in this area but the Branch maintains close contact with the Strathclyde Community Relations Council and has a responsibility for establishing and maintaining good communications and relations with all immigrant groups.

  - In the general field of community relations a considerable amount of time and importance is attached to speaking to members of the public and organisations of all types on all aspects of crime prevention, policy on child offenders and community relations.

In the pages that follow there are some criticisms of the current levels of our community development services. It is most important that these should be put into the context of the extreme difficulties of the past two years caused by local government re-organisation and the severe financial restraint which followed it. Community Education staff have had to cope with the uncertainties associated with the Alexander Report, anomalies in pay and conditions of service and the delays associated with the deliberations of the Review Group. In addition, community education was probably the most severely cut of all regional services when its budget was cut by £2 million or 25% in 1976/7. A considerable tribute must be paid to the way staff have kept the service going despite these difficulties. Similarly, community work in the Social Work Department is severely restricted by the crisis level of fieldwork staffing which has been Strathclyde's inheritance. The Police Community Involvement Branch was particularly badly affected by the restrictions in police overtime earlier this year. These have also been cheese-paring times for the voluntary organisations. In reaching our conclusions and making recommendations we have taken all these difficulties into consideration. We do not, however, believe that all would have been well if resources had been plentiful.

Having said this, the Review Group members have, in writing this Report, become even more convinced of the value of these services. The following was written in the Carnegy Report about Community Education but could equally apply to our Social Work and Police services in Community Development.

> *'The benefits of community education to society are out of proportion to the meagre expenditure of public money on it and to the small number of professional staff engaged in it. Full-time community education workers are 'multipliers' who stimulate and mobilise many times their own numbers within communities they serve – to an unrivalled degree, community education taps the springs of voluntary initiative and service on which the health of a democratic society depends, not least in times of national difficulty and crisis.'*

The Regional Council's commitment to community development is borne out by the high degree of priority which has been accorded to it, not only by making it the theme of one of the Council's first two Policy Review Groups but also through the pioneering work which has already been done in the Regional Council's policy documents on 'Multiple Deprivation' and 'Areas of Need – the Next Step'.

Among other factors, these documents identified the need for a co–ordinated effort by our departments and by regions and districts; a failure by our departments to deal in terms of people rather than tasks; poor information services; a sense of estrangement from councillors and Members of Parliament; the need for the stimulation of self-help activities and local leadership, and the need for the authorities to allow communities a genuine voice in the running of their areas.

As a result, action is now taking place in 7 selected areas of need with the joint appointment of area co-ordinators by the region and districts; intensive staff training, and positive discrimination through departments' own budgets and the use of special funds such as the Urban Programme. More action will follow. In addition to this activity, there is the regional contribution to the multi-agency approach of the Glasgow Eastern Area Renewal Project (GEAR).

The groups own work has confirmed the relevance of the analysis made in these earlier policy documents. In the East End and in those areas where co–ordinators have already been appointed, we should expect that our own recommendations would be suitably modified to take account of any special community development arrangements being made there.

THE ROLE OF COMMUNITY WORKERS

Although there is broad agreement among community workers about the short term aims of their work, there is considerable controversy about the causes of social problems and the appropriate stance of the community worker vis a vis these problems. At one extreme, problems are seen as caused by the individuals in the area themselves, i.e. they are seen as the inevitable, inadequately trained misfits of a basically just and unified society. At the other extreme, social problems are seen by some community workers as the outcome of an exploitative social system which has denied those in difficulty an adequate role in shaping their lives or an adequate share of resources and which then attributes blame to the victims themselves. It is, in the last analysis, a problem which individual community workers must face when considering whether or not to apply for local authority posts. A considerable responsibility also rests on those who train community workers. The invaluable document

Knowledge and Skills for Community Work published by the Association of Community Workers (and which we would commend to all concerned with community work in Strathclyde) has this to say:

> *"trainers should pay a great deal of attention to helping students think about their own assumptions, values and ideologies in relation to community work and community work objectives and to help them to decide what kind of community work tasks most suit their values and ideology. For example it might be difficult for a person with an anarchist personal philosophy to work for a local authority if he tried to make that philosophy the basis of his work."*

Clearly, the community worker may find himself working in politically sensitive areas especially if he is working for a local authority which he regards as part of a malign system maltreating the community. There is no easy answer to this. Each community worker has to make his own honest decision about how he maintains loyalty to his employer, loyalty to the community in which he works and his own self-respect.

At the same time, the local authority both at official and elected member level must appreciate the difficulties of the community worker, who is expected to carry out a pivotal role between community and authority. Certainly, a community worker's political beliefs are of no legitimate concern to the Region except in so far as we need to avoid appointing people whose political obsessiveness would tend to frustrate and alienate the community and so inhibit community development initiatives – but then, other kinds of obsessiveness could equally disqualify workers. There is again, however, a considerable responsibility on those charged with selecting community workers to consider this problem and attempt to ensure that those selected are mature enough in philosophy to challenge the system while living within its constraints.

Finally, we have considered the problem of setting out objectives and tasks for community workers. Because of the wide range of tasks performed by community workers and the variety of areas in which they work, we see this as being both impossible in any specific sense, and indeed undesirable in that it would prove over–restrictive in practice...

SUMMARY OF RECOMMENDATIONS

The following notes summarise the detailed recommendations

1. *Establishment of a Community Development Committee* – The Committee would be responsible for:

   (a) securing co–ordination of community development services throughout the Region

   (b) managing Community Education and Social Work Community Development, including responsibility for resource allocation

   (c) monitoring all Council policies from a 'community perspective'

(d)   working with all agencies to increase responsiveness of the authorities to pressures at local level

(e)   allocating urban aid/community council budgets and grants to voluntary organisations doing community work

(f)   receiving and discussing community reports from Area Development Teams (see recommendation 4)

(g)   arranging in service training for Area Development Teams and other staff in direct contact with local people.

2.   *Separate Budgets for Community Education & Social Work Community Development –* These would be allocated each year during the Policy Options exercise to ensure no disproportionate cuts in community development services.

3.   *Establishment of a Community Development Officer Group –* The Group's detailed terms of reference would be agreed at a later stage but should include:

(a)   Co-ordinating community development activities throughout the Region based on a joint team approach

(b)   Servicing and implementing the work of the Community Development Committee

4.   *Establishment of Area Development Teams throughout the Region –* These teams, comprising a core group of workers from the Departments of Education, Social Work (and where possible) Strathclyde Police, would be chaired by the local Regional member. The team would seek the active co–operation of District members/officers and Community Councils in carrying out its major functions viz:

(a)   to identify those community needs which require a co-ordinated approach for their solution, and to specify the steps to be taken to secure that co-ordination

(b)   to liaise and plan with community councils and voluntary organisations on the appropriate response to community needs

(c)   to study the existing deployment of community staff and other resources in the area (in conjunction with the appropriate Sub-Regional staff).

(d)   to discuss and comment on community work staffing for the area raised unilaterally by any of the participant departments

(e)   to monitor the impact of Council and other public policies on the area and to prepare a report each year on the problems of the areas; how they have been tackled and plans for the future.

5.   *Jobs and Training –* Area Development Teams must make every effort in collaboration with the Region's Industrial Development Unit and Education Careers Service, to identify possible job opportunities within their areas.

6.   *Staff Deployment –* In order to fulfil the wide ranging functions required of the Area Development Team, it is recommended that:

(a)   the proposal to reorganise Community Education staff on a field basis be approved in principle

(b)   Social Work be allowed to appoint community workers broadly-speaking in areas of deprivation recognised by the Regional Council

(c)   Management Services Department should be responsible for monitoring recommendations as to actual numbers of staff in the above categories

(d)   a rationalisation of salaries and conditions of service be carried out by Management Services for the various staff working in Area Development Teams.

7.   *Freedom and flexibility of Area Development Team staff* – Chief Officers must recognise the need to accord to staff the maximum degree of freedom and flexibility to discuss community matters with their colleagues if fresh approaches to community problems and more relevant policies are to be found.

8.   *Concept of a "Community Chest"* – The possibility should be explored of providing a fund or community chest which would enable local communities in consultation with their Area Development Teams, to decide how certain financial resources should be allocated.

9.   *The need to explain Regional Council policies and their implications* – Each Department within the Region should ensure that its policies and their implications are clearly explained to "grass roots" workers, especially those in frequent contact with the public.

10.   *Setting objectives for community workers* – Departments must ensure that objectives are set for their community workers and that these take into account the objectives and plans contained in the Area Development Team's Community Report.

11.   *Fundamental importance of premises* – The availability of suitable premises is seen as essential to Community Development and it is recommended that:

(a)   Area Development Teams assess the need for community meeting places in their areas.

(b)   Management Services Department provide a manpower structure for school premises based on the assumption that schools would be open 7 days per week, 52 weeks per year.

(c)   In the design of local authority premises equal weighting should be given by the Director of Architectural and Related Services to community use of the premises, as to operational considerations.

(d)   The needs of community groups should be reflected in the planning of community buildings and community centres.

(e)   The Education Department should prepare a report for submission to the Officer Group identifying surplus school accommodation.

(f)   Sympathetic consideration should be given to any proposals by community groups who can raise sufficient finance, to lease surplus buildings and run their own community centres.

12. *Role of schools in community development* – As schools have a significant role to play in Community Development it is recommended that:

   (a) Education should prepare curriculum proposals for schools which place a greater emphasis on informing pupils about the society in which they live and the forces which shape it.

   (b) The Review Group on Schools Councils should bear in mind our comments on the need to increase links between the community and schools, if the cause of community development is to be served.

13. *Information services to local communities* – Area Development teams should identify either on a geographic or service basis any shortfalls in information services concerning the Regional Council's policies\plans. The Public Relations Department would be responsible for making proposals to overcome these deficiencies.

14 *Central government agencies and community development* – The Chief Executive should instruct each Department to prepare a report on those matters where the involvement of Central Government departments is felt to be inappropriate or damaging to community development.

15. *Relationship to 'areas of need' policy* – Area Development Teams should work in harness with the Co–ordinators for the seven areas of need selected by the Regional Council for immediate attention. The Director of Policy Planning should report on how this will be done.

16. *Professional training for community development* – Based on discussions with appropriate Regional Departments, it is proposed that the Community Development Committee should explore with training institutions, the development of a new and more relevant foundation course for community development workers and the establishment of an adequate number of fieldwork training units in the Region.

17. *Community development and the training of local people* – It is also proposed that discussions should be held with training institutions to ensure flexible arrangements for training those unqualified local people who are interested in and can make significant contributions to development.

18. *Interim role of the Policy Review Group* – On the assumption that this report is approved by the Regional Council, it is proposed that the Policy Review Group should continue to meet in order to prepare more detailed papers for the consideration of the Community Development Committee once it has been established, relating to proposals contained in this report.

19. *Co-operation with District Councils and other housing agencies* – It is felt that the full co-operation and support of District Councils and other housing agencies is essential if the arrangements we propose are to work at local level. Accordingly it is recommended that this report be submitted formally to them with a view to obtaining this support.

THE GROUP'S FINDINGS

"... it is not enough to purge the remedies of social failure by pumping in public money; more profound remedies are required involving a much deeper understanding of the outlook and motivation, and of the social problems that produce them".

S.G. Checkland "The Upas Tree" University of Glasgow Press 1976

THE CONTEXT OF OUR COMMUNITY DEVELOPMENT SERVICES

It is artificial to think that Community Education, Social Work Community Development and Community Involvement are the only council services concerned with fostering community development. It cannot be stated strongly enough that the impact of these direct services is inevitably marginal compared with the overall impact of the Regional Council's mainstream services and that in the absence of a clear commitment throughout the Council to the idea of 'Communty", they are bound to fail. The central concern of this Council, the district Councils and Central Government should be to see that all their activities foster the corporate life of the community. Too often the community worker's task is to help people prod the authorities to provide an adequate service; ideally, the Councils and the Government should be the co-operative resource at his elbow. Every department of the Council should ensure that, by a rapid and courteous response to the public and by providing services designed to meet the needs of each community, it strengthens the sense of communal well-being in Strathclyde. Every Regional employee must come to see him/herself as a community development worker. It is recognised that this militates against a powerful trend in our society towards an increasing rigidity of terms and conditions of service of employees. The damaging effects of this trend on the ability of Council services to respond flexibly to community needs must be borne in mind by those responsible for any manpower negotiations.

It is important that Strathclyde should play a major role in furthering community development but success is likely to be limited unless we can move in partnership with the District Councils and Central Government, because their services are also crucial to the well-being of the community. During our review, those points became obvious to us in a number of ways:

–   first, it was overwhelmingly clear to us that the service where the breakdown in trust and confidence is most apparent is housing. This dominated our discussions about the relationships between Councils and the public. We appreciate that housing is the most difficult of services on which to give satisfaction since people have to live each day with the cause of their irritation. Nevertheless, it was abundantly clear to us that present systems of house letting and management give rise to anger, frustration and a most damaging sense of powerlessness in tenants. Having said this, however, we recognise a more fundamental problem namely planning – or more appropriately inadequate planning. While we recognise that some housing authorities have taken to heart the comments made in the Morris Report on the planning of new housing developments, we would urge that there should be much closer working relationship between District Councils and the Regional Council in the planning of housing developments; that adequate social and recreational facilities be made available for these developments and that, wherever possible, arrangements be made to talk to those people likely to be housed in the area in order to assess the likely needs of the community once it is established.

– Secondly, the Central Government has to pay its part in promoting more responsive government and thus, a healthier community attitude to authority. It can be more responsible in the following ways:

(a) Despite some improvement since Local Government reorganisation, there has not been the necessary devolution of power to the Regions and District that was envisaged by the Royal Commission on Local Government. Every time there is a needless referral to Edinburgh or a delay in replying, or inappropriate laws and regulations, there is an increase in cynicism about government and a damaging impact on community relations. Local Government unfairly has to take the brunt of this.

(b) Community development is not helped because many central government services seem remote and beyond influence in terms of providing a service catering for local needs. The National Health Service, the General Post Office, Gas and Electricity Boards and DHSS are extremely difficult bodies for communities to relate to and often have only a token consumers' body of which to take note in a democratic sense. Our recommendations attempt to create local structures for community development which will have the potential to relate directly to these bodies at local level. We hope that the various central government agencies will participate in these arrangements.

If we want to see a happier relationship between community and government it is essential that changes occur on the points mentioned above.

We must also, as elected members, attempt to gain a greater degree of influence (through more frequent and meaningful dialogue with the appropriate bodies concerned), over the content of Regional services which at present seem to us over-influenced by professional groups, central government and ad hoc statutory bodies and which leave us too little direct say in policy making. One has only to think of the teaching profession's overwhelming influence on school curriculum or the lack of influence the Region has over bus services (other than those of the P.T.E.) to appreciate this point.

We would also wish to make it clear at this point that the Regional Council has less influence on Police Services than other Services, and indeed less than we would like to see. We have noted the view expressed by the Royal Commission on the Police that the role of the Police and Fire Committee should extend no further than:

(a) the provision of an adequate force for its area, properly paid, equipped, housed and administered;

(b) to constitute a body of citizens (Police Committee) concerned with the local standing and well-being of the Police, interested in the maintenance of law and order and able to give advice and guidance to a Chief Constable about local problems;

(c)   to appoint and, if necessary discipline or remove, senior officers of the force;

(d)   to play an active part in fostering good relations between the Police and the public.

We accept this, but we feel there is scope for discussion between the Council and the Chief Constable on how the Councils responsibility to give "advice and guidance" can be extended, so as to increase the Council's overall influence on how Police services are provided, without interfering with the Chief Constable's own responsibility for operational deployment. We feel it essential that such discussions should take place, as the present situation, in which the public assumes that the Council exercises a degree of influence which it in fact does not, is unsatisfactory to us.

Many of the important decisions which affect the life of a community are taken outside that community, and there is usually little chance for the community to have a serious impact on those decisions. Apart from government decisions, these will pre-eminently include the employment and investment decisions of private finance and industry. Jobs are the inevitable centrepoints of a health community. The Region has done all in its power to ensure that the emphasis in terms of growth in the Strathclyde economy is in the deprived areas; it has done all it can to avoid causing redundancy and is doing a great deal to steer its own capital investment and revenue expenditure to the deprived areas, where unemployment is usually highest. However, we should be clear that local government's powers to affect the situation are limited.

The fact that unemployment and income levels cannot be significantly influenced by action at community level has led some commentators to see community development as merely a sop to society's conscience.

In many ways, we accept the judgement that it is hypocritical of society to weep crocodile tears over the deprived areas while at the same time maintaining a system of economic management which inevitably leads to the creation of these areas, since the investment decisions of industry are not necessarily geared to ensuring the welfare of local communities but more often to the maximisation of profit. (Councillor Walter Boyle recorded his dissent from the sentiments expressed in this paragraph).

We believe that, it is important for the Council to maintain pressure on Central Government to channel economic growth towards areas most in need. However there is also a great deal that community development work as organised by local government can achieve, by ensuring the delivery of appropriate levels and types of services to the community; encouraging local people to run those services which are most beneficially kept at local level; stimulating community networks and awareness so that the sick, the disabled, the young, the old, the lonely, and the delinquent are cared for more effectively; and developing the skills of individuals so that they serve themselves and their neighbours better. These are worthy aims that community development attitudes and services can do much to achieve, while the struggle to improve the general economic climate goes on. We have no control over the economic system just as we have no control over the weather but, as has been said, "If we were concerned that people get wet when it rains, we should not attempt to stop the rain, but would take steps to provide shelter".

THE NEED FOR CO-ORDINATION OF OUR COMMUNITY DEVELOPMENT SERVICES

We feel that the greatest potential for improving our services does not lie in employing more community workers – although this will be necessary in some areas – but in quite simple managerial improvements to our present system. We found that the local communities we visited were usually most reasonable in their requests – while one or two stressed the need for a greater allocation of resources to their areas, the majority merely wanted courteous treatment; replies to letters; simple explanations of the issues; consistency in dealing with requests; easy access to information; easy access to accommodation for community purposes; regular bus services; and an end to prolonged delays while Council administrations and Committees processed their requests.

A central problem with which we had to grapple was the structure of our community development services. Clearly, the Policy Review Group was set up because of concern that gaps, duplication or conflict were occurring because three regional departments seemed to be using the same language to describe the aims of their work. In addition, districts and voluntary bodies employ some community workers... At this point, we have little power to consider the Police Community Involvement Branches' place within the Council's structure since operational matters within the Police force (including the deployment of police officers) are the province of the Chief Constable himself and while we welcome the co-operative attitude that comes from the Community Involvement Branch and take this into account in our recommendations, we are not in a position to organise the branch itself. We are therefore mainly concerned in the succeeding paragraphs with the relationship between the community development services of the Education and Social Work departments.

At this time we do not consider it would be fruitful to produce a statement about the relative roles of Community Education and Community Development. There is much that is unsatisfactory in terms of the lack of overall controlled development of the services. But it would be inappropriate for us to lay down a central guideline about roles for two reasons; first, the services are so variable in Strathclyde that we could not produce definitive job descriptions which would not be needlessly disruptive in many areas – for example, Social Work community workers are so few that if we were to give a restrictive role to Community Education, this would mean withdrawal of a service already provided in some areas since Community Education staff would not be allowed to do what they are already doing and Social Work does not have the resources to fill the gap; secondly we believe it is important that both the Education and Social Work departments should contain within them workers who see their role as a wide one focused on community problems rather than being departmentally circumscribed. What certainly does matter is that there should be a co-ordinated approach which takes note of the needs of particular areas and of present levels of service.

Broadly speaking, therefore, the options open to us as far as the structure of the services is concerned are as follows:

(i)   there could be a single, independent, new department of 'Community Development' or 'Community Enterprise' responsible for all the community development services and pooling the resources of Education and Social Work,

(ii)   the Education Department could be made responsible for all community development services,

(iii)   the Social Work Department could be made responsible for all community development services,

(iv)   the status quo could be recommended, or

(v)   the status quo with amendments could be recommended.

Two other options are theoretically possible – first, that community development activities as such should not be continued. In view of our findings about the importance of this work, we now feel that this is not a practical option; secondly, we could recommend that each department of the Council should have a 'community development' section. This was not seriously considered – it would dissipate community development strength by creating marginal posts in departments whose employees should have a community development focus anyway – this should be achieved by the departments without the creation of extra posts.

We go on now to consider each of the positions mentioned above and itemise their strengths and drawbacks.

We cannot recommend the status quo: it is not possible to give our community development work a clean bill of health and say that it is working well. There was ample reason for setting up the Policy Review Group for the following reasons.

(a)   From the highest levels in the services to the face to face contact with the public there is a lack of understanding about what Education and Social Work are doing respectively in community development.

(b)   There are indeed gaps, conflicts and duplications in the provision of services, and this would continue to be so if the services continued to be planned independently of each other.

As we have indicated above, both Education and Social Work are relatively strong on the ground in some areas, while in other areas there is little or no community based tradition in either service. However, this problem is further compounded by a lack of liaison. While in a few places the liaison is good, often it is non-existent. In both cases this may be because of the personalities concerned. However, it was our experience that such liaison as did exist was rarely planned or purposeful.

(c)   The major criticism, which follows from the above, is lack of effectiveness. Both Education and Social Work said to us that Community Education and Community Development were important to mainstream Education and Social Work respectively because of the valuable community perspectives they gave the departments. However, we feel that, at present, the community educators and community development workers are often lonely people within their department – sometimes seen as the frills but not real Education or real Social Work. For example Community Education always seems to be the most vulnerable part of the Education budget to cuts. We believe the former authorities tended to neglect community development services: this should be rectified but it is not possible to do so without considerable changes to our present practices. If the lion's share of the community development budget is to continue to be spent by the Education Department, it is essential that this should be separate from the mainstream Education budget. In considering it alongside the statutory responsibility for schools, Education Departments and Councils have been unable to accord this part of the budget the significance which it merits for the community as a whole.

Should Education be the department responsible for community development? This argument has some appealing aspects. First, education is the biggest spender of our departments and perhaps the most prestigious. The bulk of present spending on community development is done by Education and by far the majority of our community development staff are employed in Education. Secondly, Education buildings are by far the most significant part of our property resources, and meeting places are crucial to community development. Thirdly, recent trends in Community Education are most welcome; these include lessening the emphasis in the duties of staff on managing centres and increasing their direct educational involvement with the public; an emphasis on increasing community control; declarations of faith that communities and individuals have very considerable untapped resources which can be utilised; a welcome broadening of the definition of Education so that all development of both individual and community is seen as education – this we see as essential if the education service is to regain contact with the many thousands who turned their backs on it on leaving school. However, while we welcome the broadening of Community Education's role, we should not welcome a situation where every community educationalist is expected to be a 'generic' or all–purpose community worker. There is considerable scope for the specialist skills of community education workers – for example, as detached youth workers or in sporting activity – but our aim is that each area should have access to the full range of skills it requires.

We reject the idea of making Education responsible for all our community development services mainly because community development work left with the Education department could never be 'the tail that wagged the dog'. Scottish education, as compared with other national education systems, has not had a good reputation for outgoing links with the community and has tended to be dominated by the professionals. In contrast, we wish to see the development of an approach in which the needs and aspirations of ordinary people determine the direction of the professionals' activities. We are saying two things. First, community development work is far too important to be left as the minority interest of the Education Department which we think is all it would be if left there alone. Secondly, Community Education, reflecting community development principles, has had only a limited impact to date on the Education Department itself though there are notable exceptions in particular areas and in particular schools.

Could Social Work take over sole responsibility for community development? After all the 1968 Social Work act does charge Social Work Departments with the comprehensive responsibility for 'promoting social welfare'. The Social Work Department through its concern for people in need, its detailed awareness of community problems and its commitment to developing and supporting the strength of local communities might be regarded as the ideal vehicle to assume total responsibility for community development.

One argument against this solution is the crisis state of Strathclyde Social Work staffing which is fully stretched at the moment, responding more on a "one to one" basis to individual client crisis in the community. Statutory responsibilities swamp area teams and hinder the necessary preventive work associated with community development going ahead. There would also be the problem that Social Work Community Development staff would be outnumbered by possibly disgruntled "Educationalists" – also Social Work does not have the same control over premises suitable for community purposes that the Education Service enjoys.

The idea of a new, independent Department of Community Development or Regeneration or Enterprise has great appeal. It is the most glamorous thing for a Review Group to do – you must mean business if you are going to create a new department! It shows the priority you are giving to community development. It would allow each and every policy of the Council to be scrutinised more effectively from the viewpoint of the community rather than that of the service departments. Such a department would have direct access to the political and administrative power points of the Region. It would hopefully end the confusion which exists at local level about who is responsible for all community work. It would allow an integrated team approach to community development using the complementary skills of educationalists and social workers.

But, we rejected this solution for the following reasons:

– Community work is, essentially two-pronged (i.e. the worker should be concerned not only with meeting the needs of the groups with which he is working in the community, but also with working within his own department so as to improve its internal knowledge of community problems and aspirations, in the hope of ultimately modifying its policies and practices in ways which are to the community's advantage.) The transfer of workers out of a service department and into an independent department would without doubt diminish the community worker's ability to bring such a "community orientation" or "community perspective" to the service department's overall thinking, planning and policy making. In addition, the feeling of being under pressure constantly from an outside agency might merely lessen the responsiveness of major departments to communities' needs.

– While a new independent Department would most certainly provide a clearly identifiable structure for community development in the Region, cohesion and unity of purpose would not necessarily follow. We feel, at this time, that there are in existence fairly strong departmental loyalties which would tend to militate against any smooth integration, and that there might be a little advantage in terms of staff morale and working relationships in the creation of an independent department.

– While it is not possible for us to carry out a detailed cost-benefit analysis of our recommendations, it is likely that the additional costs involved in the creation of an independent department would be considerable.

On balance we feel that these arguments are strong enough to dissuade us from recommending the creation of an independent department of community work. We regard the questions of securing a focus for community work, emphasising the Council's commitment to it and ensuring that resource allocations reflect that commitment as important, but we feel that these can be catered for without creating a separate department.

We believe we can achieve our aims best by major amendments to the status quo. If implemented, we believe that our suggestions would have a powerful long–term impact on the quality of community life in Strathclyde.

Our changes must seek to achieve the following objectives:

(a) A substantial increase in the importance accorded to community development in Strathclyde. We believe that this has been neglected in the past to our detriment – for example, in the construction of housing schemes which neglected first the importance of facilities of a formal kind such as community premises and secondly, took little note of the importance of stimulating small scale, social networks of friendship and acquaintanceship which enable people to feel responsibility for their environment and to care effectively for their fellow citizens especially those who particularly need the support of the community.

(b) An increase in the power of the councillor to promote and monitor policies which safeguard the interest of the community. The existing committee system needs to be considerably supplemented to give councillors more control of the direction of services.

(c) We must increase the ability of our services to respond locally to the community's needs – not the departments' needs. It is essential to have a team of officers at local level to monitor the needs of an area from the viewpoint of the community and to speak for that community.

(d) The major resource of Strathclyde is its 2,500,000 people. We must find ways of using the enormous untapped talents of these people more effectively, and community workers must see this as a priority task. If only a small extra proportion were to become more fully involved, many crushing problems – vandalism, the care of the old and handicapped, loneliness, delinquency, or anti–social tenants – could take on manageable proportions. We do recognise, however, that in many deprived areas, this is likely to be a long term task and that the initiative will rest with the professionals for some time to come.

DISCUSSION PAPER NO. 1

SCOTTISH COMMUNITY EDUCATION COUNCIL 1979

This paper represents the first thoughts of the Council on the nature, purpose and methods of community education. The Council's views will no doubt change in the light of experience and as the dialogue between the Council and those engaged in community education develops. The Council would wish actively to develop such a dialogue and hopes that any reader of this paper so minded will respond.

THE APPROACH TO COMMUNITY EDUCATION

"Community" has many shades of meaning: it should not necessarily be equated with geographical location – the source of many misconceptions surrounding community education. There are many sorts of community – local, national, international, family, friends, work, school, church, voluntary organisations, leisure occupations in great variety – all of which provide the occasion and the need for the development of mutually supportive relationships. "Education" likewise has a multiplicity of meanings: it is generally equated with schooling, but most confusion arises from the indiscriminate use of the term to denote two quite different concepts – education as a system and education as a process – education viewed from the point of view of the provider and consumer respectively.

"Community Education" has acquired widespread currency in recent years, but, not surprisingly, no precision of meaning. The title does not carry any inherent significance which would distinguish community education in Scotland from the various other kinds of lifelong education which have been adopted elsewhere under different titles. The Council recognises an affinity between its own aspirations for community education and those of, for example, the Council of Europe for permanent education, OECD for recurrent education and the Advisory Council in England and Wales for adult and continuing education. The Council will seek actively to develop productive relationships with these and other organisations concerned to encourage the development of lifelong education.

In short the Council proposes to regard "community education" as a label identifying the Scottish brand of lifelong education. The Council will formulate aims and methods for community education in the light of what it perceives as educational needs and not through seeking to interpret a theoretical concept of indeterminate and indeterminable meaning.

THE COMMUNITY EDUCATION SERVICE

Education authorities have powers and duties under the Education Scotland Acts to secure the provision of adequate facilities for social, cultural and recreational activities in their areas. They may establish and maintain centres themselves, may assist any bodies whose object include such provision and may co-operate with local authorities or voluntary agencies. It was under these powers that the youth and community service used to be supported. The facilities provided took a variety of forms. The commonest were community centres and youth centres either free-standing or incorporated into school buildings.

Traditional adult education consists essentially of leisure time classes provided under the auspices of a University Extra-Mural Department, the WEA or education authority further education centre. Most adult education classes are geared to the needs of students who have already acquired at least enough education to be conscious that they want more and are willing and able to seek it out. Adult education is still for those who have succeeded in the educational process and comparatively little continues to be done for those who need to remedy failure. Significantly more attention is now being paid, however, to educationally disadvantaged adults, particularly the functionally illiterate.

The Alexander Committee recommended that: *"Adult education should be regarded as an aspect of community education and should with the youth and community service be incorporated into a community education service."*

There are at least two interpretations of this recommendation. One suggests that a synthesis of youth and community service and adult education would produce a community education service; another that the community education service should include youth and community service and adult education together with a wide range of other agencies unspecified in the recommendation but mentioned elsewhere in the Report. Implementation of either concept would be fraught with practical difficulties. Both youth and community service and adult education are themselves loose and sometimes conflicting agglomerations of statutory and voluntary agencies, varying significantly from region to region. Neither is an entity capable of unification with each other or with other agencies with a "service" structured and administered sufficiently coherently for the name to have any realistic significance.

Even before the reorganisation of local government there was a tendency in Scotland to rename the youth and community departments of education authorities "community education" departments. The change of name did not indicate any marked development in the role of the youth and community service and in particular adult education was not integrated to any significant degree with the youth and community service. In many regions the new system of local government came into effect leaving important questions about the organisation of the youth and community service still outstanding. Some of these questions have still not been answered. In other regions difficulties of a practical administrative nature concerning particularly the management of community facilities remained long outstanding. In short, although departments of community education were established in most regions throughout Scotland, no common pattern of organisation and administration emerged which could be identified as a model to be applied generally.

Moreover, existing practice does not confine community education to a synthesis of youth and community service and adult education. In addition to activities which are self-evidently appropriate community education has an interest in what happens within educational institutions at both the school and the post-school level as well as in the activities of agencies which might not be thought to be primarily educational in nature.

Education as a matter of administrative concern has traditionally and naturally been regarded as the preserve of education departments in central and local government. As far as educational institutions administered by public bodies at public expense were concerned, it was not inappropriate to speak of an education service. But the list of activities with a claim to be classed as community education bursts not only the bounds of conventional educational preserves, but includes agencies which are not the concern of educational administration at all. It is clear that community education is so wide-ranging that it cannot be offered to the public as a service by any one agency or by any realistically correlated group of agencies.

The Council proposes, therefore, to distinguish between *"community education"* and *"community education service"*, using the latter to refer specifically to the community education departments of the Scottish Regions as education authorities. By using the term "community education service" only with this limited connotation the Council hopes both to clear up existing confusion and to clear the way for the development of productive working relationships with operators in other fields, who, it is hoped, will be happy to collaborate in ventures of an educational nature although they would not wish or would not be in a position to regard themselves as part of a "community education service".

COMMUNITY EDUCATION IN THEORY AND PRACTICE

Education is about learning; if there is no learning then there is no education. All educational structures, institutions, systems are, or should be, for the purposes of achieving learning. Community education is no exception. But learning what? And who is to do the learning? These questions, manifestly related one to the other, require an answer before community education can begin to function.

Both the youth and community service and adult education tended to provide such educational opportunities as they deemed appropriate and did not, or perhaps could not, in general attempt to assess and meet the needs of individuals. But learning is a function of the individual human mind. In a sense "community education" is a contradiction in terms; since there is no such thing as a community as such. Teaching might be individualised; learning always is. To be effective in achieving learning community education, in common with all education, must become more individualised in its approach. The community force of the educational input will be felt when individuals collaborate for their common good and the sum and interaction of the educational influence on individuals becomes an educational influence on the community.

Participation in community education is voluntary and it is not conceivable that every educational activity in which any individual might feel inclined to participate at any stage of life could be provided in anticipation of the need – defining need as Alexander defined it as "the gap between the present state of an individual and the more desirable one to which he aspires". All that community education can sensibly do is respond to need – it is essentially a consumer oriented activity. It is essential to find out what people need to learn, if necessary helping them to articulate unconscious needs, before attempts are made to provide it. Only from a dialogue of providers and learners can something emerge which would be the beginning of genuine community education. The development of positive attitudes to learning on the part of individuals would come before the provision of structured teaching.

The achievement of accord between educational provision and potential demand is, therefore, a crucial issue. Some kind of information or counselling service will be essential if prospective students are to be adequately informed of what is available and particularly if the learning opportunities to be made available are to relate to the identified needs of potential learners. A prerequisite will be a high level of co-operation among central government agencies, local government agencies and local voluntary organisations all of whom will require a willingness to work closely together. The Council sees community education as an expandable concept which allows appropriate participation by any educational agency and by any individual as in self-directed education or study.

A WORKING DEFINITION OF COMMUNITY EDUCATION

Having followed its own arguments to the inevitable conclusion that the primary criterion of success in education is not the creation of a system, but the quality and relevance of the learning that has been achieved, the Council feels ready to offer a working definition of community education. *It is the total effect on the community of successful efforts to meet the learning needs of individuals.* The Council believes that such an approach universally followed would lead to educational influences exerting an increasingly important effect on life in society. Education in general would cease to be a constrained or temporary mode of operation. Community education in particular would become the guiding principle of the educative society, postulating that in order to lead a civilised existence the individual must go on learning and will seek to do so in order to enhance the quality of personal and social life.

In short, the Council will seek to interpret community education not as an educational structure or system, but as a process affecting the individual learner. The Council hopes that this approach is sufficiently novel and distinctive to enhance the prospects of successful collaboration with other educational interests without in any way trespassing on their legitimate concerns. The Council will, naturally, wish to consider the extent to which existing organisations and agencies are meeting the educational aspirations of learners, but the Council will not confine its interests to existing agencies which might indeed not cover the whole range of educational aspirations within the community.

IAN MARTIN
SIGNPOST TO NOWHERE
COMMUNITY EDUCATION Magazine 1980

"Three out of ten. A disappointing effort." That is how I would summarise the views of a group of postgraduate students at Edinburgh University after considering the Council's "first thoughts on the nature, purpose and methods of community education" (introductory paragraph). Otherwise, there seems to have been very little response to what was presumably a widely circulated document apart from a good exposé of the main contradictions and confusions in the text by James Inglis in the *Times Educational Supplement* of December 21, 1979. The purpose of this article is to give my own reaction to the paper before rigor mortis confines it to the filing cabinet.

I should emphasize that this is the entirely personal and admittedly partial response of someone whose way into community education has been via disenchantment with the middle class, middle-aged bias of so much traditional adult education. My interest in community education centres on its potential for developing new forms of adult learning outside the conventional institutional context of courses, classes and clubs. There are obviously other perfectly legitimate variations on the theme whose enthusiasts are well able to state their own cases. Perhaps they should do so in order to convince the Council that community education in Scotland has more to gain from the dialogue its first discussion paper formally invites than the consensus it seems actively to seek to promote.

It is the misguided preoccupation with proposing a supposedly consensual interpretation of what community education is about that explains the trivial banality of much of what the paper has to say. This aspect of the discussion has been well treated by James Inglis and need not be examined in detail here. Nevertheless, the opening sortie into the definition quagmire of "education" compounded by "community" may be recommended to harassed students trying to make sense of the thing as a useful negative analogue of how *not* to go about identifying the creature. The text is not easily summarised because so little survives the exercise but four major themes just about manage to surface:

First, the conceptual difficulties inherent in the term "community education" are negotiated by the somewhat novel expedient of dismissing them and suggesting that community education be regarded as "a label identifying the Scottish brand of lifelong education" (para 3). Without further elaboration, this hardly helps because it does nothing to indicate how community education's commitment to challenge the socially regressive effects of front-end/end-on education is to be translated into operational terms. In this respect it is worth noting that the Discussion paper's cavalier neglect of current practice and critical literature (which is emerging) does nothing to help clarify the real issues.

Second, community education is presented as a consumer service. The ideology of consumption implicit throughout allows it to be discussed entirely in market terms as "provision" that is prepared, packaged and peddled by professionals trained to perceive and interpret "educational need" in the community. Divorced from the cut and thrust of the educational market place, we are apparently left with a "theoretical concept of indeterminate and indeterminable meaning". So what makes community education different from for example, traditional adult education or, for that matter, bingo?

Third, the market model provides the rationale for tidying up the community education mess which is apparently in danger of getting its grubby fingers into other people's professional pies. It must therefore ply its trade in the educational market place without trespassing on the patches of rival hawkers – good news no doubt in the staunchly defended bastion of Scottish teaching, but hardly the basis for effective initiatives in community education in the schools and colleges. The Council's concern with ragged edges seems to have more to do with bureaucratic and professional demarcation lines than with real issues in the community.

Lastly, it comes as no surprise that the paper opts for a discussion of educational input exclusively in terms of responding to individual learning needs. The treatment of this theme, incidentally, illustrates a peculiar process of what can only be called tautological logic in the way the argument is presented. We proceed from the remarkable statement that "Education is about learning: if there is no learning there is no education" to the conclusion that community education must be about individual learning because there is no such thing as the communal mind. In this way we are eventually presented with a "working definition" of community education as the "total effect on the community of successful efforts to meet the learning needs of individuals". It is this singularly unoriginal conception of passive, consumer-oriented provision which prompts the only concrete recommendation in the Discussion Paper for an information and advisory service to deal with individual enquiries.

AN ALTERNATIVE INTERPRETATION

The value of this kind of supposedly comprehensive and consensual view of community education must be questioned. What is needed is dialogue between community educators rather than a comfortable consensus among them.

The interpretation proposed here is quite simply that of community education as a flexible but holistic approach to the educational interest, learning requirements and social development of people who have gained little from initial/terminal education and the assortment of optional extras appended to it. The learning process therefore starts from where people are, i.e. with their abilities, aspirations, problems and needs as they perceive them. If there is anything "novel and distinctive" about community education, as the Council claims, it is perhaps that is does not necessarily reflect the assumptions and expectations of professional educators or the externally-prescribed curricula by means of which they impose their values in the guise of "standards". In this sense it is a direct response to the Alexander Report's concern that "those to whom adult education should be of most value are the least involved"[1] and implies a rejection of the exclusivist ethos of "education as leisure". Community education, then, could be said to be about giving people what they want from education as distinct from what they probably expect. Consequently it is characterised by a wide diversity of practice because the form and content of learning are informed by the nature of local priorities and resources – not, hopefully because community educators do not know what they are doing or because they are merely meeting the expressed demand of the most articulate and organised groups.

Moreover, community education understood in this way insists that collective forms of learning are feasible, worthwhile and often necessary. This means that community educators must refuse to accept the aggregative fallacy of the total effect of individual learning on the community which is put forward in the Discussion Paper and along with it the pathological distortions of "educational disadvantage" conceived entirely in terms of individual "learning needs". Whatever the conceptual difficulties, in reality "community" and "neighbourhood" do mean something tangible to the people who live and work in them. They mean, to put it crudely, that people are *tied up with each other* in patterns of collective interest, mutual dependence and common concern. This implies that community educators should be capable of exploiting the educational potential of local social systems. But it also means recognising how easily appeals to "community spirit" can be manipulated as a "constraint on the less privileged"[2], reducing community education simply to the level of "relevant" educational input in programmes of traditional community development. Perhaps it is precisely where planning and redevelopment or the "horizontal violence" induced by poverty and deprivation threaten community that the "basic collective idea" which Raymond Williams has identified as fundamental to working class culture[3] needs most urgently to be reasserted. This presumably is part of the logic behind the CARE Project in Northern Ireland in which local radio is being used to enable ordinary people to reflect back to one another in their own language and style the reality of community life and experience.[4]

The perception of the collective nature of people's interests and problems is crucial because it is the crunch where the cosy consensus begins to break down. As soon as we look at society in these terms we confront the fact that collective interests and conflicts of interest do exist. In this respect the Discussion paper's preoccupation with individual learning needs distorts the real context of the "educational disadvantage" with which it professes to be concerned. The community educator – given that he cannot and should not be all things to all men and that he operates under the constraint of limited skills and resources – is forced to make choices about what he does and whom he works with. This means taking sides and shedding the pernicious myth of educational neutrality. In essence community education understood in this way is an opportunity to make a decision in favour of the educational "have nots". We cannot therefore accept the consumer ideology implicit in the Council's paper because it is based on the Illichian fallacy that the educational free market of first-come-first-served operates in the interests of all equally. All this does in fact is to reinforce the initial advantage of those who in collective or class terms are best placed to exploit the opportunities it presents. It is vital to emphasize the redistributional intention, especially as non-formal education is increasingly deployed as an instrument of unemployment management.

Such a view transforms the process of community education from a passive response into an active initiative in which those ubiquitous "needs" no longer provide an excuse for waiting for people to come and express them. Initially the absence of any explicit consumer demand makes the whole learning experience more challenging and open, less predictable and safe – so much so that perhaps the validity of prescriptive generalisations about the "nature, purpose and methods" of community education is doubtful. It involves working with (not for) people towards the agreement about the nature of their collective interests and appropriate educational responses. The Discussion Paper recognises the importance of eliciting "unconscious needs" but fails to see that people might at first be hesitant about "exposing" them. This is one of the reasons why community educators should insist on the feasibility of group approaches to learning and what Freire calls "dialogical" methods in which goals and strategies are not imposed but negotiated. The point is made clearly in the following quotation from an information sheet about a new WEA venture in Edinburgh:

"We see ourselves as students who wish to develop a kind of worker's education in which all participants (students and teachers) are 'subjects who know and act', not 'objects which are known and acted upon.'"[5]

The starting point may well be what has been disparagingly but in my opinion quite acceptably called the "practical instrumentalism" of extrinsic reference to practical problems and issues in the local community. Examples of worthwhile initiatives in community education beginning in this way include work with young mothers, tenant's associations and welfare rights groups, retirement and parental education. What is quite certain is that in this essentially social process of learning, the bureaucratic language of "service" and "provision" becomes redundant. Initially at any rate, questions about quality and relevance apply primarily to the nature of the learning relationship between all the participants (rather than to content) and the social context of learning qualifies and informs the character and direction of the group's collective educational experience and development.

A PRACTICAL COMMITMENT TO WHAT?

The practical consequences of this interpretation of community education may be summarised in five basic principles:

First, community education should be understood as an attempt to redistribute and create more open access to opportunities for learning. We now accept that there is no lack of demand for education among people who would never dream of enrolling in a formal class. This latent interest in learning, however, can only be tapped effectively if we are prepared to develop curricula with the people concerned – quite different from providing "relevant"[6] education for them.

Second, educational initiatives in the community depend upon a hard-nosed definition of local priorities. In this respect there is clearly a danger that an established Community Education Service of the type that exists in Scotland will be diverted from innovation and extension by the routine demands of administration and management. Local priorities emerge from meeting people on their own ground and working with them. Pre-defined "needs" merely rationalise existing patterns of provision and legitimise the professional specialisms that service them. In addition, as Colin Kirkwood has pointed out, the bureaucratic assumption that priorities are always to be defined negatively in the language of "need" should be constantly questioned.[7]

Third, community education demands innovatory practice in a deliberate movement away from the traditional methods and values of adult education. This involves rethinking the whole spectrum of our assumptions about organisation and control (What exactly do we mean by "participation"?), the physical setting and human relationships of teaching and learning, the identification and exploitation of local skills and resources, and the entire range of issues in planning, management and research that we tend to regard as our professional prerogative. Again, the Council would not have to go far to find examples of real innovation in community education in Scotland. Indeed, the Gorgie-Dalry Adult Learning Project is on its very doorstep in Edinburgh.

Fourth, community education challenges established bureaucratic and professional demarcation lines. It is not simply a residual category for the bits left over after "needs assessment" exercises. It may well mean treading on other professional toes and certainly implies questioning the professional monopoly of teaching. This is hardly likely to satisfy the Council's apparent desire to tidy up the loose ends but it is nevertheless necessary if alternative forms of learning are to be developed with people in the community.

Finally, community education as a learning process should make it possible to combine education and action. People with interests and problems, want to do something about them. In other words, community education should embody the principle of *praxis,* that combination of action and reflection in which the purpose and relevance of learning are reformulated and extended in the process of acting upon it. The question is whether employers are prepared to follow through the logic of this and accept that if local workers get their professional hands dirty, they cannot always be expected to keep their political noses clean.

CONCLUSION

The values of individual consumption implicit in the Council's paper reinforce the dichotomy between "them" and "us" that is almost taken for granted in so much official thinking about service and provision. And yet what really matters is that community education should not be regarded as just another way of providing what we think is good for them. It is a chance to explore possibilities for genuinely participatory forms of learning in which people are active partners, not merely passive consumers or, worse still, "clients". The waters may be muddy but they are not entirely uncharted. If it would accept that community education is in a "continuous process of definition and clarification,"[8] the Council could do much to stimulate constructive dialogue and debate. After an inauspicious start it should abandon consensual approaches and invite individuals and local groups to submit their own views about community education for publication in future discussion papers. Then we might at least begin to work towards a real dialogue about a term which has indeed acquired "widespread currency" but as yet no "precision of meaning" .

REFERENCES

1. Scottish Education Department – *Adult Education: The Challenge of Change,* HMSO 1975
2. R E Pahl – *Patterns of Urban Life,* Longman 1970
3. R Williams – *Culture and Society 1780-1950,* Penguin 1970
4. T Lovett – *Community Education and Local Radio* Scottish Journal of Adult Education, Vol.4, No.2 Spring 1979
5. *Some Practical Possibilities for a New WEA Branch,* Edinburgh District WEA 1979
6. K H Lawson – *Community Education: a Critical Assessment* Adult Education, Vol. 50, No.1 May 1977
7. C Kirkwood – *Adult Education and the Concept of Community* Adult Education, Vol. 51, No.5 Sept. 1978
8. D Alexander and T. Steward – *Community Education and its Effects on University Education for Adult Educators and Community Development Workers* International Journal of University Adult Education, Vol XVII, No.2 July 1978

JOHN NISBET, LEO HENDRY, CHRIS STEWART, JOYCE WATT
TOWARDS COMMUNITY EDUCATION: AN EVALUATION OF COMMUNITY SCHOOLS

ABERDEEN UNIVERSITY PRESS 1980

This research report takes a critical look at the purpose-built community school. Is it the school of the future, or just a passing fashion?

The last twenty years have seen a rapid growth of enthusiasm for the idea of community education – an educational structure which serves the educational, social and recreational needs of the whole population, adults as well as children. In the past, community education has often made use of school facilities, for meetings, for adult classes and lectures, for social functions and for recreation. Now, an education authority planning a new school (particularly a secondary school) for an area, or an extension to a school to incorporate such features as a games area, a swimming pool or a hall which can be used as a theatre, is likely to consider whether the design should purposely take account of this growing adult use. The idea of a school which serves young and old alike has a certain appeal, and often existing schools will also aspire to the attractive-sounding title of 'community school', even without purpose-built facilities.

If community education is to develop in a period of economic stringency, there is obvious financial sense in combining the provision with the existing school system. The requirements of each appear to be complementary.

> *Schools, like football grounds, are appallingly under-used. Schools are not just educational plant: they are also – or should be – community plant. The community are stupid if they invest £2 or £3 million in lavishly-equipped modern facilities and then leave them to be used by one age-group only, and even then only from 8.30 to 4 on weekdays at certain times of the year. The first community schools are at last getting off the ground in Scotland. The hope is that eventually such schools will be open more or less all day; adults would be welcome; and the schools would eventually become the nucleus of community life. As well as theatres, swimming pools and games halls, libraries, doctors' surgeries and health centres, even bars and inter-denominational churches would be within the school complex. Indeed, the school would no longer be a 'school' as such, but a genuine community centre.*
>
> (The Scotsman, 19 August 1976)

The case for shared provision goes beyond the economic argument. The merging of school and community centre in one building is seen as a way of bridging the gap between school and community, with the optimistic assumption that both school and community life will somehow be better if the two are brought more closely together.

This is the assumption which the research project aimed to test. Clearly there is no simple answer: more precisely, the aim of the project was to establish in what ways and under what conditions and by what strategies certain objectives are likely to be achieved. Can two rather different functions be combined in one institution? Some of us are old enough to remember the first flights of the majestic airships of the 1930s – a combination of aircraft and an ocean liner in a single machine. This was a vision of the future which vanished in a disastrous inferno of flaming gas. Was the idea basically faulty, or was it just an idea ahead of its time, before the technological development of non-flammable helium which might have made it a success? In reviewing the experience of our present community schools, we should remember that we are looking at the first generation of community schools and we should not expect them to come up with all the answers. If we can at least identify the problems which they face, we may make some contribution towards the implementation of what is probably one of the most important educational ideas of our time.

TOO MUCH EXPECTED?

The advocates of community schools tend to make ambitious claims: that both school and community education will benefit from being combined in one institution; that combining the two will save money, especially in capital investment; that the effect will be to introduce 'relevance' into the school curriculum; that this is the means to achieve effective parent involvement in schools, through devolution of decision-making, resulting in a reinvigoration of local democracy; and sometimes even that community education will solve the problems of alienation, vandalism, truancy and violence.

> *Expecting too much is the perennial risk when any new fashion hits the educational scene.*

> (OECD/CERI, School and Community 1975, p134)

The notion of community education has a respectable history, dating back to the nineteenth century. Towards the end of that century, John Dewey and others drew attention to the decline of rural society and sought to preserve the virtues of the pioneer community in a period of growing urbanisation. The Cambridgeshire Village Colleges of the 1930s were the first practical implementation of the idea in England. Other elements in the development of community education have been identified: adult education, from the early years of the twentieth century; continuation classes, after the 1918 Education Act; the Physical Training and Recreation Act of 1937, leading eventually to the Wolfenden Report of the 1960s which recommended powers to local authorities to build sports centres; the Service of Youth in wartime and the youth clubs of the 1950s, and the Albemarle Report of 1958 which laid the foundation of the present youth service; the UNESCO call for lifelong education in 1972; compensatory education and urban renewal in the Educational Priority Area programmes from 1969; and more recently, the Taylor Report on school managers, and the Russell and Alexander Reports on adult education. This long series of events has been brought together in the 1970s in the community school movement. The movement, with all its popular appeal, is a gift to the politician or administrator who wants a jewel for his crown. Taking an idea which is philosophically respectable, has a sound historical background but is highly topical, and promises economy in expenditure, wrapping it in the concept of local democracy and spraying it with the aerosol work, 'community', he has an irresistible package to offer. But the dangers are of offering too much, of failing to reckon the necessary steps between the aspiration and its realisation, of ambiguity or vagueness which encourages people to expect fulfilment of conflicting objectives.

It is time for a critical look at the proposals for community schools and a review of developments where such schools have been established. In no sense does such an investigation reflect hostility to the ideal of community education: rather, it is a rational step in trying to ensure its implementation. Without such monitoring we risk being launched on the too familiar sequence of the 'bandwagon' effect which leads into disillusionment and backlash.

THE RESEARCH PROJECT

The research which is reported here was a three-year project, funded by the Scottish Education Department with the collaboration of Grampian Regional Council. An early statement of the objectives read:

> *A central part of the research will be the observation, analysis and evaluation of school-community relationships in areas which have been recently provided with purpose-built community schools or community facilities. One task will be to clarify what is meant when people speak of 'community schools' and 'community education' ... there is also the question of how the relationship between school and community operates: does it reinforce established values, or does it lead to a radical change of emphasis in both school and community? And how important are the purpose-built facilities in the community school, and how are they most effectively organised?*

Though the research was confined to one Region, the aim was to identify the basic issues which would emerge in any Region adopting a community schools policy.

An initial hypothesis, soon confirmed, was that each community is unique, in that the relationships of school and community depend on specific features in the area, its social context, the geographical setting, the nature and history of the community and possibly the personal qualities of the individuals. Particular strategies likely to be effective could be expected to differ in a variety of settings, and general principles could be derived only from detailed analysis of a number of case studies. Consequently, a main element in the research design was the study of five locations in the Grampian Region which afforded contrasting interpretations of the community school idea:

- Aboyne, in the rural area of upper Deeside, where a combined secondary school and community centre had been opened in 1975;

- Linksfield, in the city of Aberdeen, where a new purpose-built community school planned in 1971 was now nearing completion;

- Dyce, in a rapidly growing suburb of Aberdeen, where community provision had been integrated with a large new primary school;

- Bankhead, a nearby suburb with a recently extended secondary school and the Beacon Centre, a sports and community centre, about a mile distant;

- Powis, a city area with pockets of severe social problems, where the pre-war secondary school building has no special community facilities.

These individual studies were set in the context of surveys of Regional policy and of provision for community education in other secondary and primary schools throughout Grampian Region. A number of other special studies – on attitudes of young people and College Council members and on the training of community education workers and teachers, and on other topics – were undertaken to investigate special aspects which emerged as the research proceeded.

WHAT IS A COMMUNITY SCHOOL?

A declared objective of the project was 'to clarify what is meant when people speak of "community school" and "community education"'. There is no shortage of definitions: one of the classic studies in 1955 by Hillery distinguished 94 definitions of 'community'; the total by 1970 probably exceeded 300 definitions; and in 1978 Newby commented: *The analysis of various definitions still remains a thriving industry.*

One reason for ambiguity in the use of the terms is the variety of elements which have contributed to community school thinking: various exponents of the idea attach different weight to each of the elements. Different recipes for mixing these ingredients result in quite different products.

Six elements can be distinguished:

1. Mutually supportive relationships between school and community;

2. A sharing of facilities between school and community;

3. A community-oriented curriculum;

4. Lifelong education;

5. Community involvement in decision-making and management of schools;

6. Community development.

Clearly there is overlap between the elements: for example, the sharing of facilities (element 2) may involve the community in the management of resources (element 5) and may lead to community development (element 6). Some teachers interviewed equated the 'community school' almost exclusively with opportunities for adults to attend day classes (element 4), or with a harmonious relationship of a school with its community (element 1). There is no necessarily correct combination of elements, nor does it follow that the ideal community school has all six. Each area is unique: different types of community will emphasise different types of provision. Indeed, a single blueprint for community education may hinder rather than promote growth.

The crucial issue is not how many of the elements are included, but how they are interpreted. When we first began to use this framework, we thought of it as a progression from marginal change to radical change, or from evolutionary to revolutionary. Thus element 1 is an example of 'good practice' in existing schools, elements 2-5 leading progressively to the radical element 6. On this interpretation, schools limit their aspirations to 1 and 2, a few incorporate 3 and fewer still 4 and 5, and the majority would not regard 6 as a legitimate part of their function. But this can be misleading: each element covers the whole range from marginal to radical change and can be developed either to maintain the status quo or to initiate fundamental change.

Thus the sharing of facilities may mean school use until 5pm, and community use in the evenings, or it may involve school and community in integrated use with consequent sharing in management and policy. Community involvement may be limited to invitations to parents to discuss their children's progress or it may extend to community participation in school policy. The point may best be illustrated by contrasting different interpretations of the sixth element, community development.

The terms 'community organisation' and 'community development' are used to distinguish these different interpretations. Community organisation means strengthening existing social groupings to help them co-ordinate and expand their activities and so extend their influence. The old-style community apparently provided for all the needs of its members, while demanding from them an acceptance of social norms and moral values. That bond of community has been lost through urbanisation; community organisation aims to recreate it, to re-establish values and restore consensus. In contrast to 'community organisation', 'community development' on this interpretation, aims to challenge and change social structures. There are disadvantaged, disenfranchised and alienated groups within communities, whose problems will not be solved by an appeal to traditional mores and values or by strengthening the established constraints of law and order. Extending opportunities to these groups means trying to build a different kind of community, involving a shift of power in our society. Whereas community organisation aims at consensus, community development adopts a conflict model in its search for solutions to social problems. Education traditionally has adopted the consensus style of working, and many of those who work in education are both uneasy in handling conflict and inept in using it in ways that make it constructive.

WHAT IS COMMUNITY EDUCATION?

These general issues, which have to be expressed in an abstract form, underlie many of the practical problems which we have encountered in the course of the project. An alternative way of expressing the point at the end of the previous paragraph is to ask: is community education complementary, something added on to existing provision, or does it imply a redefining of education?

Among those engaged in community education, teachers, community workers and administrators, we met some who saw it as complementary and some who saw it as redefining. For those in the first group, the aim of community education was to provide a service which would improve the quality of life in the community by opening up access to a wide range of facilities which education had to offer. For those in the second group, community education seemed necessarily to involve a new approach and a style of working quite different from that conventionally adopted by professional educators. For them, the prime task was to effect a change in the community, a change in relationships and attitudes which enable people themselves to improve their quality of life and create opportunities and demands which an education service would then meet.

In general – though there were exceptions – the first view was commonly held by the teachers whom we interviewed and who joined in our discussion groups, and the second view was more widely found among the community education workers. Many of the practical difficulties and conflicts which arise in the day-to-day management of a combined school and community centre are attributable to these two contrasting philosophies of education. If community education is to be implemented, these two philosophies must be brought together somehow in a new theory of community education.

Community education itself is uncertain about its identity. Is it a social movement or a profession? This was the question posed by Specht, the Professor of Social Welfare at the University of California, Berkeley, in 1975 when he addressed the Association of Community Workers and reviewed community development in Britain. He attributed much of the 'gloom and doom', the sense of frustration among community workers, to their ambivalence on this question. Community work in Britain, he said, has many of the qualities of a social movement, a spirited feeling among youthful members inspired by an ideal:

> a collective effort to bring about social change ... spurred by strong feelings of discontent ... in combination with an ideology.

But community work as a profession is:

> a body of knowledge and skills used in an articulated framework of values and ethics which society recognises as being useful.

In our work in community schools, a disturbing discovery was the lack of understanding by teachers and community education workers of each other's philosophy. Relatively few teachers were aware of (or were sympathetic to) the principles which guided the community education workers; and many community workers were critical of the schools' mode of operation. Consequently, one of the special studies undertaken was a review of the training of community education workersz and teachers. Although both groups are trained in the same colleges, there was little contact between the students, and the styles of training differed sharply in the college where we conducted this study.

INTEGRATED FACILITIES

The practical question at issue was whether community education facilities should be built into new schools, or whether it was better to locate community provision apart from the school. The advantages of combining are obvious, and though given brief mention here they are important. The school has the use of more extensive and more varied facilities than it could otherwise hope for; and so has the community. Where existing schools are opened to community use, community education acquires instant accommodation without having to wait for buildings to be planned, approved and erected. Indeed, for community education now, the sharing of facilities is Hobson's choice. Beyond this immediate bonus, integration opens up possibilities of revitalising the school through a closer involvement with its community, and of reinvigorating the community through the resources of formal education.

The case studies identify the many practical difficulties, for both teachers and community workers, of operating in an integrated community school. As long as there is a dual structure of organisation, school and community centre, the sharing of equipment and accommodation is likely to result in recurring friction between the two groups of users. To whom do things belong? More important, whose is the responsibility for care and maintenance? The examples quoted in the case studies are only a few of many instances, seen as interference or irritation; and though a specific instance is usually a trivial incident, the accumulation of such events drains morale. Such difficulties arise in every large organisation, but where there is a divergence of aim between school and community work, the issues are sharpened. Schools are expected to provide a disciplined framework for children, to teach respect for buildings and equipment, to set standards, and teachers are given the authority to require compliance. Community education is a voluntary commitment, is more flexible in its organisation and priorities, and expectations are often different. Explicit training and pre-defined standards are often seen as short-term, greater emphasis being given to the long-term goals of self-help, to the developing of relationships and allowing people to learn responsibility for themselves, even if time, organisation and equipment have to be sacrificed in the process.

These are matters which have to be resolved by management. Whatever the structure of management, a community school with integrated facilities requires the highest personal qualities from those who have the responsibility of management. In the Grampian Region during the period of our study, the issue of dual versus single management was a recurring controversy. Where a school and a community centre are combined in one building, should there be a single person with over-all responsibility for the complex, or should each 'side' have a 'manger', a head teacher for the school and a community education worker for the centre, the two sharing responsibility and consulting regularly? There is no one right answer, for the answer depends on the values and criteria adopted in reaching a decision. A single management structure seems necessary for day-to-day decisions, many of which require quick and painless resolution; general policy and long-term planning fit a dual management structure. The case for single management of a combined school and community centre is strong, if the criteria for judging the effectiveness of the complex are smooth operation, maximum usage and minimal conflict. Whether this is the right way for community education to develop, is a separate question.

If an education authority opts for purpose-built community schools, a major issue is the size of the unit or scale of integration. The large institution has immediate attractions, particularly because of the range of facilities which it can incorporate. Our interviews showed that there are groups (old age pensioners, for example, and mother and toddler groups) who prefer small-scale separate accommodation, even if it is inferior. The larger the organisation, the more has to be done by professional staff (programming in advance, for example), and this has the effect of diminishing local initiative. With a large building, there is also a risk of neglecting those who do not come to the centre, providing instead for those who are already skilled in taking advantage of opportunities. The existing club organisations can readily take over the facilities, unless there is positive discrimination in favour of the individual, and in several centres in our project the balance between club and individual rights has proved a controversial issue. For the community worker, the need to fill the large building in order to demonstrate its success is a pressure which may lead to neglect of area work; and managing the building may by default become more important than achieving the social purposes for which the building was established. Buildings also may outlive the purposes for which they were provided.

For reasons such as these, the large multi-purpose community school should be regarded with caution. If the risks are seen, they can be avoided: in the Aboyne district, for example, we found no evidence that local community activity in the surrounding villages had diminished with the opening of the centre. This was the result of a deliberate policy, depending on the availability of a wide variety of community provision of varying size in different localities. The need for a diversity of provision is a matter which is considered in the following section.

Nevertheless, there are certain advantages in relatively large units, and clear benefit from integrated facilities. The dangers to be avoided may be summarised as risks of monopoly: monopoly by professionals, who are thrust into an organising role; monopoly by the articulate, who are able to exploit access to facilities; monopoly by the institution, in that buildings (like all formal structures) tend to take over from relationships; and the monopoly of paternalism of a single agency, instead of a response to the varied needs and wishes of the community.

THREE RECOMMENDATIONS:

The Need for Diversity

The need for diversity in the provision for community education is a consequence of the range of differences in areas, in people and in activities. Our research project started with the assumption that each area is unique: even among the small group of areas which were studied intensively – rural, urban, suburban, housing scheme, inner city, new communities, established communities and areas with several communities – the variety was so wide that generalisations were only possible at an abstract level. Our interviews demonstrated contrasting interests, aspirations and expectations within each group of people, and of course between adolescents and older members of the community. Activities such as competitive swimming, diving, athletics and gymnastics, and advanced or specialised education courses, can only be provided centrally. Other facilities in the middle range, like the specialised classroom or games halls, are too expensive to be duplicated unnecessarily. Simple meeting places and accommodation for play-groups are usually available locally and must be local to serve their function properly. This diversity is a source of strength for community education: resources must not be channelled exclusively into large units. We found good examples of the larger unit being used as a resource centre to strengthen local groups.

The Need for Support

Community education will not just 'happen' by building facilities into schools, appointing staff (however excellent) and leaving them to work out a mode of practice. An infrastructure of support services is needed, particularly if the aim is to bring different services together. The OECD report, "Co-ordination of School and Community Facilities: Implications for Policies" (1978), suggested a scale from co-operation through co-ordination to integration. To move along this scale requires a support system of information and communication, and structure for decision-making and management for planning and policy, and for training. Community education at present is inadequately developed, especially at the intermediate level between policy-makers and practitioners.

The Need for Policy

It is not enough to have the 'climate for discussion' which such an infrastructure would promote: the discussion must lead to guidelines and a direction for policy. This is easier said that done. Somehow a clearly defined policy must be compatible with flexibility in its local interpretation, to allow for the diversity of situations within any one Region. Consequently, it is more important to clarify policy issues at a general level than to establish precise rules for organisation and management.

Many of those whom we have interviewed expressed the view that a clarification of policy on community schools was urgently needed. They found themselves often working in the dark, uncertain as to what was expected of them, what lines of action were open to them, to whom to refer, or how best to resolve the practical problems which they encountered daily. But in calling for a statement of policy, many quickly added that they wanted guidelines for action and not a straitjacket. Sometimes we suspected that what they wanted was a statement which would strengthen their own positions in dealing with contrary views; but in response to this challenge, the general view was that firm decisions on principles, favourable or not, were preferable to ambiguity and doubt.

The final section of this report therefore attempts to analyse the general questions which require to be faced in establishing a policy for community education.

ISSUES

The underlying issues are: what are the purposes of the school system, and of community education, and what is the common purpose of an integrated provision? It is unreasonable to hope that clear agreement can be reached on such fundamental questions, but it is important that the questions should be faced squarely, for much of the present confusion originates from the lack of consensus on the function of community education when an attempt is made to integrate it with existing formal education. Earlier in this summary of the report, a distinction was drawn between evolutionary and revolutionary patterns of change. Less dramatically, the question which requires to be settled as a starting point in formulating a policy is: shall community education be brought in to supplement, strengthen and extend the existing education system, or shall the purpose be to redefine existing education, to introduce a new and challenging interpretation, a new approach which will encourage – or compel – people to re-examine what education is all about.

If the aim is to supplement, we can take the existing school structure and the whole system of classes, timetables, organised groups, examinations, professional training and the hierarchy of authority through committee structures and appointed personnel as a basis to build on. There is then a good case for co-ordinated development under single management and central planning. This is likely to improve existing provision cumulatively in the long run – a 'marginal' effect, which suffers the disadvantage that it may be seen as a dispensable extra in times of economic stringency.

If the purpose is to redefine education, to break away from existing patterns and to reach out to alienated sections of our population, then swimming pools and show-piece buildings are irrelevant – unless only as a political strategy to win recognition and acceptance of the idea, or as an initial focus of attraction. The relevant action is to create a new sense of self-hope and responsibility, a basic change of attitude leading to new patterns of relationships. Thus the educational issues cannot be separated from political questions of power and authority: essentially, what kind of society do we want?

Popper, in *The Open Society and its Enemies,* (1945), contrasts the open society in which issues are debated and there is no dominant ideology, with the closed society with its clear lines of authority. The community school is supported by many in the hope that it will transit a consensus of values, now sadly vanishing from modern life, more efficiently to all members of society. If community education is brought firmly within the framework of the established educational system, this is what it may achieve. But if it is allowed to develop with a degree of autonomy from our conventional school provision, it may reshape our ideas of the function and purpose of education, and may in the long run contribute to a reshaping of the society we live in.

THE SCHOOL OF THE FUTURE?

Thus if community education were to lead to a fundamental redefinition of the aims and functioning of the whole educational system, this would be an important step towards a new pattern of schools for the 21st century. But the evidence from our surveys suggests that there is no wide understanding of the idea, nor acceptance of its aspirations either among the public or among teachers. Such changes as have occurred are incorporated within the established system rather than changing it fundamentally. Earlier in this chapter we asked: can two rather different functions be combined within one institution? What seems to have happened in most instances is that the two 'educations' exist side by side, with relatively little interaction as yet. But we also pointed out that we are looking at the first generation of community schools.

The most difficult question is whether the way ahead is to pursue the policy of integration in purpose-built community schools in which school and community centre are combined, or whether each should have a degree of insulation, in separate institutions, possibly adjacent and (one hopes) collaborating. The argument of the previous section is that the answer depends on our values. But we can be more definite than this. The purpose-built community school is a sensible provision for larger and expensive facilities, though the provision of facilities is of less significance than the way in which the two 'sides' are managed. The management style must be compatible with the aims of community education, and with the public's expectations of the school also. The large centre must not monopolise community education resources: the strength of community education is in area-based work as much as (or more than) in centre-based activities. A diversity of provision is an essential requirement.

In a period of economic constraint, possibly none of the options for new provision is open. The time can be put to good use to clarify issues, to define policy, to improve local co-operation and to extend mutual understanding. Each of the contrasting perspectives can gain a new dimension from taking some account of the other. In the meantime, little of significance will happen without changes of attitude: consequently, development is likely to be incremental rather than radical, and it will be slow. We should therefore take care not to expect too much too soon of the community school movement, nor make the opposite mistake of underrating its educational significance because of its apparently slow rate of growth.

CHARLIE McCONNELL
COMMUNITY EDUCATION IN SCOTLAND
IN DEPRIVATION, PARTICIPATION AND COMMUNITY ACTION
Eds LEO SMITH AND DAVID JONES. ROUTLEDGE AND KEGAN PAUL 1981

PRIMING THE PUMPS

The following case study, the Strone and Maukinhill Informal Education Project, covers the period 1973-78, during much of which I was the action/research worker with the project. This project has already attracted significant interest in Scotland and Professor Alexander has himself written of the project:

> '*I see the project as a small part of a group movement for and by people who, through lack of an effective power base, were by-passed and neglected by those operating the machinery of local and national government.*'[1]

The use of social indicators to designate certain 'areas of need' or more pejoratively 'areas of multiple deprivation' is standard practice in Strathclyde Region. One such area is to be found in the Inverclyde district of Strathclyde. It was a 'labelled' area many years prior to the introduction of social indicators. Known simply as 'The Strone', the area is more correctly Strone and Maukinhill.

In the field of neighbourhood community work the main inputs in the area during the time of the case study project came from the Local Authority Community Development Unit and The Rowntree Trust. The Community Education Service was a late arrival on the scene in Strone and Maukinhill.

The Community Development Unit in Inverclyde is now the largest in Strathclyde. Since its inception in 1972 it has grown to a team of a dozen community workers plus secretarial staff and a recently developed Fieldwork Teaching unit with one full-time Fieldwork Teacher (an ex-CDP worker). The Unit is part of the Strathclyde Regional Social Work Department and is formally accountable through the District management structure in Inverclyde. It operates throughout the District (independent of but in co-operation with area social work teams on the basis of the principle of positive discrimination).

With the background of this official approach to community development we should place the other major input, the Rowntree Trust-financed Strone/Maukinhill Community Action Project (SAMCAP) out of which developed the Strone and Maukinhill Informal Education Project (SMIEP). The Rowntree project was initially independent of the local authority and thus one could assume less tied to the corporate planning model adopted by the Local Authority Community Development Unit. The possibility of a more radical model working in the community alongside the local authority input thus existed.

In much of the community work literature there is reference to the greater freedom of action for workers not employed by the bureaucracy they seek to challenge. This was not really the case for this project. The origins of the Rowntree input lie with a local councillor who successfully applied for the finances. Besides Jo Grimond MP as symbolic but absent chairman, the councillor, also convenor of social work, along with the director of social work were on the management committee alongside a priest, a vicar, a doctor, an academic and two residents. It seems that most of the committee knew little of community development except for the director and convenor. They thus tended to view the process as one within the sphere of social work with the additional belief that it could lead to improved dialogue with and through the local councillor.

ADULT EDUCATION NEEDS LOCATED

If the Local Authority Community Development Unit and SAMCAP were largely the brainchild of the labour convenor of social work and the director of social work, the Strone and Maukinhill community development experiment in adult education, SMIEP, clearly emerged from the grass roots, developing from the growth of community groups and being identified as important by them.

The Strone and Maukinhill Informal Education Project developed from almost two years of community work inputs in the area. Of primary importance in this respect was the work of the SAMCAP community worker. She considered that her task was to encourage residents to work together for various social and environmental improvements which were important to them, whilst at the same time promoting a spirit of optimism in the area. This was simply translated into making herself available to any group of residents who wanted to start collective action.

By summer 1973, there was a range of new activities and associations, attracting residents who had not previously been involved in the existing tenants' association. '*Not all groups were successful and relations between groups were not always harmonious but nevertheless a mood-for-action was developing. People were becoming involved in the organisation of the groups - writing letters, planning meetings, reading council minutes; government reports, legislation.*' (2)

It was at this time that an identification of a need for particular knowledge and skills began to be articulated. It was thus suggested to participants within these groups, by the community worker, that they might like to join an English FE class run by a local further education lecturer in the local community hall. In other words introducing more structured learning experiences alongside community action. Several people joined this group, including a 76-year-old. Of this the local press wrote '*it enables people in the area to take up further education in surroundings familiar to them.... In fact, its aim is to bring education to the people rather than have the people go to the education centres.*' (3)

It was this aspect more than possibly any other that made SMIEP an extension of the community development process. From the outset its aim was to de-institutionalise and demystify education and to elicit demand without pre-empting response. These points are seen most clearly in the process by which this almost insignificant English class grew by Autumn 1974 into a unique experiment in community adult education in Scotland.

In March 1974 a short, open-ended questionnaire was put to the participants of the class to test opinions as to extending this experiment. From this questionnaire evidence for a significant 'demand', initially from local activists, was located. The SAMCAP community worker, a college lecturer and a number of her colleagues in the English and General Studies Department, then approached the college principal to seek approval for extending the principle of adult education located in a community. Thus the FE college would be seen as a teaching resource centre and its lecturers as advisers/community workers. The support of the college authorities was secured and the Regional Education Department's support for this scheme came through in the early summer of 1974.

ASSUMPTIONS CHALLENGED

In a report on the project prepared by the college lecturers involved, (4) they say that this change in attitude by a college towards a community was important because it challenged many assumptions and traditions of the educational establishment including:

- that education must be conducted within an educational institute;
- that education must be controlled by an educational institute;
- that further education establishments are limited to certain types of courses;
- that classes should bear no relation to need.

With these assumptions now challenged the next hurdles were public participation and resource support.

The debate as to financial support will be dealt with later, but one area, the 'selling' of the SMIEP idea to the community highlights the role and style of the community worker. Initially the community worker had a meeting with the English lecturer and her colleagues in the English and General Studies Department to discuss:

- how best the community might be approached and involved;
- the structure of any possible community committee;
- the relationship of the committee to the college and the Community Action Project;
- selling the project to the different community groups and organisations within the area, publicising in particular the idea of the college coming into the area as a local resource.

The college's direct approach to the community was absolutely crucial, it being felt that the success or failure of the project depended on the skill and sensitivity with which this was tackled. To this end the community worker arranged meetings between representatives of the college and existing groups in the area, from which emerged a committee.

The majority of the new committee were from the English class students, with the 76-year-old acting as honorary chairman. It must be added here that this committee structure concept was itself debated; the danger of potential cliques emerging which could be unrepresentative of the community was acknowledged, and the requirement for a regular turnover of officers and an annually rotating chair was written into the constitution.

The committee had three main functions. Firstly, it aimed to perpetuate the project through obtaining necessary finance, and satisfying existing demand as well as stimulating further demand. Secondly, it had to administer finances to provide for all classes (accommodation, equipment, texts, materials) and to liaise with the college administration, through whom teachers were paid by Renfrewshire Education Department . Lastly, it had to decide with the advice of the heads of department and the principal upon the staff to be employed for each class

The aims of SMIEP by 1974 were:

> '*to elicit and respond to the needs, individual and collective of the community, and to enrich, enlighten, develop and involve on a practical, political, social, cultural, and academic basis. The types of education offered aim to appeal to individual needs and interests, community needs and interests, practical needs and interests, and to prepare people for future education/employment. Further, all classes offered aimed to develop their members emotionally and intellectually through sharing and challenge, and hopefully to further confidence as well as offer a new vision of and for themselves and their children. This stimulus cannot help but lead to the action necessary to create a more inspiring environment.*'

With an organisational structure and these aims SMIEP as an embryonic English class became a potential community development and adult education medium for Strone and Maukinhill.

The next major step was to get participants and to choose courses. It was agreed that if it was essential to elicit demand without pre-empting response then the list would have to avoid at all costs looking like a set of classes that the middle classes thought the working classes ought to be interested in. At best that would be patronising, at worst, disastrous. Education should be relevant to the needs of the community and where desired related to social action. It was decided that three approaches at publicity and demand elicitation could occur. '*The View*', a newly formed community newspaper run by the SAMCAP community worker and some of the students of the English class, would include a tear-off questionnaire section to try to obtain some idea of what might be wanted. Alongside this a little brochure was produced by the committee listing some ideas, telling people of the project and giving the venue and date of an enrolment night. This brochure was then distributed by the committee to all the houses in the community. The community newspaper questionnaire and the brochure contained only two sentences for completion by would-be students:

> 'I wish I could..............'
> 'I wish I knew how to...........'

Although the response rate of returned slips was not great, almost all the responses contained constructive if somewhat traditional suggestions - typing, car maintenance, English, home maintenance, dressmaking. The major litmus test was to be the enrolment night, however. Held in a local hall and in conjunction with a free film show and tea, three hundred adults and unnumbered children turned up - and in the event 223 adults enrolled for twelve classes.

It seems that this number exceeded all expectations and necessitated a search for tutors. Besides the college teachers, two local residents volunteered as tutors, plus some local teachers. As to other resources, typewriters, etc. were provided by the Education Department, some classrooms in a local primary school were utilised, and two local halls. These resources were, however, often inadequate, e.g. at the primary school desks and chairs were too small for adults; the project had only one cupboard for storage; the local halls were at the same time used by numerous youth clubs, luncheon clubs, social events etc.; and SMIEP had to compete for its limited use. The janitor for the largest hall was a committee member which proved crucial.

A question must be answered concerning the relative success in attracting the community along to that enrolment night. The considerable publicity has already been discussed. The interest in the English class was important, as without doubt was the word of mouth network within the community. The tacit support of the other community groups brought with them considerable interest, whilst the location of the project was of major influence, located as it was within the centre of the community. But alongside these the question of finances cannot be ignored not merely the considerable expense of travel to the FE College as an alternative, but also and chiefly, a no-fees policy of SMIEP.

The first English class had always had as a hallmark the fact that it should be free. The SAMCAP community worker, college lecturers and primarily those early interested tenants were fully aware of the constraints inherent in fee-paying education and its equation with educational opportunities. These early participants would term themselves 'socialistic', although within a broad political spectrum on the left. In common, however, was a clear commitment that any education experiment should be free and any minimum attendance levels applicable at the college should not apply in areas of need - in other words a real commitment to positive discrimination. This belief has remained a central tenet of this project (and as a precedent has possibly been SMIEP's greatest influence upon the development of the Community Education Service throughout the Region).

Until 1975 the community worker had secured Rowntree Trust financial support for the SMIEP venture of £500, but this was only of a temporary nature and in order for this project to continue, a project which was by now reaching hundreds of people, security in terms of finances was necessary. Although tutors were paid for out of the college and later the Community, Education budget, non-tutoring costs, e.g. for equipment, books, hiring of theatre groups and primarily the payment of rents for the use of community facilities, were not covered. In all, these accounted for several hundred pounds - nearly half going on the rent paid for the use of the halls alone. With the support of their Regional councillor (also secretary of Strathclyde Labour Group and a significant factor in the project's development) the SMIEP committee approached the newly formed Strathclyde Regional Education Department in early 1975 for financial assistance.

It has been stated already that the ruling Labour party in Strathclyde were heavily committed to positive discrimination and community development and following this meeting with SMIEP the following clause was passed on 16 April 1975 by the Regional Further Education sub-committee in relation to areas of need:

> 'The education service should provide adult courses and a tutor service wherever the need arose be it within or without education authority premises and that in such cases no fees be charged, the education service being responsible for providing a 'tutor service' and paying the tutor's fees. '(5)

A few months later an annual grant of £1000 was assured. Although this precedent set by SMIEP did not cover those non-tutorial costs mentioned, it was a crucial precedent that in subsequent years has enabled community education both from the statutory and non-statutory sector (e.g. Workers' Educational Association) to make inroads in areas of need.

The financial grant given to SMIEP and this commitment to positive discrimination was only half of the package required by the project in its approach to the Regional authority. The position of the Rowntree Trust and the College of Further Education towards SMIEP had led to a situation whereby control and finance were in the community's hands. This of itself was a significant innovation, behind which was the belief that, as the 'SMIEP committee grows in maturity, the college loses more and more of its monopoly of educational expertise'. The policy of the Rowntree Trust to SMIEP was that 'The Trust does not attempt to control operations which it funds other than having the theoretical right of suspending any grant made .... We also receive reports on the progress of the Projects, as they are prepared. But essentially control remains with the Project Committee.' (6)

And even when the funding body after one year became the Region these principles were accepted by the Education Authority with direct funding being made available to the committee to allow them to continue to develop their programme; although the local authority insisted upon regular auditing, querying the various purchases and vetting the accounts in considerable detail. One should add that although this funding was only on an annual basis, considerable time and energy was taken by the committee in having constantly to justify themselves during subsequent years.

EXPERIMENTING

By 1975 SMIEP witnessed a shift towards experimenting with less traditional media for learning – moving away from what Alexander had called didactic methods of somewhat formalised classes towards increased community action, political theatre, video, etc. This change was the result both of dialogue between the students, the committee and the community educationalists and of an increasing influence of experiments from elsewhere, particularly Ashcroft, Jackson and Lovett in Liverpool and Freire in Latin America, (7) and recurrent education theory, especially the analysis of the importance of 'language' for the educationalist, SMIEP having also begun to identify that words such as school, course, class and even teacher seemed to stifle interest.

In her book *'Adults Learning'*, (8) Jennifer Rogers discusses what motivates adults to education and suggests several reasons: vocational, self-development, captive wives, social motives, remedial, the facilities: and one could add a seventh - social action. It would seem for SMIEP that the preponderance of traditional leisure activities, e.g. dressmaking, initially desired by the participants was of importance to them for many of the first six, but could these classes be translated into catalysts for social action? The committee felt this was possible and desirable. Dressmaking, for example, was also used as an approach to consumer education, as a way of cutting costs for many participants, and as a potential forum for women's studies. In terms of a greater political content both 'Writing for the Press' and a series of meetings on understanding local government and community councils were sharing with the participants necessary skills in producing a local paper or in setting up pressure groups. Discussion groups, sometimes held in pubs or people's homes, about industrial democracy or the work of John McLean (a socialist educator of the early twentieth century),and the introduction to some groups of 'neighbourhood action packs', all developed knowledge, confidence, political consciousness and experience of the participants. And one important area of experimentation was political theatre put on by the project and the 7:84 group which attracted audiences into the hundreds on several different occasions.

The 7:84 theatre company was set up in Scotland under the direction of John Magrath in 1973. They were a clearly socialist political theatre company (7 per cent of the population own 84 per cent of the wealth) who used the theatrical/ music hall genre to politicise their audience. SMIEP, along with other community groups in Scotland have utilised this approach on a number of occasions, covering issues such as multi-nationals in Scotland and alcoholism. On each occasion over 200 local folk turned up. It seems that one element in the success of this group has been the utilisation of a language that people understand. Through music and dialogue placed in a working-class milieu crucial issues, often complex economic and political issues, are discussed.

On the question of alternative educational media, reference should be made to the projects' use of audio-visual aids. In early 1976 an opportunity arose for access to video equipment from the Scottish Council for Educational Technology at very little expense. (9) Because of the ease with which anyone could be taught how to use it local people in Strone and Maukinhill were able to film their community as they saw it – producing instant television of the community, by the community, for the community. This process at the same time helped to demystify film production and in a very short time one could observe individual confidence growing amongst the users. On the other hand the very fact of seeing one's neighbour walking around with a film camera could produce both interest and entertainment. One of the films on the question of housing was also utilised by community workers in the area to present and 'bring home' important issues to some of the senior officials and elected members at the council offices. The researcher attended this meeting and undoubtedly the showing of this film at the end of a somewhat turgid meeting led to great interest and an uncomfortable defensiveness on the part of the Director of Housing.

In the early days of SMIEP a community newspaper, *'The View'*, was begun by the SAMCAP community worker. This paper was utilised in a number of ways by the project:

to include questionnaires on SMIEP, publicity and advertising, arranging courses in 'Writing for the Press' for contributors and producers alike, as a learning medium itself. It has been noted elsewhere by Ensor (10) that community newspapers emerged as a reaction to the complacency of the provincial press. From the outset the SMIEP committee and the other community development experiments saw it as a reaction to blatant political bias in the local press and thus as an alternative source for information and comment. But also to counter the constant labelling of this community by the local press. The reputation of the area, for example, on issues of vandalism or alcohol problems or 'scroungers' was felt to be largely the creation of the press. Thus, for SMIEP in particular the question of 'image projection was crucial if any changes in local authority attitudes were to occur. In addition, through involvement in the community newspaper and on the 'Writing for the Press' course several residents emerged as confident and articulate spokesmen for the area through the publication of letters in the local press and this was undoubtedly not a small influence on the interest taken by the rest of Greenock, and indeed Scotland, in this project.

ACTION RESEARCH

During most of the period covered by this experiment there was a monitoring input by a research worker. To a large degree the researcher's own close involvement had an effect upon this project's development. Indeed this was in part intentional if the evaluative action research process is correctly understood. (11) Some examples highlight this.

In drawing up questionnaires the researcher worked closely with the committee over design and implementation. The undertaking of door-to-door surveys and interviews was a communal process with the researcher sharing his skills with the committee's intimate knowledge of the people and of the area – a two-way process. The co-option of the researcher as a non voting observer onto the committee led to numerous occasions where opinions of the researcher were sought. This opinion seeking was of influence on the question of the relationship of the project with industry, with the local schools, and over experimenting with alternative media.

In 1976 the researcher, following interviews with local trade unionists and members of the Trades Council, made suggestions to the committee that some educational links between the community project and the trade unions could occur. An interesting discussion followed and these ideas were brought together in a document. A course was then run on the theme of 'Industrial Democracy' and an open debate in the local community hall was prepared. A local environmentalist gave a session of talks and slide shows on pollution in the area - relating this to immediate issues like dirty laundry and pollution in the Clyde. And one result of this was the drawing up of a list of all responsible authorities, phone numbers and addresses so that the project might act as a watchdog. As to numbers coming along, on each occasion up to twenty adults and children got involved. On the topic of profits and commerce in general the 7:84 theatre group appeared with their production 'Honour Your Partners', this play being about the role of multi-nationals in the Scottish economy, and of particular relevance to this area in terms of employment.

The concept of 'action research' adopted by the researcher has become increasingly common as a methodology for community development. Lambert has written (12) that the criteria for good research are: 'care' in a search of inquiry, 'science' guiding the endeavour of discovery, 'criticism' informing any investigation. Yet, as he notes, there is a dilemma here for the researcher in a community project between the action and the research. Care and insistence on method means that the researcher cannot be too hasty, yet the action worker or community group often needs information urgently. As to the scientific nature of social inquiry one repeats that communities are not laboratories, 'facts' don't necessarily speak for themselves and the claim that, methods can be divorced from values and ideology, (both the researchers and his employing agency), is to be doubted, whilst critical investigation through elaborating on the nature of questions and answers can only aid rather than remove difficult decisions about what needs to be done. (13)

Research findings are not neutral since intelligence and understanding are a part of control and power. It was this awareness plus a wish for the research itself to reflect the community development process of encouraging participation and demystifying that 'power centre' that led me to the action research methodology.

A close affinity between the activities of community work practice and social research has already been acknowledged in much of the recent professional literature. Rapoport (14) describes 'action research' as aiming to contribute both to the practical concerns of people in an immediate problematic situation and to the goals of social science by joint collaboration within a mutually acceptable ethical framework. This type of research does not therefore merely provide a purely detached assessment over time of some aspect of performance but rather sets up a dynamic interaction between the researcher and the practitioner as part of the ongoing experimental process.

At its roots this approach also aims to engage practitioners, volunteers, action groups in enquiries about matters that are of interest and importance to them. Thus for example, the use of a questionnaire survey engaged over a dozen local residents in drawing up the questions and processing the questionnaire with the researcher. In this process the participants were encouraged to think and work systematically and with clarity. Research method is as a result demystified and seen to be available to all. Research becomes a form of action that is no longer merely the domain of experts but of the people who themselves must act. In this defining of problems and finding of facts, research itself becomes a form of empowerment and action.

For this reason action research has a high potential for becoming political; the simple phrase 'knowledge is power' is crucial. Anyone who has ever watched an unprepared community group without information and facts at their fingertips, confronted by experts from the council, is witness to this. Knowledge is power therefore in the sense that it gives a group real confidence to participate. There are difficulties for the researcher here, but possibly Rapoport's concept of 'mutually acceptable frameworks' meets these. There is the obvious danger of the researcher having over-biased support for the community he is working with, particularly if he uncovers 'evidence' which it is not 'political' to publish.

Fortunately the goals of this project were ones with which I could work - relatively clear and not, for example, as ambiguous as those set for CDP. But the techniques of evaluation are problematic; for example, where one used existing sources of data great care had to be taken. Frequently data had only been recorded haphazardly. Often availability of data was the result of accessible evaluative material on some poor experience, whilst good experiences were unrecorded. One should add here that almost the first input of the researcher here was to suggest regular, well-kept recording of the project.

EVALUATION

It is necessary now to make some brief comments upon the effectiveness of such a project. We have noted already some of the processes involved and the roles and activities of the various 'professional' workers - for example, the community worker and the action/research worker - in stimulating and sustaining participation of various kinds. Does the SMIEP experiment and others like it have anything to tell us concerning participatory democracy and political education? I would wish to argue that community education/ community development has a major contribution to make in this respect. Community education workers, whether termed community workers, adult educationalists or even action/research workers, accomplish change by enabling the people in a particular community to clarify their own objectives, improve their own relationships, and overcome for themselves any obstacles in their way. Community educationalists are not leaders inspiring people with their goals but they can be catalysts helping groups to diagnose, clarify and implement their own goals. Community education involves, therefore, the sharing of knowledge, skills and experience in language and form people can relate to. There is a recognition inherent in community education that to be committed to participatory democracy the community educator must not indoctrinate or condition, because to indoctrinate would involve treating the group as a means and not an end. For SMIEP the relationship to participants, whether it be the committee or others involved, was one of dialogue and respect between equals.

Hampton, in the journal 'Teaching Politics', (15) remarks of this process that 'in some cases the adult educator may attempt to create the community atmosphere which will encourage political action as a basis for educational activities.' In all this, says Hampton, the educator must be concerned with the growth of the learner's self confidence to engage in social or public activities. In this sense all community education is political, although not all community education is about politics. It recognises that politics is life and that for the community educators, whether working with young people on an adventure playground, or tenants over the publication of a community newspaper, education is geared to social action, to individual and communal creativity and participation in the decisions which affect everyone's life.

REFERENCES

1   K. Alexander, Foreword to C. McConnell (ed.), *'The People's Classroom'*, Dundee College Publication, 1979.
2   B. Darcy, *'The Relationship of S.M.I.E.P. to Community Development'*, 1973-74, S.M.I.E.P., 1977, page 2.
3   Greenock 'Telegraph', 24.8.74.
4   M. Kay and J. Jackson, *'A Greenock Experience'*, Scottish Journal of Adult Education September,1975.

5   Strathclyde Regional Council, Education Minutes, Clause 5, April 1975.

6   The Joseph Rowntree Social Trust Ltd, letter to Researcher 7.3.77.

7   B. Ashcroft and K. Jackson, *Adult Education and Social Action*, in D. Jones and M. Mayo (eds), '*Community Work One*', London, Routledge & Kegan Paul, 1974; T. Lovett, '*Adult Education, Community Development and the Working Class*', London, Ward Lock Educational, 1975; P. Freire, '*Pedagogy of the Oppressed*', Harmondsworth, Penguin, 1973; V. Houghton and K. Richardson, '*Recurrent Education*', London, Ward Lock Educational, 1974.

8   J. Rogers, '*Adults Learning*', Harmondsworth, Penguin,

9   This type of equipment is now much more readily available in Scotland – see '*Video in Scotland*', Scottish Film Council, 1976.

10   Ensor, '*Community Newspaper Kit*', Community Service Volunteers, 1976.

11   R. Lees, '*Research Strategies for Social Welfare*', London, Routledge & Kegan Paul, 1975.

12   J. Lambert in C. Briscoe and D. Thomas (eds), '*Community Work: Learning and Supervision*', London, National Institute and George Allen & Unwin, 1977.

13   Ibid, p.114.

14   R. Rapoport, *The Dilemmas in Action Research*, 'Human Relations', vol.23, no.6, pp.499-513.

15   Hampton, *Adult Education and the Teaching of Politics*, in 'Teaching Politics', no.6, 1977, p.139.

THE RIGHT TO LEARN – A STATEMENT ON ADULT EDUCATION

SCOTTISH INSTITUTE OF ADULT EDUCATION 1981

ADULT EDUCATION

Definitions of adult education are manifold. In Scotland the term has frequently been used in a restricted sense to refer to a particular kind of liberal academic education. In this statement a much broader definition has been assumed – something along the lines of that used by the Organisation for Economic Co-operation and Development:

> *"Adult Education refers to any learning activity or programme deliberately designed by a providing agent to satisfy any training need or interest that may be experienced at any stage in his or her life by a person who is over the statutory school leaving age and whose principal activity is no longer in education. Its ambit, thus, spans non-vocational, vocational, general, formal and non-formal studies as well as education with a collective social purpose".*
>
> (OECD, Learning Opportunities for Adults, Vol. IV: Participation in Adult Education. Paris: OECD, 1977 p. 11)

THE SCOTTISH INSTITUTE OF ADULT EDUCATION

The Scottish Institute of Adult Education is the principal national body in Scotland specifically concerned with the promotion of education and training opportunities for adults. The Institute arranges conferences and training courses, promotes research, acts as an information centre, publishes the Scottish Journal of Adult Education and maintains links with international bodies in the adult education field. It is responsible for administration of the Scottish Adult Basic Education Unit and for the management of "NETWORK", the Glasgow-based Telephone Referral Advice and Information agency which provides support services for broadcast radio and television programmes.

EDUCATION IS FOR PEOPLE

Education is something for children and young people: that is the common assumption – made by educators and decision-makers, as well as by the general public at large. This papers argues a contrary view. It argues that education is for people – for everyone – and it points out that most people at the present time are restricted in gaining access to educational opportunities. Provision of education for adults has not received adequate attention in Scotland. In so far as our college and university institutions make provision of post-school and post-experience education, they do so mainly for those who have already done well at school.

Our aim is to promote the development of an open and comprehensive system of education within which initial compulsory schooling plays only an introductory part and in which ordinary people have the opportunity, at any time of life, to participate in formal education or informal learning programmes on either a full-time or a part-time basis. Such educational opportunities would not be restricted by the immediate demands of the labour market. Adult education is essential to the development of a democracy at all levels, to the development of the individual and to the general culture of the community.

Education must be seen as part of each person's total life experience and should not be confined to traditional educational institutions and patterns. Work-based and community-based education programmes, for example, have an important part to play. The day-to-day learning needs of people will often best be met within their own communities, and the statutory services must be prepared both to assist voluntary organisations and associations and to operate in a variety of settings – including community centres, private houses, churches, pubs, social clubs, hospitals, prisons, etc., as well as in educational premises.

RELEVANT EDUCATIONAL POLICIES

Whilst recent years have witnessed an increasing tendency to question the effectiveness of present educational performance and educational structures, inadequate attention has been paid to the implications for the education system of other major social and economic changes. The educational policy issues receiving attention have tended to be those relating to general ideological conviction – equality of opportunity, maximisation of parental choice and so on – or to financial and administrative matters.

The need for policy discussion and policy formulation in the field of adult education is closely related to wider policy issues and general social trends. The kind of adult education policies required are those which take account of factors like industrial change and the development of new economic opportunities; the changing role and expectations of women; the needs of the unemployed; the changing age structure of the population and the role of retired people; the growing importance of leisure; the need for social education, health education and consumer education; the problems of inner city areas and the problems of isolated rural areas. Undoubtedly these factors also have implications for the nature and content of initial schooling. Of more importance in this context, however, is the current neglect of educational provision for the community at large. The nature of tomorrow's world is determined by today's adults, more than by today's children. The absence of coherent policies for adult education must now be seen as something of an embarrassment.

The statutory framework for Adult and Further Education in Scotland is incorporated in the Education (Scotland) Acts of 1962 and 1969 and the Further Education (Scotland) Regulations 1959-1979. The Education (Scotland) Act 1969 stipulates (Part 1, 1) that "It shall be the duty of each education authority to secure that there shall be made for their area adequate and efficient provision of school and further "education". Under the Education Acts, 'further education' includes both vocational education and 'social, cultural and recreative activities either as part of a course of instruction or as organised voluntary leisure-time occupation'. For administrative purposes the tendency has been to identify two distinct types of education: vocational work-orientated education ('Formal Further Education') and leisure-time non-vocational education ('Informal Further Education' and

'Community Education'). However, analysis of recent developments in adult education suggests that these distinctions may now be inappropriate – even unhelpful. Basic Education, for example, or Women's Education, or Trade Union Education, or Retirement Education, or Health Education, fit comfortably in neither category.

Perhaps of more importance, however, is the question of 'adequate and efficient provision'. On the one hand the Acts and the Regulations make no distinction between the continuation of initial education for the young and the provision of post-initial education for adults, and on the other they give little indication of the expected range or extent of provision. In the absence of up-to-date and clear guidance on Adult Education policy issues it is, therefore, not surprising (particularly during a period of severe financial constraint) that Education Authorities and individual providing agencies and institutions have difficulty in judging what is expected of them. This is a matter requiring clarification.

The diversity of adult education makes it impossible to distinguish completely separate and mutually exclusive categories of provision. At this stage, however it may be helpful to identify the following types of education:

(a)   **Basic and Second Change Education**
A great many adults when contemplating a return to education, training or employment feel the need to start again, almost from the beginning. They may require help with Literacy and Numeracy, Study Skills and other Basic Skills and need to benefit from a general confidence-building process. For these the traditional 'O' Grade starting level of many Second Chance programmes in Further Education Colleges is too high. Expansion in provision of Foundation courses, Preparatory Courses, New Opportunities Courses and Basic Education Programmes of all kinds must be seen as an essential element in any coherent pattern of Adult Education provision.

(b)   **Continuing Education**
This category includes a wide range of vocational, professional and general education courses provided mainly in Further Education, Higher Education and University Institutions for adults who have already reached a minimum level of general education and who wish to improve their qualifications or to train (or re-train) for a particular career. Access to such courses, for mature students, depends on recruitment and admissions policies, on the availability of appropriate Information, Guidance and Counselling Services, on provision of Study Skills and 'Return to Study' courses, on policies with respect to grants, allowances and entitlements to Paid Leave, and on the availability of part-time courses.

(c)   **Post Experience Vocational Education and Training**
Often organised on an in-service basis for particular groups of employees or for member of a particular profession, Post-Experience courses are associated variously with up-dating, refresher education, acquisition of new skills and knowledge, re-orientation or retraining. Courses are frequently much shorter than conventional academic courses and in some cases may involve Paid Educational Leave of one kind or another. Participation in regular short, specialised in-service training

programmes of this nature is sometimes as effective as some of the more prolonged forms of initial education and training.

(d) **Liberal Adult Education**

A number of educational agencies, including adult education bodies such as the Workers' Educational Association and the University Adult Education Departments, have a long tradition of providing courses for adults concerned particularly with promoting greater understanding of both the physical and the social environment and of international affairs, with the deepening of intellectual and cultural experience, with general personal development and with the broadening of horizons. Many would argue that subjects such as politics, psychology, economics, literature, music, history, sociology, etc. require maturity for full understanding and appreciation. Undoubtedly many pupils find their school and college experiences of these subjects less than satisfactory. Regrettably, however, official support and public subsidy for liberal adult education has markedly declined in recent years and opportunities for people to broaden their general education during the years of adult maturity are currently being severely curtailed.

(e) **Adult Education in Community Contexts**

The past decade has seen a significant move on the part of adult and community educators to take learning opportunities to ordinary people in the community wherever they are, rather than expect people to enrol on conventional courses at educational institutions. This kind of Non-Formal 'Outreach' activity has been associated with attempts to make contact with groups of people previously ignored by the education system, to involve people in planning and controlling their own learning and to make education relevant to every-day concerns and activities, Programmes include Trade Union Education, Civic and Political Education, Health and Consumer Education, Parent Education, Social and Life Skills, Community Arts activities – as well as more conventional education courses, though organised in places such as pubs, clubs, works canteens, private houses, etc.

(f) **Social Cultural and Recreational Education**

The informal Further Education (mainly evening) programmes provided by Education Authorities in schools, in community centres and other local premises offer to the general public a wide range of subjects and activities for those who wish to extend their knowledge, pursue new interests, practise and improve useful skills, maintain health and physical fitness, or participate in recreational, cultural and social activities. Regrettably, during a period of steady increase in both the numbers of the unemployed and in the size of the retired population, provision of Informal Further Education by the Education Departments of Regional and Island Councils has substantially diminished.

RECENT DEVELOPMENTS IN ADULT EDUCATION

The past decade has seen a number of significant developments in education and training provision for adults. Whilst some of these have originated within the mainstream education system, rather more have come about as a consequence of initiatives taken outside the system. It could be argued that these ad hoc developments represent evidence of a typically British pragmatic approach to the wider concept of Lifelong Education. However, in Scotland as elsewhere in the United Kingdom, it is difficult to detect signs of any substantial modification of educational policies or educational structures designed to take account of these new developments and new demands. The paragraphs below describe a number of these developments and give some indication of the extensive nature of the current Adult Education agenda.

THE OPEN UNIVERSITY

The setting up of the Open University represents perhaps the most important commitment of public expenditure to Adult Education in recent years. Flexible modes of study, multi-media methods, open admissions policies, counselling and support services – all these have helped to stimulate new approaches to relevant learner-centred education. However, despite intentions to the contrary, the successful growth of the Open University has primarily extended the range of up-market higher education opportunities available to those who are already relatively well-educated by average standards. It remains to be seen whether the expansion of the O.U. Continuing Education and Community Education programmes (the latter quite clearly designed for rather more down-market audiences, yet paradoxically receiving no public subsidy) will significantly extend educational opportunities to a much wider adult audience. Clearly, however, the education and training needs of the majority of people manifest themselves at a very different level.

ADULT LITERACY AND BASIC EDUCATION

Most of today's adult population left school at the minimum leaving age, with no certificates or qualifications. A substantial proportion of these find themselves unable to take advantage of even the lowest level of existing further education and training courses, the starting point of such courses being too high for them. Of this number a significant minority, perhaps 200,000 in Scotland (or possibly even twice that number) have problems of one sort or another with basic numeracy, reading, writing or other communication skills – problems that local Adult Literacy and Basic Education schemes have only begun to tackle. The Adult Literacy Campaign was initially promoted by a voluntary organisation (the British Association of Settlements) then raised to public consciousness in 1975 by the BBC television series, "On the Move", and the BBC's subsequent three-year broadcasting project (supported also by independent broadcasting agencies). Support from public funds followed. In Scotland in the five-year period from 1976 to 1981 £525,000 of government money was channelled into pump-priming activities by the Scottish Education Department, via a succession of central agencies attached to the Scottish Institute of Adult Education (first the Scottish Adult Literacy Agency, then the Scottish Adult Literacy Unit and now the Scottish Adult Basic Education Unit). At local level Education Authorities throughout Scotland have supported the development of a network of Adult Literacy and Basic Education Schemes. It is noteworthy, however, that the total of public funds devoted to Adult Education of this kind is only a small fraction, for example, of the annual budget of a single university.

THE TRAINING OPPORTUNITIES SCHEME AND PROGRAMMES FOR THE UNEMPLOYED

For a variety of historical reasons Britain maintains a clear distinction between 'Education' agencies and 'Training' agencies. The launching of the most ambitious adult vocational education programme during the last decade was the work of the Training Services Agency (now the Training Services Division of the Manpower Services Commission). The Training Opportunities Scheme (TOPS) launched in 1972 aims to

- provide individuals with 'training on demand'
- enable the adult population to change occupations quickly in the face of increasing industrial change
- promote the general idea of adult re-training

Courses funded under TOPS may be provided in public and private educational institutions, in government Skill Centres and in employers' premises. They range in length from 4 weeks to 12 months and can cover anything from Communication Skills and Basic Education to post-graduate Management Studies. Courses are full-time and those attending receive a living allowance or grant.

Although the channelling of 'Education' money through agencies of the Manpower Services Commission (MSC) has been resented by bodies in the education field, undoubtedly the Training Opportunities Scheme has brought opportunities to thousands of people who, in some cases, might not otherwise have been provided for by conventional further and higher education institutions. MSC Special Programmes for the unemployed have had a similar effect – though the old special Temporary Employment Programme and the new Community Enterprise Programme for the long-term adult unemployed offer virtually nothing in the way of education and training compared with the more ambitious Youth Opportunities Programme for Younger People. This being so, the planning and provision of education programmes for the adult unemployed must now be treated as a matter of the greatest urgency by the MSC and the various branches of the Education Service.

EDUCATION FOR SELF RELIANCE

"Education for Self-Reliance" was the theme of a conference organised in Glasgow by the Scottish Adult Literacy Unit in 1979. The recognition that large-scale unemployment is likely to be with us on a long-term basis has prompted a number of agencies to promote activities designed to stimulate self-employment, co-operative enterprise, community business ventures and other alternatives to conventional paid employment. In the north and west of Scotland the Highlands and Islands Development Board has initiated a number of such schemes. In urban areas Local Authorities, public development agencies, voluntary associations, community organisations and large industrial concerns whose workers are being made redundant – many of these have begun to take an interest in the promotion of new kinds of Self-Reliance programmes. In Glasgow the Co-operative Movement employs a Co-operative Development Officer to encourage and support such activities. Throughout Scotland membership of "Community Business Scotland" (serviced by the Scottish Council of Social Service) has been steadily increasing.

The demand for new kinds of Adult Education and Training to meet these growing needs is only now beginning to be felt. It will, however, be a challenge to educational providing bodies to see how far they are capable of meeting the small scale problem- orientated learning needs of individuals and groups, some of whom may have had little experience of further education since leaving school at the minimum age. Towards the end of 1981 the Scottish Adult Basic Education Unit expects to publish a training pack for those involved in the promotion of such community business ventures.

TRADE UNION AND WORKERS' EDUCATION

Education for trade unionists and for working people has been a concern of the trades union movement and of bodies like the Workers' Educational Association for many years. In the mid-1970s, however, new developments took place which may turn out to have considerable long-term significance in a wider context. Under new legislation Trades Union representatives were granted a statutory right to paid educational leave for attendance at approved education and training courses (concerned mainly with the industrial relations role of shop stewards and with the provisions and implications of Health and Safety at Work legislation). Central government grant was made available for the development of a coherent trades union education programme (through both the TUC and the STUC), and a three year broadcast-linked project involving the BBC, trades union movement and the Workers' Educational Association provided an opportunity for experimenting with new multi-media approaches in this kind of educational programme. In 1977 Glasgow Trades Council in association with the Scottish Trades Union Congress established a residential trades union college, Treesbank, near Kilmarnock.

Until recently educational opportunities for rank and file trades union members (as opposed to trades union representatives and officials) have received far too little attention. However, the publication in Spring 1981 of a collection of essays on trades union education in Scotland ("Is Knowledge Power", edited by Tom Schuller and published by Aberdeen People's Press) and the joint sponsorship in May 1981 by the Scottish Institute of Adult Education and the Scottish Trades Union Congress of a national conference on Paid Educational Leave give promise of possible new developments on this front.

Management Education is already a well-established element in the curriculum of Colleges and Universities. The developments referred to above have now begun to stimulate a growing interest in Trades Union Education amongst both statutory and voluntary educational providers. Central to any significant extension of such provision, however, is the question of entitlement to Paid Educational Leave. Only in the last two or three years has Leave for Education and Training begun to figure in any significant way on the trades union bargaining agenda.

EDUCATION FOR WOMEN

Educational programmes for Women Returners have been the subject of steadily increasing demand for a decade or more. Elsewhere in Britain courses with titles like

"Wider Opportunities", "Fresh Horizons", "New Opportunities for Women (NOW)", have been offered by a variety of education and training agencies. Some aim specifically at preparing women for a return to employment, others for a return to learning, whilst others are primarily concerned to provide a confidence-building, stimulating experience encouraging participants to explore new interests and engage in new activities. The supply of such courses in Scotland has been sparse.

A conference on "Women, Education and Training in Scotland", jointly sponsored by the Equal Opportunities Commission and the Scottish Institute of Adult Education in March 1979, helped to map out the wide range of educational needs in this area. A follow-up seminar on "Women Returners" held in Glasgow in February 1981 (and sponsored jointly by the SIAE and the Scottish Council for Community Education) considered current examples of good practice and examined obstacles in the way of more extensive developments. As part of the follow-up to this seminar a guide to courses for Women in Scotland has been commissioned. In south-east Scotland the Extra Mural Studies Department of Edinburgh University has been the pioneer of such courses north of the border; in Aberdeen and the north of Scotland the Workers' Educational Association has also made a particular contribution to this kind of work.

OUTREACH PROJECTS IN ADULT EDUCATION

Over the past few years Scotland has see a number of experimental 'Outreach' projects aimed at extending educational opportunities to sections of the population normally unable or unwilling to make use of conventional courses in colleges, schools, or community education centres. Although some of the projects developed have been for people requiring Literacy or various kinds of Basic Education, others have been designed to meet practical learning needs arising in everyday living and working situations. The Maryhill Project in Glasgow, on the other hand, offers a programme of relatively ordinary courses – English, Arithmetic and so on (extending to 'O' Grade and beyond) – and caters for several hundred students. The success of the Maryhill Project and others like it suggests that the demand of ordinary people for ordinary education has been seriously underestimated. The secret has been in the use of flexible approaches and modes of operation which our formal education system at present seems ill-designed to adopt. It is noteworthy, moreover, that a number of projects of this sort have not been funded from the normal Local Authority education budget, but from Urban Programme money.

RETIREMENT EDUCATION AND EDUCATION FOR THE ELDERLY

Although the work of the Glasgow (now the Scottish) Retirement Council over a period of several decades has given Scotland a lead in the provision of Pre-Retirement Education courses, still only a small percentage of those approaching retirement age are offered places on such preparatory courses. The numbers participating in educational programmes during retirement are similarly limited. However, the proportion of the total population aged 55 or above has been growing year by year. Between 1978 and 1980 a Scottish Working Party on Retirement Education, convened by Age Concern Scotland, met to consider the educational needs of older people and to formulate appropriate recommendations. The Report of this Working Party, published in mid-1981, is to form the agenda for a top-level Scottish symposium sponsored by UNESCO later in the year, under the title "Education for the Elderly: A National Policy Framework".

It is important to remember that the majority of those entering retirement are fit, active, entering a period of new opportunity and ideally placed to play an active contributing role in society. A wide variety of education and other agencies will have something to offer to this often neglected age group. In later years programmes organised in association with Health, Social Work and voluntary agencies will need to be provided for those whose activities become more restricted and for older people resident in homes and other institutional settings.

PARENT EDUCATION AND HEALTH EDUCATION

A number of organisations including the Scottish Health Education Group, "Family Network" (National Children's Homes), the Open University and the Scottish Pre-School Playgroups Association, have put a considerable amount of effort into highlighting the need for Parent Education and into the provision of appropriate educational programmes (including various forms of Health Education).

Parenthood occupies a sizeable proportion of an adult's life. It demands maturity and a high sense of responsibility by the very fact that it can make or mar the life of another younger human being. Yet one enters into parenthood without having to satisfy any objective criteria for assessing one's fitness to do so.

Health education is of prime importance; yet those parents who are in greatest need of guidance on ante-natal care, child care and child safety are those who, often through a lack of awareness or their social isolation, either do not benefit from it, or reject it as it is presented to them.

Parents of handicapped children require support in the additional responsibilities they face; parents whose children have difficulty at school must be helped to gain confidence to work along with teaching staff to try to resolve a problem such as truancy, or slowness to learn; parents must learn how to cope with the widely differing mores of a younger generation which may unsettle or totally disrupt the life of a family.

The mopping up process undertaken by social work departments, police, children's panels, teachers and youth workers indicates that very many parents have found the onus of parenthood to be no easy task. Also, many of these difficulties do not reach the casebooks of the social services, some parents seeking help from voluntary caring organisations.

Adult education has an important role to play in this part of adult life, not least to support the contributions already being made by the organisations referred to above. Education is required within the whole range of activities concerning preparation for and the undertaking of responsible parenthood. After all, parents are the main educators of their children.

RECURRENT EDUCATION PROGRAMMES

There is a growing awareness that the efficiency of initial professional training does not last forever. Practice and technology change; individuals feel the need for updating and refresher courses. Post-experience programmes in Medicine, Architecture, Education, Accountancy, Pharmacology and many other areas of professional activity are increasingly the subject of discussions between educational institutions and professional groups. The Finneston Report on Engineering Education paid particular attention to the 'Continuing Formation' needs of engineers. In Scotland all universities and some Central Institutions have been reviewing their role in the provision of Continuing Education and recurrent Post-Experience education courses. After a prolonged period of intensive planning and discussion Heriot Watt University has recently made public its commitment to the development of "Through Life Education" programmes. A research project at the University of Strathclyde is currently exploring the scope for similar developments in the west of Scotland.

OPEN LEARNING

It has long been recognised that many people unable or unwilling for one reason or another to attend college courses on a regular basis may prefer to enrol on distance learning or correspondence courses. However, the success in recent years of the Open University and (mainly below degree level) of the National Extension College in developing courses and learning packages for individuals and small groups has stimulated a much wider interest in individualised learning – and in other forms of flexible learning programmes where those engaged in home study receive occasional or regular support from Colleges, from Libraries or from other tutor-support services. Dundee College of Education, Napier College in Edinburgh, Glenrothes and Buckhaven Technical College in Fife, and the Scottish Business Education Council (through its special Directed Private Study scheme) have all made substantial contributions to developments in this field. In early 1981 the Scottish Council for Educational Technology announced its intention to sponsor a three year development project involving the appointment of an Open Learning Systems Officer and in May 1981 the Manpower Services Commission, at the request of the government, published an important consultative document outlining pilot proposals for an 'Open Tech'. Whereas most of the previous schemes referred to are predominantly concerned with certificated formal education courses. In the last year or two we have also begun to see the development of Flexistudy and open learning materials for use in basic education and community education programmes. The creation of learning packages for widespread general use should now encourage a number of agencies, including public libraries, to consider how best they might contribute to the effective promotion of open learning opportunities for adults. The arrival of microelectronic individualised learning programmes will shortly add an exciting new dimension to this area of work.

BROADCASTING AND ADULT EDUCATION

Adult broadcasting constitutes a particular kind of 'open learning'. Broadcasting reaches into every home. The effective potential of collaborative ventures between broadcasters and local educational or community agencies is very considerable indeed, as projects concerned with such widely differing subjects as foreign language learning, unemployment and mental handicap have shown. On radio and television both the BBC and Independent Broadcasters have not only made a very significant contribution to adult education over recent years, but have also provided deliberate positive stimulus to other social and educational developments.

New arrangements for adult education broadcasting on ITV and refreshing new approaches to community education programming on the part of BBC Scotland are now opening up even further opportunities. There are, however, two fears: that economies forced on the BBC may weaken the commitment of Management to promote the educational responsibilities of the Corporation; and that the educational work will fail to make effective use of the initiatives taken by the broadcasters. In this connection it has to be said that, with one or two notable exceptions, adult educators and Education Authorities in Scotland have not so far developed the kind of close collaborative arrangements with Local Radio that are required to exploit the full educational potential of that medium.

ADULT EDUCATION AND THE COMMUNITY ARTS

Community Arts projects are now familiar in many areas of Scotland. Those involved with the Community Arts take the view that art (like education) is for everyone, not merely for the well-educated minority. The impact of projects like the Arts in Fife, Edinburgh Craigmillar Festival Society and the Merkinch Community Arts Project in Inverness has been very considerable. However, development in this field is very uneven and it is time for educational agencies and adult educators to consider ways in which they might give positive support to activities aimed at promoting art within local communities (and indeed within their own educational programmes).

PLANNING FOR THE FUTURE

Very few of those to whom this statement is addressed can have been aware of the variety of provision in the Adult Education field or of the scope of the new initiatives as outlined above. The conclusion might be drawn that we have been living in an age of expansion in Adult Education. The facts are quite other than this. Except where special funding has been secured the strenuous efforts of adult educationists to cope with new demands have, as a result of inadequate resources, merely resulted in a redistribution of provision.

THE NEED FOR NEW POLICIES

Adult education has rarely received serious consideration in a national policy context. The 1919 (Smith) Report of the Ministry of Reconstruction, an inspiring as well as a comprehensive document (reprinted in 1980 and once again available), like so many other post-war blueprints fell victim to the depression years. The much later Alexander Report on Adult Education in Scotland ("Adult Education: the Challenge of Change", HMSO, 1975) has received little serious attention from either Labour or Conservative governments.

Concerned particularly with informal and non-vocational adult education the Alexander Report called for new approaches, the appointment of 200 additional adult educators in Scotland and the doubling of provision between 1975 and 1980. The extra staff have not been appointed. In the majority of Education Authorities the Youth and Community Service (re-christened "Community Education") has been expected to take responsibility for new developments with few, if any, extra resources, and the very principle of public subsidy for adult education provision has come under serious attack as more and more class programmes have been required to operate on a commercial self-financing basis.

The implementation of the Alexander Report recommendations (had this taken place) might have constituted a significant first stage in the development of new policies for adult education. However, the Alexander Committee was restricted to a consideration of non-vocational adult education. Indeed the distinction between vocational and non-vocational education can now no longer be regarded as meaningful, either from the providers' or the consumers' point of view. For administrative purposes the distinction should be abolished.

What is now required is a second stage of development involving a reassessment on the part of all education and training agencies of their role in the promotion of learning programmes for adults, as opposed to any role they may have in the provision of initial education for young people. Such a reassessment must take place in the overall context of social and economic policy. Many adult education programmes, for older people, for women, for workers, for the unemployed, indeed for ordinary people generally, are unavoidably linked to some of the fundamental questions now facing us concerning the pattern of 'work' and 'non-work' activities in our society and the changing relationship between them. Within the world of education itself what we must look for is a shift from the prevailing view which stresses the once-for-all nature of school and further education to one which is based on a philosophy of lifelong learning. Current economic changes and financial pressure may make such a shift more difficult; they also make it more imperative.

A FRAMEWORK FOR POLICY PLANNING

The starting point must be a process of discussion and policy formulation – at all levels and by a variety of individuals and agencies. There is a great deal of thinking to be done. The CBI, the Trades Union movement, the Political Parties, the Scottish Education Department, the Manpower Services Commission, a wide variety of statutory and voluntary organisations concerned with education and training – all of these, and others, must be expected to contribute towards the process of policy formulation. In a number of cases it may be necessary to cut across normal lines of communication and responsibility. Within the Scottish Education Department, for instance, separate Divisions deal with Colleges of Education, Central Institutions, Student Grants, Research and Development, Further and Community Education and so on. No part of the organisation is concerned with the provision of education for adults across these institutional boundaries. It may be that new structures and new procedures will be needed if the issues referred to in this paper are to be adequately dealt with by some of the agencies concerned. The end product of this process of widespread discussion and policy formulation must be debate in Parliament of appropriate proposals and government implementation of policy decisions.

It is recognised, however, that a great many practical decisions about education in Scotland are made at local level. Every Regional and Island council should therefore be encouraged to institute locally a complete review of policies for both formal and non-formal adult education. If such a review process is to be effective it will need to involve discussions within local political party groupings, and amongst elected members, as well as discussion by officers, administrators and practitioners.

In each area of Scotland considerable progress could be achieved in Education Authorities, if consultation with the Scottish Office, were to establish Regional (and Island) Development Councils for Adult and Continuing Education. Under the auspices of these Councils the various agencies concerned with provision of education and training for adults would meet to plan a coherent pattern of provision on a regional and local basis, including appropriate arrangements for collaboration.

CONCLUSIONS

Many different education and training agencies and a number of other statutory and voluntary organisations have a contribution to make to formal or non-formal adult education: Technical and Further Education Colleges, Central Institutions, Colleges of Education, Universities, specialist adult education bodies, Community Schools, the Community Education and other Services of Local Authorities, Women's Organisations, Trades Union bodies, Industrial Training Boards, the Training Services and Special Programmes Divisions of MSC, Health Education bodies, the Open University, the Library Services, Broadcasting agencies, etc. Diversity is the greatest strength of adult education: it is not merely another administrative sector within the education or training system. However this can also be its greatest weakness. In the majority of cases contributing agencies see Adult Education as only a small part of their overall activities; and it is an area of work easily overlooked in circumstances where there is an unbalanced commitment to initial education.

Some have argued that adult education should be the responsibility of a separate Department and should not be left in the hands of Education Departments which see their role as providing for children and young people. It is germane to that argument and to the policy debate that we propose that so much of the recent development in adult education has been funded from sources, including government sources, other than the Scottish Education Department and the Education Authorities. However, the kind of collaborative machinery suggested above would be intended to provide all agencies with an opportunity to make their own relevant contribution to adult education in Scotland or to support the contribution of voluntary non-institutional providers like the Workers' Educational Association.

Our argument is that education is for everyone, but that the present education system operates in such a way as to exclude the majority of people from participating in the benefits and opportunities commonly associated with education and training. This comes about partly because of the mistaken assumption (on the part of providers and public alike) that education is mainly about formal courses held in institutional settings, partly because of the firmly held belief that education is predominantly for the young and partly because those who control the education system have ensured (whether by design or by default) that it provides most benefits to the minority who are able and successful and least to the remainder.

First we must learn to envisage the possibility of providing education for adults as well as for children. Then we must be convinced of the desirability of providing for ordinary people opportunities for learning at any stage in life. Finally we must be persuaded to recognise the greater efficiency of arrangements within which education and experience, learning and living, reflection and practice are set in fruitful juxtaposition.

The proportion of manpower and financial resources currently devoted to education other than initial education is small – reflecting presumably the view that provision for adult education should constitute only a minor part of total educational provision. That view is now challenged. The piecemeal improvisatory tactics of the past must be replaced by a considered policy agreed by government after a well-informed public debate.

RICHARD BRYANT & BARBARA HOLMES
A STUDY OF COMMUNITY WORK IN GLASGOW:
CHANGE AND CONFLICT

ABERDEEN UNIVERSITY PRESS (1982) pp 60-87

DAMPNESS: ORGANISING A MASS CAMPAIGN

Of all the issue-centred action which was supported by Crossroads, the Gorbals Dampness Campaign was the most successful and controversial. The success of the campaign in exposing the city's 'new slums', obtaining rehousing for tenants and winning entitlements for compensation, has implications for housing policies which extend far beyond the boundaries of Glasgow. The political conflict generated by the campaign was of an unusual degree of intensity and resulted in a backlash which almost led to the closure of the Gorbals Unit.

The campaign started by seeking a collaborative relationship with the authorities – get the facts straight and the problem will be solved – and rapidly moved into a conflictual relationship. According to the authorities there was no dampness issue. It was a personal problem of condensation, caused by the tenants' living habits or 'heavy breathing' as one official suggested[1] Schattschneider points out that;

> *'an issue does not become an issue merely because someone says it is. The stakes in making an issue are incalculably great. Millions of attempts are made but an issue is only produced when the battle is joined.[2]'*

The campaign, therefore, had not only to force the authorities to acknowledge the issue, but had also to push them to take action to alleviate the dampness – a formidable task. The strategies employed involved selective law-breaking and the violation of social norms; withholding rent; organising demonstrations and making personalised attacks on power holders. This rule-breaking was always issue-centred. The aim was to force concession on housing policies and not to overthrow the power structure. These reformist goals were often interpreted by the power holders as expressions of 'revolutionary militancy' and the campaign was, at one time or other, labelled as a front for almost all the left-wing groups and 'tendencies' which seek to challenge the status quo. The Gorbals tenants only wanted 'dry habitable homes'.

THE PROBLEM[3]

Dampness had proved to be a problem in many parts of the Gorbals. During the 1970s well over 1,000 individual complaints were registered with either the Glasgow District Council or the Scottish Special Housing Association. The majority of these complaints were from new blocks of flats in a development officially known as the Hutchesontown-'E' estate. This estate consisted of twelve blocks of seven-storey low-rise and two twenty-four storey high-rise blocks; in all, 1,143 flats. The flats were constructed of prefabricated heavyweight concrete panels, and solid precast concrete floors, walls and ceilings. The external walls were of a sandwich construction, with a layer of polystyrene insulation incorporated within the concrete. This prefabricated design is known as an industrialised building system and the proprietary name, in the case of the Gorbals flats, was Tracoba.[4] This system was developed in France and the sole concessionaries in Britain were Gilbert Ash (Structures) Ltd. Industrialised building systems were introduced into the United Kingdom in the early 'sixties and they were viewed as a cheaper and speedier response to the housing demands which prevailed at the time. They also offered the prospect of increased profitability for private contractors, especially in terms of cutting labour costs and increasing site labour productivity.

The first tenants moved into the new flats late in 1971 and, within months, complaints about dampness were being reported. The term 'dampness' was used by the Gorbals tenants to describe the conditions of their flats; wet walls, fungal growth on furnishings and musty smells. Most tenants experienced considerable financial loss because of damage to furniture, clothing, carpets, the cost of redecorating frequently, and because the flats were extremely difficult, if not impossible, to heat to a tolerable level. They experienced social embarrassment about the conditions and there was the added problem of being unable to position furniture in a way which would be considered normal. It was not unusual for tenants to move their beds into the living room, because the bedrooms had become uninhabitable and had to be vacated. Most distressing of all, was the damage to health. Local doctors stated that the dampness was a health hazard;

> 'This woman suffers from recurrent bronchial and urinary infections which in my opinion are being aggravated and caused by the dampness of her present home due to condensation.'

Professional opinion finally agreed that the cause of the dampness was excessive condensation, due to the structure of the flats.[5] They were built of heavyweight concrete, which is a material of high thermal capacity, and which creates extremely cold surfaces. The sandwich of polystyrene in the concrete panels was an insufficient form of insulation. At the edges of the panel joints, in areas of unknown size, there was solid uninsulated concrete, known as 'cold bridging'. Insufficient insulation, combined with the inadequate natural ventilation of the rooms, resulted in high humidity and excessive condensation.

THE CAMPAIGN

Pre-Organisation

> 'It all started through Jimmy Carlin. You ought to see his house, the wife said. So I went round and I really was appalled at the conditions – it wasn't fit for an animal to live in it, and his whole family were living in one room. I reported the problem to the Hutchesontown Tenants Association and then I went to the Information Centre. (Chairman, Dampness Campaign)'

From the earliest days of occupation the tenants had complained about dampness. The only response from the authorities was a visit from a housing official and advice to turn up the heating and open the windows. The Laurieston unit, opened in Summer 1974, had received sporadic complaints about the problem, and, when a local resident approached the staff in February 1975, a student was asked to explore the problem further.

'As I chatted and took photographs of the conditions of houses of people already known to the Unit, I discovered that already the problem was fairly widespread, but very patchy and few people know of other people's problems. An article in the 'View' served to publicise the issue. I not only followed up local leads, but started to research the causes of dampness. A common view shared by many local people with experience in the building trade, was that the dampness was caused by a combination of pre-cast concrete and poor insulation. Further research revealed that low cost design was frequently the cause of such condensation, so it was easy to argue the Corporation's responsibility to clear it up.'

Specht points out that perception determines response.[6] The perceptions of key activists and the Unit staff were identical and, now that the fault was seen to be with the authorities, combined action was possible. The early moves in organisation building had been initiated and the student began to plan for collective action.

'The student unit had a discussion along the 'where do we go from here' lines and agreed that I should encourage enthusiasm for a public meeting and investigate ways of getting the principal activists together, perhaps with people from the Laurieston Tenants' Association and the Hutchesontown Tenants' Association to discuss the tactics and organisation of such a public meeting. I also felt it was about time to get some expert opinion on the condition of the flats, so we contacted ASSIST – a community-based architectural service – to see if they could suggest anyone. This contact resulted in an 'alternative' expert report pinpointing design problems as the cause of the dampness.'

The Campaign is Launched

The informal gathering of contacts agreed to invite local councillors and the city architect to a public meeting which would be convened by the two tenants' associations. The Unit organised publicity and made copies of the expert's report on the flats available for the meeting. The public meeting, in May 1975, marked the beginning of the campaign. The councillors attended, but the City Architect refused the invitation – the first of many occasions when representatives of this department would decline to meet the Gorbals tenants. Over a hundred tenants attended the meeting and various suggestions for action were advocated, including a call for a rent strike and the taking of legal action under the 1897 Public Health Act. This meeting also identified potential activists.

'I'll never forget it – this chap stood up and what a speech he made – speaking on behalf of his mother and father, and when he finished speaking everyone just clapped. I remember saying to the student – who is this? I thought you knew, he said. I've never seen him in my life, but I'll tell you one thing, he's not getting out of here tonight until I find out who he is because I think he would be a big asset to our campaign.' (Committee member)

The mystery man was a Gorbals resident and trainee lawyer who was to eventually become the Secretary of the dampness campaign. Despite militant suggestions, the public meeting only endorsed a suggestion for a deputation to the authorities and the sponsoring of a further meeting. Battle had now commenced, even if very quietly. The deputation to the authorities achieved little.

> *'I think they thought it was some wee thing that would blow over – they say they'll do what they can but as soon as you're out the door, they've forgotten your name. I don't think anyone realised the severity of the problem and they didn't want to know. I think they thought if they just kept putting us off, we'd forget all about it.' (Committee member)*

The early initiatives taken by the embryonic campaign represented an attempt to establish a collaborative relationship with Glasgow District Council. The Secretary, who joined the organising committee early in the autumn of 1975 recalls the frustrations of this period.

> *'I got invited to a meeting after the first attempts had failed – the normal channels, deputations, petitions etc. They knew these attempts had failed in the past, but they tried them for 3-4 months as a final attempt.'*

In October a second public meeting was held. The 150 tenants who attended instructed the organising committee – which comprised a triumvirate of Chairman, Secretary and Treasurer – to take more abrasive action and investigate the possibility of initiating legal action against the District Council. Within three weeks the first moves had been made under the provisions of the 1897 Public Health Act. It was not surprising, with a trainee lawyer in the triumvirate, that a legal strategy was adopted.

> *'I saw it as a straightforward thing – these houses are defective – there is a dampness problem – let's take legal action or whatever we require – call in the experts, ascertain the problem and repair it. But then I realised it was not so – you had the political problem which I didn't know anything about. I may have read guys like Dahl, but that's entirely different from politics in Gorbals. There is no comparison between political theory and the real life politics that goes on – just none.' (Secretary)*

Fortunately, the Crossroads staff and the other committee members understood the political problem (if not the legal process) and when, in December, a local authority 'Combat Condensation' exhibition visited the Gorbals, the community worker saw it as an excellent opportunity to develop the local organisation and, simultaneously, put pressure on the authorities. A two-day counter-demonstration and picket publicised the campaign's views on the causes of the problem, ridiculed the Council's insistence on 'heavy breath', and achieved press, radio and television publicity for the campaign. The picket also convinced the Secretary of the value of direct action.

> *'I used to think once you took your cause to the streets you were defeated, but then I saw that it was important to the local people – they can see it and can in fact do something Moreover, it brings publicity which is one of the most effective tactics. Mind you, the stuff on the streets is only successful to a point – you can't march every day, but you can write every day.'*

from then on both legal and direct action tactics were used to pressurise the authorities.

RENT STRIKE

In February 1976 a third public meeting attracted 300 people, but the committee once more rejected a call for a rent strike and work continued on the legal case. When, however, the campaign discovered that a tenant had gone on rent strike after the February meeting, in the mistaken belief that most people at that meeting would be doing the same, the committee not only provided legal support, but an enthusiastic band of local tenants, complete with banners, arrived at the small debt court when the striking tenant received a summons from the District Council. The District Council withdrew their action and the tenant was awarded a decree of absolviter (acquittal) with expenses – a significant moral, if not legal, victory for the campaign. This case occurred in June and, over the next six months, three other tenants were taken to court for withholding their rent. On each occasion the District Council withdrew action before the Sheriff could consider the cases. The rent strike tactic, rejected for almost a year by the campaign, now began to be considered as an effective strategy.

> *'We never intended it at the beginning – I didn't think it was a good thing myself because I thought it might get people into a mess – use their rent money and never be able to make it up. Mr Carlin was the first to do it, and then another lady was taken to court and we won – then another tenant, so then it began to seem a good thing – maybe they'll take notice if we withhold rent. So we put it to the people – it was entirely up to them – if they wanted to withhold their rent and put their money by, then by all means do so. We also started the dampness clinic one night a week. We felt it was very important that the people had somewhere to go where the advice was immediate and accurate.' (Committee member)*

The campaign was gaining local support and was acquiring a reputation with the media. It was also gradually absorbing and using more militant tactics but, despite eighteen months hard organising, no tangible results had been achieved.

THE ISSUE IS RECOGNISED – THE COMMITTEE IS DIVIDED

In June 1976, the Chief Executive of Glasgow District Council published a report admitting that 'modern building methods' could be one of the contributory factors causing the dampness problem. Limited recognition perhaps, but the ensuing 'commitment to take action to combat the dampness effectively undermined the campaign's attempt to take legal action under the Public Health Act, yet committed the authorities to no specific course of remedial action. A proposal by the authorities to undertake another survey, this time by the National Building Agency, split the campaign's committee. In a period of disillusionment, when so much action had produced so few results, recrimination set in. Should there be a more conciliatory attitude to the authorities, or were more militant tactics called for? The committee threatened to split over the issue. Angered by the suggestion, made by a local authority official, that they did not have the full backing of the people in Gorbals, the committee managed to patch up a compromise and agreed to organise a major public meeting to demonstrate, once and for all, that the campaign had the popular support of the people in the area. The move to mass organising had been taken. Pressure on the authorities was to continue and the displacement to ritualism had been avoided.

MASS ORGANISING

The background work undertaken for the public meeting, which was planned for the 28 November, gives some idea of the tasks involved in mass organising. A student reports;

> '*The main brunt of the responsibility for organising for the public meeting fell on the Action committee and a group of about fifteen tenants, but often escalating to forty or fifty when leafleting or postering had to be done. No decisions were to be taken, no press statements made no interviews given without a decision being made by the committee first. All statements of intent, press releases etc. were thoroughly prepared in advance. The preparation for the meeting started in earnest about three weeks before and the Wednesday night dampness meetings were of vital importance. At these meetings the Action committee delegated responsibility for making posters, distributing leaflets, etc. Tasks included leafleting certain blocks, fly posting at night, arranging for volunteers to assist at the actual meeting and the week before the meeting, arranging for people to speak from the floor. The speakers were to raise specific topics so as to avoid a clash of questions. In an effort to step up activity and make people more aware, corridor meetings were arranged. These took place on the two Sundays previous to the meeting. Several tenants paraded round the area. Using loudspeakers and leaflets they carried out door-to-door deliveries, holding short meetings in the corridor with those interested enough to listen. We printed 250 posters, and some members of the community made huge banners out of sheets.*'

Over 600 people attended the meeting, which was one of the largest and stormiest in the Gorbals for many years. Television, press and radio were present and the meeting was reported on the national ITN news. The elected representatives stated from the platform that they full supported the tenants' action and considered the flats were uninhabitable. It was a watershed in the history of the campaign. Results followed quickly; the local M.P. brought the Scottish Minister for Housing to the area in December; the District Council agreed to rehouse tenants living in damp houses – the first tenants were moved in December – and local councillors persuaded the District Council not to re-let flats badly affected by dampness.

THE USE OF POWER

> '*The purpose of an orgnaisation is not only to have the power to effect a commitment, but also to make sure the commitment is carried through.*'[8]

The tenants had gained considerable experience and the same people were still the key leaders in the campaign. Theoretically, they had achieved many of their objectives, but the fight to have these gains implemented demanded hard negotiation and recourse, on occasions, to direct action. The leaders were now agreed on the need to negotiate from a position of strength.

> '*To begin with, when the Council asked for a meeting, my attitude was, never meet them – the others' attitude was that we must meet. I saw this as weakness but they saw it as co-operation with the Council. Eventually though we agreed.*

When the Council asked for a meeting, we delayed it – it was tactically good to delay, and eventually there was a degree of equality. There was a bargaining about date and time and what was to be discussed, instead of just being invited to an open-ended meeting, given a chocolate biscuit, a cup of coffee, a two hour lecture and you're out the door with nothing.' (Committee member)

The campaign had also uncovered some unexpected weaknesses in the opposition.

'I learnt in the early days, much to my surprise, that these guys (the politicians) don't like heckling – they didn't want verbal combat. There was a lack of verbal skills that I would have assumed they would have had as a natural gift.' (Committee member)

A public meeting, held at the Citizens Theatre on 1 May 1977, was a further demonstration of the campaign's ability to mobilise mass support and expose the politicians to uncomfortable public pressure. This meeting was designed to keep the pressure up on the authorities and was deliberately held on the day before the local elections for the Glasgow District Council. In addition to mass leafleting and door to door canvassing several new tactics were used in the preparation and organisation of the meeting; street theatre, campaign songs composed by the '7.84 theatre company' and local residents, a pipe band, a motor cavalcade and even disruptive interruptions of the meeting itself.

'During the actual meeting there was a number of pre-arranged and rehearsed events. These interludes included a skit between Mr Mould and the Housing Manager and also a rendering, by a local tenant, of the dampness song which he had composed. There was also a number of unrehearsed and unexpected interruptions, especially when impromptu fights between Mr. Fungus and Mr Anti-Dampness occurred on the stage of the theatre and interrupted the course of the meeting. The interruptions caused considerable consternation amongst most of the speakers who were on the platform.' (Job Creation Worker)

A thousand tenants attended this meeting, which proved to be the zenith of the campaign's public events. For the politicians, the penalty of refusing to offer support was to incur public odium and the possibility of opposition at the next local elections. Following the meeting the rehousing of tenants speeded up. This was a positive gain for the campaign, but the action almost inevitably resulted in a gradual undermining of the mass base. Most tenants were rehoused away from the Gorbals because of the shortage of suitable local accommodation.

THE COSTS OF SUCCESS

In our typology the dampness campaign represents a clear-cut example of a conflict relationship. The key parties in the relationship were polarised over their perception and response to the issue at stake. The possibility of a collaborative agreement was minimal and the community organisation had to adopt contest strategies, in an attempt to force the power structure into recognising the issue and taking action. By 1977 the dampness campaign had achieved this goal. The Glasgow District Council had, with great reluctance, accepted the building design explanation of dampness, had agreed to rehouse tenants and had acknowledged, in principle, the tenants' entitlement to financial compensation. These objectives were achieved only after an intense struggle which left a legacy of bitterness, damaged reputations and simmering tensions. Local leaders feared that they might suffer a backlash at some later date;

> *'If you are a local leader, you worry that the authorities might take a chance to get back at you. Maybe they wouldn't dream of doing that, but it's always at the back of your mind.' (Tenants' Leader)*

The friction became most immediately apparent in the relationship with the local M.P. and some other members of the constituency Labour Party.

> *'Some members of the local Labour Party resented the style and tactics of the campaign. It was too abrasive, bloody minded and went over the score in the demands it made on the local councillors. Others alleged that it was really a front for a left-wing sect or a rival political party. It is likely that the campaign upset some people because it could not be disciplined or controlled by the established political power structure of the Gorbals. The campaign was an independent organisation which showed scant respect for reputations or political orthodoxy. In short the campaign was seen as a threat.'*[9]

These tensions also surfaced in a public form when the SWSG attempted to close the crossroads Gorbals Unit.

THE INFLUENCE OF THE COMMUNITY WORKER

The Importance of Relationships

> *'When people are brought together or organised, they get to know each others' point of view; they reach compromises on many of their differences, they learn that many opinions which they entertained solely as their own are shared by others and they discover that many of the problems which they had thought of as only 'their problems' are common to all. Out of this social interplay emerges a common agreement and that is the people's programme.'*[10]

The organiser is an important element in the social interplay, and it is through this interaction that influence is exerted. Whether or not this influence is absorbed into a campaign depends largely on the relationship which the worker has with key local activists. These relationships can be closely guarded. The Gorbals fieldwork teacher comments;

> *'The areas which were inaccessible to students were the very intimate relationships I had with about half-a-dozen leaders. These little tete-a-tetes were crucial to the dampness campaign, and this was an area I was not prepared to delegate to students.'*

Relationships provided the cornerstone for the various and diverse roles which the community worker performed with the dampness campaign. In this section we have attempted to describe the main roles which the worker played and also we consider how these roles changed over a period of time.

Organisational Role

Prior to the local organisation being formed, in what we have described as the 'pre-organisation state', the community worker was the organiser.

> *'You've got no option – the very fact of moving into the area and then initiating makes you a leader. It's just a question of deciding when, at various stages, you should draw back.'*

The community worker had the big advantage of time to contact the little isolated pockets of protest, who were ineffective on their own and rapidly becoming frustrated.

> *'If it hadn't been for the student putting me in touch with all the other tenants, I don't think the dampness campaign would have started.' (Committee member)*

The staff continued a direct organising role by calling informal meetings of those contacts who were concerned about the dampness problem and used their relationship, with the two local tenants' associations, to persuade them to sponsor the campaign and to organise the preliminary meetings. The unit also provided somewhere for the tenants to hold committee meetings. Once the committee began to effectively organise itself, the organising role changed to one of support for the local leaders.

> *'It's sort of a supplementing of direct organisation. I help the committee to organise public meetings, committee meetings, the odd demonstration. It's knocking on doors; putting up posters; chasing up local contacts; making sure the people know the time of the meetings and that the person is well briefed to talk to the press. I also fill in 'gaps' when people are unavailable for work or domestic reasons.'(Community worker)*

This supplementing of the direct organisational work of the committee continued throughout the campaign. The hard, unglamorous work was valued.

> *'The Unit did a lot of the leg work – going round doors, going up to the City Chambers for information – we've got families and couldn't possibly do this all the time, but the Unit took some of the pressure of us. They also did a bit of the paper work which we couldn't have done.' (Committee member)*

At times, the community workers became more assertive;

> *'When to draw back is a very difficult decision which involves delegation, a highly skilled task. You need a degree of confidence to do it. The other thing is the ability to move back into the leadership position for one meeting and move back out immediately. You have to know which meeting – you can see the thing is going to collapse – they've reached a stage now that they're all so determined they're not going to back down, so you move in, solve the problem and move back out again.'*

In the latter days of the campaign, when many tenants had been rehoused, the Unit again assumed a more direct organising role.

Tactical Role

The tactical role of the community worker involves looking at the total situation, as far as it is possible. Tactics cannot be transferred, without thought, from one situation to another, and community workers must understand the organisational implications of certain tactics

> 'Attempt to use a variety of simultaneous strategies when putting pressure on the authorities and seeking to gain public attention for your cause. There is nothing a politician or official likes less than pressure coming in from a variety of sources, particularly when these different types of pressure are sustained over a long period of time. To sustain different forms of action at the same time calls for considerable commitment and generates a high workload. It is not a general strategy which we could recommend for groups which have a very limited support and only a handful of regular activists.'[11]

The tactical role was sustained throughout the life of the campaign. At the pre-organisation stage, however, it was largely hidden from local activists and took place, mainly, in student supervision sessions. With the formation of the group the tactical influence, which could now be accepted or rejected by the local leaders, was exerted through informal discussions with key people.

> 'I was involved in a sustained dialogue on a week by week basis, not necessarily with everyone, but with twelve people who were very prominent in the campaign. Sitting down and discussing what had gone on, what options were open to people, providing them with a sounding board to bounce ideas off, providing someone for local activists to talk with and test out ideas. It's a sort of rehearsal process and a means of clarifying your thinking.' (Community worker)

Obviously these discussions influenced the committee.

> 'One of the things that always upset me was that you have to spend so much time working to get support – it seems almost ridiculous to have to sell the dampness campaign – people are getting something for nothing. Eventually, listening to the people in the Unit, who have more experience in dealing with problems like this, I got the message – retarded possibly, but I got the message – that's the only way to sell the campaign and then you might get somewhere.' (Committee member).

Regardless of intent, the community worker is likely to be seen as the expert and his advice is given more weight than the worker may expect. Tactical advice is not only selling ideas, but also backing these up with action, e.g. the community worker suggested the picket of the condensation exhibition and the staff and students joined the picket line. At times, the 'pupil' may educate the teacher. The unit 'sold' the Secretary the value of direct action, but the staff were soon to learn much from him about organising techniques, fund-raising and the tactical development of a large organisation.

Mediator Role

The diversity and talents within the committee was one of the strengths of the campaign. The Secretary comments;

> *'Possibly one of the reasons we succeeded was we were able to bring together things from various approaches in order to work. The Treasurer was able to attract the women and the Chairman called on his trade union background and the administrative work was left to me simply because no one else would do it and I happened to enjoy it.'*

But, at times, there were acute tensions within the group. One activist describes the community worker as a type of 'community glue';

> *'The Unit was helpful in keeping the various personalities together because you're going to get strong personalities coming to the forefront in any kind of group. We didn't have the opportunity to get to grips with each other's difficulties and that's where the community worker helps – he bonds things together – gets things. A lot of my attitudes were an anathema to the rest of the campaign – but eventually we reached a compromise, and without the information centre I wouldn't have compromised and therefore, possibly, I would have got fed up and moved on.'*

The community worker reflected on this role;

> *'This keeping a foot in both camps and trying to get the group to compromise about their tactical or, at times, ideological differences was very important, and one which depended upon you knowing the individuals very well indeed, helped by having been associated with the campaign and leaders for some time. The underlying tensions within the group came to a head when the group had done a lot of work, but, had achieved no concrete results. This period of disillusionment was turned in on the group. To illustrate how difficult this period was, two or three of the key people in the group became so antagonistic to each other that they would only meet together when I was present – almost as a referee- as an interpreter to try to keep the temperature down. If the split had occurred at this time, I guess the campaign might just have fallen apart and a lot of the work might have come to nothing.'*

Research Role

The community worker comments;

> *'There was a lot of legal research – checking out public health legislation; research of causation of dampness – a voluminous amount of material. Some of that work was done by local people – more often than not by myself or students who had the time to go and sit in the big Glasgow library all day long. A very vital if invisible role – very important slogging, dull work which went on behind the scenes to prepare the arguments which the local activists would be using when involved in legal debate or negotiation with the Council. That persisted throughout the campaign.'*

Keeping up Morale

This role was singled out by the Community worker as being of key importance;

> '*If I reflect on some of the most important work I did in the Gorbals, it wasn't necessarily the political and analytical roles which some attribute to me. My main quality as a community worker was a capacity to develop a positive and emphatic relationship with local people and, also, almost a personality thing, of being an optimistic character with high expectations and a lot of patience. I'm in danger of saying that my most crucial role with the dampness campaign was almost a case work role, because there are certain case work skills which intuitively I utilise, although community workers are rather embarrassed talking about them! It is rather similar to giving tactical advice, but rather more emotional – keeping enthusiasm going; trying to stimulate local people when they feel low and depressed and feel their work hasn't achieved any concrete end. It is a role I found myself playing quite a number of times throughout the campaign.*'

The community worker also identified certain roles which he refused to perform.

Permanent Go-Between

> '*At times, especially in the early days, the campaign needed advice from experts on architectural or legal matters. Often the search for the appropriate expert took time; frequently the community worker negotiated the first contact, but this contact was quickly passed on to local people who thereafter retained the link themselves. Frequently, community workers maintain some power by remaining the permanent go-betweens. This was a role we rejected.*'

Formal Leadership

> '*We also rejected a formal leadership role. We weren't involved in fronting the campaign at public meetings or dealing with the media, although we would often help organise the events, and prepared information.*'

Negotiator Role

> '*We deliberately kept out of the twenty or so delegations to senior officials or to the Housing Minister – we didn't even attend these meetings. It was partly a principled commitment that we should not act as a negotiator to allow residents themselves to acquire these skills; it was also partly a tactical decision because we feared, on previous experience,* [12] *that the politicians would use our presence to deflect the aims of the delegation.*'

WHY WAS THE CAMPAIGN SUCCESSFUL?

Local residents and Crossroads staff attribute the successes of the campaign to a combination of five main factors. The emphases given to these factors vary, but all stress a combination of the following ingredients; the severity of the problem; an active committee; the mass support of the tenants; the back-up of the information centre and the role of the secretary in the campaign.

The Severity of the Problem

The sheer misery of living in a damp ridden house pushed the tenants to become involved and forced them to continue fighting. In Glasgow, where only 10% of housing is allocated to transfer cases, there is virtually no chance of easily moving to another house.

> *'We felt like giving in so many times because we got so frustrated banging our heads against the brick wall of the authorities. And then you'd go back to your house ... God no, I can't give up or I'll be here for the rest of my life. You felt you had to grit your teeth and get on with it – push and push and push to open every door. We just couldn't give up – the authorities would have loved it if we had.' (Committee member).*

An Active Committee

The key committee of three was supplemented by a support group of up to thirty residents, who were active on a week to week basis. It was the work of this committee, described in the text, which developed the mass support of tenants.

The Mass Support of Tenants

The sheer hard work of door to door contact gradually developed mass support for the campaign. Apart from the 'big occasions', described in the text, the weekly committee meetings doubled as advice clinics for between thirty and a hundred resident. During most weeks, over seven hundred homes were visited for fund-raising or organising purposes.

The Secretary

Unfortunately, the secretary was a rarity in Gorbals; born and bred in the area, living in a damp council house, he was also young and an apprentice lawyer. His contribution was outstanding;

> *'He was one of the greatest things that ever happened. He was a big asset to our campaign because he had a fantastic legal brain, and he opened up a lot of doors we could never have opened. He worked all the time – we'd pass the information centre at 11 pm and he'd be working. He got the services of all sorts of professional people who seemed pleased to work for just a nominal fee.' (Local resident)*

Most tenants attributed his capabilities to his education and legal training. The secretary felt that many younger people in Gorbals would have adopted similar attitudes if they had been suffering from the problem.

> *'People like me weren't involved in a Tenants' Association in the first place, but were willing to react strongly to the problem when it hit them.'*

He did, however, feel that his influence in threatening legal action and bringing in other professionals was important since 'it brought a degree of fear from the Corporation'. The Staff came to value the Secretary most as the nearest person to Saul Alinsky, the American community organiser, that they had ever met. He had an innate tactical sense for building large organisations.

The Support of the Information Centre

The importance of the Unit has already been stressed, especially in the early stages of the campaign. The presence of a fully staffed information centre, open five days per week, prepared to devote a considerable amount of its time to supporting, administratively and emotionally, the efforts of the Dampness Campaign cannot be under-estimated. The practical help is most often mentioned.

> *'People would have learned to live with the problem – people would have accepted it as they accepted everything in this area – they just feel they're working class folk – we're supposed to live like this, we're supposed to accept these things. But with the Information Centre at their back, it gives people that bit of support. They feel they're doing the right thing. They begin to find some way of fighting.'*
> *(Committee member)*

The staff also felt that one of their main contributions – via the mediator role – was keeping the Secretary involved in the campaign, without allowing him to dominate it completely.

> *'At times, I think the Secretary would have been quite happy to run the whole show himself and I don't think this would have been a good thing – it would have alienated his other committee members and other people if he was doing everything and they weren't doing anything. I think the Unit played an important role in preventing this happening without him leaving.' (Staff member)*

The secretary resembled Hoffman's all-purpose leader – both an asset and a danger to the campaign.[13]

ACHIEVEMENTS

We interviewed the three formal leaders of the Dampness Committee and the chairmen of the supporting tenants' associations. There was a large measure of agreement between the local activists and the staff over the achievements of the campaign.

Material Gains

All were agreed that the belated recognition by the authorities that the dampness was due more to design faults than to 'living habits' was the crucial breakthrough. In 1980, officials of Glasgow District Council acknowledge this fact.

> *'For too long it would appear that officials in all Departments have avoided the issue by placing the blame almost exclusively on condensation as a result of tenant lifestyle; other causative factors have thus received scant attention. This approach has in turn led to ad hoc responses to major problem areas, resulting in the current chaos.'[14]*

Thereafter the list of successes is impressive;

(a)   The rehousing of tenants living in damp houses. By the summer of 1982 over 1,000 households have been rehoused from the Hutchesontown 'E' estate.

(b)   The granting of certain concessions in the policy and procedures for rehousing, e.g. taking into account past as well as current lengths of tenancies when offers were made; the setting up of a special inquiry desk at the Housing Management Office for dampness tenants.

(c)   Following reports by the National Building Agency the Glasgow District Council committed itself to exploring the feasibility of a remedial programme. At 1978 prices, the cost of a full remedial programme would have been over £2 million. The flats cost £5 million to build. By 1982 the Council had still to decide whether to implement a remedial programme or demolish the flats.

(d)   A ban on the reletting of damp flats once they become vacant.

(e)   The non-eviction of tenants who are withholding rent because of damp conditions. At the end of 1978, the arrears resulting from the rent strike totalled over £50,000.

(f)   The recognition of the tenants' rights to compensation. Entitlement to compensation was originally won in 1977, but it was not until 1980 that a detailed scheme was finally negotiated. This settlement had two major elements; firstly, that all past and present tenants of the damp flats will receive a back payment of one third of their rent, paid from their date of entry into the estate and, secondly, that claims for damage up to £300 will be met by the District Council and that claims in excess of this figure will be subject to negotiation with the city's legal department.

(g)   A reduction in rateable values for 500 tenants. This reduction ranged from 5%-7%.

Political Awareness

Any attempts to assess developments in political awareness is an infinitely more complex and speculative task than is the evaluation of the practical gains which can be achieved through community action. At a general level, the dampness campaign did succeed in mobilising and involving a large number of people who were new to either traditional or extra-political activity in the Gorbals. Many of these tenants, especially the women, had no previous experience of organising public events, lobbying politicians, running committee meetings and taking any form of direct action. This unleashing of new leadership and the creation of new opportunities for participation illustrated one of the major strengths of community action – its potential to draw into association people who do not figure as active members of political parties and who may also have little or no contact with the established institutions of the British Labour Movement (e.g. the trade unions). For many residents in Gorbals – housewives, pensioners, the unemployed – community action represented the most immediate and accessible arena for political involvement.

> 'One thing about the campaign is that the majority of the people who were vociferous were people who weren't involved in any Tenants' Association before – probably they were willing to react strongly to the problem when it hit them, but after the problem had been solved they just disappeared. It is important, though, particularly with the younger people in some other area, maybe when in the years to come they find themselves with a problem of some size they will know what worked in the past. If they describe, for example how to go on rent

> *strike, or how to use professionals, such as lawyers, that many people have not come across before, then it will carry much more weight.' (Committee member)*

Whether this involvement will lead to a wider set of commitments and an awareness of the inequalities of society remains an open question. Community action tends to be issue-centred and, once the issue which precipitates action is resolved or partially treated, the momentum needed for further developments can be lost. Thus, in the dampness campaign the rehousing of tenants – which was a symbol of success – served to undermine the collective strength and future political potential of the campaign.

> *'Once the dampness campaign had achieved what it set out to achieve, that's the end – there's no lasting effect, and that's reinforced by the fact that many of the stronger members of the campaign are spread throughout the city once they've successfully achieved rehousing.' (Committee member)*

There was, however, agreement that, in the short term at least, people had lost their deference to the 'higher ups'. This was singled out as a major achievement.

> *'Everyone lost their fear of officials after a while. To begin with I felt kind of intimidated, which got me nowhere. As time went on I thought 'I'm not going up there, explaining problems to them just like a silly wee girl, because they're probably laughing at me anyway, so I went up with the direct approach – and if they were getting nasty, got nasty as well. After a while your approach did change. I think they began to realise that they couldn't intimidate us and get rid of us, so they began to act nicer and show more respect for us – I think that was when I began to realise we were beginning to win a wee bit.' (Committee member)*

Wider Achievements

Both Crossroads staff and the committee valued the assistance the campaign had provided to dampness groups in other parts of Glasgow and Scotland. On the local Gorbals and Govanhill front four other tenant groups have organised around dampness complaints and, throughout the city, some thirty different local campaigns had developed by the early 1980s. The Gorbals campaign had also been frequently approached for support and assistance by groups in other parts of Scotland.

> *'I'd never in my life talked to the press – and it was a great experience to speak on television. It was one way of getting things across and telling other people about the conditions that people in Glasgow were suffering. I think we're the only place in Britain that has achieved so much and through the press and media there's quite a lot of Tenants' Associations throughout this country who know of our victories and have formed their own associations to do the same.' (Committee member)*

This rather puts into question the criticism that local community action is 'parochial'.

REFERENCES

1   *Sunday Mail*, November, 1975.
2   E.E. Schattschneider, *The Semi-Sovereign People Hold*, Rinehart and Winston, 1960, p 72.
3   The sections of this chapter on 'The Problem' and 'The Campaign' draw upon reports by J. Gracie (student), D. Anderson (student) and J. Bain (Job Creation worker).
4. For details of this building system, see: R.M.E. Dimont, Tracoba *The Architect and Building News*, 26 June 1963.
5. For details see: National Building Agency, *Technical Report on Hutchestown 'E' Scheme*, April, 1977.
6. H. Specht, Disruptive Tactics. In R.H. Kramer and H. Specht (Eds) *Readings in Community Organisation Practice*, op. cit.
7. For details see: R. Bryant, *Rent Strike in the Gorbals*, Community Development Journal, Vol. 17, No. 1, 1982.
8. S.D. Alinsky, *Reveille for Radicals*, Vintage Books, 1969.
9. R. Bryant, *The Dampness Monster*, Scottish Council of Social Service, 1979, p 32.
10. S.D. Alinsky, op.cit., p 54.
11. R. Bryant, *The Dampness Monster*, op. cit., p 55.
12. For an example of the problems which can arise when community workers are members of delegations see: S. Jacobs, *The Right to a Decent House*, Routledge and Kegan Paul, 1976, Ch. 8.
13. N. Van Hoffman, The Good Organizer. In J. Ecklein and A. Lauffer (Eds) *Community Organizers and Social Planners*, op. cit.
14. Glasgow District Council, *The Dampness Issue: Position Statement*, 1980.

RONALD YOUNG
A LITTLE LOCAL INEQUALITY

IN SCOTLAND THE REAL DIVIDE
Eds GORDON BROWN AND ROBIN COOK MAINSTREAM 1983 pp 223-252

STRATHCLYDE'S DEPRIVATION STRATEGY: 1977 TO THE PRESENT

Strathclyde Region's deprivation strategy has been *area based* – operational in 45 areas (most council estates) judged serious enough to warrant priority treatment. This simply because of the geographical polarisation which was such a feature of the West of Scotland. We were appalled by the myths about money being poured into these areas and by the patronising attitudes of many people to the competence of the residents of the areas which seemed to place the blame for the poverty on the poor themselves. The reality was administrative, political and professional neglect creating a group of second-class citizens.

We had more sympathy with the few which pinned the blame on the government – with its responsibility for economic policies and social security. But as these areas always had unemployment running at two or three times the regional average, which in turn was twice the national average, we could not accept that central government action, if and when it came, would be sufficient to overcome the deep-rooted problems of these areas.

We were convinced that local authorities – particularly one as large as Strathclyde – *could* and *should* do more within its existing resources and skills to ameliorate conditions in these areas. *When* and *how* such resources and skills were made available was the crucial question which local government seemed to have ignored – thereby ensuring that it compounded rather than ameliorated the effects of inequality.

In 1976 the Regional Council drew up its strategy to tackle multiple deprivation. This has five basic elements:

1. To bring pressure on central government and its agencies – the DHSS, the Health Boards, the Gas and Electricity Boards – to deal with the problems of poverty.

2. To pressure the government and – through our own efforts – to tackle the severe unemployment problems of the poorer parts of Strathclyde.

3. To encourage district council housing departments, the Scottish Special Housing Association and the new towns to stop concentrating disadvantaged families in selected areas. We also asked them to try to achieve a more balanced community mix.

4. On our part we would try to make sure that the services we provided in the poorer areas were as good as – if not better – than those in the better-off places. These services would be run well, more accessible and relevant to the people's needs.

5. Finally, we would back up communities which wanted to plan and run their own projects to help their own areas.

What we were asking our staff to do in 1976 was to accept that fairly simple things were needed from them in the first instance: not massive spending but just a commitment, firstly to those who lived in these areas, secondly to attempting new relationships both with their colleagues in other departments and with residents. We were also asking for a bit of imagination and courage, in encouraging staff to bring forward proposals for better practice despite the discouragement we knew they would encounter from the rules, traditions and prejudices which seemed deeply engrained in certain departments.

Even then, we had examples of good practice developing in some localities by dint of individual officers, politicians or activists being prepared to roll up their sleeves and try something different. In some places it had been police initiatives; in others adult education and in yet others health initiatives. In many cases, these were accompanied by rapid improvements in the indices of social malaise. The tragedy, however, is how isolated such simple initiatives were – and how many obstacles seemed to be placed in their way. We always seem to be wishing to reinvent the wheel.[1]

ITS CRITIQUE OF LOCAL AUTHORITY MANAGEMENT – AND CONSEQUENCES

Behind all this lay a fairly coherent critique of local authority management which it is important to spell out; it came very much from the experience of councillors and officials struggling in the early 1970s with rehabilitation schemes and has found expression – in a rather bland and diluted way – in such different national documents as the Seebohm and Paterson Reports.[2]

- The boundaries between local authority departments are too strongly defended.

- the professionals who inhabit them are too blinkered in their perceptions of problems; and too casework orientated;

- the departments are too hierarchical (and therefore oppressive of initiatives);

- it is the better-off who make most use of our services and are quickest to articulate demands for more.[3]

Since 1977 Strathclyde Region has been involved in a range of apparently unrelated innovations which have, however, all stemmed from this simple critique, and a belief that unless that machine was fundamentally changed socialist programmes would be distorted out of all recognition.

These activities have been:

Urban Programme activities;

Community Development;

Area Initiatives;

Member/Officer working groups.

The following section will look briefly at each.

Urban Programme
Since 1968 central government has made available special 75% funding to local authorities for projects relating to social problems: in such areas they require to be individually approved by the Scottish Office and are then funded for three to five years. Thereafter if they are to continue, they become part of the local authority's normal rate-borne expenditure. Prior to reorganisation this fund was not really used by Scottish local authorities. Since 1976 Strathclyde Region has changed all that and is now guaranteed about £6 million each year for new projects in its areas of priority treatment. While this is:

(a)   a small fraction of what we have lost in central government financial support recently;

(b)   considerably less than we were promised in the 1977 White Paper on inner Cities;

(c)   small beer compared with Strathclyde's annual budget of £1,500 million;

its significance should not be underestimated.

It constitutes, after all, a major part of the development money at the Region's disposal and, properly used, can exercise important "leverage" in changing traditional practices, policies and resources allocations of departments. Almost 1,500 staff are employed on 600 schemes in Strathclyde's urban programme.

There have, however, been various problems associated with it.

(a)   **Types of projects:** in theory we have adopted a "bottom up" approach, viz. projects were to come from local staff and community groups in APTs. In fact, for various reasons, the programme was in the early years used more as an alternative source of funding for the mainline activities[4] and some considerable difficulty has been experienced in attracting well-designed, innovative projects for areas where the need was greatest.

(b)   **Support:** those projects which were clearly innovative have not always received adequate management support.

(c)   **Staffing:** many of the urban programme posts are the most demanding in the Region, yet salaries and conditions (limited contracts) have been such as generally to recruit only inexperienced (however committed) staff. Naturally, as a project approaches the end of urban aid funding and uncertainty arises about its absorption by the Region, staff tend to leave for more secure jobs – and considerable difficulty is experienced in replacing them. The subsequent underspending is then flaunted at local authorities by central government as proof that they are at the limit of their spending!

(d)   **Timing:** looking at the most appropriate way of responding to local problems in APTs is time consuming – not least because of inter-departmental tensions. A lot of people have to be consulted, premises found, architectural briefs for conversion jobs agreed and leases negotiated. Then the submission has to survive the various hurdles of council and Scottish Office approval.

Community Development
"Inside every fat man", Cyril Connolly once wrote, "is a thin man struggling to get out." For such a large authority Strathclyde has a major commitment to local action. It has:

- established in 1978 a Community Development Committee which has acted as a "friend at court" for community groups and organisations;[5]
- appointed an increased number of community workers;
- set aside more than £1 million a year for community projects;
- established 20 area development teams:[6]
- organised six community conferences during 1982 to feed into a major review of the deprivation strategy.[7]

The "community approach" has become a fashionable phrase which conceals more than it reveals.[8] There seems to be a consensus about the desirability of something called community development/ involvement/participation. But behind that consensus lies confusion. At one extreme it may reflect a deliberate or unconscious attempt to ensure a more orderly acceptance of the agency's policies and services,[9] at another it might express a genuine desire to shift the balance of political power. In between there is a lot of confusion – and no little paternalism with assumptions that it is communities, or groups within communities, who need changing or developing.[10] As far as Strathclyde Labour councillors have been concerned it was the institutions, policies and procedures of *government* that needed changing or developing. In espousing community development we were recognising simply that in such an endeavour we needed the active support of residents. Support here does not mean harmonious consensus. Many people in local government seem to think that clients of statutory services should have a subservient and grateful relationship to local government and that collective organisation and protest is impertinent and unseemly. What they seem to want from community involvement is public approval if not applause! By "support" we mean strong collective organisation to press from below – whether by example or by argument – for the sorts of improvements we indicated in 1976 we wished to see from our nominal positions of power. because what many of us have recognised is the illusion of being able to use such power or authority to engage *on our own* in significant change.[11]

In as much as community workers were a group of staff whose training role and location identified them closely with our commitment, they have tended to be seen as the "front line" troops in the strategy. It is here, however, that dangers lie. Many of them are young and inexperienced and working in the most difficult jobs! They are not necessarily familiar or even sympathetic to the detailed workings of bureaucracy. In many cases they lack supportive management and have been left to fend for themselves. In some cases they are just glorified youth workers and some serious questions have to be asked about their qualifications. We have expected too much of them. The time has come to ensure they work in a clearer policy and management framework and receive more support.

Area Initiatives

Since 1978 the Region has established at a local level a variety of neighbourhood structures (Area Initiatives: Area Development Teams) to break through bureaucratic inertia and professional myopia, in particularly the APTs.

In January 1978, as a result of negotiations with the six District Councils who indicated their agreement with the Regional Strategy, seven joint Area Initiatives were established on an experimental basis – in the first instance for three years. They reflected a belief that many field officers were frustrated in their desire to work with one another and local people in a more reactive search for relevant solutions to local problems by petty administrative controls and over-sensitivities about "setting precedents". Area Initiatives were, in one sense, invitations to local staff and residents to think creatively to take initiatives without being hamstrung about precedent and to demonstrate more effective ways of running services which might have implications elsewhere.

Each Area Initiative had certain common features, viz:

- an Area Co-ordinator;
- appointed by the two respective Chief Executive Officers;
- with special links to the Policy Committees;
- and to senior levels of the relevant departments;
- a support group of local officers;
- and a reasonable guarantee of Urban Programme support for the new projects.

Lessons from the subsequent five years' experience of these initiatives are at various levels – first, about the precise shape of such interventions: second, about the detailed implications of that experience for policy, procedures and structures in local government generally and, finally, about the nature of – and potential for change within – local government[12].

The second level lessons are incorporated in a later section: at the most fundamental level it could be rather cynically said that the Area Initiatives served merely to confirm our analysis of the essential obstructiveness of the present administrative system within local government. A couple of years ago Robin Hambleton of the School for Advance Urban Studies reviewed the British Inner City Programme and the following excerpt should be pinned to the noticeboard of politicians and officials who profess their commitment to such programmes:

> *Area approaches, like the American Model Cities Programme and the current British Inner City Initiative, by attempting to build positive discrimination in favour of specific areas into existing services, by insisting on a more co-ordinated approach to the problems of these areas and by attempting to open up the processes of decision-making, challenge three fundamental organising principles*

of urban government – uniformity of service division, functional service management and formal political and departmental hierarchies of control .

In these circumstances it is inevitable that new initiatives will be faced with formidable opposition from entrenched interests. Whilst some opposition may take the form of hostile resistance, a more subtle and probably more widespread response is to absorb the threat – to defuse, dilute and redirect it.[13]

Member/Officer Groups

In the last few years a large number of proposals for change have derived from reports produced in the Region by small working groups of councillors and officials in such areas as Child Care, Addiction, Disablement, Further Education, Community Business, Pre-Fives and the first two years of the secondary schooling. Generally after the approval of the recommendations in the reports, monitoring groups had been established to oversee the translation of the recommendations into practice – whether by negotiation with such agencies as Education, Health and Housing (and government and social work staff) or by extra finance for new programmes – and to monitor their implementation. This experience breaks with local government convention on at least three counts:

(i)   Members and officers are working as equals in a task-oriented framework.

(ii)   New policies are assumed to derive from such a *joint search* and not from circulars, professional or political prejudice.

(iii)   New emphasis is given *politically* to the process of implementation.[14]

Such structures reflected the discontent in the Region in the mid-1970s with the committee system and departmentalisation which was sustained by it.

The committee process itself, with its predetermined agendas, its rules of procedure, focuses upon itemised decision-making at the expense of policy-making, becomes a substitute for real action. It does little to encourage constructive communication between the two main participants – councillors and officials, let alone the public at large – or to bring together and exploit their special skills and experience.

The other criticisms we were making in 1976 of the committee system related to:

(a)   **Size.** An average of 15-20 councillors plus twelve or so other officers gives three times the effective number for creative exploration of issues.

(b)   **Role.** To take decisions. Councillors become impatient with colleagues who question fundamental issues and are generally keen to move on to "next business".

(c)   **Collusion** of chairman and chief officers. Basic political loyalties, if not whips, can be guaranteed to carry the day for predetermined recommendations.

(d)   **Inertia.** Officers can generally rely on the caution of the average member to act as a brake on the dangerous, radical idea.

(e)   **Professional control.** Committees relate to and are controlled by a single department organised around a set of professional skills and perceptions.

(f)   ***Cinderella issues.*** Those issues which are low in the priority of professionals or overlap with other deparments create rivalry and therefore fall into the cracks between departments and committees.

This last point is particularly the case with the problems experienced in working-class areas.[15]

WHAT HAS THE REST OF THE MACHINE BEEN DOING?

These have, of course, been special initiatives, attempting to change by various means – persuasion and exhortation, financial incentives, new structures and grassroots pressures – not just specific policies and resource allocations but the whole basis of professional thinking about, and response to, urban poverty. One of the most important areas has been the way officials see their own and others' role and expertise.

There is still too easy an assumption that only those with certificates from professional training schools can solve problems: that individual therapy and treatment is as much as one can or should offer: that the residents of areas such as Strone have no skills to offer.

Having said this one must recognise the valiant attempts made by departments to reallocate resources and to make their services more relevant.

The *Education Department* has moved, since reorganisation, towards providing comparable or better staffing in the APTs than other areas. The effect of declining rolls and the ability to recruit and deploy staff across the whole Region have helped the Education Department to eliminate part-time education and achieve national standards of staffing in APTs. In addition the extra staffing provided through the Urban Programme have been entirely deployed in areas of need ensuring a slightly better pupil/teacher ratio in most schools serving APTs.

Other progress has been made largely through use of the Urban Programme – thus new nursery schools, home/schools link teachers, extra careers staff and the development of community centres have all been largely dependent upon the Urban Programme. The development of Community Education Services, particularly in the field of adult education, has been considerable and largely funded through mainline resource provision.

On the other hand the combination of threat of school closures and the new Parents' Charter has in some cases lessened rather than increased social mix. Equally there is still too much of an inclination in the system to blame problems of uptake on behaviour of people in these areas rather than on attitudes, structures and practices within the educational system.[16]

The *Social Work* Department has also been able, in a period when the basic grade establishment has increased from 289 to 712, to divert staff to the APTs. Again they often started well behind but areas now have a better level of staffing per head of population than other areas – not that this is totally adequate as the scale of problems is dependent on factors other than the total population. Unlike Education, Social Work has been growing during the five years since the strategy was introduced. Community Work and Welfare Rights have expanded almost ten-fold and the majority of the new staff have been deployed in the APT areas. Other developments, mainly funded through the Urban Programme, include Children and Family Centres, Social Group workers, Family Aides, Homemakers and a number of projects aimed at special client groups such as Single Homeless, Battered Wives and Alcoholics.

On poverty we mounted a series of massive campaigns to make sure that people were getting their full rights from the DHSS.

For example, we distributed tens of thousands of claim postcards which put £4 million into the pockets of people who hadn't been claiming their rights.

We sent "Benefit Buses" into every APT to show people how to get their entitlements. As a result the image of the unemployed as "scroungers" has taken a severe knock.

Regarding employment, with unemployment of over 200,000 or 19% of the working population, the need to retain and create new jobs remains a key objective of the council. The Policy and Resourcs Committee of the council has established an Economic Strategy Subcommittee and has launched a *Strategy for Joint Economic Initiatives* for twelve areas of the Region. The council have also pioneered a £2 million *Employment Grants Scheme* using the European Social Fund, and has taken an active role in defending the loss of jobs in steel and shipbuilding. The council also blazed a national trail in the development of *Community Businesses.* [17]

REFERENCES

1　See Paragraph 10 for an except from S. M. Miller's *"Reinventing the Broken Wheel"*. It is also salutary to reread the classic *Dilemmas of Social Reform*, published in 1968 by Marris and Rein.

2　*The Reorganisation of the Social Services* (HMSO, 1968); *The Management of Scottish Local Authorities* (HMSO, 1973).

3　Studies on this phenomenon have reached saturation point: they range from the seminal book Conviction edited by Norman McKenzie in 1959, through Townsend's work to Julian le Grand's recent book on equality.

4　See the book on the urban programme by Edwards and Batley. The best critique, however, of the British Approach to urban strategy probably still remains Joan Higgins' *The Poverty Programme*.

5　The was the result of a councillor review group on Community Development.

6　The establishment of these teams requires a submission to be made by a regional councillor with local staff to the Community Development Committee of the Region who must be satisfied that there is a manageable task for such a team to perform which is not property being carried out by existing machinery. It is a simple but powerful device for cutting through inter-agency inertia and departmental hierarchies!

7　See the special August 1982 issue of Strathclyde's Digest for details.

8　See, for example, the confused debate which arose during 1982 following on the publication of the *Barclay Report* on Social Work: the June/July issues of *Social Work Today* contain a particularly interesting debate.

9　One of the best surveys of a complex and confusing literature on participation is Peter Hain's *Neighbourhood Participation* (Temple Smith, 1980). *Public Participation in Local Services* by Boaden et al (Longman, 1982) is also a useful overview of the different forms participation has taken in Britain in the last decade. It is, however, salutary to read the Fabian Tract 419 of 1973, "Towards Participation in Local Services".

10　See the author's article *"Community Development: its administrative and political challenge"* originally published by Social Work Today in February 1977 and incorporated in *Readings* in *Community Work*, edited by Henderson and Thomas (Allen and Unwin, 1981). Again it is salutary to look at Fabian Tract 400 on *Community Action*, edited by A. Lapping, which appeared in 1970.

11　See the author's *"Must the System always win?"* in Community Care, September 1977.

12　An evaluation of four of these initiatives was carried out by the Institute of Operational Research.

13　R. Hambleton, *"Inner City Policy – Reflections from experience"*, Policy and Politics, Volume 9, No. 1 (1981).

14　This is taken from the author's *"The Management of Political Innovation – The Strathclyde Experience of New Devices for Policy Making"*, Local Government Studies, November/ December 1981.

15　A neglected report on this issue was that from Southward CDP, *"The management of deprivation"*.

16　For a critical look at the Scottish Educational System, see T. Worthington's *"Life Long Learning: The Enemy Within"*, in the Times Educational Supplement for Scotland, February 1981.

17　A copy of the Region's review of the nature of future support for Community Business is available from the Chief Executive's Department. More than three-quarters of community enterprise projects in UK are to be found in Strathclyde – due in no small measure to the Local Enterprise Advisory Board headed by John Pearce and located at the Local Government Unit, Paisley College.

CHARLIE McCONN[...]

DEFINITIONS, METHO[...]

IN COMMUNITY EDUCATION AND C[...]

Eds LAURIE BIDWELL & CHARLIE McCO[...]

EDUCATION 1982

AN INADEQUATE CONCEPTUAL FRAMEWORK

One of the main recommendations of the 1975 Alexand[...]
Change[1] was to advocate the involvement of larger num[...]
activities, particularly the disadvantaged. The major recommend[...]
integration of informal adult education with youth and commun[...]
foundation for community education, an intergration that only partiall[...]
government re-organisation in the same year.

Although much of the Report was to do with organisational reforms an[...]
expansion, generally the Report did not adequately draw up a conceptual framew[...]
which to understand and develop effective knowledge and skills. The Alexander R[...]
therefore, gave little lead by way of practice and theory. David Alexander and Tim Stew[...]
of Edinburgh University have highlighted this weakness well:

> *"No matter how many well intentional structural and organisational reforms are carried out, it is the nature and quality of the approach of the ... educator to this work and to the people he works with that are the most fundamental factors in achieving learning programmes."*[2]

At conference after conference, since the publication of Alexander, debate has raged and confusion has ensued because of a lack of some basic understanding of what community education is all about.[3] It seems that at least two schools of thought concerning general definitions, principles and methodology have prevailed:

1. It should be left to each practitioner to work out his/her own definitions and methodology (or by default their employing Authority).

2. By defining community education one might be putting needless constraints on employment prospects, training parameters and future expansion.

Both of these responses are of importance and we appreciate their caution, but we feel they are unrealistic for at least two reasons.

(a) Policy decisions and some understanding of what constitutes community education cannot be separated.

(b) Ambiguity leads to the unsatisfactory position of it being 'all things to all men' and to a situation where any authority or group can spray the term community education onto their work with no real thought as to what this implies. This inevitably leads to confusion.

lucation [4] came
sted in the field,
h contemporary
ompounded the
ixed boundaries
needs of people
an ethos of self
is an adjustment
nding were to be
h of the positive
ted social policy

tish Council for
t of community
' or 'Recurrent

e lifespan of the
ucation with the
individual's other activites – for example his or her work, social, cultural and political life. [7]
Education is seen as a life-long process and is prescribed as the organising principle for all education. It includes formal, non-formal and informal patterns of education. It includes planned or educational learning as well as the incidental or educative aspects of learning. Great emphasis is also placed upon the importance of the community (whether geographic or interest group) and this includes the home, the workplace, peer-groups, social and political groups. There is, implicit in this change, the belief that there should be equality of access to education at any stage in life. The education system becomes more open, flexible and diverse with a challenge to the traditional, more monolithic and uniform systems. Undoubtedly this is a prescription for total educational change rather than a description of current practice, administrative or organisational structure. Nonetheless, we are at least closer to some understanding of the long term aims of community education, which as it suggested includes the total incorporation of the formal education system!

It is clear that community education, as viewed from Alexander to the present, is something much wider than any existing local authority Community Education Service. This is very significant, for the general view [8] is now that commuity education is a concept embracing an enormous spectrum of the total educational needs of individuals and groups and not merely the administrative and structural arrangements of any given historical period or functional department.

PARTICIPATORY DEMOCRACY AND SOCIAL CHANGE

Recurrent Education lays great emphasis upon the active participation of the learner in the decisions affecting his or her learning. This idea has long roots in education thinking and practice within the writings of Dewey, Mead, Bently, Pierce, Ferrer, Neil and others[9]. This growing libertarian influence emerged strongly in the latter part of the 1960s and 1970s in Britain. Community education in Scotland has attempted to fuse together many of these ideas and experiences. A great many individuals and groups have influenced practice and theory in community education. Of particular note are the Home Office's Community Development Projects (CDPs), the National Institute of Social Work (NISW), the National Youth Bureau (NYB) and the National and Scottish Institutes of Adult Education (NIAE and SIAE). Professional and training agencies such as the Association of Community Workers, the Central Council for Education and Training of Social Workers and the Standing Consultative Council for Youth and Community Service should also be mentioned.

Numerous practitioners[10] have reflected and written upon their experiences ranging from Fordham, Jackson and Lovett on adult education; Cox and Goetschius on youth work; Jones and Mayo on community work; and Midwinter on the bridge between the formal and informal. Special note should also be made of Batten and Freire who had significant influence upon practice and theory in Scotland in the 1960s and 70s respectively. The methodology of these practitioners is similar with a central emphasis upon participation and dialogue between the community educators and learners throughout the education process. The starting points are *the problems and needs of people's lives.* For them the emphasis was, as Freire stated, that learning could only come about through an increased awareness of one's life situation that resulted from action upon it. This, says one writer, is a perspective that respects the inevitable unity between subjectivity and objectivity in the act of knowing. And the only significant objectivity for all humans are their working, living and social situations.[11]

Education in this sense becomes a vehicle for change and not for standing still. This is the central philosophical point, and one that Houghton and Richardson's publication, *Recurrent Education – A Plea for Life-long Learning* makes so emphatically. A community education system is, therefore, founded upon open and competing claims for knowledge. Knowledge – and by this we include both curriculum and hidden curriculum, content and structure – is seen as fallible. In practical terms this means quite simply that the traditional approaches to learning – the didactic teacher/pupil relationship, formality, institutionalism, subject-centred approaches are challenged. Ivan Illich has written that "an age-specific, teacher-related process requiring full time attendance at an obligatory curriculum which requires its students to submit simultaneously to custodial care, sterile competition and indoctrination"[13] is now rejected. Whether most community educators are aware of this or not, it represents a major cultural and ideological challenge to Scottish education and will be of tremendous significance to the developing practice and theory of community education.

COMMUNITY DEVELOPMENT

Although it has been stated earlier that the Alexander Report did not draw up an adequate conceptual framework, one section of that Report is nevertheless of very great significance, and that is the section termed "Community Development".

Alexander had made some brief attempt at outlining the historical development of these informal education services in Scotland. If we add to this the historical reviews from other sources, what we see is the disjointed incrementalism of policy developments throughout this century[14]. Indeed, not until the Post-War development of the Welfare State did these aspects of Social Policy begin to be systematically formulated by the state and even then they were based largely upon non-statutory foundations. Towards the end of the 1960s, *Positive Discrimination, Public Participation and Corporate Management* began to emerge as key elements of social policy, against a backcloth of economic decline, the re-discovery of poverty and the emergence of dissenting groups in society.

It was the publication of the Gulbenkian Report *Community Work and Social Change*[15] in 1968 which established in Britain a methodology which would attempt to tackle both multiple deprivation and public participation, and which became an important part of various government, local state and voluntary sector programmes initiated in Britain over the last decade. This methodology was termed community development.

The publication of the Alexander Report for Scotland was, therefore, merely one of the many reports grounded within this particular socio-political framework. Alexander, in attempting to discover some methodological common denominator between Informal adult education, youth work and community work quite consistently, therefore, adopted community development ie:

> *"The process by which those who live in a community (defined in either geographical or social terms) are helped or encouraged to act together in tackling the problems which affect their lives has come to be called Community Development. Implicit in this process is the assumption that having been helped to solve one problem those involved will be suffficiently motivated and will have acquired sufficient skills to tackle other problems. The educational character of community development is, therefore, readily recognised and the youth and community service has long been involved in the process. Much less obvious is the precise role that the adult educationalist should play in it. Involvement in community development calls into question traditional didactic approaches and emphasis on classes and class numbers; but it provides new opportunities for reaching large sections of the population hitherto untouched by adult education."[16]*

That commuity education would be informed by and based on the philosophy of community development or problem solving education was in line with social policy ideologies in Scotland at that time.

The Essential Features of a Community Development Approach
While there is no single authoritative opinion as to what constitutes problem-solving education, some consensus is common to a number of publications about its essential features[17]:

1. **Holistic.** It is an holistic approach emphasising the relationship between a person and his immediate environment, often with the adherence to some undefined value of the

desirability of commuity solidarity and co-operation. Problems are seen to be inter-related and not compartmentalised into the traditional boundaries of health, housing, education and social welfare. Any attempts to bring about change are fully based on the culture and beliefs of the community.

2. **Responding to needs.** Rather than impose specific programmes the community educator engages in a dialogue with the residents, community activists and community organisations and responds to their established needs. When there is no clear consensus on the needs, the community educator attempts to help the community reach one. In cases where the perceived needs of the community differ from those of the community worker he/she either attempts to convince the community of the superiority of his/her own perception of needs or helps them to achieve theirs. Emphasis is on the process of defining needs and finding ways of meeting them, which build up community organisation and power as well as achieving particular end points. Batten describes this process as the 'non-directive' method. This dimension of the community development approach implies a different kind of relationship between the community educator and the people from that of teacher and pupil, or professional and lay person. Instead, the relationship is seen to be that of equals engaged in a dialogue.

3. **Mutual aid groups and volunteers.** Mutual aid groups such as playgroups, food co-operatives, gingerbread groups are frequently set up in community programmes and these can be seen as a way of demystifying highly-professionalised education, health and social services. In addition to using mutual aid groups and volunteers, lay members of the community can be employed and given basic training as para-professionals.

4. **Pressure, conflict and participation.** Within a community development approach there can be the creation of pressure to improve both the quality of the different services and the participation of the community in the planning of health, education, housing and environmental services, for example. While a successful outcome from a community's point of view may arise through consensus between state and community, conflict through community action may be necessary to bring about change.

5. **Action – Research.** Inflexible conventional evaluation methods are considered inappropriate for community development programmes because they usually require the goals to be set in advance and rigidly adhered to. This rigid adherence to goals hampers flexibility and is difficult to reconcile with community participation, and can ignore unforeseen spin-offs. It is also usually impossible to set controls. Action-research is the name given to the research approach where the role of the community educator and researcher are fused; and a participant observation approach, supplemented where possible by 'hard' data, is used to evaluate a programme.

At each stage in the 'developmental process' the interaction is between identifying problems and needs and through activity based learning, raising the consciousness of the group and the individuals therein through the process of problem-solving.

Kenneth Alexander has commented:

> *"The central point for modern educationalists is that problem-oriented teaching, which helps people solve problems, is not only the best way to interest people in learning but also gives the individual a greater contribution in the development of society. Therefore, I see a community educationalist as someone who, in the process of dialogue and discussion, gets involved in the analysis of problems facing the community and attempts to find ways of solving these problems."[18]*

This process, therefore, is centred on socio-political activity based on an identification by the worker with those who are oppressed and powerless. Through this process the participants are made aware of their dignity and liberty and of social justice and equality. Through what Freire has called the process of conscientization, the group eventually perceive more clearly their needs and understand how to demand their satisfaction. But as Freire stresses, education cannot occur through intellectual effort alone; it must be a union of action and reflection.

THE ROLE OF THE COMMUNITY EDUCATOR

It is useful now to explore more fully the community educator's role in this developmental process. One group of practitioners in a recent study suggest the following stages in this problem solving process which can be applied to the tasks of the worker[19].

- Defining the problem(s) to be addressed and the nature of the worker's association with the social change process;

- Aiding the formulation of the community group's goals;

- Supporting or building an organisational structure that is suitable for tackling the problem(s);

- Aiding the community group's selection of strategies and use of resources in implementing plans;

- Monitoring and helping the community group to evaluate the impact of its activities and in the light of this, to revise plans for future action.

From this model it is clear that we are not talking about a single work role but a multiplicity of roles which necessarily form part of good community education practice.

> *"Workers, like groups themselves, adopt a range of different strategies in operationalising their role. On some occasions a worker might act directly, he may base his actions on intuition, knowledge and experience, or on rational criteria; at one time the focus might be on the development of group processes, at another, more explicitly on facilitating task achievement; he might adopt a provocative style or move towards smoothing tensions over and resolving conflict."*

His justification for "involvement" might rest on a radical political perspective which views collective action as tackling deficiencies in the "system", or on a more conservative welfare perspective which expresses a general concern for people and how they can effectively adjust to the ever-prevailing changes in a modern industrial society[20]. This multiplicity of roles is nothing new to good community based work, but for many workers it involves not merely a change in ideological models but also in style and context of work. Implicit in this community development approach is the need for workers to adopt more of an outreach role. This is not to negate the need for community centres as a resource for community groups, because they are just that, one amongst the network of resources within the community, that can assist with group and learning processes.

David Thomas, who recently spoke to over 150 workers at a Scottish Conference at the Dundee College of Education[21], has suggested that in adopting a more flexible approach, which allows for both centre-based and outreach work, the learning processes can more effectively be promoted. Thomas has elaborated upon this work and has produced some of the most recent writing about this intervention process.[22]

He suggests that the developmental process can be broken down into several not necessarily sequential stages, many of which are, of course, overlapping; but as with Batten he stresses that the early preparation stages are crucial to a successful learning programme, to social action and awareness. Each of the planning stages involves skillful intervention by the worker.

1. **Planning and negotiating entry:** The worker plans his/her intervention and negotiates entry, with e.g. community groups and relevant agencies.

2. **Getting to know the Community:** The worker begins to collect relevant information concerning the needs and problems facing people in the community. The community educator observes and records the life of the local people. Freire emphasises that this is a stage of Co-Investigation and involves close inter-relationships with the people.

3. **Working out what to do next:** The worker and community group come together to begin to decide what are the main issues, concerns, problems, hopes and themes facing them. The worker begins to identify his/her particular role and priorities.

4. **Bringing people together and building organisations:** The worker assists the local groups if necessary to become a more constituted organisation, eg. a youth unemployed action group. Contacts with other people within or outwith the area who can assist takes place.

5. **Helping to clarify goals and priorities:** The goals of the group are more sytematically identified.

6. **Keeping the group or organisation going:** The worker provides resources, information, is supportive, co-ordinates help and develops confidence and competence.

7. **Leaving and ending:** Here the community educator plans and prepares, where applicable, for gradual withdrawal from the group.

A recent policy document from Lothian Regional Council[23] entitled simply *Community Education* has encompassed well the current application of this approach in Scotland.

"Community Education is about learning – it is about the total effect on the community of determined efforts to meet the learning needs of individuals of all ages who participate voluntarily. The end result should enhance the quality of personal and social life through the greater understanding of human relationships and through the promotion of wider involvement in the democratic and bureaucratic processes of society.

In the context of community education the word "community" need not necessarily be equated with geographical location; although it does require to be grounded in the cultural envionment of the people with whom it works enabling them to deal with issues which concern their own lives. However, these local issues should not detract from a need to take account of the inter-relationship between the local and global issues.

The promotion of a learning activity of this nature requires that maximum access to learning resources be secured for all members of the community, particularly those who currently may be excluded from them or to whom they are least available. Community education is directed towards participation in the design, content and implementation of education programmes in which students are involved, based on the belief that an authentic dialogue should exist between educator and learner.

The above statement is informed by and based on the philosophy of community development which sees the educational task to be that of developing skills and knowledge of individuals and groups in order to enable them to identify and move towards the attainment of their goals."

THE DEFINITION AND VALUES OF COMMUNITY EDUCATION

We can now therefore set out a summarising understanding about Community Education.

Community Education:

- is a life-long activity;
- is an activity that lays great emphasis upon the learner's active participation in learning and decision-making;
- is an activity that lays great stress upon the problems and needs of people as starting points for learning – in particular, though not exclusively, of disadvantaged, deprived and powerless groups;
- is an activity that can be identified as being based within identifiable communities, whether these be neighbourhoods or communties of interest;
- is an activity that lays great stress upon the process of change as well as the achievement of change in itself;
- is education, yet claims to encompass more informal and non-formal methods and contexts.

By definition, therefore, community education is the *developmental process of life-long learning and social action relevant to the problems and needs of individual and groups.*

Underlying Community Education are thus statements of values:

- The first of these is that education throughout life is a right with an emphasis upon open access, ready availabilty and social relevance;

- The second is that people acting together develop their capacities as human beings. Society should give the maximum opportunity for the active participation of people in decisions affecting every aspect of life;

- The third relates to the sharing and redistribution of power, including knowledge, in pursuit of the search for greater equality and social justice and in minimising a culture of silence, deprivation and powerlessness.

These values are very close to those agreed by the 1973 Report *Current Issues in Community Work*, published by the Calouste Gulbenkian Foundation.[24]

As we now have a definition and the value assumptions underlying community education, our conceptual framework has begun to emerge.

THE OBJECTIVES OF COMMUNITY EDUCATION

What do these aims and values of community education mean when translated into concrete objectives?

The Association of Community Workers, a major body representing community educators in Scotland, has suggested several objectives for this work.[25] These include:

- To engage in an educational process aimed at increasing people's awareness of social, envionmental, class and political issues.

- To encourage citizen participation as a way of gaining greater control over resources and decision-making processes.

- To work with people so that they can influence the course of change in ways which seem desirable to them.

- To work with consumers to ensure a fuller take-up of services; to press for better service delivery and more comprehensive provision.

- To work with providers of services and/or to engage in inter-organsational work with a view to defining common goals, improving consultation or developing or changing policies, procedures and structures to make them more responsive to needs.

- To increase people's capacity to discover, define, pursue and achieve common objectives, and in the process to develop more confident relationships with one another and the outside world.

For the community educator whether full or part-time, paid or volunteer, these objectives necessitate a whole range of tasks.

IS THIS AN ACCURATE DESCRIPTION OF CONTEMPORARY COMMUNITY EDUCATION IN SCOTLAND?

As I have said, by equating community education with recurrent education, the Community Education Council are making long-term prescriptions as to the general direction in which they see education developing in Scotland in the decades to come. We are very much at the beginning of this development, and there is some evidence to suggest that in the last year or two the pace of change has slowed somewhat. That said, however, at the level of rhetoric at least, the major political parties in Scotland have paid lip-service to this change and direction. Certainly we have not yet re-organised our system of education to the extent that recurrent education is now commonplace, but the process has begun. The case studies in this volume are, we hope, examples of what we would argue are good practice. The various chapters describe work that is typical of some of the community education going on in Scotland in Local Authority Community Education Service Departments, Social Work Community Development Sections, or the numerous voluntary agencies in the fields of adult education, community work and youth work.

On the other hand, trainers, students, employers, community educators, local groups and others including teachers would be correct in saying that there is much going on in the name of community education that does not yet encompass the range of processes described.

Alan Barr, a lecturer at Glasgow University, suggests that not one but several models of community education in fact co-exist. However, these are not arbitratily equally good. One can and one must make choices and our belief in this volume is that the developmental model allows for a more open, flexible yet systematic approach to community education. We strongly believe this to be a model of good practice – creating the opportunities for the developmental processes of life-long learning and social action relevant to the problems and needs of individuals and groups.

In 1978 the *Worthington Report*[26] on the future of Community Development for the largest local Authority in Scotland concluded that it hoped that the developmental methodology would be adopted. Several other major employers have also come to this conclusion. Indeed, the 1979 Salaries Agreement (Circular SO/43 from the National Joint Council for Local Authorities' Services) now obliges staff to undertake developmental work within the community. But this model of community education is not simply the preserve of the existing local authority education departments. History, tradition, attitudes and a general resistance to structural change make it doubtful that mainstream education departments in Scotland can, alone, make the transformation that is necessary. Social work, leisure and recreation, housing, planning, libraries and museums, health, voluntary agencies, trade unions, the training agencies, central government and others all have and are having a central part to play. It may well be that in the near future service provision will have to be fundamentally re-organised and that the present structures and functions, which are generally quite arbitrarily distributed, will require major change and redistribution. If community education practice aspires to be analogous to our working definition then it has a long way to go. A much more serious application of the strategies and tactics of social change will require to be adopted before that claim can become a reality.

REFERENCES

1. Alexander K, Chairman: *Adult Education, The Challenge of Change*, HMSO. 1975
2. Alexander D and Steward T *Community Education*, Scottish Radical Education Review. 1977
3. McConnell *On Defining Community Education* Dundee College of Education. 1978
4. Carnegy G, Chairwoman *Report on Professional Education and Training for Community Education* SED. 1977
5. Such public expenditure cuts have had a decimating effects upon participation. See Horobin J in Scottish Journal of Adult Education. Spring 1980. Vol 4. No 4.
6. Scottish Council for Community Education *Discussion Paper No. 1*. 1979
7. Houghton V and Richardson K *Recurrent Education – A Plea for Lifelong Learning*. Ward Lock Educational. 1974
8. SCCE *Discussion Paper No. 1*. op cit.
9. McConnell C *The Community Worker as Politiciser of the Deprived* CEC. 1977. Chapter 3
10. Fordham P et al *Learning Networks in Adult Education* RKP. 1979
    Jackson K in Jones D and Mayo M *Community Work One* RKP. 1974. Chapter 3
    See also Thompson J *Adult Eduction for a Change* Hutchinson. 1980
    Lovett T *Adult Education, Community Development and the Working Class*, Ward Lock Educational. 1975
    Cox D *A Community Approach to Youth Work in East London* TWCA. 1970
    Goetschius G W and Tash J *Working with Unattached Youth* RKP. 1967
    Edginton J *Avenues Unlimited* NYB. 1979
    Jones and Mayo M *Community Work* One RKP. 1975
    Mayo M *Women in the Community* RKP. 1977
    Midwinter E *Patterns of Community Education* Ward Lock Educational. 1973
    Freire P *Pedagogy of the Oppressed* Penguin. 1975
    Illich I *Deschooling Society* Pelican. 1976
11. Richardson K in Houghton V and Richardson K op cit pp 11-21
12. ibid
13. Illich I *Celebration of Awareness* Pelican. 1976
14. Thomas J *Adult Education for a Change* op cit. pp 19-31, 83-109, 219-225
15. Gulbenkian *Community Work and Social Change* Longman. 1968
16. Alexander. op cit. p31
17. Hubley J *Health Education and Community Development* Paisley College. 1980
18. McConnell C *Multiple Deprivation and Community Development in Strathclyde* Dundee College of Education. 1978
19. Butcher H et al *Community Groups in Action* RKP. 1980
20. ibid. p220
21. *The Development of Community Work in the 80s* Conference Report, Dundee College of Education. 1980
22. Henderson P and Thomas D *Skills in Neighbourhood Work* George Allen and Unwin. 1980
23. Lorimer G *Community Education* Lothian Regional Council, Community Education Service. 1981
24. Gulbenkian *Current Issues in Community Work* RKP. 1973
25. Association of Community Workers *Knowledge and Skills for Community Work*. 1975
26. Worthington T, Chairman Policy *Review Group on Community Development Services* Strathclyde Regional Council. 1978

WORKING WITH YOUNG PEOPLE

STRATHCLYDE REGIONAL COUNCIL, 1984 pp 7-8, 26-41

AIMS OF YOUTH WORK

It is important to state at the outset the broad aims prescribed by the Community Education Service in relation to youth work and in particular to those areas of youth work promoted directly by the Education Department through a range of youth services. We believe that effort should now be centred on the needs of the individual on a personal basis and on the role of each individual in relation to wider society. Youth work should be seen:

(a)   as being responsive to the personal educational needs of the individual whether social, intellectual or recreational; and

(b)   within a community development context, so that it is concerned with the individual's role in relation to the wider society and his or her active participation in it.

It is vital to underline these fundamental aims as they are not always easily identified in working practice nor translated into working objectives by field workers.

The first aspect of youth work is concerned with the individual young person and his particular needs throughout adolescence. These needs vary constantly from one young person to another. Within the framework of youth provision, contact is made with young people in a variety of settings, the most common one being through traditional centre-based work. Participation and democracy should be encouraged by a variety of methods and approaches through discussion, personal counselling, and a progressive programme of planned activities. Through this process it is hoped that young people are exposed to a number of experiences all of which will contribute to their personal development. Only in this way will youth provision become responsive to the varying needs and views of those it seeks to affect.

The second aspect, the community development context, is the subject of increasing debate and frequently reflects concern about a lack of participation in and even alienation from the decision-making processes affecting individuals and the community in which they live. One cannot, however, simply ask for participation in the democratic processes. If people are inexperienced in this process they are less likely to participate, but if they have grown up within surroundings which offer such opportunities then they are much more likely to understand its significance and participate more effectively as adults. With imaginative and dynamic leadership, youth work can offer worthwhile opportunities for young people to participate in decision-making. An important aim of youth work, therefore, should be to offer opportunities for critical and responsible participation among the rising generation.

Inherent, too, in this community development approach in community education is the emphasis on self-help. This means that members of a community are helped to express their needs through active participation and are then stimulated towards local initiative and producing their own leadership.

Adolescence is characterised by both physical and emotional change, sometimes difficult or confusing to young people and not always understood by the adults surrounding them. It is important, therefore, that those working with young people do not lose sight of the fundamental objectives around which work with young people is developed; that is, to work with them to create opportunities through which they can:

(a)   gain positive self-esteem,

(b)   acquire skills in managing their own affairs,

(c)   establish satisfactory relationships,

(d)   gain a sense of worth from belonging to group activities,

(e)   recognise the contribution they can make to society,

(f)   understand their own physical and emotional capabilities, and

(g)   develop a set of social and personal values that provide a suitable framework both for their own lives and for the needs of others.

This inevitably means that work with young people has to begin with their own interests and experience, and be sensitive to their hopes and aspirations. It has to take their contribution and potential for leadership seriously. Since groups of young people will differ in all these aspects, it cannot be expected that neat youth work programmes will necessarily emerge. The enterprise of contacting, befriending and co-operating with young people in these ways may sometimes seem distant from the objectives, but in reality it is the basis for their successful achievement.

It is against this background that there is a clear wish by the Regional Council to think deeply about the position of young people in society so that the services are supportive and as enriching as possible. There are both positive and negative forces behind all this. Positively, there is the desire to help young people to develop and find valuable interests and skills to sustain them in their lives, and complementary, the rest of society needs the vigour and talent of young people applied to community development. Negatively, there is great apprehension about pressure on young people today. In particular, current youth unemployment seems unlikely to fall in this decade and consequently large numbers of young people seem likely to be deprived of the full participation within society that fulfilling paid work has been seen to give. There is also concern about the vulnerability of young people to delinquency, drug abuse and other prevalent problems.

FUTURE DEVELOPMENTS

Youth Development Teams

The Regional Council has placed great emphasis on the need to develop an area approach to services. This is particularly desirable in terms of opportunities for young people. If young people are interested in any particular aspect of the arts, physical or recreational activity or interest, it is largely accidental whether or not such opportunities exist within an area. In many parts of the Region, there has been no mechanism for bringing together different agencies which look coherently at provision for young people. Schools, community education, careers, further education, social work and District Councils have largely ploughed their own furrow.

We have, therefore, looked at the arrangements that have been recently implemented for planning post-16 education and training services. In 1982, the Regional Council agreed a policy on post-compulsory education and training which proposed the creation of local area planning groups. It was intended that the groups would comprise a number of key professional staff within designated geographical areas responsible for the planning and implementation of educational services. The purpose was to ensure that there was coherent planning of services based on the areas by increasing the number of persons involved in identifying provision and thus extending community participation.

However, in January 1983, the Scottish Education Department issued a document *"16-18s in Scotland – An Action Plan"*, which set out proposals for improving the quality and co-ordination of educational provision for the 16-18 age group. This Action Plan, whilst relating closely to the Regional Council's Strategy for Post Compulsory Education and Training, laid a greater emphasis on the involvement of secondary schools and further education colleges. Unfortunately, it made little reference to the range of activities which would form the framework for youth work provision currently under review by this Member/Officer group.

Following these two developments, the Regional Council in April 1983 agreed a new structure for planning educational provision. The structure included the establishment of 46 Area Curriculum Planning Groups covering the whole Region with each group comprising professional staff and local Regional Councillors. The groups have a responsibility for identifying post-16 education and training needs and for devising a range of opportunities through which these needs can be met.

It seems, clear, however, that the present Area Curriculum Planning Groups will be concentrating on issues affecting the development of vocational and academic education opportunities for the 16-18 age group and to a lesser extent opportunities for adults within this educational provision in the foreseeable future.

In the longer term "youth work" must form a vital part in the planned services for 16-18 year olds and consequently Community Education Services must maintain involvement in the Area Curriculum Planning Group arrangements.

We feel, therefore, that for the successful co-ordination and development of youth work programmes involving community education, social work, police and voluntary agencies an additional framework is required to the present Area Curriculum Planning Group. It is proposed, therefore that:

(a)   Within each of the 46 areas of the Community Education Service a Youth Development Team should be established which will be concerned with the development of a coherent and responsive range of opportunities and activities for young people.

(b) Each Development Team should involve education, social work, police and the voluntary sector and the Community Education Service should be responsible for convening and supporting the work of the team.

(c) Each Development Team should produce a strategy and working objectives for the area.

(d) It is important that working links are established with the Area Curriculum Planning Groups, thus ensuring that there is co-ordination within the education programme. Similar links should be established with the appropriate management structures in other departments.

(e) The Development Teams should seek to involve local young people.

(f) The Development Teams should seek to involve local Regional Councillors as far as possible in their work, given the many competing demands on councillors' time, and ensure they are kept fully informed.

We would expect that the issues raised in this report become the starting point for the work of the Youth Development Teams. We suggest that this Member/Officer Group (perhaps suitably augmented) should monitor the implementation of the recommendations in this report for the life of this Council until May 1986.

Community education must see its central role as ensuring that young people have access to a comprehensive range of opportunities and not just as the development of a traditional youth service. There is a danger of being over concerned with general youth clubs, rather than meeting the particular needs of young people. By establishing Youth Development Teams there will be an adequate framework for developing a coherent strategy for meeting needs and providing opportunities.

We also believe that young people can benefit from the Development Teams. We stated earlier our desire to give young people the power to cause change and to work actively towards meeting their own needs. This will involve the formation of youth forums or councils. There is little point having such structures unless the young people feel that the authorities are responding and that action can follow quickly from their expressed wishes and needs. The Development Teams should ensure this happens.

We are also determined that, in any development which may occur in youth work, we are not obsessed with building up a professionally dominated youth service. To make this statement in no way lessens the need for professionally trained workers. Indeed there is a considerable need for a further provision of such workers because of the skills involved in recruiting and supporting part-time staff and volunteers; analysing and making appropriate responses to developing counselling and support skills; and providing skills in the arts and outdoor activities for young people and staff.

Young people will benefit if the Regional Council successfully develops appropriate provision for the entire community. For example, access to schools, colleges and other educational establishments is important to the whole community – not just the young people. A good community transport policy, the development of resource centres, and staff support generally for local community groups and projects, should also be of benefit for young people. The system of decentralised local grants should help young people as well as others in gaining access to pump priming funds. We must ensure that on each of these aspects of our services the particular needs of young people are not forgotten.

COMMUNITY INVOLVEMENT AND PARTICIPATION BY YOUNG PEOPLE

We stated earlier that all the material we have read stresses the importance of young people's involvement in running services and participation in community life. We recognise participation as fundamental to the future of youth work. We stress the need to go beyond the rhetoric of participation by giving young people the power to cause change and to develop their own services by creating opportunities that emphasise the strengths of young people and by encouraging contact with adults.

We are conscious that many of the terms used in this section can sound institutionalised or bureaucratic. We do not intend them to be taken this way and are aware that structures alone will not solve the problem. New ways of involving young people must be found that adopt a direct political approach which, like a trade or student union, ensures young people "educate, agitate and organise" themselves as a force for change.

There can be no standard formula for strengthening participation. In political terms, a number of positive steps can be taken:

(a)   In any existing settings where young people meet, they should have a high degree of control over programming, activities and finance and be actively encouraged to assume management and leadership roles.

(b)   Youth Action Groups or Youth Councils should be established. Some areas have such groups, but in many areas there is no mechanism for young people to meet and organise. We consider it essential that young people have a collective voice to identify what services and activities they want in an area and to campaign and organise for change. The Youth Development Teams will be responsible for ensuring support for existing groups and for setting up new groups or Councils where none exist.

(c)   Youth Enquiry Services attract young people initially around the need for advice and information. This has led to a number of initiatives developed by young people themselves including newsletters, cafes and meeting places in addition to providing youth information in a form young people want and understand.

The Education Department has stressed that the work carried out to date by YES in Strathclyde, with its strong emphasis on the participation of young people, has proved to be an excellent springboard from which to make progress in tackling the problems young people face. We endorse this view and support further development.

(d) The local grants committees can provide grants of up to £1,500 to groups of young people and for projects devised by young people. This system has not yet been used extensively, largely because young people are not aware of the availability of or how to get access to finance. Often the constitutions, audited accounts and other requirements for grant applications put young people off applying. We consider that the role of staff is to assist and encourage the education of young people in how to become constituted and organised and thus gain access to grant aid.

(e) We recognise that participation is a two-way process. Ideas and proposals made by young people need to be followed up quickly. It is important that there is rapid feedback so that reasons for any delays are explained by staff to sustain interest.

(f) We appreciate that for effective participation young people need meeting places. We know there is a serious lack of informal meeting places and wish to emphasise the need to increase the numbers of these types of places.

(g) The active involvement of young people in community groups should be encouraged, for example in community councils, tenants' groups, centre management committees, community associations and service to the community in their own area. Young people are often under-represented in community development activities and we wish to see this changed.

(h) The promotion of leisure activities that interest young people as well as adults is also important. This is particularly desirable where young people area accepted on equal terms with adult members. Outdoor activities, fishing, computing, martial arts, cycling, motorbikes, drama and chess clubs are examples of these types of activities. They are also important in bridging the gap between school and adult life when many young people give up or lose interests. Staff should look at ways of encouraging adult clubs in their areas to develop activities for young people.

YOUNG PEOPLE AT RISK

Young people may be at risk in a number of ways – through offending, truanting, problematic behaviour at home or school – and this can be picked up by a number of agencies including the police, the childrens' panels, social work, schools, community education and education psychology. The Social Work Department's 1983 Youth Strategy Report emphasises the dangers of defining a child as problematic or "having a problem" too soon. Once so defined, the label can become self-reinforcing as the child's subsequent behaviour is no longer compared with his peers but seen as evidence to confirm the label.

Children who are genuinely in need of individual help or control are the legitimate concern of the "helping" agencies, but there is a growing view that some young people are being labelled inappropriately or too soon, often through genuine concern for their welfare. This can negatively affect their chances of outgrowing the behaviour and being accepted as normal young adults.

There is, therefore, a need to develop new kinds of preventative work with young people at risk or thought to be in danger of offending, which is inter-disciplinary and can offer help and support without any hint of labelling or stigma.

These types of young people would include those known to associate with delinquent peers, or referred for voluntary supervision by the Reporter, or known to police through their warning system, or their families are already known to the Social Work Department.

This type of work necessitates a joint approach from community education, social work, police and other agencies in terms of joint planning and agreement on the approach, identification of young people at risk and shared use of premises and equipment. This will be the responsibility of the Youth Development Teams.

Clearly local circumstances will dictate how each Team will approach its task. A joint approach to work with young people at risk needs to consider individual young people as well as general principles. Therefore, the size of the area and the number and specialisms of staff available will need to be taken into account in the structures set up. Small groups of selected staff may be needed in some areas.

We are aware of good examples of this kind of work, taking place in several parts of the Region, particularly where community education have specialist workers with a youth focus. In other areas there is a lack of penetration by the service to young people at risk and in some areas community education is alleged to wash its hands of young people who cause problems. We should not minimise the dilemmas faced by part-time workers who may be compelled to exclude some young people from premises because of their disruptive influence on the majority of the users. However, we cannot just exclude certain young people as very often this merely transfers the problems and trouble from the inside to outside the building.

The principles involved in work with young people at risk are similar to those we expect in all future youth work developments. They are, however, particularly important for work with young people at risk. The main principles are:

(a)   It is neighbourhood based, relating to young people in their own communities.

(b)   It involves making informal contact with those young people who reject, or are rejected by, existing youth facilities through, for example, developing drop-in-centres, YES points and cafes.

(c)   Workers should discriminate in favour of young people thought to be at risk.

(d)   This approach aims primarily to develop and reinforce young people's competence and skills as young adults, rather than to treat their problems and weaknesses.

(e)   Young people should identify issues and problems themselves and be encouraged to organise and tackle them. This may involve challenging the relevance and appropriateness of existing youth facilities.

It has not been part of the remit of this group to look at the major social problems some young people experience, for example, drug addiction, under-age drinking and criminal acts. We recognise that often experimenting with drink and soft drugs is part of growing up and thus part of the educative element of youth work must involve discussion of the potential problems of drink and drug abuse. We are conscious of the growing concern about, for example, the increase in heroin addiction among young people. There are no simple solutions for dealing with young people in trouble and thus a separate Officer Group, involving social work, education, police and the Reporter, has been set up to look at this issue in depth.

YOUTH WORK: GIRLS AND YOUNG WOMEN

Despite changes in legislation, the status of women in our culture is still adversely affected by deep rooted prejudices, attitudes, customs and conventional beliefs. These are often unwittingly and, occasionally, deliberately reinforced in the socialisation process within schools and youth work settings.

Activities which at present predominate in youth work programmes are male orientated and attempts to develop work with girls are often frustrated by physical and emotional demands upon scarce resources of time and space from more assertive male members. In this atmosphere, girls adopt a secondary role. They have learnt to watch, not to take the lead; to be apathetic and uninterested – all of which underwrite a further lack of confidence and belief in their own ability.

It is possible that this situation is exacerbated by youth workers of both sexes who interpret this role response as proof that girls are simply apathetic, and consequently believe that "something for girls" on the periphery of the programme is the best that can be achieved.

A further factor could be the ratio of male to female staff in youth work. We estimate that overall the ratio is now about 50:50, if we include all full-time and part-time staff. However, this hides the tendency for males to dominate the hierarchies. At a club level, leaders-in-charge tend to be male and at senior management level in community education there are very few females.

We are optimistic that the old myth that you have to be a man to work with young people, although not quite dead yet, is certainly dying. This is reflected in some current college courses where females outnumber males by 2:1. Although no college operates a discriminatory policy, this is a major change from the situation 20 years ago when the early Youth and Community Work courses were made up almost exclusively of male students.

However, a more realistic and dramatic approach is required if there is to be a change in practice and thus more female orientated activities and programmes. For this reason, we would like to see a vigorous debate taking place in the following three areas, leading to positive action for change.

(a)   It is important for service providers and youth workers to examine their attitudes towards the education, development and personal needs of girls and the ways in which inappropriate assumptions are translated into programmes.

(b)   The tone and emphasis of youth work programmes should change to allow more intensive work with girls within mixed-sex settings and also for the development of single sex groups for girls. Where such work has been sensitively established, notably with small groups, we have evidence that girls have developed new interests, increased self-confidence and felt able to discuss topics relevant to their own life experience. Clearly, such work demands appropriately trained female leadership, but we hasten to emphasise that consciousness of the importance and necessity of this work is the responsibility of male youth workers also.

(c)   There appears to be a real need for learning opportunities for staff to:

    (i)   become more aware of the special needs of girls, including emotional needs and development;

    (ii)   acquire practical skills in work with girls;

    (iii)   develop listening and discussion skills; and

    (iv)   become competent in social education practices to encourage girls to evaluate their own circumstances and make decisions appropriate for themselves in relation to their own lives.

We are conscious that despite the fact that these points have been made many times in the past, youth work with girls and young women is a neglected area. We feel, particularly dissatisfied with the level of debate on the issue. We, therefore, charge the Youth Development Teams with the responsibility of rectifying this.

Each team should critically examine youth work in its area with the view to producing and testing out ideas for positive action in working with girls and young women. We intend to hold a seminar to look at good practice and to discuss this issue in more depth. For this seminar, which will be held in about a year, each Team will be expected to produce a report on their response and how their ideas worked in practice.

POLICE INVOLVEMENT

We have noted the valuable work being undertaken by the Police Community Involvement Branch.

One approach to the youth in the Region is made through the schools. In the primary school, the main emphasis is laid on the film "Don't go with Strangers", but the initial contact which is provided by this film is built upon in an attempt to create a good relationship between the police and the primary school child. General road safety and cycle proficiency are also part of the primary schools programme.

At the secondary level there is more educational content in the presentations given by the police, for example, Evolvement of Law, The Police and Law Enforcement, Children's Hearing Systems, Vandalism, Truancy and Solvent Abuse. Nevertheless the main objective of involvement in secondary schools remains that of creating a rapport between pupils and police and should be aimed at younger pupils (S1 and S2).

While there is merit in meeting the youth of the Region in a school environment, the police are also very much involved with those youths who have committed offences or are "at risk" in society for some other reason. In this area, the police work very closely with the Reporter's and Social Work Departments and, indeed, have their own Strathclyde Police Youth Advisory Service which attempts to divert youngsters from criminal activities at an early stage.

Within the general field of youth work, police involvement tends to be on an "ad hoc" basis within the authority's own youth clubs with a greater commitment being made to the voluntary youth organisations.

The concept of "community policing" is a valuable one but it has become a cliché. We believe the police are taking practical steps to improve the quality of relationships between the force and the local community. The recent (November 1983) increase in the number of police community projects in the APTs from 12 to 27 demonstrates this. The discussions about community policing, however, have all focussed on the role to be played by other local government services and local people themselves. We believe it to be extremely important that we should find a local forum that is not just a talking shop but seriously tackles the whole area of relationships between young people, the community and the police. We are concerned that all aspects of these relationships are examined including the issue of young people feeling harassed by some adults' response of continuously phoning the police about young people hanging around the streets in groups, although committing no crimes.

We believe that there are initiatives which show such progress is possible. For example, in some parts of Strathclyde, the Police Community Involvement Branch has developed a programme for working with secondary schools and establishing junior crime prevention panels. This is a start and could be repeated elsewhere.

In looking at the relationship between the police and the community, it should be emphasised just how pivotal to this issue is the relationship between the police and young people particularly young men in some areas. The recent British Crime Survey (although covering only England and Wales, a Scottish survey is to be published soon) is interesting in this respect:

> "The findings on contact with the police consistently showed that young men had a disproportionately high number of unsatisfactory contacts with the police. Urban and inner city police also tended to receive less positive ratings than elsewhere. Three things should be borne in mind in interpreting these findings. First, young men were not universally condemnatory; they reported incidents which pleased them more frequently than any other group. Secondly, young men are involved in law-breaking more than any other group and some antipathy and conflict between them and the police is probably inevitable. Finally, many young men's commitment to the social order is very tentative and their dissatisfaction with the police may simply be an expression of this more general disaffection. Nevertheless the findings give some cause for concern. Policing needs consent and it is by no means clear that the police have been able to secure or sustain this consent amongst the young."

It is clear that we need to make a major effort to ensure that the relationship between the police and young men is a healthy one.

But it should not be thought that this is an issue that relates only to these two parties. It is a matter of importance to community development, as a whole since, as the British Crime Survey again says, the fear of crime in Britain is becoming as great a problem as crime itself – "that fear is needlessly reducing the quality of people's lives and that fear of crime can itself lead to crime – by turning cities at night into empty, forbidding places."

That fear of crime by others is largely centred around the activities of the young. Clearly we need to ensure that older people have the opportunity to see youth on the many occasions that they are acting positively and that the resources of the whole community are used so that the streets are both safe and believed to be safe to use.

As with youth work with girls and young women, this is an issue that requires a critical and wide-ranging debate, an examination of local practice and the development of new ideas and approaches. In order to encourage this, we need to look at ideas and discuss this issue further with Youth Development Teams and other interested parties.

RURAL YOUTH WORK

We have studied some of the problems associated with youth work in rural areas and conclude that the basic needs of young people are the same wherever they live in the country, town or city. However, some profound differences will remain. Living in the country still makes, and will continue to make, a difference to personal development and social attitudes and this needs to be recognised when developing opportunities for young people in their leisure time.

Some differences which affect opportunities are that:

(a)   The village is more conscious of itself as a community than the town neighbourhood. This is particularly reflected in the problems of leadership and youth work. There could also be resistance, especially among the traditionally influential residents, to any change which may conflict with the special character of the village.

(b)   The population of a village is relatively dispersed. This is even more true of the village hinterland and should not be forgotten.

(c)   The number of young people in any one area may be small, allowing little scope for group activities.

(d)   Distance of travel is still a major problem.

(e)   The availability of suitable premises for association and activities can be a major problem.

Our study leads us to believe that, as with all youth work, rural work cannot be successfully undertaken without regard to the wholeness of community life and that the needs of young people can be best met by encouraging them to participate in village activities and, ultimately, to provide the opportunities for young people in rural areas have to be just as flexible and diversified as in town and cities.

A major problem is that young people are adversely affected by the lack of transport in rural areas. Scarcity and cost of transport also presents special problems for unemployed young people in reaching places where they can take part in activities, look for work or seek further training. It is difficult to provide a comprehensive youth work programme in rural areas and it is, therefore, essential that maximum use is made of existing community facilities including schools, community centres and village halls. Easy access to resource materials and equipment is also difficult. Equipment stores are generally located in the main centres of population and the collection and return of such equipment often involves travelling long distances. Consideration must, therefore, be given to providing additional community buses through either Regional transport departments or assisting voluntary organisations to buy their own transport through grant aid. In addition, the Community Education Service should examine methods of decentralising pools of equipment to suitable locations which will permit easier access by villages in rural areas.

We have noted that the comments of the Working Group on Resource Centres on provision in rural areas. This report also highlights the acute problems relating to the transport and other resources although not specifically in the context of youth work.

In view of the particular issues identified we propose to make a further and more detailed study of the needs in rural areas and will be interested in seeking the views of the appropriate Youth Development Teams, when these have been established.

VOLUNTARY YOUTH GROUPS

The majority of voluntary groups are connected either with a church or with a particular field of activity or tradition. To this extent the voluntary organisations differ from each other, providing a variety of opportunity within the community. To be successful in attracting young people, these groups must not only be different but be seen to be different and, to survive, must be able to meet the challenge of competition for some of the leisure time of young people. Providing variety is part of this, rethinking methods even though a traditional aim is maintained is another, whilst accepting the need for experiment is a third.

National statistics indicate that the voluntary organisations attract for the most part the younger age group within the community. Consequently, if they are to attract the older young person they must be encouraged to be more forward thinking, and experimentally minded in their approach which will make them sufficiently attractive to the young person for him to join on merit or join initially because of church, family or other connection. Their task is to retain this membership and involvement.

There are three main categories of voluntary groups:

(a)   Long-established uniformed organisations with national structures. These organisations tend to appeal to younger age groups and to young people with particular interests and attitudes. In many cases that are relatively well-supported financially and by voluntary adult leaders, largely as a result of church affiliations and also often through a tradition of family connections with the organisations. In other areas, however, they find it very difficult to get established or existing groups are in decline. There are various reasons for this, for example, competition from schools and other groups for young people's time, difficulty in attracting sufficient leaders and the lack of appeal because of the ethos of the organisations in some parts of the Region.

(b)   Voluntary youth clubs. Many different types and sizes of youth groups exist, organised by voluntary adult help and many are connected to churches or have national structures. Others are not linked to any parent organisation or ethos, but are formed as a response to unmet local need.

(c)   Specialist youth organisations, developed round specialist activities such as football and other sports, drama and music. Although existing mainly to promote their particular activity, they often fulfill a wider social function. Again groups range from well-organised national groups like the Scottish Youth Theatre to street football and netball teams.

It is of prime importance that fieldworkers continue to foster and develop close relationships between the statutory and voluntary groups, thereby ensuring that there is a maximum variety of opportunity to meet the demands of the young person. There must be no sense of competition between the statutory service and the voluntary organisations, rather they should be complimentary to each other.

But what additional support should the Council give voluntary groups? What scope is there for collaborative work and how should this be organised? What lessons can the Community Education Service learn from the voluntary organisations?

In practical terms, the working relationships with voluntary groups should be strengthened at an area level. Voluntary groups should be included in the Youth Development Teams and thus involved in discussions on local youth work needs, priorities for future work and on the issues raised by this report. Local discussions should also include the promotion of joint training opportunities, shared resources and the priorities for grant aid for voluntary groups.

At a Regional level, we are aware of some pressure from the voluntary organisations for liaison arrangements to be set up. It is not clear what would be the purpose of, and most suitable structure for, any region wide liaison. For example, should the Council meet representatives of voluntary organisations separately or collectively? Voluntary organisations are, therefore, invited to submit their arguments and ideas for liaison arrangements to the Member/Officer Group. With the financial constraints currently imposed on the Region, priority will be given to the organisations whose aims and objectives meet with the Council's.

SABEU – SCOTTISH ADULT BASIC EDUCATION UNIT

A POLICY DOCUMENT SCOTTISH COMMUNITY EDUCATION COUNCIL 1984

WHAT IS ADULT BASIC EDUCATION? (ABE)

In terms of requests from the adult public at large (and currently over 18,000 ABE students receive help annually in Scotland), ABE means:

> *help with literacy, numeracy, communication and learning skills, basic life management skills, preparation for a new start in life, or a serious transition; preparation for a return to community life, or to formal education, or to training and employment opportunities.*

WHAT IS SO SPECIAL ABOUT ABE?

Adult Basic Education has grown out of the Adult Literacy Campaign of the 1970s. It represents an approach to adult learning that focuses on

- helping students acquire confidence in themselves as valuable, capable people
- enabling people to make use of and improve their capacity to learn
- encouraging people to be active and co-operatively supportive when tackling issues in their lives that might be helped through educational means
- helping people acquire the knowledge and skills necessary to manage their lives and feel they are productive members of the community.

WHAT ARE THE CHARACTERISTICS OF AN ABE APPROACH?

ABE has an identifiable style. It is informal and confidential. It recognises that an adult's own experience of life may be a more important resource than qualifications or expensive equipment. It is egalitarian, and the roles of tutor and student, or group leader and participants, frequently change. It is open and responsive, being offered where and when it is most convenient for the beneficiaries; the learning process is supportive in such a way that all participants are encouraged to take over control and responsibility for their own learning.

In greater detail, an ABE approach realises the following principles:

(a) **The student is paramount**
Experience gained during the "adult literacy only" phase, and confirmed by more recent experience in ABE, shows how important it is that a person's own views, needs, expectations and abilities should determine the kind of support for learning he or she gets. Many people looking to ABE for help have found previous contacts with education demoralising.

(b) **The focus of the relationship between students and tutors is on learning**
A good relationship is the ground for learning to take place. The tutor's/worker's role is that of supporting learning, which means helping learners identify learning strategies that work for them. The attitudes of those doing the supporting are a critical ingredient if a learning exchange is to take place.

(c) **All participate on an equal basis and the learning programme is negotiated**
'Tutor' and 'student' are roles, not ranks, and can be freely exchanged. What is shared is usually experience or the fruits of learning. All participants should see themselves as contributors. The benefits of the learning exchange should be

- enhanced self confidence and responsibility
- new knowledge/a sense of personal development
- new skills
- new contacts and networks.

Negotiating takes place on the basis of

- the real needs, abilities and commitment of all those involved in the 'contract'
- recognising choices, responsibilities and realistic objectives
- recognising the true nature of the barriers to personal development.

(d) **There are real barriers to personal and social development.**
In the attempt to break away from a 'remedial' or 'deficit' view, and so help people escape from labels that stigmatise them, ABE workers look squarely at two things,[1] the actual barriers people face[2] the actual capabilities, experience, knowledge and sources of satisfaction people have, which will form the basis for their 'attack' on the barriers.

For example, an individual may have to confront one, several or all of the following barriers:

(i)   impairment or disablement

(ii)   communication/relationship difficulties

(iii) symbols (as when reading, writing or using numbers)

(iv)   systematic social exclusion or stigma

(v)   inadequate income, food and shelter (which may absorb his/her available time, energy or interest)

(vi)   ignorance, alienation and powerlessness.

(e) **Basic adult skills are essential adult skills, and basic information is information which is essential to all adults**
The following diagram attempts to represent the main barriers people face, and which therefore determine the skills and knowledge they must acquire to be full members of a democratic society:

ESSENTIAL ADULT LEARNING

Participate in democratic processes

Live a productive life (through work, expression, recreation and community involvement)

Manage your life (through organising, budgeting, catering, dealing with agencies)

Use symbols – through reading, writing and computing

Communicate and relate with confidence

Personal, family and social barriers

Symbol-systems, formalities and institutional restraints

Geographical communal and economic constraints

Systemic national and international barriers

Institutions, social and political barriers

OR

BARRIERS TO ADULT DEVELOPMENT?

(f) **Stigmatising labels, ranking and generalised criteria have proved unhelpful**
Labels such as 'remedial', 'a reading age of 7', 'an IQ of 60', have proved to be more of a hindrance than an insight when applied to adults. They not only tend to block sympathetic observation and obscure the resources existing within a person, but to tie people to criteria which may have served a purpose only at school, at the expense of focusing on adult needs and potential now.

Even labels like 'unemployed', 'ethnic minority', 'mentally handicapped' can distract both learners and helpers from recognising the particular individual barriers a person is confronted with, and should be regarded as, at best, only administrative labels. Unfortunately, the people given such a label tend to be seen as the 'problems', rather than the barriers they face.

(g) **Formality is itself a barrier to many**
Many of the people seeking or finding help from ABE have experienced failure and frustration in earlier encounters with education. Many, as a result of lacking confidence, knowledge and skills, have developed dependent relationships, and are 'intimidated' by any situation or context that threatens to reveal their sense of inadequacy. Confidentiality and informality have proved to be powerful ingredients in encouraging such people back into a "learning situation"; whereas imposing buildings, complicated enrolment, authority figures, registers, and programmes that roll on irrespective of whether people learn, only serve to confirm their worst fears.

(h) **ABE is not an adult version of Remedial Education**
People who become involved in ABE are not a minority tribe, made of illiterates and those with a "remedial" background at school. They are people from all classes and groups in society whose only shared characteristics are a lack of confidence, at least one important channel of communication closed to them, and a feeling of frustration at not being able to realise their full potential. Our society is constantly generating new demands upon adults, both in terms of new knowledge and skills, new attitudes and patterns of living, and yet the majority of adults have no further contact with any educational support after their teens. ABE is often the only effective way forward.

WHO HAS BEEN HELPED IN SCOTLAND? WHY DO THEY NEED HELP?

We have said that many of the people coming forward for help express a lack of confidence. Yet, paradoxically, those people who have had the courage to refer themselves to regional Adult Basic Education Schemes represent only the bravest of those believed to need help. We know from national statistics and from outreach projects that the proportion of people who would benefit from ABE support is much higher than the 4% figure invoked at the outset of the Adult Literacy Campaign (Which predicted 200,000 adults in Scotland).

Since 1976, when the Adult Literacy Campaign got under way in Scotland, some 45,000 adults have been helped by regional schemes and voluntary organisations. Yet, new students are still coming forward at the rate of 18,000 each year, even though the number of voluntary tutors has remained static at about 4,000. Why has the early dream that "Adult illiteracy and innumeracy would be eradicated within a few years" not been realised?

Firstly, the overt and latent needs are greater than was first realised. Consider the following statistics:

> *Over 30% of adults cannot correctly complete first time a tax return or census form ...*
>
>

Administrative Forms in Government
Sir Derek Rayner's White Paper.

> *Over 30% cannot understand or use concepts like percentage, inflation or ratio ...*
>
>

"Mathematics Counts – Report of the Committee of Enquiry into the Teaching of Mathematics ... 1982"
– The Cockcroft Report.

> *Over 20% cannot read with understanding a sentence like:*
> *"This coupon entitles you to a specimen of our delicious toffee ..."*
>
>

Holborn Reading Test

In addition

> *Over 30% of young people leave school with nothing to show for their attendance*
>
>

Regional Trends HMSO

> *Over 50% of all adults have no further contact with educational provision after the age of 16.*
>
>

Regional Trends HMSO

Social changes have resulted in raising demands for qualifications, as well as for literacy and numeracy (particularly in relation to form filling, claims for benefits, access to employment). At the same time, social changes are also removing opportunities for practising skills, particularly with the rise in unemployment and the popularity of media which make few demands (radio, television and video) on literacy skills. In particular, many young people who would previously have made a transition from school to work, where such skills would have been demanded and applied, are now finding that post-school unemployment rusts their basic skills, and they are in danger of lapsing into illiteracy and innumeracy.

The Regional ABE Scene

All the Scottish Regions and Island Councils make some provision for Adult Basic Education, though the levels of funding, staffing and support, and the style of each scheme, vary considerably from area to area. Some areas have barely developed from offering basic help with reading, writing and numeracy, while others (generally with the benefit of outside funding) have evolved more comprehensive services, covering a wide range of learning, available in many contexts, at any time, and offering collaborative links with training, employment and further-education agencies. In 1982/83, there were some 4,000 volunteers active throughout Scotland, supported by 235 paid ABE workers, helping 17,855 students. Most of these students have been attracted from those groups traditionally regarded as non-participants in adult education. Contrary to popular myths, their non-participation has not been the result of apathy or indolence on their part but the lack of suitable learning opportunities. At present, unfortunately, under-resourced teams of workers are finding it difficult to cope with demand.

Within Schemes there are two broad categories of work:

(a)   provision for self-referring students, and

(b)   outreach provision for dealing with latent demand.

GENERAL PROCEDURES FOR THE SELF-REFERRING STUDENT

In responding to students who themselves seek help (and motivation is best when people refer themselves), ABE Schemes must be sensitive and confidential in the way they handle enquiries, interviews and introduction. ABE workers do not necessarily plunge into identifying learners' "problems". A great deal of sensitive work is needed to build up confidence and much time may be spent raising success and satisfaction before the cognitive process of learning can be applied directly to overcoming identified barriers. For many people, their energy is tied up in holding daily problems at bay, and energy can only be released to begin solving them through success and relaxation in some 'sector' of their lives. Educational counselling is therefore an important element in ABE support, and much of the provision is on a one-tutor-to-one-student basis. An important ingredient in creating responsibility is the fact that any learning programme or course is negotiated by the student(s) with the ABE worker(s). This may at first be alien to a learner's previous experience of education, but it is a vital step if students are to assume responsibility for their own development.

The role of the tutor is expressed through:

- caring
- listening
- identifying strengths and sources of satisfaction for a learner
- supporting learning
- suggesting learning strategies
- devising learning strategies
- devising learning materials and experiences
- tackling real problems in the student's present life (eg a lack of essential skills) through a negotiated programme
- promoting self-help, empowerment and increased independence.

WHAT THE STUDENT WILL EXPERIENCE THROUGH ABE

In general, students report that the most important benefits of ABE are improved confidence and a sense of success and personal worth. They also appreciate the fact that help focuses on their individual needs and is confidential. They find the programmes they have negotiated enjoyable and relevant, particularly because they have progressed at a rate they have determined and have concentrated on 'problems' they have identified. They also comment favourably upon the approach to assessment, which encourages them to evaluate their own performance. Finally, where provision is able to be fully 'open', they appreciate the flexibility as to location, time and duration.

TRAINING

In order for students to feel these achievements, tutors need to learn a wide variety of skills. Tutor training will involve elements of:

- Helping someone learn

  - English   ie understanding & speaking
  - Reading   English as a first or additional language
  - Writing
  - Spelling
  - Numeracy

- Negotiating a programme
- Listening Skills and Educational Counselling
- Learning Strategies
- Inter-personal skills
- Simple materials development
- Dealing with other workers and agencies
- Finding resources
- Useful learning aids (recorders, video, computers)
- Working with students
  - one-to-one
  - in groups
- Working with students at a distance
- Working with women
- Working with slow learners
- Working with ethnic minorities
- Working with unemployed people
- Working with people with physical impairment

The duration of a training course and the number of elements within it depend largely upon the time volunteers have at their disposal and the number of trainers a Region employs. The Adult Literacy and ABE 'traditions' have been for trainers to emerge from or be tutors, and so, through experience, to remain responsive to tutor's needs.

THE OUTREACH APPROACH

As we have already shown, public statistics and reports indicate "inadequate levels of educational competence in the adult population", whether the source is a government department lamenting wastage in form completion by the public at large, or particular research exercises examining competence in limited but essential skills. However, there are many other indicators of latent needs. Employers and college lecturers, for example, report difficulties arising from employees and students lacking knowledge and skills pre-requisite for certain jobs or courses. Counter-staff in Department of Health & Social Security Offices report difficulties stemming from illiteracy and innumeracy: in fact, many professionals whose work brings them into daily contact with those members of the public faced with most barriers comment on the lack of essential adult skills.

The effects of such disabling factors can range from a sense of frustration, inadequacy or exclusion on the part of the individual, to local and national wastage in terms of bureaucratic processes (costing Britain hundreds of millions of pounds in useless forms, because they have failed to effect desired results for either the public or the agency); to danger, low efficiency and productivity in relation to manufacturing processes; to effective disenfranchisement in a democratic society, through lack of awareness of rights, obligations and responsibilities.

Yet, until the early 1980s, ABE was dependent upon people having the courage to overcome stigma and seek help themselves. In a country with a recent tradition for educational excellence, it took a great deal of courage to admit that one was not attaining national expectations. Pilot surveys conducted by one or two regional schemes indicated that, if provision could now be offered in neutral settings, where the focus of learning was not directly on adult literacy and numeracy needs, then more people would come forward for help. ABE schemes were thus presented with a clear challenge:

How are people needing help with essential knowledge and skills to be reached?

This was a challenge to reach people who

* on the whole expressed negative reactions to their previous contacts with "education" and who saw no role for "education" in their lives

* had acquired little sense of personal worth or social potency from their contact with "officials"

* were often beset with problems of unemployment, unsatisfactory living conditions, poor health or limited opportunities

* had poor support (like child care or informal learning bases)

* were concerned about the cost, proximity and style of any kind of help

Obviously terms like "adult literacy" or "basic education" would not help. People with a tradition of co-operative action might be encouraged by group events rather than one to one provision.

Various initiatives, some more 'structured' than others, but virtually all dependent upon injections of extra-regional funding, were developed in a few areas with the aim of reaching out into community settings or institutions eg hospitals, prisons, residential homes, etc. and developing provision for those who would not otherwise come forward.

The most commonly used strategies were for workers to:

* get to know a particular area well, by spending time outside schools in shops, pubs, public places (like job centres and libraries), rent offices and bingo halls

* make themselves known to local networks, by chatting to residents' associations, community 'leaders', teachers, social workers, health visitors etc; find out about existing local, informal groups

* stimulate curiosity and discover local concerns by getting local people's opinions on what kind of learning opportunities might be appreciated: and involve any volunteers who show interest

* find suitable friendly, informal accommodation where those who have expressed an interest can meet together

* find ways of creating crèche and child-care facilities.

(This whole process is a long one, if local confidence and a sense of local control are to be established.)

Once people had shown an interest and tentatively voiced their needs or aspirations, workers could begin to negotiate social learning programmes with them. Early activities might focus on generating pleasurable, group 'events' – like keeping fit, organising 'away days' – or might focus on urgent local issues, like a lack of employment opportunities or even training initiatives.

The directions and content of programmes cannot be predicted in advance of the negotiating process. However, once under way, people will feel more confident about revealing personal interest and needs, even suppressed ambitions – like a desire to write, to do 'O' Grades or prepare for the Open University. Their needs may be functionally specific, like coping with particular forms, or letters to school, or helping children with homework. They may be generalised, like relating to teenagers, understanding social security information, finding out about health or the Women's Movement. The skill of the workers lies in building up good relationships, good networks and good support, so that both group and individual learning can be supported. Whenever possible, resources within the group are identified and tapped, in order to create responsiveness, co-operativeness and confidence.

Key factors in all these outreach initiatives are

• informality and friendliness

• responses are local and flexible

- accommodation is accessible and non-threatening
- people can feel and see how learning relates to their immediate lives.

They must above all, experience being responsible for their own programmes and outcomes.

These early forays into popular learning programmes have shown the importance of being responsive to personal and local needs and aspirations. There is no standard format or 'course', yet ABE's contribution is helping people make fresh starts:

- to renew their confidence in their ability to learn
- to prepare for a return to first informal and then formal educational opportunities. (Here ABE acts as an indirect recruitment service for formal education)
* to prepare for a training opportunity
* to participate in the local community
* to acquire new knowledge and skills (eg computer literacy)
* to meet social changes
* to get involved in skill sharing, new hobbies or voluntary activities, and so live a more productive life.

In terms of its contribution to adult and continuing education, ABE's role is to help people tackle those barriers which prevent them developing personally, or exclude them from existing social opportunities.

REGIONAL SCHEMES AND SABEU (SCOTTISH ADULT BASIC EDUCATION UNIT)

In relation to regional ABE schemes, SABEU's role is a supportive one, attempting to help with resources, training, information exchanges and innovations in programmes, research and publications.

However, SABEU can also play a collaborative role with regional schemes when they are developing ABE initiatives with new groups or in new contexts, and also with professionals in hospitals, social work centres, penal institutions, community settings and voluntary organisations.

Together with regional schemes and other professionals, SABEU can tackle some of the social barriers affecting learners, and:

- work with the media to reduce stigma, to raise awareness and increase essential skills

- collaborate with workers in libraries and other public amenities to improve access, resources and user figures
- collaborate with agencies like SCSS, Community Business Scotland, the Scottish Consumer Council, MSC, SHEG etc., to raise confidence, awareness and basic skills
- offer 'Plain English' services to originators of public literature, like forms and brochures, to make such documents more accessible. (Money saved nationally in this area alone, through improved public success rates with forms, could more than pay for national ABE staff and resources.)
- promote research and innovation in building popular learning programmes in communities.

No one could have foreseen that the adult literacy campaign of the middle seventies would lead, by the early eighties, to a student-centred style of provision for adults that encompassed such skills as ABE is now concerned with. Yet ABE in Scotland is only at the beginning of its potential development. If we are to approach the characterisation of ABE given by UNESCO, we still have a long way to go:

"Basic education has three essential objectives; the imparting of skills to communicate, skills to improve the quality of living, and skills to contribute to, and to increase, economic production. The communication skills, at the minimum, include literacy, numeracy and general civic, scientific and cultural knowledge, values and attitudes. The living skills embrace knowledge of health, sanitation, nutrition, family planning, the environment, management of the family economy, and creation and maintenance of a home. The production skills encompass all forms of activity directed towards making a living or producing goods and services, at whatever level of economic sophistication".

"Basic education, therefore, is a relative, and not an absolute process. The character, degree and method of basic education will vary according to the country, the group selected for education, and their particular needs. Basic education is similarly diverse in its levels of planned activities, comprising formal, non-formal and informal offerings. Its different elements are assimilated over a lifetime and can lead, incrementally, to an individual's material welfare, increased productivity, and ability to earn a living from self-employment."

(From "Managing Adult Literacy Training"
in 'Prospects' Vol XIII, No 2 UNESCO)

However, what is evolving in Scotland has a less directive approach, and is, as yet, very patchy.

RALPH WILSON
THE SCOTTISH COMMUNITY EDUCATION COUNCIL

IN POST 16 – DEVELOPMENTS IN CONTINUING EDUCATION IN SCOTLAND
Eds D COSGROVE AND C McCONNELL DUNDEE COLLEGE OF EDUCATION
1984 pp 77 – 80

INTRODUCTION

In March 1975 the report *'Adult Education – the Challenge of Change'* was published. The major recommendation of this report, which has come to be known as the Alexander Report, was that:

> *'Adult education should be regarded as an aspect of community education and should, with the youth and community service be incorporated into a community education service.'*

The publication of this report coincided with the re-organisation of local government in Scotland and while certain Regional authorities had already been moving towards the introduction of a Community Education Service, the report resulted in authorities developing an integrated service which most called community education.

In considering a national structure for community education, the Alexander Report said the following:

> *'We therefore recommend that the Secretary of State should establish a Scottish Council for Community Education to assume the present functions of the Standing Consultative Committee (on Youth and Community Service) and in addition to carry out for adult education the functions outlined in the following paragraph. The members should be appointed by the Secretary of State and should be selected for the personal qualities they can be expected to bring to the work of the Council rather than as representatives of particular associations or groups, but the Council as a whole should be broadly representative of the various interests concerned with community education. It should also include some members with other relevant interests The Council should have its own staff including a chief officer who should maintain close contact with developments in community education. Its expenditure should be met by the Secretary of State.'*

The first Council known as the Scottish Council for Community Education, was set up in 1979, and serviced not by its own staff but by staff of the Scottish Education Department. During its three year life this Council funded and completed a number of projects; research was carried out into the methods of collection and collation of community education statistics and a substantial report[1] published; a three year project 'The Scottish Community Education Microelectronics Project', SCEMP, was established under its own management committee and located at Dowanhill, Glasgow sharing premises with the

Scottish Microelectronics Development Programme; funding was made available to establish a radio studio within the premises of the Scottish Community Education Centre in Edinburgh enabling 'live' inserts about community education to be broadcast on a regular basis on Radio Scotland; a two year Telephone Referral Project was set up through the Scottish Institute of Adult Education.

The Council, from within its own resources, published a number of reports – on community schools in Scotland, on the social benefits of community education and on community education training.

As a result of its policy considerations, the Secretary of State decided to reform the Council by merging it on the 1st April 1982 with the Scottish Community Education Centre, a body which had for a number of years been responsible for supporting the development of community education in Scotland by disseminating information, providing advisory and training services and by co-operating with other bodies in Scotland and abroad through exchange of information and through comparative study visits. During 1982 further restructuring proposals were considered and these resulted in the transfer of management responsibility of the Scottish Adult Basic Education Unit from the Scottish Institute of Adult Education to SCEC as of 1st April 1983.

The constitution of the new Council defines two prime objects:

- to advise the Secretary of State for Scotland on all matters relating to community education and

- to promote the development of community education. Five areas of activity are listed by which the Council may pursue its objects:

  – fostering co-operation among statutory and voluntary organisations

  – providing information, advice and services

  – informing itself of developments, national and international

  – providing training services and resources

  – encouraging, sponsoring or undertaking research.

In the first year of its existence the Council identified three broad themes to underpin its policy making work. These were:

  – promoting lifelong learning;

  – confronting social change;

  – releasing local dynamic and liberating local resources.

The themes are being developed in the contexts of the two committees of the Council, the Training Committee and the Adult Basic Education Committee which are composed of members of the Council along with representatives from both sectors, statutory and voluntary, of the community education field and, in the Council's working groups. In 1982 three working groups were formed.

The *Communications Group*, containing a large number of members co-opted from the media, has been engaged in the area of the application of new technology to community education. Amongst its many interests are cable television, in relation to which it prepared a discussion paper for publication; in radio broadcasting through the provision from the radio studio of a weekly ten minute slot called 'community desk' to BBC Radio Scotland's popular morning programme, 'The Jimmy Mack Show'; in computing where the group has responsibility for future developments relating to the SCEMP project. The group has also taken on the task of submitting advice to the Home Office on the laws of copyright, and to the Convention of Scottish Local Authorities on the development of computing in schools.

Issues related to unemployment and the programmes created by the Manpower Services Commission in relation to it have dominated the work of the *Employment, Education and Leisure Group*, although the group also has a strong interest in education for older persons, in which a joint research project with Age Concern has been undertaken. The unemployment interest is reflected in the staffing structure of the Council by the existence of an MSC funded unit originally named the Community Schemes Resources Unit but recently retitled the Youth Training Unit in recognition of the importance of the Youth Training Scheme. This unit acts as a two way channel of information between MSC and the field, providing information to the community education services through conferences, publications and training consultancies and at the same time transmitting to MSC the needs and concerns of the practitioners in the hope of influencing future developments in the programmes.

The Unemployment Initiatives Unit, supported by Council funding carries out a similar role in relation to non MSC unemployment work such as co-operatives and community businesses. Again the emphasis is on the provision of information to the field through the publication of occasional documents such as a register of unemployment initiatives and through the publication of a four page review of unemployment issues in the monthly community education newspaper, SCAN.

In the latter half of 1982 and into 1983 the *Youth Affairs Group* was particularly active. On the advice of the Council, the Secretary of State for Scotland approved the setting up of the International Year of Youth Committee, to oversee and co-ordinate preparations for this major event in 1985. The themes of IYY, as outlined by the United Nations are 'participation', 'peace' and 'development'. The first of these. 'participation' is reflected in the composition of the IYY committee which comprises twenty young people, chosen from applicants from throughout Scotland, along with four 'older' persons selected because of their proven ability to motivate young people to participate. Nine consultants, experienced in various fields of Scottish life have agreed to advise and support the committee, and the Scottish Education Department has funded a three year full-time post to cover the administration of the committee. The committee commenced its work in June 1983.

The twenty young people who form the major part of the Committee were selected after they had applied to the Council in response to a publicity campaign mounted through the press and, in particular, through the Independent Local Radio Stations with whom the Council has established useful relations. As a result, the International Youth Year Committee contains young people, ranging in age from 16 to 25 from all over Scotland.

In October 1982, the Thompson Report—a review of the Youth Services in England, was published. After studying this report the Youth Affairs Group set itself the task of conducting a similar review with reference to Scotland. This Report entitled Youth Enquiry Report[2] being published in 1982.

THE COUNCIL'S SERVICES

The Council supports the development of community education in Scotland in several ways: by disseminating information through publications, publicity, and conferences; by providing advisory and training services through seminars and consultations; and by co-operating with other bodies at home and abroad, through the exchange of information and comparative study visits.

Information Services

The Council operates an enquiry answering service based on its resource library which operates a free book and document loan service. A new service, recently developed, is Community Education Briefing—an abstract of recent articles, research reports and books of interest over the entire field of community education which is distributed monthly to subscribers, who then request copies of articles of particular interest. Overall, the enquiry service handles around 10,000 enquiries annually.

The Council has two regular publications. SCAN is Scotland's monthly newspaper on community education, leisure and health, and has a circulation of over 6,000 copies each month. Each month SCAN highlights national and local news, with features, information and reader's enquiries. Several pages are devoted to a review of unemployment and responses to it. Frequent supplements on special interests are included in SCAN on subjects as diverse as multi cultural education, planning youth exchanges, arranging a club programme and children's play.

The Scottish Directory of Community Education, published annually, is an invaluable reference book for anyone working in community education and related fields. The latest edition lists national Councils and committees, schools, further education establishments, voluntary organisations, community centres and community education and development staff throughout Scotland. In addition, there are useful addresses for community service, arts, sport, travel and adult literacy.

In addition to its regular publications, the Council produces special publications on an ad hoc basis to respond to particular issues as they arise and to meet specific needs within the community education field.

'Young Scot', an annual information booklet of over 120 pages aimed at young people in the transition from school to adult life is issued to all 16 year olds through the secondary schools, and through Youth Training Programmes, youth clubs and Independent Local Radio who co-operated with the Council in mounting a media publicity campaign, achieved a distribution of over 150,000 copies in 1983. Printed in colour, in a handy pocket size, 'Young Scot' has received acclaim from young people, teachers and parents throughout Scotland, and has generated much interest in Europe. Support has been given by other national organisations such as the Scottish Arts Council, the Scottish Sports Council and the Scottish Health Education Group as well as commercial interests. One of the undoubted advantages in Scotland is the manageable size of national initiatives of this kind, where co operation between national agencies and the 12 Regional and Island Councils responsible for education is relatively easy to organise.

A substantial range of materials in support of 'Young Scot' is also available including a tutor's handbook aimed at teachers using 'Young Scot' in school social education classes or guidance and counselling groups and a series of social education kits on topics such as 'A Place to Love', 'Sex and the Sexes', 'Money Matters', 'Good Health', 'Rights and Obligations', 'Drugs, Drink and Tobacco', and 'Carry on Learning'.

The demand from the community education field for information publications has become increasingly wide and diverse in its subject matter and the Council staff have recently responded by publishing booklets such as 'Urban Aid Explained'—a guide aimed primarily at voluntary organisations and community groups. In his foreword, Allen Stewart, Minister for Home Affairs and the Environment at the Scottish Office writes

> *'Urban Aid has been in existence for more than 10 years now without very many people being aware of it. That did not matter a great deal when the sums of money were small and when it was all spent directly by local government. This has changed. In 1983-84 we shall be providing £35 million, and I am keen that voluntary bodies and community groups should have access to a fair share of the money. While Urban Aid can seem simple to officials who handle it daily, it can be rather perplexing to a community group with an idea for a project. So I welcome the initiative of the Scottish Community Education Council in producing this booklet, and I am confident it will quickly prove its worth'.*

There is no doubt that this information dimension is a vital part of the Council's contribution to the development of community education in Scotland.

Training and Consultancy

The Council staff are frequently approached by organisations in the field to provide training services on a consultancy basis, either in the Council's premises or by contribution by Council staff to seminars, conferences and training sessions throughout Scotland.

In the area of training, the radio studio has proved of particular value. Community educators have come to realise that if they are to get the message of youth work, adult learning and community participation over to people, then they must become skilled in their use of the media. The Council offers this training in its studio, frequently combined with training in the use of press publicity, in one or two day training sessions.

Promotion of Practice

While the Council supports, through its information and training roles, existing practice in the field it also plays an important part in the development and promotion of practice. One example is found in the efforts made to develop the Youth Enquiry Service (YES). In essence the Youth Enquiry Service requires the setting up at local level of YES points where young people themselves are able to research and collate information materials about their own local area. Implicit in these schemes is the idea that young people, once involved in information services, are stimulated to consider self help programmes of action. The production of a local youth newspaper; the initiation of useful discussions with police over the improving of relationships in an area between young people and the police are two practical examples of recent action.

In most cases support is given locally to emerging YES initiatives by local Community Education Services and/or by local voluntary organisations, and it is through advising these support organisations, often over a period of many months, that the Council is able to achieve its objectives of developing good practice in the field.

To enable the staff of the Council to anticipate trends and developments, various national groupings and working parties are convened on a regular basis. Examples of such groupings are the Regional Principal Community Education Officers Group; the Community Service Forum; the Opportunities for Older Person's Group.

THE FUTURE

The pattern of Scottish education is likely to undergo considerable change in the 1980's and 1990's. Flexibility and diversity of provision would seem to one developing theme; another is the development of a more effective partnership between the formal institutions, such as schools and colleges and the community education field, including the voluntary organisations as well as the Community Education Services.

The front-on model of education is likely to give way to a more flexible pattern of continuing lifelong learning, based perhaps on modular courses from which credits can be accumulated, as envisaged in the recent Scottish Education Department report '16 – 18's in Scotland – an Action Plan', and in the Council's Training Committee's Report 'Training For Change' due to be published in Autumn 1984. The Scottish Community Education Council, with its strong links to the community education field, its relationship with schools and colleges, and its well developed information and resource services, is well placed to make a major contribution to these future developments.

REFERENCES

1. Horrobin J, *Community Education Statistics, SCCE* (1980)
2. Youth Enquiry Report. *A Discussion Report SCEC* (1982)

TRAINING FOR CHANGE
SCOTTISH COMMUNITY EDUCATION COUNCIL 1984

WHAT DOES THE WORKER IN THE COMMUNITY DO?

A recurrent theme in our consultations was that training should be relevant to the functions and tasks which the community education worker undertakes. But before devising a system of training, there are prior questions to be answered. "What does the worker in the community actually do and what ought the worker to be doing?" The questions are simple. The answers, we have found, are complex.

Essentially, a community education worker is an individual who engages in

(a)   a developmental process which is often but not always located within

(b)   a specialist setting.

The process, we believe, is common to all community education although the degree to which a particular worker is able to verbalise the developmental process and make it explicit will depend largely on the worker's own perspective and training. The specialist settings are enormously varied, ranging over the fields of education, health, social work, leisure activities, housing, employment issues and so on.

The process can best be described as a set of six functional tasks or stages of intervention.

(a)   Identification of the issues, the demands and needs of the situation

(b)   Design and planning of programmes or structures of development and learning to meet the needs

(c)   Promotion of the programmes or structures to meet the needs of individuals or groups

(d)   Managing, supporting, administering and delivering the programmes or structures including tutoring, guidance, and counselling of the participants

(e)   Publicising the programmes or structures to extend their usefulness

(f)   Continuous assessment and evaluation of the programmes or structures, as they develop.

As we have indicated earlier, it is a principle of community education that the participants are involved at every stage of the process, not merely in dialogue but in decision making. In carrying out the functional tasks the community educator fulfils, at various times, roles as an educator, as a communicator, as a facilitator, as a manager and as a trainer of part-time and voluntary colleagues.

SOME EXAMPLES MAY BE HELPFUL

(a) A community education worker, employed full-time by a Regional Council, is approached to set up some support, including learning opportunities, for the unemployed in the area. The worker engages in the following process:

- setting up a group of people, including the unemployed, to assess the needs of the unemployed in the area;

- designing and running, along with the group, a programme of developmental and educational work to meet the needs which may involve consideration of funding, acquisition of premises, employment of part-time staff, programmes of activities and so on;

- promoting involvement in the programme;

- managing, administering and supporting the initiative, at least in its early stages;

- assisting the group to publicise the initiative;

- co-operating in monitoring and evaluating what has been achieved.

(b) A youth worker is employed by a Voluntary Youth Organisation, under Urban Aid Funding, to set up a programme of detached youth work in an area of urban deprivation. The youth worker engages in a process of:

- contacting young people, and attempting with their co-operation, to identify issues and needs. It emerges that one need is for social and recreational space to be created for the young people, and a major issue is the beginning of an increase in drug abuse in the area;

- in co-operation with the young people, planning and running a programme of education about drugs and their misuse, and designing with the group a plan to acquire the use of an empty flat from the District Council;

- promoting the drug education programme through a variety of agencies;

- supporting and administering the programme at least in its early stages;

- publicising the programme;

- monitoring and evaluating the programme.

(c) A community dietician, employed by a social work department, is asked to intervene in a family situation in which dietary problems have been identified in a young child. The dietician may engage in the process which may involve:

- assessment of needs and issues, with the family, to determine the roots of the problem which may be located in poverty or caused by lack of knowledge of how to acquire benefit entitlements or lack of knowledge of basic nutrition, or mental health problems related to the internal stresses of the family or many other possible causes;

- designing of a programme of development, which depending on the assessment, may involve the family in a variety of practical learning situations within the home or outside it; in actions related to health, or to marriage guidance;

- promoting and facilitating a group learning situation of benefit to other families with similar problems;

- supporting the individual family and managing and administering a programme set up to meet the general problem;

- publicising and informing others who might require to join the programme;

- assessing and evaluating the results of the initiative.

It would be possible to construct a large number of varied examples in which the worker requires, in addition to general knowledge and skills relevant to the process, a level of specific knowledge of one or more areas. In the first example the community education worker, in addition to generic training, requires specific training in the techniques of basic education. In the second example in addition to generic training, the worker requires specific skills in group work with young people and access to training related specifically to health and drug abuse. In the third example, the dietician would have received the specific knowledge from professional training as a dietician, and requires from community education access to general knowledge and skills related to the community education process.

The first general conclusion which we draw from our consideration of what workers in the community do is that there should be two aspects to training

(a)   a generic training relevant to the community education process as a whole;

(b)   a wide variety of training options to acquire knowledge and skills related to specific settings or arenas, and of how the community education process can be applied within the specific setting or arena.

We are inevitably drawn to a core and options model of training, in which generic training forms the core and the training in specific settings forms the options.

The second general conclusion we draw is that the training system required must be a flexible lifelong system, into which and through which there is a variety of routes:-

- a route through training is required for the person already trained and qualified in some specific area such as health, arts, technology, sport or business who wishes to practice that specialism in a community context;

- a route through training is required for the individual who wishes to become a full-time qualified community education worker and who, having achieved that aim, may at different career stages wish to acquire additional training in specific arenas to meet personal development needs or new employment opportunities;

- a route through training is required for the person who having developed an interest in some particular setting, for example, youth work – perhaps through experience as a volunteer or as a part-time unqualified worker then wishes over a period of time to either deepen that knowledge, or to acquire a new specialism or indeed to achieve professional qualification with a view to full-time employment.

We recommend that the system of training should avoid unnecessary distinctions between initial and in-service training with respect to the various routes through training.

The community education worker may not however be a free agent but, as an employee, works within the policy framework set down by the employer and is accountable to the employer. In the next section we attempt to analyse the needs of the various employers and the implications of these needs for the training system.

WHAT DO EMPLOYERS REQUIRE FROM TRAINING?

The Employers

In Scotland, the local government authorities remain the main employers of community education workers. The Education Departments of the Regional and Islands Councils are the principal employers, although a substantial number of qualified community education workers find employment in the Social Work Departments. A smaller number find employment with District Councils, mainly in Leisure and Recreation Departments. Currentiy we estimate that nearly 900 people are in full-time employment within the Community Education Departments of Regional Authorities in posts funded by 'mainline' funding, and a further 400 are employed in posts funded through the Manpower Services Commission and Urban Aid. A national survey conducted in 1983 indicated over 200 workers employed in Social Work Departments, and we were able to estimate that around 50 worked in Leisure and Recreation.

In addition to full-time employees we estimate that there are over 9,500 part-time employees, with almost 7,000 of these employed in youth and community posts, and around 2,500 in tutoring and/or organising roles in adult education and adult basic education. At any one time a substantial number of voluntary workers operate within the statutory services in this arena.

The voluntary organisations are major employers of qualified community educators in full-time posts, and, in addition use the services of thousands of volunteers. And, since our report also relates to the training of volunteers, it is necessary to point out that a vast army of people are engaged in work in the community in organisations of many kinds – engaged in youth work, in community businesses, in community arts projects, in unemployment initiatives, in education and in leisure and recreation. We are unable to quantify the number of people involved, but feel confident that they account for a very large part of the total community education effort in Scotland. At least 300 fully qualified workers are employed in the voluntary sector.

Through the Manpower Services Commission's Youth Training Scheme, and employment measures such as the Community Programme and the Voluntary Projects Programme, increasing numbers of people hitherto uninvolved in education or community work are finding employment as supervisors and training officers responsible to the sponsoring and managing agents, in both the private and public sector, for the delivery of services which are educational or community based and sometimes both. This must, we believe, represent a considerable training task, to which elements of community education training could provide a valuable input.

Because of the ever increasing restraint on local government expenditure, and the channelling of central government funding through agencies such as the MSC and through voluntary organisations, the trend is for a smaller proportion of employment opportunities to arise in local authority services, but for this to be compensated for by a larger number of opportunities arising in other ways. Again we are unable to obtain data to quantify this trend, but can only indicate it in a qualitative manner.

The Regional Community Education Services as Employers

About 80% of the full-time employees of the Regional Community Education Services work in the urban and semi-rural areas of the central belt of Scotland, or in and around the major cities on the edge of or outwith the central belt such as Aberdeen, Dundee and Perth. The remaining 20% are scattered throughout the more rural areas of Borders Region, Dumfries and Galloway, Argyll and Bute, Highland Region, Shetland, Orkney, Western Isles and the rural parts of Grampian Region. It is hardly surprising that the organisational structures and methods of working adopted, even when similar on paper, are quite different realities in the areas where, geographically, community education staff are widely dispersed. This has important implications for training, particularly in-service training and staff development, and we recommend that the content, method and style of training should be strongly influenced by local needs.

The Regional Community Education Services, initially formed from, in the main, youth and community staff accustomed to providing what was fundamentally a centre based service, offering a limited range of educational, social and recreative activities had to respond rapidly to an expansion of services to cover a new and varied range of tasks. This had to be accomplished in a period during which finance and resources have become increasingly constrained. In response to this situation we can identify four approaches to the management and organisation of practice which have a bearing on training.

The Development of Area Teams

A number of Regional Community Education Services in attempting both to be responsive to the needs of a particular geographic locality and to provide a range of specific expertise in the various areas of youth work, adult education and community work have adopted the concept of the Area Team as an organisational structure. In general an Area Team, under the leadership of an area community education officer, assumes collective responsibility for its geographical area, but an attempt is made to identify specific skills and specialist interests within the team so that individual members of it can be associated with particular specialist areas. As a result within the total resource of the team, the individual worker has a general geographical responsibility and a specific functional responsibility. This organisational method reinforces our belief that training should comprise a generic core and specific options, in such a manner that a wide range of options is available not merely during initial training but also in creating in-service opportunities for workers to retrain in specific areas to meet the needs identified by the employer, in this case the Regional Community Education Service.

Creation of Specialist Posts

A further strategy adopted by the Community Education Service is the creation of specialist posts, usually in functional areas which have been given a special priority. At present around 670 full-time education department workers are employed in area team work, with or without specific functional responsibility, and around 130 are employed in specialist posts. The main areas of specialisation are adult education (27), adult basic education (27), secondment to voluntary organisations (22), outdoor education or related services (15), community schools (20), recreation management (11) and community arts (5). We believe this trend towards the creation of specialist posts, at an early stage now, is likely to increase in response to the identification of new priority client groups, such as the elderly, or in response to advances in methods such as the use of information technologies and microcomputing in the learning process. This trend again reinforces our view that, in training, specific areas should be identified as options and that the system of training should allow for the development of new specific options as these become identified by the employers as priority areas within mainstream practice.

The Use of Alternative sources of Funding

With restrictions in mainline funding, an attempt has been made to develop the provision of community education by using alternative sources of funding. In the main, this funding has come from the Urban Programme, from temporary employment schemes operated by the Manpower Services Commission and from the European Social Fund. Figures for Jordanhill College of Education indicate that, in 1982, nearly 30% of newly qualified workers were employed in projects of this nature. Since much innovative and developmental work is carried on within these types of project, this is a situation which has serious implications for training and management. Such projects have aims and objectives located in one or other of the specific arenas of community education, and this further reinforces the need for a degree of explicit specialism in training.

The Introduction of a 'Brokerage' Role

A further effect of the new demands has been the gradual move of emphasis for some community education staff, away from being direct providers in face to face contact with their clients, and into a brokerage role. In this role, the community educator is involved in identifying and assessing the learning needs of individuals or groups and then linking with other services or agencies who have the expertise and resources to meet these needs. A second part of this brokerage role is the involvement of the community educator in marketing the opportunities created through linkage with other providers, to increase accessibility and take up by the general public. This function has involved community educators in establishing and maintaining links with press, local radio and television; in the production of publications and exhibitions and more recently in the creation of specific units and centres devoted to providing information. Increasing use is being made and will continue to be made of new technology in the collation and dissemination of information. It is our view that elements of information expertise should be included in the core of training for community education, and that it should also form the basis of one or more options at a more advanced level.

RELATIONSHIPS BETWEEN THE STATUTORY AND THE VOLUNTARY ARMS OF COMMUNITY EDUCATION

The diversity of demands which followed the acceptance of the Alexander Report's recommendation to combine youth and community work with adult education within a community education framework, and the responses of the Community Education Services outlined in the previous four paragraphs have highlighted the need for an effective partnership between the services and the voluntary organisations. This is not an easy area. Each voluntary organisation tends to have its own specific area of interest and the structural framework of the voluntary organisations at local level may not mesh firmly with the structural framework of area teams responsible to a Regional Community Education Service.

The evidence available to us indicates that many of the voluntary organisations do not see the expectations they had of the Community Education Services achieving proper fulfilment.

(a)   The Scottish Institute of Adult Education, representing individuals and voluntary organisations throughout Scotland, responded to the earlier report of the Interim National Training Group of the Scottish Council for Community Education in the following terms

> *"adult education work is neglected, either because adult education workers are missing from the staffs of Community Education Departments of Colleges of Education or because no adult education training is available for such other existing staff as are asked to undertake adult education work. Until appropriate staff are appointed and until new kinds of training have become available, the sorts of adult education programme listed below are not likely to be effectively provided in many regions of Scotland:*
>
> * *retirement education*
> * *education and training programmes for the unemployed*
> * *adult basic education*
> * *outreach "second chance" education*
> * *language and life skills education for ethnic minorities"*

While we believe that the situation is improving, our consultations with those representing adult education, and in particular the voluntary organisations interested in adult education, indicate that many would agree with the Institute's response.

(b) While adult education agencies were concerned about the lack of emphasis on adult education, many youth organisations have also indicated that they felt that both the quality and the quantity of youth work provision has been impaired, as a result of the introduction of the Community Education Service. While each sector will have its own views on the allocation of resources, the one thing in which both are agreed is the need to translate the concept of a statutory/ voluntary partnership into a reality. The Scottish Standing Conference of Voluntary Youth Organisations Report, *"Voluntary Youth Services in Scotland – A Policy for Action"* which was published in May 1983 stated that

> *"partnership is seen as the complementary working together of the voluntary and statutory. It is about consultation as equals concerning policy development. It is about planning provision and co-operation with one another to provide a service which is relevant to the needs of young people. It is about statutory resources being available to the voluntary to support their work and to encourage development and experimental work .... it is important for the voluntary sector to develop a greater understanding and appreciation of statutory sector provision but there is also a failure in some parts of the Community Education Service to appreciate the nature and contribution of the voluntary sector in meeting the needs of young people".*

(c) Voluntary organisations which are neither adult education organisations or youth organisations, tend to find expression of their views through the Scottish Council for Social Service, and much community development work is undertaken by these organisations. Again the evidence we have been able to obtain suggests the view that community education remains overconcerned with the provision of services and that this role inhibits the community education worker from fulfilling the community development potential of the enabling role. The local authority Community Education Services are seen, from this viewpoint, as the greatest potential resource available for community development work. Essential elements in training for this role are perceived as a core of hard knowledge of social and political sciences; knowledge and skills in group work and the processes of decision making and organising; maturity and confidence gained from well supervised and supported fieldwork practice.

In relation to the voluntary/statutory partnership we recommend that, as part of the core of training, there is a need to include knowledge of the voluntary organisations in general and the role that they play in the various aspects of community education.

THE VOLUNTARY ORGANISATIONS AS EMPLOYERS

The voluntary organisations employ, in both full-time and part-time posts, many qualified community education workers and many workers who do not necessarily possess community education qualifications, although they may possess professional qualifications in related fields. The evidence from our consultations suggests that the elements of training which the voluntary organisations wish to see strengthened are

(a) *Training in Management*

Even in first appointments, many of the community educators working for voluntary organisations are in posts in which they have to advise on policy matters, on the setting of priorities, on the aims and objectives and have to execute decisions which involve considerable knowledge and skill in management. In this respect the Scottish Standing Conference of Voluntary Youth Organisations believe that

> *"many youth workers and officers in the Voluntary Sector have developed management and administrative skills through business experience and through their work in the voluntary organisations. Some have also received administration training outside the youth work field. There is, however, a need to develop more formalised training to meet the needs of those without such training and experience".*

While, as a Committee, we agree with the need for formalised training in management theory and practice, we believe that such training must be in considerable depth, greater indeed than could be justified by placing management training only as part of the general core of training. But in recognition of this need, we recommend that management training should be provided as an option, and should be available in initial training and in in-service training also.

(b) *Training in the particular area of interest of individual Voluntary Organisations*

Quite clearly such specific training would be of value to individual voluntary organisations and many of them have devised excellent induction and in-service programmes within their organisations. It is equally clear that no initial training scheme could possibly cover the diversity of organisations. We believe, however, that the inclusion of options in training will go a considerable way towards meeting this need.

(c) *Training in Training Others*

A feature of employment in many voluntary organisations is that the full-time qualified employee, even in a first post, may be expected to provide induction training and staff development training for the part-time employees and volunteer workers. A view expressed to us suggested that the current system of training seemed to assume that face to face work was the more important objective, and that 'working through others' was somewhat neglected. Once again we consider that the solution may lie in the inclusion as an option of a course or module on the training role that the full-time worker may be asked to fulfil.

THE PARTNERSHIP BETWEEN THEORY AND PRACTICE

In a time when community education work is changing rapidly in response to changing needs, it is clear that training requires to be closely allied to and responsive to developments in practice. In the course of our consultations, the question of links between the training institutions and the field was raised frequently and a number of tensions identified. These tensions related to:

(a) selection procedures;

(b) linking theoretical learning to practice;

(c) reflecting employers' needs in training;

(d) improving fieldwork practice undertaken during training, and, in particular, supervision of that practice;

(e) assessment, and, in particular, the relative weight to be given to theory and practice in the assessment of students.

In relation to selection procedures, linking theory to practice, reflecting employers' needs, and devising balanced assessment procedures we believe that there is a need, within a new system of training, to create structures within which employers, fieldworkers and the training institutions can, at local level, work together to make decisions on selection, on content, on assessment and on resourcing.

Fieldwork Practice

Fieldwork practice has long been seen as an important element in training. Indeed the organisation and supervision of fieldwork practice has been a major area of co-operation between the training institutions and the field. The need to improve fieldwork practice was nevertheless raised frequently in our consultations. Arranging placements and providing adequate supervision of placements involved a heavy administrative workload both in the field and in the training institutions. Because of this, the tripartite negotiation of suitable placements involving the student, the fieldwork agency and the training institution does not always take place, leaving all the parties involved unclear about the purpose of the placement and about their individual roles in the process. Too often, it is left to the students to make what they can of the situation.

We believe that in moving towards a system of training which encompasses initial and in-service training for full-time, part-time and voluntary workers, it is crucial to re-emphasise the importance of fieldwork practice and its supervision, and to indicate that a major effort should be made to improve the arrangements for it.

We make three recommendations:

(a) that supervised fieldwork practice should be a major element of all training and that around 50% of the training time should be devoted to it;

(b) that an increase or reallocation of resources is needed to support fieldwork placements in two ways:

  i improving the administration of placements;

  ii improving the training of fieldwork supervisors;

(c)   supervised fieldwork training should be of sufficient length to ensure that learning is achieved and supervision ensured.

In addition we suggest that it is necessary to re-examine at a local area level how best to structure the fieldwork practice element of training. There is support, for example, for the creation of student units along the lines of those that exist in social work education. A student unit is an agency set up with specific responsibility for fieldwork training in an area. But we do not consider that this is the only approach which should be examined, or indeed that the method used to support fieldwork training in a rural area where there is a wide dispersion of the population should be the same as that appropriate in an urban area. For that reason we would place the responsibility for devising methods of improving the fieldwork element of training at as local a level as possible.

SUMMARY

We have recommended that a new system of training be set up in which:

(a)   there is a balance between a generic core of knowledge and skill required by the worker in understanding and practising the process of community education and a set of options which provide the worker with expertise in one or more of the specific settings within which community education takes place;

(b)   training is seen as lifelong, with initial and in-service training linked as a continuum which is developmental in nature, and with linkage created between the training of full-time, part-time and voluntary workers;

(c)   the needs of the employers, both in the statutory and in the voluntary sector, are given greater recognition; and

(d)   fieldwork practice is seen as a crucial element and efforts are made to improve its effectiveness in delivery.

TOWARDS A FLEXIBLE TRAINING SYSTEM

Elements of the System

In this section of the report we set out proposals for a system of community education training, which is continuing and coherent. We believe the system of training must possess the following features.

It should provide training opportunities at all levels, from the most elementary to the most advanced.

It has to cater for the needs of a wide variety of people, and we have identified the following groups:

(a)   voluntary or part-time workers wishing to enhance their knowledge and develop their skills in a particular area or arena of community education in which they are already engaged;

(b)   voluntary or part-time workers, engaged and trained in one area or arena, who wish to extend their knowledge and skills into other arenas, perhaps with the aim, ultimately, of acquiring a full community education professional qualification by part-time study;

(c)   people engaged in related fields of activity such as leisure and recreation, social work, teaching or health, who require knowledge and skills in a particular area or arena of community education to enable them to undertake a particular function;

(d)   people who seek full community education professional qualifications by the shortest possible route, i.e. by full-time study;

(e)   existing fully qualified community education workers and trainers who are seeking to enhance their knowledge and skills in particular areas or arenas, as part of their career development.

It has to cater for a wide variety of interests which we see as falling into three broad categories:

(a)   training in the process of community education

(b)   training in the application of the process of community education in the broad arenas of adult education, community work and youth work;

(c)   training in the application of the process of community education in a wide variety of specialist settings such as adult basic education, children's play, health education, leisure education, training related to employment and many more.

It has to be easy of access, readily available to all who require training. This we believe implies a variety of provision including training based in educational institutions such as colleges of education and universities and training based in the field, within both the statutory and voluntary sector. Variety in the ways of gaining access to training for example through full-time study, and through part-time study by means of short courses, regular evening provision over a period of time, distance and open learning is essential.

It has to be flexible and able to adapt quickly as the training needs change in response to changing priorities of practice and policy.

For the individual, the training system should provide a cumulative record of training credits achieved within the system proposed, and recognition of other training, education or experience relevant to community education.

The system of training has to be based on nationally recognised and comparable standards of quality, and yet reflect local needs in its content, methods and organisation.

OUTLINE OF THE PROPOSED STRUCTURE

The notion of arriving at decisions by a process of discussion and negotiation is central to community education. The structure of training which we propose embraces this notion in two principal ways.

Firstly we propose that decisions about community education training should be taken by discussion and negotiation amongst the fieldworkers, the employers and the trainers and to achieve this we propose the setting up of four Area Training Councils and a Scottish Community Education Training Council as forums within which the discussion and negotiation can take place and in which decisions can be taken. Secondly we believe that in the delivery of training a process of discussion and negotiation between the trainers and the learners is essential with regard to the content of training, its context and methods, its assessment and its evaluation. This process of discussion and negotiation is, in our view, an essential feature of the modular training, which we recommend should be introduced. We believe that the setting up of training councils and the introduction of modular training must be linked. Modular training, imposed from the centre without the benefit of the knowledge and experience of the people who work in the field, the employers to whom they are accountable and the trainers themselves would be ineffective and unacceptable.

If all the features outlined are to be developed, we believe that the introduction of a modular approach is one essential. The concept of a modular training is not new. It was proposed in the Carnegy Report; it is practised within many of the community education courses currently offered in colleges of education; increasingly it is being adopted in other areas of education and training, for example in non-advanced further education. What we are advocating in this report is the development of a more systematic structuring of modular training on a Scotland wide basis.

A modular structure does not itself imply any particular content, or method of learning, or method of assessment. These remain matters to be determined by the trainers, in discussion with the field and with those being trained. What modular training implies is a structuring of training into components called modules, each of which is sufficiently autonomous and defined to be a self sufficient unit of training, capable of being related to other modules in a systematic and coherent progression, and capable of being fitted into any individual programme of learning in a variety of ways. In creating a modular system of training it is necessary to have an agreed shape or structure within which each module is designed. To ensure comparability on a national basis, guidelines for module construction require to be created. We see this as a task for the Scottish Community Education Training Council working in co-operation with the Area Training Councils.

D J ALEXANDER, T J I LEACH, T G STEWARD

A STUDY OF POLICY, ORGANISATION AND PROVISION IN COMMUNITY EDUCATION AND LEISURE AND RECREATION IN THREE SCOTTISH REGIONS

DEPARTMENT OF ADULT EDUCATION, UNIVERSITY OF NOTTINGHAM. 1984.
pp 2-3, 430-439, 445-448, 463-466

INTRODUCTION

Aims and Objectives of the Research Study

The aims of the research were to examine the effectiveness and efficiency of the provision of Leisure and Recreation and Community Education Services in selected areas of the Tayside, Central and Fife Regions of Scotland. The project, therefore, studied the various organisational structures and policies at Regional and District level for leisure and recreation and community education to reveal how these, together with professional orientations and attitudes affect the objectives and quality of work done. The project was particularly concerned to study the range, nature, quality, balance and purposes of the programmes offered by the services and to study the nature and patterns of participation. The study involved an examination of linkages, actual or potential co-operation and integration between elements within each service and between the two services.

Community education and leisure and recreation activities undertaken in leisure time are not treated as isolated categories of activity since we perceive them to be related to the social locations of individuals and groups. These activities are considered from the point of view of their social functions, and their contributions to personal growth and development. Leisure activity is seen as part of a spectrum of linked educational, community, recreational and sporting activities related not only to individual psychologies, concepts of "individual sovereignty" and freedom of choice but also to the varying patterns of activities, opportunities and range of choices which are influenced by socio-economic, cultural and historical conditions.

The project examined the aims and objectives of programmes in community education and leisure and recreation and the extent to which those programmes may be seen as "developmental" for individuals and groups in terms of the development of physical, creative and reflective skills, knowledge, confidence and social awareness...

Conclusions on Overall Patterns of Policy and Organisation

Evidence ranging from interviews with senior staff, participants and studies of particular community education and leisure and recreation centres indicates that policy is made in very general terms. Where priorities are laid down, staff frequently report that little guidance existed as to how they should be pursued or about adjustments in existing programmes to accommodate them.

Policy may be seen as emanating from

(a) long-term perceptions and assumptions concerning the functions of youth and community work, informal further education, adult basic education and leisure and recreation in society. Views and values held by staff on these matters affect the nature of provision and practice and the development of links between the various areas of work, yet they are often reluctant to be explicit. This is because long-term policy matters are conventionally the preserve of elected members and because, especially amongst community education staff, there is the view that provision and policy should be responsive to the particular requirements, needs and interests of the people in the localities in which they work.

(b) In the context of 'responsiveness', management does not wish to constrain fieldworkers from developing relatively autonomous and flexible modes of provision by imposing more specific policy objectives, but, does at the same time wish to provide support and guidance so that the worker does not experience isolation in the face of the myriad of demands and needs he or she faces in the task of decision making on the allocation of financial and human resources. Our evidence from all three regions in community education and leisure and recreation indicates that workers do express their need of more support and guidance in this decision making. Policy at this level is then not only to do with views and assumptions about long-term functions but also to do with the organisational frameworks in which staff operate, with staff deployment, with the types of facilities in and with which they operate and the allocation of financial resources.

(c) It is evident in all three regions that policy and the workers' perceptions of their long-term functions are fundamentally affected by the structures and professional orientations which existed prior to local government reorganisation, as well as the development of Community Education Services and more composite departments of Leisure and Recreation.

While much consideration is given to the ways in which policy and structure might lead to more efficient and effective cooperation, practice is dominated by disparate professional traditions in youth and community work, informal further education, adult basic education, and leisure and recreation. In overall policy and organisational terms there is a pressing need for better cooperation, understanding and coordination between the work of different local government services if balanced and effective programmes of recreational, educational and youth and community work are to become more accessible. There is a lack of conceptual understanding of the potential links between the various areas of work.

Workers' perceptions of long-term functions and policy stemming from historical and professional traditions and orientations may be characterised as follows:

(a) *Youth work* has consisted of heterogeneous fields of activity resulting largely in the provision of social and recreational activities for young people but significantly affected by the importance given to 'social education' and to the importance of raising self-confidence through 'non-directive' contact and group work. The work is seen as being responsive to local needs and as contributing to individual and social development. *Community work* has been added but concepts and practice in neighbourhood work, outreach, participation and community development have not been fully analysed or followed through. Inherent tensions and ambiguities as to the long-term purposes and functions of youth and community work continue – compensation, care, support, socialisation, policing, enriched recreation and leisure, 'non-directive' social education, more structured and rigorous education are all areas which contribute to the problematic nature of defining objectives, policy and priorities. The role of 'facilitator' for example is clearly an important and valid one particularly at the point of initial contact and confidence raising; however, in the context of community education, if the functions of the worker are limited in practice to that of a facilitator and manager of social, community and recreative services, a major and significant part of his function disappears. He or she as an educator must be concerned with the scope and range of the programme of community education activities to develop work of genuine educational value as well as recreative participation in pastimes, information giving and social participation. These objectives and activities may be linked and lead onto one another. It is recognised that one of the major strains on the community educator in the field is a proliferation of tasks and a frequent absence of prioritisation, guidance, appropriate support and effective in-service education. But if the service is to be an educational one then clearly educational objectives must not be submerged and should be more carefully delineated and prepared for.

(b) *Informal further education* or non-vocational adult education has employed very few full-time professionals in regional and district authorities and there is little sign of a secure career structure developing. Educational programmes have been and continue to be based largely on a 'for leisure' view of education and have not involved a significant amount of outreach, issue-based or more cognitive work, although a certain amount of work with 'disadvantaged' groups has been developed. More responsive outreach and community-based approaches to provision still need to be developed. (Adult basic education has in some cases developed more responsive approaches and has educational objectives which supersede 'for leisure' approaches).

(c) *Leisure and Recreation* provision has been based largely on a tradition of making facilities available to the public on an open 'democratic' basis. Outreach and participatory approaches are being developed in some areas and more recent objectives have involved notions of learning and personal growth but these have not significantly affected large areas of practice.

All three areas of work then converge in practice on 'leisure' and 'the problem of leisure' but from differing perspectives, purposes and professional traditions. There is no agreed and comprehensive view of community education and its relationships with leisure and recreation, nor is there a clear consensus on its values, functions and purposes. In terms of its effectiveness different criteria may be adopted. If a recreational 'for leisure' view is taken together with ideas concerning 'social education' in which, for example, informal group contact between full-time and part-time professionals and youth groups is, on its own, defined as 'education', then the provision of recreational and physical activities together with confidence raising group work of various kinds at a basic level may be perceived as sufficient. It frequently contains little that can be described as developmental although viewed within the context of the traditions referred to it is valid in terms of a basic level of provision. The evidence is that the emphasis of programmes in community education and informal further education in the three regions fall largely into this category as do district leisure and recreation programmes. The quality of much youth work and 'social education' is questionable and a high proportion of senior and field level professionals express their legitimate concern for this area of work as do participants. Programmes do not adequately take into account the range of functional and developmental objectives in education which the Alexander Report recommended community education should contribute to an active participatory democracy and individual growth. Issue based and more cognitive educational work have not developed significantly and community education workers from youth and community traditions have understandable difficulties in adding or integrating educational orientations and skills into their practice and policy objectives, given the wide range of demands already made on their time.

Despite the differing organisational arrangements (characterised as 'comprehensive' in Fife with ABE under FE; 'separate' in Tayside but with a comprehensive CES including ABE' and 'unintegrated' in Central Region), linkages both between component parts of community education (youth and community work, informal further education, ABE) and between Community Education Services and Leisure and Recreation are rarely very strong. Where they do exist and work well the linkages depend largely on individuals who have worked out clear purposes for co-operation (eg. a youth and community worker and an ABE worker cooperating to develop a programme of women's education).

Organisational arrangements do not of themselves create effective collaboration and the ways in which staff see their functions are of central importance. To assume a commonality of aims and approaches may well obscure understanding. Co-operation depends on a clear specification of functions and purposes at district and regional levels of local government services. A clearer understanding of differences in functions would assist collaboration and help to avoid territorial conflicts which have been evident between, for example, youth and community work, youth and informal further education and ABE workers. This analysis does not imply a concept of either generic community education or leisure and recreation work but a differentiation of functions and degrees of specialisation. This might foster the development of functional cooperation which could achieve a higher quality of work in community education and leisure and recreation. Youth work for example, could benefit from collaboration with informal further education and/or ABE workers in developing valuable educational programmes in community centres and elsewhere. The informal further education and ABE workers would benefit in terms of learning from face-to-face contact with young people and the development of more responsive community based educational strategies useful for other areas of their educational work.

Specialisation of functions does however depend on how effectively staff are able to decide on priorities, and overall policies do not provide clear advice and support in this task. But informal prioritisation of a kind does take place between what we term 'mainstream' and 'special' provision and there is a tension between the two.

In Leisure and Recreation Services 'mainstream' consists of the provision, management, maintenance and improvement of facilities for indoor and outdoor recreational and sporting facilities. 'Special' provision is made by sports officers, leisure-leaders and others involved in face-to-face work with members of the public.

In Community Education Services mainstream provision differs between different branches in the service. In youth and community work 'mainstream' provision consists of a relatively fixed weekly programme of activities in community centres involving youth clubs, mothers and toddlers, OAPs lunch clubs, an unemployed group and a Family Night. Keeping the door open to all is seen as an essential part of the task. In informal further education 'mainstream' work consists of conventional, largely physical and craft based leisure classes. 'Special' provision involves work with 'disadvantaged' groups such as the 'unemployed' and 'women' and issue-based and outreach work of various kinds. At times part of the mainstream work becomes 'special' in the sense that many workers feel that youth work for example is not being given sufficient attention.

What is clear is that if 'disadvantaged groups' and traditional non-participants are to benefit more and if a greater degree of distributive justice is to be achieved in both Community Education and Leisure and Recreation Services then clear priorities will have to be developed and that on the basis of these priorities, resources and support reallocated. To argue in policy terms that facilities are 'democratically' open to all is insufficient and leaves out of account:

(a)   the concept and fact of latent demand demonstrated in, for example, responsive and community based adult basic education in Central Region and in the Stirling district Sports Scheme.

(b)   the pattern and nature of participation which is largely determined by the professional suppliers and by the patterns of existing and previous usage. This demonstrates neither responsiveness nor more genuinely democratic and innovatory approaches to provision but the views of professionals as to what should or can be feasibly supplied.

(c)   the importance of national and local social, economic and cultural forces which fundamentally influence patterns of participation and the nature of expressed needs.

The issues involved in the tensions between 'mainstream' and 'special' provision relate to problems of 'outreach' work and responsiveness and to problems of organisational change and development. Staff in both Community Education and Leisure and Recreation Services claim to be 'responsive to local needs' and responsiveness is perceived to be an important target of organisational and staffing arrangements. All of the organisations and units studied exist within hierarchical local government structures but there are, in overall terms, differences in approach and organisation between both Leisure and Recreation and Community Education and among the units of each service. These are characterised as follows: Leisure and Recreation operates largely on a line management structure in which relative to Community Education and youth and community work, there are fewer professionals in the field and more manual workers, sports officers, leisure leaders and sports instructors who have innovatory and outreach approaches and are concerned with the development of 'special' provision, are frequently separate from the main management structure which is concerned largely with the maintenance of 'mainstream' facilities and provision and so may be marginal to decision-making structures concerned with policy, programmes and the allocation of financial and human resources.

In Community Education and youth and community work a main component and principle of policy is that the services should be responsive to local needs. There are many more full-time professionals in the field and it is recognised in principle that community education workers should have a degree of responsibility, autonomy and discretion in the allocation of resources based on negotiation with members of the public on their terms, with Centre Management Committees and with other appropriate organisations in the community.

In district Leisure and Recreation departments the notion of responsiveness differs in that there is a planning orientation and responsiveness enters into the planning process through consultation between senior staff and elected members, discussion with voluntary organisations and clubs, informal discussions between staff and participants and, infrequently, questionnaires and surveys. Goals are set by policy-makers. The process of policy-making is conceived as one in which needs are taken into account and are then implemented by locally based staff at lower levels of the hierarchy. Negotiations at field level with members of the public at the point of contact with the service is then constrained organisationally within narrower limits than in Community Education and Youth and Community Services. There are fewer professionals available to develop outreach and more responsive approaches and they are in terms of time and practice concerned with the maintenance and efficient management of facilities. Having said that, it is clear in practice that due to the tensions between 'mainstream' and 'special', the lack of prioritisation, the proliferation of tasks and the emphasis by senior and middle management on the importance of the efficient maintenance and management of facilities, many community education and youth and community workers find themselves similarly constrained in relation to negotiation, responsiveness, effective outreach work, and innovation despite stated policy principles.

Both Community Education Services and Leisure and Recreation organisational structures attempt to be responsive; both have hierarchies of decision-making and accountability at the top of which are elected members and senior management and in theory policy is arrived at through negotiations with officials and members of the public at different levels of the organisation. But some of the more important responsive, innovatory, outreach and 'special' programme developments in community education and leisure and recreation which have involved traditional non-participants and disadvantaged groups and have moved away from 'for leisure' and 'mainstream' programmes to varying degrees of developmental work, have been implemented through different kinds of organisational structures.

In the past local authorities have frequently developed extended decision-making structures and lines of authority which tend not to be efficient in responding to changing circumstances. Responsiveness requires organisational flexibility, information about local purposes and needs and the capacity to act quickly in response to changing conditions. Our research shows that effective change occurs where channels of communication are short; when a latent demand is systematically uncovered by a programme with clearly defined objectives; and where staff have a degree of specialism, commitment, self-confidence, and the resources to negotiate programmes with members of the public where need may not be initially openly expressed or made explicit.

The various constituent elements that have historically come together to form a Community Education Service together with the development of adult basic education, of sports provision and of Leisure and Recreation departments serve a wide range of complementary and often overlapping purposes and functions. However no single organisational model is suitable for achieving such diverse purposes and functions and the effective development of practice throughout the range of these areas may well demand the creation of different and appropriate organisational structures.

With much of the introductory work, either in a social or leisure setting, confidence building efforts and responses to local needs may be best met by small locally based specialist teams. That is where goals and objectives cannot be pre-determined small specialist teams are necessary to negotiate with potential participants at the point of delivery.

However, it is equally clear that specialist units are necessary not only at a local centre level but also at a District and Regional level and that hierarchical structures must emerge in many areas to link and coordinate these specialist units...

On the Need for the Creation of Developmental Structures and Specialist Functions

What emerges from this overall review of policy, organisation and participation in Community Education and Leisure and Recreation is the lack of functionally linked and developmental structures and programmes in both Community Education Services and Leisure and Recreation which are capable of providing effective access, especially for the disadvantaged and poorer sections of society. As stated elsewhere, this conclusion neither implies that workers are generally complacent nor that they lack a developmental intent but that they are hampered by a variety of factors ranging from the lack of defined priorities and of appropriate allocation of resources to the inherent tensions and ambiguities involved in overlapping areas of work. There does exist a basic level of provision but there is not an overall tendency for taster or confidence building programmes to lead any further. Fairly low level introductory programmes frequently continue virtually the same in nature year after year with few developing or linking programmes for cognitive, cultural, sporting and recreational growth. For example, there is a massive educational opportunity gap between 'social education' in community centres for young unemployed people and effective access to credit or non-credit courses in FE, College and University programmes or more advanced art, craft and drama work.

As participation in Central community education and leisure and recreation programmes is more representative of the population in terms of age and social class than in either Fife or Tayside there is no simple relationship between more apparently integrated structures of youth and communty work, informal further education, ABE and leisure and recreation and the quality of work done or participation by lower income groups.

Attempts to create organisational integration and cooperation between previously distinct traditions in youth and community work, informal further education and adult basic education have not been generally effective in the field. A 'community development' approach to adult education has failed to emerge. There is generally little effective contact between youth and community education workers and informal further and adult basic education workers at field level. Constructive signs of cooperation do appear but are often dependent upon particular individuals.

Effective corporate management of resources in the Regions in terms of linkage between Regional educational authorities and District Leisure and Recreation is slow to merge. With a number of exceptions again largely dependent upon individuals there is little effective contact between leisure and recreation workers and youth and community, informal further and adult education workers. The development of functional links between these areas remains of real importance to the creation of effective access to a range of linked and developmental opportunities. Our evidence points to the effectiveness of relatively small specialist teams which have informal network management styles providing both a high degree of autonomy and support. Such teams in ABE, Sports Development, the Arts and the Countryside Ranger Service have created often small but recognisable structures of opportunity for growth and development and have uncovered latent demand attracting traditional non-participants and members of 'disadvantaged' groups . . . .

Conclusions on Policy, Organisation and Programmes in Adult, Community and Informal Further Education, Youth and Community Work

This section is concerned particularly to examine how far effective access to developmental and linked structures of cultural, cognitive and issue based education have been developed in the three regions and to examine what might be done to improve on the present situation. It is recognised that there have been major financial constraints but a crucial evaluation of the Alexander recommendations is the evaluation of the various forms in which local government has organised provision and of the pattern, nature and quality of programmes of community education involving youth and community work, informal further education and ABE workers. Attention is also paid to the nature of Arts programme in this section.

The evidence shows that in all three regions there exists a basic level of 'mainstream' youth and community and community education work based on community centres, with programmes which are often recreational and social, but with some developmental and educational programmes. However, there is little sign in mainstream youth and community work and communty education of deliberate and systematic programming for the creation of developmental work.

By training and experience, most youth and community work and community education workers do have a general developmental focus and intent, but the burdens of administration and the difficulties of prioritisation in terms of objectives, prevent them from decisively creating, with participants, more purposive and balanced programmes. The majority adopt what are termed 'non-directive' approaches to educational work. They tend to see more cognitive and structured educational work as being 'elitist'. Though it has traditionally attracted and continues predominantly to attract people with higher levels of formal education, more cognitive education is not of itself elitist, although patterns of access have been seen to reinforce existing educational inequalities. But, if the Community Education Services are to establish more developmental and educational structures, the creation of effective access for all members of the community to a more cognitive and intellectually challenging curriculum is essential. If there are valuable areas of knowledge to which only some sections of the community have traditionally had access it is not 'elitist' to suggest that those areas of knowledge are equally valuable to those who have traditionally not enjoyed such access.

The 'non-directive' approach is in a sense confusing in that it implies that what the professional workers say is likely to be more influential in a group of people than what anyone else says. Perhaps more important is that individuals have frequently interpreted the approach to mean that structured teaching and the development and creation of knowledge and learning through such methods are almost forms of 'cognitive imperialism'. Frequently youth and community workers and community education workers view and have experienced teachers as people who impose their knowledge upon others and who have failed in the past to benefit many participants in youth and community work. Youth and community workers therefore often wish to care for people in other ways which are frequently non-challenging, which provide comfort and assist people to resolve their difficulties. While non-directive methods have their place, workers frequently do not have sufficiently developed areas of knowledge and skills to create appropriate curricula and learning methods for particular groups of participants or for non-participants. *In sum, they have not been adequately prepared and trained to develop effective learning and do not have effective educational approaches to their work.*

The tendency to confuse with 'elitism' intellectually valuable and more cognitive educational work, which may well be issue and community based, is unfortunate because its absence does contribute to a reinforcement of educational disadvantage. Many youth and community work and community education workers see, with some justification, traditional adult education and informal further education as tending only to assist individuals rather than the 'community' as a whole. Workers emphasise their commitment to development of inter-personal and communication skills and the raising of social confidence and esteem through non-directive group work and see 'teaching' and systematic structured learning as inappropriate. There are however dangers in basing a programme of activities and learning solely on a locally defined community and on the understanding that it must be 'relevant' to the local culture. 'Relevance' only to a local and 'deprived' sub-culture may mean a narrow and third rate programme of activity and learning which once more reinforces educational disadvantage and denies access to an analysis of why it is 'deprived'. Such programmes do not challenge elitism and educational inequalities but reinforce them.

In evaluating the balance of a broadly defined curriculum of learning and activity in community education it is necessary to seek a vital strand of work in the area of systematic learning and analysis which may be related to identified needs and social issues in the community and to work concerned directly with intellectual development. The development of an understanding of wider social issues and of an active participatory democracy requires that learning and analysis of a rigorous and systematic nature are a recognisable part of the structure and programme, and are accessible in real terms to all adults. This essential strand of work is frequently absent. The major objective of the recommendations in the Alexander Report and of the reorganisation of adult education and youth and community work, which was to develop a strong, broadly based and highly professional system of education for adults providing effective access for the majority and for 'disadvantaged' groups to balanced and developmental programmes of social, cultural, recreational and cognitive education has not been achieved to a significant extent. To repeat, there is an enormous gap in educational opportunities between 'social education', confidence building, and much adult basic education and informal further education and the credit and non-credit programmes of further and advanced education to which the majority who leave school with little or nothing in the way of education qualifications do not have effective access. Neither is there effective access for this majority to programmes and activities which derive from local issues, concerns and needs, nor to programmes which would assist individuals to develop skills to enhance their participation in their community, family and personal lives. The structure, staffing and programmes in community education in the three Regions do not adequately fill this gap, so that the possibilities for the vast majority of individuals and groups to develop educationally beyond basic levels are not sufficiently provided by local authorities nor by any other agency.

Alexander was also concerned to allocate educational resources in Scotland in such a way as to promote personal development, discussion of operative social issues and an active democratic society.

It is necessary at this point to say something further about the functions of education. Education is concerned to develop effective and systematic learning. That is the objective. Education is organised so that learning may take place. Learning does of course take place outside educational structures but may be incidental to the activity of which the major objectives may be social, participatory, recreational or enjoyment. The educator may hope and plan that participants enjoy the process of learning and develop participatory or discussion methods. These may be useful and necessary for the attainment of educational objectives but the major purpose of the activity is the quality of learning and not recreation, social participation or enriched leisure. Learning may sometimes be difficult and painful although it may be argued that much satisfaction, pleasure and confidence are derived from the achievement of difficult tasks in an appropriate curriculum. These arguments apply to, for example, social education with unemployed groups who are frequently well aware that they are being sold short educationally as well as in other ways.

In the light of this, a significant part of the task of community educators is to create situations in which young people and adults learn systematically what they and the educator jointly agree it is useful for them to learn. Education may well involve emotional and social learning as well as cognitive development but the latter must not be by-passed because it appears to be more difficult. The objective of the educator is to develop skills, abilities, and understanding of fields of knowledge whether issue or subject based, as far as the educator and the group can or decide to go. In the absence of a linking and developmental educational perspective there is a danger of producing an array of discontinuous and ad hoc activities.

The following points concerning education in the context of community development are in our view crucial to an understanding of the meaning of community education. Participants must also be able to place what they learn in an intelligible context, in which their interests become clearer and more surely understood, in which their awareness of society or the physical world is increased, and in which their consciousness of their own position is heightened. Contact and communication between community education professionals and members of the public and the development of good relationships are necessary activities and may be perceived as one basis for developmental and educational programmes. But of themselves they are not sufficient, and they may be linked to educational programmes which lead to further growth, involvement and change. These programmes may involve practical and participatory activity related to the nature of the issues, subject matter and the present ability and knowledge of participants.

Community education, like leisure and recreation, should not be perceived as a commodity for passive consumption, but as a programme of active development. Having said this we can identify a list (not exhaustive) of functional objectives which may assist in examining the nature, quality and balance of activities in both community education and leisure and recreation.

These functional objectives are placed in hierarchical form but are clearly inter-related and overlap so that, for example, an individual or group may be gaining information and data concerning welfare rights and in addition be engaged in an educational programme concerned to identify and analyse the causes of current high levels of unemployment. In youth and community work an individual or group may be participating in recreation in the countryside and at the same time developing their understanding of the nature of the environment and issues in conservation. In addition, the model assists us to perceive interconnections between community education and youth and community work objectives and between physical, emotional, social and intellectual development.

Whereas in introductory programmes, the objectives may well be related to both the development of personal confidence and skills, abilities and knowledge, in other programmes and activities, the principal objective is the development of more advanced levels of skills, ability, knowledge and analysis, and confidence raising may well be an effect, rather than prime objective . . . .

General Implications and Recommendations for the Future Development of Community Education

If a more balanced developmental programme of community education is to be created constructive discussion could take place around the following:

(a)   Given our conclusions on the need for a more responsive and developmental structure to emerge in both Services, it is suggested that more specialist teams with clearly defined tasks, objectives and priorities be created with specialist workers developing functional cooperation with other teams as necessary and appropriate. These teams would have an important contribution to make to the quality of youth work, recreational sport and informal further education for example. Teamwork with other workers outside each unit in this context implies cooperation between specialists, who have a clear overall view of relationships between different areas of work, towards linked objectives.

Integrated teams made up of workers with different specialisms or teams made up of generic workers with little effective specialism based on an assumption that all workers can tackle a wide range of recreational and educational tasks do not appear to succeed in creating effective contact for particular purposes. What appears to be required is the development of clear policy priorities followed up by support and allocation of resources and the appointment and training of specialist staff capable of conceptual and practical understanding of the relationships and links between different areas of work.

(b)   The evidence then points to the need to educate, train and appoint workers with specialist skills rather than generic community education workers and leisure and recreation managers who both tend to have less direct face-to-face contact with members of the public. This vital and fundamental task is frequently left to part-time workers, private instructors or volunteers, while full-time professionals spend very high proportions of their time managing facilities and resources. This emphasis on facility and resource management does not effectively create responsive and developmental programmes. As noted in (e) below part-time voluntary workers clearly do have a significant and valuable role to play. However in our view the role of the full-time professional in creating innovatory work and developmental structures is crucial.

c)   There is a need to prioritise educational and youth and community work objectives more clearly and to allocate resources and in-service and pre-service education and training on that basis. Workers cannot be expected to take on everything and specialisms need to be developed if the capacity to work effectively with particular groups, issues and interests is to be created. This applies to youth work and to outreach work in responsive community based adult education and/or informal further education. More full-time specialist staff are required for these areas of work and these might be obtained (i) through releasing youth and community workers and community education workers from centre based administrative work and providing them with appropriate specialist training, (ii) through the nature of future appointments which need to be based on a variety of qualifications. Appointments should be made more open and the notion of basing the profession of community education, with its requirements for varying specialism and expertise, predominantly on one major qualification needs to be changed, (iii) through the development of specialisms in pre-service and in-service training.

(d)   Priorities emerging from our study are for the creation of appropriate systematic learning for (i) youth work, particularly 'outreach' and work with the so-called 'unattached'; (ii) the unemployed (particularly the mature male and female unemployed, and young female unemployed); (iii) women; (iv) persons with low levels of formal education and functional literacy and numeracy; (v) the retired, particularly women.

These programmes of work all require the development of social awareness and a cognitive understanding of the causation of difficulties and problems experienced.

(e)   Effective educational work and activity in the areas indicated in (d) require face-to-face work by full-time community education, youth and community, informal further education and ABE workers. In some instances this might mean serious consideration being given to the possibility of changing the balance of part-time paid workers to full-time professional workers in order to pay for the employment of full-time professionals. Serious consideration might also be given to the nature of part-time work and the variety of skills both required and available. Education and related activities for the young unemployed, women and the elderly for example frequently cannot be effectively carried out by enthusiastic but not sufficiently skilled part-timers and volunteers. Such programmes require highly motivated and skilled full-time educational workers if the excellence and high quality which participants deserve are to be created. This is in no way to suggest that part-time workers and volunteers do not have a major and qualitatively significant role to play, but to emphasise the importance that full-time workers have in the creation of innovative, responsive and high quality programmes and in the training of part-timers and volunteers. It is also recognised that there are policy difficulties in employing more full-time staff even if overall costs are not increased but the issues must be raised if the question of the quality of work done is to be addressed.

(f)   If responsive developmental and linked programmes of cultural, recreational, educational and issue-based activity which derive from local and national concerns are to be created, workers must have the skills and the time to develop with individuals and groups an analysis of needs, issues and latent and expressed demand in the area in which they work.

(g) All of the above imply that community education, informal further education and youth and community workers have education and training needs which are not at present being adequately met.

The evidence points to the following requirements:-

(i) *Skills and knowledge related to particular subject areas,* which can be applied to the creation of appropriate curricula based on needs, issues and problems. For example it is perfectly possible in youth work to base systematic learning leading to social awareness, scientific, musical and technical skills on an analysis of popular music. However the fundamental task of ensuring that adequate physical provision of a social focus for young people remains, together with the challenge of creating appropriate curricula of learning and activity for young people that will truly assist them in their personal, social and educational development. That curriculum should clearly be related to the concerns, interests, purpose and problems that actually confront young people in their everyday lives. Related to this is the need for professionals to develop an appropriate range of informal and more formal educational methods. Unemployed groups, young and old, can develop work of genuine intellectual and social value through structured study of the causes and effects of unemployment. 'Social education' for such groups as presently conducted is less than adequate. Health education and women's education are other examples of work which require systematic learning leading to both social awareness and potentially to material improvements.

(ii) *Skills in teaching and tutoring.* A wide range of participatory and structured teaching and learning methods should be a major part of the workers' equipment. The essential art is the development of the capacity to flexibly move from one method to another as the situation changes. This requires confidence and practical experience.

(iii) *Skills in social and economic analysis.*

(iv) *The necessary conceptual and theoretical background for the understanding of links between the various areas of work.* The lack of this background has serious practical effects in that it creates continual confusion amongst workers as to their functions and priorities. The conceptual confusion and the proliferation of tasks often leads to a decline in morale; a retreat into administration and day to day management; a submersion in routine tasks; and a significant movement away from face-to-face contact with members of the public. If the worker understands more clearly his functions and purposes he has the conceptual tools and the knowledge to avoid these tendencies. If workers grasp the often problematic nature of relationships between various objectives and functions in community education and leisure and recreation they are clearly better equipped to deal with them and are better protected against loss of morale. In addition to this understanding, the development of specialist skills and work will enable the worker to enjoy a sense of satisfaction derived from involvement in high quality tasks directly with members of the public.

(v) *Training, both in-service and pre-service, for the effective management of the development of innovatory and responsive educational programmes,* and for decision making in the crucial area of prioritisation of objectives, programmes, groups and future development.

(vi) *Education and training in the area of evaluation, both formative and summative.* This implies the necessity of developing a range of skills and procedures with which to test out the extent to which overall programmes reflect existing and latent demand, and inform future policy and programme development. Clearly professional staff have a significant role to play in the active development of research, in the normal process of programme and policy development and planning.

COLIN KIRKWOOD
KEY TEXTS IN COMMUNITY
VULGAR ELOQUENCE

EDINBURGH: POLYGON. 1990

What we are going to do is try to trace, mainly from written evidence – from three key texts – the evolution of a new profession, which is just twelve years old. It is a profession, or service, in which a lot of hopes were invested. In a sense it belongs to that era, the late 1960s, when hopes were high and central government set up committees to investigate and restructure various aspects of public service provision. You could argue that The Alexander Report, *Adult Education: The Challenge of Change*, arrived too late. The Committee of Enquiry was established in 1970 and didn't report until 1975, by which time there was an economic crisis, which persisted and worsened. It was hardly an auspicious time for a new service to get off the ground, a service which depended for the realisation of its hopes not only on the integration of two previously separate services but on the expectation that the state would invest substantial amounts of new money. Alexander spelled out what was wanted: an extra million pounds per year at 1974 prices as a permanent addition to the bill, plus an extra £70,000 a year for five years.

Before we begin to look at the Alexander Report in depth, let me remind you of two important human factors. We shouldn't over-estimate their importance, but we should be aware of them. The world of the youth service and the world of adult education were very different. Adult education was organised by men in suits, well-groomed men in collars and ties and polished shoes. They ran classes in evening institutes, usually in schools used at night, or in a few cases in specially adapted adult education centres. They were a respectable lot. They saw themselves as educators. They had degrees. The youth service was different. It was also run by male workers, but they tended to be more informal, with open-necked shirts, jerseys and sleeves rolled up. They ran youth clubs, with table tennis, dancing, football, other sports and perhaps work-camps or community service. They had youth work training. There was often a social class division between these two services, a blurred division rather than a sharp one. Adult education classes attracted more middle-class, better-educated, older people, while youth work had a rougher element along with the respectable kids; it had more of a working-class presence and, of course, by definition, it was young.

These two worlds had fairly negative views of each other. Adult education tended to look down its nose at the youth service. It wasn't rigorous, it wasn't education, just containment. Ping-pong and coca-cola. The youth service regarded adult education with a certain amount of contempt: it was too formal, too polite, nose-in-the-air, middle class, cut off from real people with real problems in the real world. This factor of inter-service rivalry really existed, but has now largely receded into the background. It's reflected to some extent in the other human factor I want to touch on: the rivalry between the two types of training agency. By and large adult educators got their training in universities. Youth workers were trained on the job, as assistant leaders, and got in-service training at weekends, or else through doing full-time training courses at Colleges of Education. There was (and still is) a rivalry between these two types of training agency. It is not the same as the first rivalry, but it influences and is influenced by it. It wasn't only a matter of degrees: most college staff did have degrees, though they often got them by routes other than that of going straight from school to university. It had to do with the relative status of the two types of agency and with the orientation of the training provided. The universities had a basically conceptual and historical orientation, whereas the colleges were centred more on practical skills.

I don't want to over-emphasise these factors, but they are there, and they have been at work in some of the difficulties and conflicts experienced in community education over the past twelve years. It could be argued that, even if you agree with the Alexander prescription for an integrated Community Education Service, it singularly fails to take into account as a factor in the process of integration, the human relations issues arising out of these inter-service and inter-institutional rivalries.

Turning to the Alexander Report, it is worth stressing that it is a report about adult education. Its aim is to advance the cause of adult education, and its chosen method is the creation of a Community Education Service incorporating adult education with youth and community work. It is concerned with voluntary leisure time courses for adults which are educational but not specifically vocational. It takes careful note of the present position: a provision involving just over 4 per cent of the population, 72 per cent of them women, mainly middle class, generally well educated, and with a disproportionately high number of people over fifty-five. The report describes adult education students as 'the older, the better educated, the more affluent.' (Brian Groombridge was making a similar point when he asserted that adult education was stuck in a lower middle-class ghetto.) The main subject areas are categorised as physical training, needlecraft, and handicrafts and hobbies. Local Education Authorities provide for 87 per cent of the total number of students, Extra-mural Departments 10 per cent, the WEA 2 per cent and the central institutions 1 per cent.

Alexander wants to expand the volume of provision, and to redistribute it. He aims to double the number of students by the mid 1980s. He calls for 200 more full-time workers, and for emphasis generally on the socially, educationally and economically disadvantaged, and specifically on such special groups as young mothers, the elderly, those with literacy problems, immigrants, prisoners, the physically and mentally handicapped, shiftworkers, those working unsocial hours, people in long-term residence in hospital (whether physically or mentally ill, or geriatric), and people living in what are described as areas of multiple deprivation. The report has a cultural deficit view of these groups: it uses the phrase cycle of deprivation, leading to a notion of education as remedial.

Returning to the key structural prescription, listen carefully to the words used. Adult education is to be seen in community education as an element with specific characteristics and requirements, but sharing common aims with the other element (youth work), and needing its resources and expertise. You'll notice how far this is from the later concepts of generic community education and a single community education process. As I've already said, Alexander is not calling just for crude expansion, but for change and qualitative improvement. He suggests that the universities should use a community development approach to stimulating involvement. He argues for research into what subjects, themes, activities and methods will prove attractive in different areas and different social milieux. He attacks the division between intellectual and practical provision. He proposes certain new structures: a National Community Educational Council (happened), Scottish Education Department grants towards the teaching costs in developmental work (didn't happen), regional advisory councils (tried in one region but didn't really prosper), and the creation of adult education centres (hardly any).

Although the report touches on the question of the numerical balance of full-time staff as between adult education and youth work (1:7), it doesn't tackle the problems of integration inherent in such an imbalance, contenting itself with soft soap about both services having the same objectives, and the potential gains through economies of scale. As you know, this was the argument used in every case of structural integration and increases in scale in the organisation of government services in the 60s and 70s, often – incredible as it may now seem – in combination with arguments about the devolution of decision-making to local levels.

At the time, Henry Arthur Jones, quoting the limerick:

> 'There was a young lady from Riga
> Who went for a ride on a tiger.
> They came from the ride
> With the lady inside
> And a smile on the face of the tiger'

implied that there was a danger of adult education getting swallowed up by the youth service. He was proved right in one sense but wrong in another, for it was generic community education that was to swallow up the resources available for both adult education and youth work, as we shall see.

In discussing the development of training the report called for flexible entry so that people without first degrees could get in, and for expansion in the role of the Universities. Universities, Colleges, employers and the Open University were to collaborate to provide in-service training for full and part-time staff. With regard to the principles underlying training, the report called for a common purpose, cutting out wasteful duplication and competition. It argued that training for each sector (adult education, youth work, and community work) should not be isolated, and

> 'the common core of knowledge and expertise concerned with adult education
> should be included within training schemes for each of the other sectors.'

Discussing how the sectors should relate, Alexander describes adult education and the youth service as having overlapping functions and that there should be common elements in the training of both groups. These terms common elements and common core, used in evolving and finally quite different ways, reverberate down the history of community education in Scotland over the last thirteen years. The struggle around their meaning was the focus of a running battle between colleges and universities seeking to defend or expand their share of the market for training in a context of shrinking resources.

Here are a few of the remaining Alexander recommendations:

–   a dual fee system, of economic fees side by side with aided fees, whose aim was to free resources for priority work;

–   fees to be waived altogether for the sixteen to eighteen-year-olds, pensioners and the disadvantaged;

–   flexibility on minimum class numbers;

–   incentives to employers to grant paid educational leave;

–   management councils for adult education centres, with staff and student representation;

–   students' associations where centres were big enough;

–   the WEA to concentrate on the educational needs of the socially, economically and educationally disadvantages; education authorities to seek its help in making the relevant provision;

–   the establishment of a residential college for industrial relations training;

–   education authorities to establish counselling services;

–   each education authority to appoint an Assistant Director with specific responsibility for adult education.

How are we to assess the Alexander Report? My view is that it is a workmanlike job, well researched and thorough. Its various recommendations hang together, and all run in the same direction. The whole package depends on the availability of a considerable amount of new investment in full-time staff, buildings, and training, which never appeared. In another sense it is very much of its time. It is structural, integrative, expansionist, top-down, and male. It has a passive-objects-of-improvement attitude to people. It avoids saying anything about class or other conflicts of interest. It is outer-orientated, rather than inner-orientated. It is rational and orderly in the Scottish way, but it is not philosophical: it doesn't wrestle with questions of value or ideology. It speaks the language of service and provision. Finally, its key recommendation, the integration of adult education and the youth service, failed to achieve its stated aim of the expansion, redirection and qualitative improvement of adult education in Scotland.

Let's pass on to the report of the Working Party on Professional Training for Community Education, known as the *Carnegy Report*. The Working Party was created, very shortly after Alexander was published, by the Scottish Institute of Adult Education and the Standing Consultative Council on Youth and Community Service, and it reported in February 1977, reflecting an eagerness to get training for the new Service under way. We are only a little way into Carnegy, however, when we realise that things have moved on. There is reference to:

> the common core of knowledge and skills required by almost all community education workers

already a fundamental departure from Alexander. Grand claims are made for community education:

> the significance of community education for the well-being of society, for the quality of life in communities, and for the personal fulfilment of individuals is now widely recognised and

Community education taps the springs of voluntary initiative and service.

This is clearly promotional hyperbole, since, at the time of writing, the Service was just getting off the ground. It may be that it was felt necessary to hype community education in order to gain extra resources in a time of economic stringency. But the trouble with hype is that gaps can open up between claim and performance. Carnegy sets itself the task of creating a general impression of what community education is, but not giving a precise definition. This is justified, it claims, because

> it is the needs and responses of individuals and groups which must determine the nature of community education ...

This is the first of many refusals to define community education. As the needs and responses change, the report goes on, so should the nature and specific aims of community education. Having refused to be specific, the report proceeds to produce a very clear statement of the general characteristics of community education:

> We consider the concept of community education to be consistent with current international thinking about education as a whole, as represented for example by the phrases 'education permanent', 'recurrent education', and 'continuing education'. It reflects a view of education as a process (a) which is life-long; (b) in which the participants should be actively and influentially involved and the traditional stress on teaching outweighed by the emphasis put on learning; and (c) in which the needs of the participants rather than academic subject divisions or administrative and institutional arrangements should determine the nature and timing of provision.

> The distinctive contribution which the concept of community education may be said to bring to these international concepts is its emphasis on the process as one in which the benefits to and the contributions of the individual are matched by those of the groups and communities to which he or she belongs; and one which can be enjoyable as well as beneficial, relaxed as well as rigorous. Community education recognises the educative influences and the educational potentialities

inherent in a local community and operating through multifarious groups and agencies, formal and informal, industrial, commercial, religious, social and recreational as well as explicitly educational.

We therefore see community education as a constantly evolving process of interaction between the needs of people and the educational resources of the community, a process to which fixed boundaries cannot be set ...

This is elegant and clear, and much of it is admirable. As an abstract statement, it says nothing about the concrete realisation of its ideals. Perhaps we cannot take it to task for avoiding what it does not set out to do, but the absence of any models of practice fills me with unease, because it opens the gate to omnipotence. The association of the educative and the educational is valuable, insofar as it brings closer together categories traditionally kept apart. But I suspect that it conceals a confusion of learning with experience. While all learning involves experience, not all experience results in learning. Finally, a service which refuses to define the boundaries of its own process is a service which is going to have problems.

The report proceeds to a statement of general aims, which can be summarised as follows: to involve people as individuals and in groups and communities in, first, ascertaining their needs for opportunities to:

(i)   discover and pursue interests;

(ii)   acquire and improve knowledge and skills;

(iii)   recognise their personal identities and aspirations;

(iv)   develop satisfactory inter-personal relationships;

(v)   achieve competence in their roles in the family, community and society;

(vi)   participate in shaping their physical and social environment and in the conduct of local and national affairs

and second, *meeting* these needs, once ascertained, in co-operation with others, and by finding appropriate educational resources.

Once again this statement cannot be faulted for its clarity, its comprehensiveness, or its ambition. But is it realistic? Can it be done by one service? Where are people to find these resources? I want to spell out what I suspect you will already have guessed about my own view. I would prefer the adoption of a more modest list of aims combined with some sense of how they might be achieved. There is a virtue in making choices, prioritising objectives and concentrating resources, rather than spreading the butter so thin it disappears. To use a different metaphor, the Carnegy Report had its eye on the beautiful panorama, rather than on the road ahead.

Proceeding further, we come across another feature that has become characteristic of community education: an excessive admiration for the effectiveness, the untutored brilliance, of voluntary participants:

circumstances will occur where the proper role of the professional should be at most that of releasing and supporting voluntary initiative and ... admiring and learning from the insights and natural skills of non-professionals.

Now, this is true, and worth stressing, but it can also contain something unhealthy: a negation of the positive aspects of professionalism, a romanticising of 'the people' and their 'natural skills'. This is connected in my mind with what was to become the caricature of the community education worker: a scruffy, unkempt individual who gave no lead and upheld no standards of performance. This negation of professionalism, which I confess I shared for a time, can be seen as an antithetical reaction to the experience of the paternalistic professional. Its *reduction ad absurdum* would be to hand back the salary.

Later, an attempt is made to categorise the kinds of full-time workers the report envisages will be required. The four categories proposed are staff concerned with:

- animation, groupwork and tutoring;
- organisation and management;
- advisory and specialist functions at a remove from participants;
- formulating policy, administration, and managing staff.

In one sense this is accurate enough, but in another it subtly presages the process of devaluing practice. I am referring here to that process, found in most professions in the last twenty years, and specifically in community education, of leaving the practice work to the lower grade or part-time staff, and the other side of the coin being the scramble to get into policy-making, administrative and managerial positions. Is this an aspect of the process of bureaucratisation?

The central shift from Alexander in Carnegy is the introduction of the concept of a common core of knowledge and skills required by all categories of community education staff, which include education, psychology, sociology, social administration, community work, group work, politics, and leisure. This list is so long that it leads me to wonder about the danger of the dilution of quality, of a relatively shallow *tour d' horizon* approach being adopted in all these areas. Yet the Carnegy Report claims to be concerned with high standards.

The list of areas of knowledge is followed by a list of skills, which is very impressive, but also very long. Again I ask myself, how could people learn *all* those *skills*? I was very aware, in the late '70s and early '80s, of the annual trail of newly trained or just-appointed community education workers coming to see me at the WEA. The story was always the same: I'm supposed to be doing adult education but I've got no idea how to go about it.

It should be stressed, however, that Carnegy does recognise the existence of processes specific to each of adult education, youth service and community work.

An unfortunate though presumably unintended effect of the Carnegy Report's rejection of the binary system of training was to give a further twist to the destructive competition between the colleges and the universities.

The Carnegy Report introduced the word 'generic' into the glossary of community education. As first employed, it is inter-changeable with the word 'common' and used to refer to the skills held to be shared by those professions said to be 'related' to community education: teaching, social work, and leisure and recreation.

In summary, the Carnegy Report opts for an idealising description of community education, using hyperbole to sell the fledgling service, with the danger of opening up gaps between claim and performance. At the same time, training in the original areas of practice, though still held to be important, can be regarded as having been diminished in value as the concept of the common core of knowledge and skills required for community education is introduced.

The evolution of community education - and the process of revising Alexander – takes further steps in *Training for Change*, subtitled *A Report on Community Education Training*, issued eight years later, in 1984, by the Scottish Community Education Council. By this time the service has had a chance to show what it can do, still without the hoped-for extra cash.

The key concept is now *core plus options*, with core defined as relating to the process of community education, and options to the wide variety of specialist settings in which the process is put into practice. We are moving further away from Alexander towards the concepts of generic community education and generic workers, to whom specialists are in some sense inferior. The net effect is to raise the status of community education and community education process, and to lower the status of adult education, youth service and community work. They are no longer areas with their own processes, they are mere settings, equivalent in status to other settings like outdoor activities, dance, play leadership, and adult basic education.

As a document, Training for Change is full of contradictions. One moment it recognises adult education, youth service, and community work. The next, we are back to the community education process. There are moments of self-critical frankness such as this:

> 'It is not surprising, therefore, that the introduction of a Community Education Service led, initially, to confusion amongst staff as to their roles. Previously a youth and community worker or an adult education organiser, the newly designated community education worker was now to deliver lifelong learning, supporting individual and group development from pre-school children to the elderly, incorporating, along the way, provision for disadvantaged or special needs groups. In this 'cradle to the grave' education, the possibilities were endless, and the generic community education worker was born. For some time the experience was overwhelming and they retreated to what they knew best, while others began to exploit the freedom of their role by carrying on within their traditional areas of activity but with some new emphasis in their work. In the early stages after re-organisation there was little evidence of the formulation of new policies or practices which might reduce the tensions faced by the community education worker. Some of the tensions remain today, and there is

evidence that a recognisable and accessible developmental structure of education has not been fully achieved. There is substantial evidence that the mainstream curriculum tends to be static, ad hoc, remains located in leisure, social and recreational areas avoiding cognitive and issue-based learning.'

There is an attempt to look at the third strand - community work - and a recognition that community education staff feel they lack the skills to tackle it. But the report doesn't draw the obvious conclusion: that there is a particular set of skills, and a process, in community work, which people need to learn in depth, and which differs from, though it overlaps with, the processes of youth work and adult education. Instead, reference is made to the need for trainees to learn about local authority structures and social policy issues.

Training for Change goes on to sketch in some of the 'additional responsibilities and interests' which community education has 'developed' in the last eight years: ABE, vocational training, unemployment, poverty, welfare rights, information technology, resource centres, women's education, children's play, the disabled, multi-cultural education, older people, community schools, and so on. It summarises community education as a 'rapidly expanding field of practice', meaning of course not more workers but more responsibilities for the existing workers. We are close, in fact, to the rag-bag concept of community education, and to a picture of a passive profession with a low self-image which gets new tasks flung at it whether it wants them or not. The report does not complain. It classifies all such work as community education, and in the same breath, not surprisingly, asks itself what the central concept of community education is.

In seeking to answer its own question, *Training for Change* starts off with a pretty hard challenge from Professor Nisbet, who lambastes community education for failing to define its theoretical basis and the anti-theory attitudes of its practitioners, and specifies four 'fears' which are in fact criticisms aimed at the heart of community education . These are:

1. Practice without theory leads to judging provision by scale rather than purpose;

2 community education is in danger of becoming a series of unco-ordinated and unrelated responses;

3. community education is in danger of being seen as only for people in deprived areas;

4. practice paid for by public funds must be theoretically justified.

Instead of responding to this challenge in a lively fashion, the report says, simply, that it agrees with Nisbet. Seeking to restore community education's dignity, it embarks on an attempt to define its aims, starting with those identified by Carnegy. This is followed by a list of people and activities to which these aims are said to be applicable. They are applicable to *everybody* and to a vast range of activities: leisure and recreation, knowledge and skills, personal and social learning, environmental and political change. They are appropriate to other professions as well. What the report succeeds in doing here is reverting to the Carnegy position and somehow evading Nisbet's challenge. I ask myself: what is the meaning of this repeated concern with other professions? Is it the anticompartmentalising tendency, or does it in fact reflect community education's continuing uncertainty about its own professional identity? Are they trying, by association, to borrow status from professions like social work which have succeeded in establishing a core of task and expertise? Is community education really aware of its lack of coherence and is this the drive behind the insistent search for a common core of knowledge and skills? The report seems unable or unwilling to make exclusive choices.

Training for Change concedes that community education is seen as an umbrella term but asserts that there really is a central process, visualised as the hub of a wheel, holding all the activities and settings together. They offer a definition:

> 'Community education is a process which involves the participants in the creation of purposive developmental and educational programmes and structures which afford opportunities for individual and collective growth and change throughout life.'

The process is described as having six functional tasks:

1. identification of issues, demands and needs;

2. design of programme /structure /learning to meet the needs;

3. promotion of these;

4. managing, supporting and delivering them;

5. publicising them (the difference between tasks three and five is not made clear);

6. continuous assessment/evaluation.

The report admits that workers will need specific knowledge of one or more specific areas, as well as a knowledge of the generic process, and this leads them to their conclusion: that what is required is a core-plus-options model.

For a moment we are allowed again to glimpse some of the evidence demonstrating the unwisdom of the whole drift of *Training for Change's* thinking. Reference is made to the fact that the national bodies representing both adult education and youth service feel that the quantity and quality of work in these areas is being impaired. Again, they deal with the damning criticism by agreeing with it.

The cure is threefold. First, it is recommended that the amount of training time spent in fieldwork placements is to be increased to 50 per cent of the total, thus bringing about a different relationship between theory and practice, and a greater attention to the employer's requirements with regard to training. It is recognised that the quality of placements and of fieldwork supervision will have to be improved. Secondly, the modularisation of training, that is to say the adoption of a system of free-standing forty-hour units of learning which can be articulated (joined up) in what is held to be a flexible variety of ways, thus improving access and reducing rigidity. Thirdly, the creation of a national-and-regional training scheme structure consisting of four area training councils and a national training council.

Course members must decide for themselves what to make of all this. I confess to a distrustful attitude towards pseudo-scientific, ultra-rational, totalising systems. Modularisation can be regarded as a diversion of time and resources away from the long-overdue task of mobilising everyone available to train the vast body of part-timers on whom the community education service depends. The aim of changing the relationship between theory and practice is a good one, and it is right that there should be a greater emphasis on fieldwork practice experience. I argued at the time that the resources called for in the report to create the structure of national-and-regional councils should be diverted into the creation of fieldwork teaching units located in practice agencies throughout Scotland. These considerations, however, must be regarded as academic in the light of the fact that the whole package of recommendations was rejected by the Secretary of State three years later. Yes, three years later, an illustration of the masterly use of delay as an instrument of policy perfected by British administrators in colonial settings, and applied with devastating effect throughout the whole community education period in Scotland.

How are we to assess *Training for Change?* It reflects the anxiety of a profession about the core of its identity, the quality of its practice, the absence of boundaries, and the poverty of its theory. It attempts to identify a core. It can be seen as grasping at the quasi-technological straw of modularisation as a means of prising resources for training from a tight-fisted central government.

Widening the lens now, how can we summarise the development of community education from Alexander through Carnegy to *Training for Change?* We have been watching the formation and early stages in the evolution of a new profession, with dimensions of internal conflict, identity uncertainty and a search for identity, with moments of omnipotence and grandiosity, alternating with moments of doubt about competence and direction. More specifically, we see a shift from the initial focus on adult education and its expansion and redirection towards those who are disadvantaged, towards a view of adult education and youth service as regions of the wide, newly designated territory of community education, and a further shift towards the notion of a single imperial entity – generic community education - with its single process, its collection of settings, and it hierarchical ranking of generalist over specialist workers.

There is one final pressing question. Suppose the notion of a single process proves to be unhelpful in the longer run? If so, is the concept of community education still valid? If it is, how can the identity of the Service be strengthened, boundaries set, and the self-worth of the staff established in their own eyes? If it is not, how are we to promote the causes of adult education, youth work, and community work? So many questions, as Brecht wrote – and behind them, such a lot of anger.

JEAN BARR

KEEPING A LOW PROFILE: ADULT EDUCATION IN SCOTLAND

ADULT EDUCATION VOL 59. NO 4. (N.I.A.C.E.) 1987

One of the less discussed problems of adult education in Scotland at the moment is that it is hard to see.

The political and administrative context

1. There is no separate budget for adult education (at national or local authority level) and
2. there is no coherent national policy for adult education.

At national level money for adult education comes out of the SED's division 6 budget which covers Sport, the Arts and Community Education (which includes Scouts and Guides). At local authority level money for part-time tutor costs comes out of budget heads like 'grants to voluntary organisations', 'other bodies' – or 'miscellaneous'. It is impossible to get hold of a figure which represents expenditure on adult education in Scotland.

The reluctance of government to develop a coherent overall policy for adult and continuing education looks no more likely to be overcome now than it did when the 'Our Right to Learn Campaign' first drew the public's attention to it. A great deal of muddy water has passed under the bridge since then, including the consolidation of the MSC's role as a major provider of vocational training and the fuller development of the concept and practice of continuing education.

Since the publication of the Alexander Report on Adult Education in 1975 the provision of education for adults by Scottish local authorities has been embedded within an all-embracing concept of 'community education'. Alexander recommended that *'adult education should be regarded as an aspect of community education and with the Youth and Community Service should be incorporated into a Community Education Service'*. This is now the position in most education authorities. However, Alexander's recommendation that 200 specialist adult educators should be appointed never materialised and since the publication of the Report the principle of public subsidy for adult education provision has been seriously eroded, as more and more programmes have had to become self-financing. Even adult literacy, one of the few areas of expansion since 1975 has, in its widened form as adult basic education, suffered severely from local authority cutbacks; the Scottish Adult Basic Education Unit (SABEU) no longer exists as a separate unit, having been integrated into the Scottish Community Education Council (SCEC) with accompanying staff losses.

The Alexander Report had, in any case, a narrow focus on 'non vocational adult education', whereas most new demands and recent developments do not fit easily into that category. Developments by the WEA and others in women's education, basic education courses, unemployed courses, 'Second Chance to Learn', open learning and the whole spectrum of 'continuing education' provision, cannot simply be categorised as vocational or non-vocational. In any case the distinction between vocational and non-vocational education has lost its validity.

No mechanism for policy

There is now a structural, financial and administrative lacuna between adult education/community education and adult education/continuing education in Scotland which is obstructive, frustrating and harmful for all concerned. The necessary mechanisms which would assist the formulation of a coherent policy on adult and continuing education simply do not exist. SCEC, the body which was set up to advise the Secretary of State on all matters of policy relating to community education and (ipso facto) adult education in so far as it can be viewed as part of community education, is structurally unsuited to the task of devising a policy on adult and continuing education. The SIACE which only recently changed its name from the Scottish Institute of Adult Education does not have the required powers relating to policy matters. The SED has so far been unwilling to initiate the process of policy development either by itself setting up an appropriate mechanism or by commissioning an existing body to do it. The WEA now sees this lack of policy as a cause for real concern.

The WEA has a long history of involving working people – whether waged or unwaged in a wide range of adult education provision. But it is chronically under-resourced, starved of access to development funds and burdened from year to year with the uncertainty of whether it will be able to continue to exist at all. It is continually told that its gain will be somebody else's loss – somebody paid out of the same budget head. An associated problem for the WEA in Scotland is its lack of Responsible Body status and its consequent reliance on financial support for its programmes on the local authorities, a problem which has become more acute during a period when most local authorities have reduced their support for adult and continuing education.

Ad hoc development

Meanwhile, in the absence of such a mechanism and of a coherent overall policy for adult and continuing education, developments are ad hoc, uncoordinated and fragmented. Short-term funding via the MSC and EEC continues to create havoc in various places, raising expectations which are short-lived and which have no connection with any collaborative national or local strategy.

The latest news is symptomatic. Announced with no prior warning or consultation, the four Extra-Mural Departments which receive SED funding are to have their grant for 1986/87 cut by fifty three per cent and phased out completely next year. The effect will be to reduce access to the Universities' teaching services for ordinary people at a cost they can afford. The money 'saved' is to be put into a new Scottish scheme for continuing vocational education modelled on the PICKUP programme which was launched in England and Wales in 1982 without reducing aid to other areas of adult continuing education. The 're-ordering of priorities within existing resources' is justified in the name of the recent Scottish Tertiary Education Advisory Council Report which emphasised the importance of retraining, skills updating and continued professional development. Nobody would deny the importance of this but robbing Peter to pay Paul is not a sensible strategy.

The 'community' context

'Adult education by stealth'

Ian Bryant, describing community education initiatives in Glasgow,[1] draws a distinction between those in which the adult education component is explicit and all those community-based programmes in which there is an adult education component which is undefined and secondary to the achievement of other objectives, where learning proceeds 'by stealth'.

John Horobin,[2] after showing the decline in traditional adult education between 1976-1981, notes that 'there is more to adult education in Scotland than is revealed in these figures'. Much of the 'more' is what Ian Bryant is referring to.

There is very little of the explicit sort of adult education in an area like Strathclyde. There is of course some limited provision of free 'basic education' in APTs and other 'Areas of Need' and there are a few community-based adult education projects. But there is a great deal of the other – undefined – sort. In Strathclyde, for example, community education is conceived of as part of the Region's Community Development strategy to combat deprivation. A 'community development' approach to adult education is very firmly advocated and located centrally in its Social Strategy. This being the case it seems likely that working class participation in adult education activities has been underestimated. For by far the greatest number of 'educational' activities engaged in by working class people in Scotland, certainly in the West of Scotland, takes place in a myriad of community schemes or projects in which adult education is not the main activity but where the workers involved in running these schemes see educational aims in some sense as an important, but unstated, part of *their* agenda.

Some see in this a cause for celebration, believing that working class people are turned off adult education by its formality, its elitism and lack of relevance to real life experiences. Many who take this view would no doubt align themselves with the 'radical' rather than 'respectable' traditions in adult education as outlined below. I believe that there are very real dangers in an interventionist educational strategy which pretends not to be one.

(i)   It means that the vast bulk of the 'educational' work which is undertaken by working class people, especially women, remains hidden from view, unrecorded in the statistics and seldom the subject of systematic research, appraisal or evaluation; it is seldom carried out by people who are trained as or who regard themselves first and foremost as adult educators and it is usually subordinate to some sort of community development aims. This in itself may not be worrying, but when it is allied to a second kind of invisibility it is profoundly so.

(ii)   This is when the adult education component remains hidden from the participants themselves. The Open University course 'Education for Adults' describes education as 'deliberate, planned and organised with the conscious . . . . *"slipped in between the afternoon cuppa and the organisation of the jumble sale ... fearful of being seen to be serious and as a result failing to take seriously the educational needs of the women involved*[3]. . . . intention of bringing about change in knowledge, attitude or skill' and where 'the learner as well as the educator is involved in this conscious, deliberate process ... *Thus (it) assumes the willing, conscious involvement of the learner in the process of his (sic) learning'. (my italics).*

Although unsatisfactory in some ways (failing as it does to draw attention to the mutuality/interchangeability of 'learner and educator' roles in adult education) this description highlights an essential feature of any educational transaction: it is something consciously and deliberately entered into. This may admit of degrees, of course, and nobody may *call* what's going on 'education'. But there is a minimum level of complicity required in one's own learning which, if breached, turns it into something quite other than education and more akin to treatment.

Jane Thomson has spoken scathingly of adult education of the 'low profile' variety introduced by stealth into community centres, mothers' and toddlers' groups and gatherings of women on housing estates.

This clandestine 'education' often attaches to the community schemes which involve women as others or as members of community groups, where significance is attached more to the women's influence on their children's or community's development than to the needs of the women themselves for their own intellectual or creative progress.

Open to challenge

One of the more extreme manifestations of the 'hidden curriculum' is found in some informal parent education schemes (they are never called this) in deprived areas where parents (mainly mothers) are encouraged to drop in to community (or 'family') centres with their young children and where they are supposed to pick up good parenting practice from watching how the worker deals with the children. If the notion of role model were made explicit it would be rejected out of hand by the women, who might, with justification, say that if they wanted to know about parenting they could do a course.[4]

Because the educational element is hidden it is not open to challenge by the people subjected to it. (I do not use the verb casually.) I sometimes find the notion of informality in adult education disquieting. It is in danger of becoming a new orthodoxy and one which patronises people no less than the formality it supersedes.

Of course, easy access and styles of learning and teaching that encourage a relaxed sharing of views, experiences and ideas are essential features of good adult education.

Developments in women's education by the WEA and others in community settings provide some of the best models here. But too often informality can be a very effective cloak for a hidden curriculum; it can mean that the educational element remains implicit, never surfacing sufficiently to become the subject of serious negotiation.

The alternative to the 'education by stealth' approach, that of trying to convince people that there are real benefits to be got from education for more than a tiny minority, is more difficult. 'Schooling' has left most of them uninspired and many believing themselves to be failures. Learning itself can be a difficult process; so can creative effort. The process of developing a learning programme requires negotiation. Negotiation requires mutual and explicit respect between educational workers and participants. both sides have to know what the process is, and the participants have to be, in the end, the best judges of what they need. Until working people take up education in their own terms with the help of sympathetic professionals adult education will remain a lost cause.

The two traditions

The most familiar way of depicting the history of adult education in Britain is to see it as having dual roots – in groups of workers and women and other social groups demanding education or providing it for themselves as a means of liberation and social change; and in governments, the Church and other Establishments using education as a means of 'domestication' and amelioration. Ian Bryant has similarly divided the historical process of adult education in Scotland into 'Radical' and 'Respectable' streams.[5] And Raymond Williams had distinguished between a 'social conscience' approach in the history of adult education and a quite different approach which sees the point of adult education as the building of an adequate *social consciousness* – a real understanding of the world.

There is a kind of community education for the 'disadvantaged' which sells people short by concentrating on 'life adjustment skills and diminished cognitive content';[6] it is part of the ameliorative, 'social conscience' tradition. I would guess that much of the 'invisible' type of 'educational' work going on in the many community schemes up and down the country has strong links with this social conscience/ameliorative approach. This happens, I believe, less through conscious intent than through the workers involved not having the orientation or skills which are necessary to develop learning programmes from the issues raised by participants.

Given the well-documented educational disadvantages experienced by working class people, in particular women, it is important to be clear about how much education is being presented in working class areas, the quality of what is on offer and its purpose.

I believe firmly that any adequate education practice must be explicit about educational content and underlying ideologies; it should involve a careful articulation of aims and objectives so as to make the curriculum open to negotiation, challenge and change. It should also be underpinned by adequate provision for tutor training. The amount of education with adults in Scotland which fits the description is minuscule – and shrinking.

Not surprising given the absence of a sensible framework for adult and continuing education, the lack of resources devoted to it and the poverty of policy.

REFERENCES

1.   Bryant, I. *'Educational Initiatives for the Adult Unemployed'* – Handover copy of contribution to OU Reader.
2.   Horobin, J. *'Adult Education in Scotland from 1976 to 1981'*, Scottish Journal of Adult Education, Vol. 6, No. 1.
3.   Thompson, Jane L. *'Adult Education and the Disadvantaged'* in *Adult Education for Change ed.* Jane L. Thompson (Hutchinson).
4.   Scribbins, Jenny. *'Education for Women and Parent Education'* a paper given at the ILSCAE Conference at Nottingham University in July 1986.
5.   Bryant, I. *Radicals & Respectables – the Adult Education Experience in Scotland,* SIACE, 1984.
6.   Alexander, D. and Stewart, T. *'An educational perspective on community education in Scotland'* in Scottish Journal of Adult Education, Vol. 5, No. 3.

GERRI KIRKWOOD/COLIN KIRKWOOD
LIVING ADULT EDUCATION: FREIRE IN SCOTLAND
OPEN UNIVERSITY PRESS 1989

The writings of the Brazilian adult educator, Paulo Freire, have been available in English as a source of inspiration and encouragement to students, teachers and trainers since the early 1970s. In spite of the cultural gap between Brazil and Britain, and the difficulty of his language, we knew that Freire was speaking to us. Interest in his work has grown steadily. Today there are few writers on adult education who do not acknowledge his influence. Freire has been no instantly disposable prophet.

Yet all along there has been a problem. Although, from time to time, word was out that such and such a project was struggling to apply his ideas, after the initial flurry of excitement, little further information would emerge. It was as if the gap was too wide to bridge. It was as if Freire belonged to another world. He faced south, towards Africa and Latin America, and although he visited North America and many European countries, and for ten years was based at the World Council of Churches in Geneva, doubts were expressed as to the relevance of his interesting ideas about oppression, liberation, and the culture of silence in the high-tech democracies of the north. The opposite view was also held, that Freire was saying nothing that was not embodied in the work of the best exponents of the liberal tradition in British adult education. For whatever reasons, it seemed that his vision and our reality were doomed to remain apart.

In the Lothian Region of Scotland, as elsewhere, there was an existing interest in Freire's ideas among community education workers, which was further encouraged by a series of courses offered by the Workers' Educational Association. It was this interest which led to the successful efforts of Fraser Patrick (Community Education Officer) and Douglas Shannon (Senior Community Education Worker) to obtain funding for a project which would put his ideas into practice.

This book tells the story of how, in 1979, the Adult Learning Project (ALP) came to be created, as a systematic attempt to implement Freire's approach in Scotland. It sets out to explain his ideas as simply as possible, and to show how they have been adapted and applied by the ALP workers and participants in learning programmes in the Gorgie Dalry area of Edinburgh.

It is written by practitioners for practitioners, trainers, managers and policy makers, and tries to answer the questions which have been directed at the ALP workers over the years. The authors have attempted to communicate the experience of taking part in Freire type learning groups, the process that has been developed, the issues that have arisen, and the lessons that have been learned. They have tried to represent the contributions of everyone: ALP workers, participants, and resource people. It has been a difficult but rewarding job.

ALP is a part of the Community Education Service of Lothian Regional Council. A word of explanation about the meaning of community education in Scotland may be helpful. The Community Education Service was established in the years after 1975, following the publication of Alexander Report which recommended the integration of adult education and youth and community work into a single service. It is promoted at national level by the Scottish Community Education Council. The specific interests of adult education in community, further, and higher education, and in the voluntary sector, are promoted by the Scottish Institute of Adult and Continuing Education.

ALP was set up in the first place as an Urban Aid project. Essentially this means that it was financed jointly by central government (the Scottish Education Department) and local government (Lothian Regional Council) on a 75/25 per cent basis. After an initial three-year period of funding, a two-year extension was given. At the end of five years, Urban Aid projects sponsored by local government either close down, or else the local government body involved assumes full financial responsibility, integrating the project into its own mainstream provision. The campaign by ALP participants to secure the future of the project in Gorgie Dalry received widespread support from adult education bodies throughout Britain, and was successful.

The Story of ALP

Origins and aims

The Adult Learning Project in Gorgie Dalry was started in 1977 by a small group of women supported by a neighbourhood community worker and a community education worker. A street-based survey was carried out, asking people what classes they would like. The demand was for classes such as English 'O' grade and yoga. They were to be free, put on at times and places convenient to residents, and managed by local people. Tutors were to be responsive in their approach, prepared to negotiate the content of programmes with students. Initially, tutors were paid, but the idea was that some students would themselves become volunteer tutors.

The community education worker hoped that, as an atmosphere of learning developed in the area, people would begin to explore personal, local and national issues in a more systematic way.

This early ALP, then, was based on ideas of self-reliance, popular demand, local access and local control. It was quickly successful, with nearly 200 people taking part in the first year. Already demand was outstripping resources in the form of the time the women and the community education worker were able to give to the project, and the money available to pay part-time tutors.

Lothian Region's Community Education Department, with the agreement of the women, made an application for urban aid funding to the Scottish Office. They asked for three community education workers, a secretary/receptionist, a shop on the main road, and a budget for books, publicity, tutors' fees, and equipment. The stated aims were to provide cheap learning opportunities locally, in response to requests; to create a network of local tutors; to develop issue-based education; and to publicise the project effectively.

During the following year, while the urban aid application was being processed, changes took place as a result of which these aims were modified. Community education staff were deepening their interest in the work of Paulo Freire, and joined an in-service training course on his ideas and methods organised by the Workers' Educational Association (WEA). The influence of Freire led to a shift away from the idea of classes provided in response to popular demand, towards programmes aimed at exploring themes and concerns identified by residents. In practice, this meant moving away from vocational and leisure-and-recreation classes towards issue-based education. Classes would still be provided in the area, but by other community education workers, outside the framework of ALP.

The proposed role of the full-time workers was also changed in emphasis, from responding to demand, organising classes and supporting volunteer tutors, to playing a key part in every stage of what later came to be called the ALP process: investigation, building learning programmes, and supporting action outcomes.

Gorgie Dalry: The place and the people

Gorgie Dalry is a densely populated inner area of Edinburgh, sandwiched between the west end of the city centre and the suburbs. Built between 1880 and 1900 for the families of workers employed on the railways and in local factories, it was for years solidly working class. People lived close to where they worked. The area was the centre of their social life. Hearts Football Club had its home here and still does.

In the 1960s this picture was disturbed when many families moved out to Wester Hailes and other peripheral council housing schemes. Local works closed down- the rubber mill, the biscuit factory, a glue works, laundries, engineering works, the railway sheds. Breweries like Scottish and Newcastle became automated and needed fewer workers. Other employers like Ferrantis required a highly skilled workforce and recruited from all over Lothian, not just locally.

Today, Gorgie Dalry is not one community but several. The old population of skilled and unskilled working class people remains, reduced in numbers. But new people have been moving in, attracted by the relative cheapness of the housing and its nearness to the city centre. Many residents now work elsewhere, and many of those who work locally live elsewhere. The majority of existing working class residents are middle aged to elderly, while most often incomers are younger, often with more education and white collar jobs. Some are single, some couples without children, some have one young child. The percentage of households with children is small. In the last few years there has been an influx of young unemployed people, sharing rented accommodation.

Despite these population changes, the physical character of the place and its reputation for friendliness remains intact. First impressions are of a crowded area of tenements, small shops, factories and breweries, churches, schools and other public buildings, on either side of a busy main road. The narrow side streets are lined with parked cars, many belonging to people working in the area or in the nearby city centre rather than to residents. The smell from the breweries and the noise of the traffic are constant factors. There is an impression of lack of greenery, in spite of the Victorian graveyard on the main road (hidden behind a high wall), the small park in the Muriestons, and the Gorgie City Farm.

The whole place has a feeling of being on the move. Rehabilitation of the housing stock by Gorgie Dalry Housing Association and Edinburgh District Council, begun in the late 1970s, is well advanced. Tenants, owner occupiers and private landlords are benefiting, despite the stress and upheaval of decanting or living on a building site. Many environmental problems remain, like the smallness of the flats and the lack of play space for children, but – despite grumblings – these seem to be accepted, along with the benefits, as part of the cost of living so close to the city centre. Some important distinctions are not obvious to outsiders. Gorgie and Dalry are two distinct areas, separated by the traffic junction at Ardmillan Terrace. Defining other boundaries is not so easy. Shandon, an area of terraced houses with small gardens just up the hill. can be considered part of Gorgie or of Merchiston, depending or where you send your children to school, do your shopping, and feel you belong.

The ALP workers

Gerri Kirkwood, Stan Reeves and Fiona O'Kane started as ALP workers in September 1979. Joan Bree, the ALP secretary and receptionist, arrived six months later. All are still in post, except for Fiona, who left in 1984. Their backgrounds are very different. Gerri is married with two teenage children. She has a degree in modern languages, and post graduate training in adult education and community development, and human relations and counselling. She has previous experience as a teacher, community worker, reporter to children's panels, and tutor on return to learning courses. Stan is married with two school age children. He trained as a photographer and then as a youth and community worker. He has previously been an adventure playground organiser and a community development worker. He also plays the melodeon in a ceilidh band. Fiona is married and has a degree in English language and literature, with postgraduate training in community education. She has previously worked as a literacy tutor/organiser, and is now in mainstream community education. All three had prior interest in the work of Paulo Freire. Joan Bree is single. She trained as a secretary and has previously worked in a bank and as a mother's help in Canada.

The ALP process

What follows is an outline of the ALP process of building programmes of learning and action as it has been refined during the life of the project. This represents ALP workers' understanding of Paulo Freire's approach to education as they have adapted it in Gorgie Dalry in the 1980s.

The stages in the process are:
>secondary source investigation
>primary source investigation
>finding co-investigators
>co-investigation
>building codifcations
>decoding
>building the curriculum
>learning programmes
>action outcomes

Secondary source investigation

The workers begin by doing research on the life of the area using secondary sources, that is material written about it available from local and central government departments, libraries, universities, and so on. They meet regularly to share their findings and begin to build up a composite picture, which may include such dimensions as the built environment, work, schooling, planning, census information, health profile, employment and unemployment, and so on.

Primary source investigation

The workers get to know the area at first hand by walking about and observing the physical environment and the way people relate to each other in public. They make contact with key professionals, clergy, the local politicians, and residents involved in community organisations. They visit workplaces and make contact with managers and with trade unionists.

The questions asked in this stage are: how do people see the area, its boundaries, its physical and social characteristics, its history? What are their feelings about the area and their hopes for its future? What is their personal experience and knowledge of its problems? The aim is to build up a picture of the people, the area, its background and its difficulties as experienced by those who live and work there, to set beside the factual information gathered from secondary sources.

Finding co-investigators

The next task is to invite a cross-section of residents to join the workers in the investigation process. At the beginning of ALP this was done by knocking on people's doors, explaining the purpose of the project and inviting them to attend a public meeting. Once the project got into its stride, co-investigators were recruited from those who had participated in earlier ALP programmes.

Co-investigation

The co-investigators meet regularly with the ALP workers, one of whom leads the group with the other as observer/recorder. Co-investigators are invited to say how they experience life in the area. The aim is not to come to conclusions but to formulate questions which the co-investigators in their turn will ask other people.

In general ALP workers and local volunteers share all the tasks of this stage. Co-investigators interview their own contacts in the area: relatives, neighbours, shopkeepers, and so on. These interviews take the form of conversations: the co-investigator takes notes or may use a taperecorder, asking a series of broad open questions and paying particular attention to matters of special concern to the individual being interviewed.

Another dimension of co-investigation is the observation of moments of life. This involves visits to public places in the locality where people come together. Participants are encouraged to make these visits in pairs, to overcome diffidence. Where visits are made to settings attended by members only, some advance preparation may be necessary. The purpose is to observe the nature of the activities, how they are organised, the communications between participants including the words, phrases and gestures used, and the emotional content of the encounters. Co-investigators are given guidance on how to observe but not what to find. Co-investigators continue to meet as a group to share their findings with one another. One ALP worker listens for common concerns, linking interviews and observations together. The meetings are taperecorded so that no important material is lost. The aim now is to begin to identify key themes which will be codified at the next stage.

The worker leading the group encourages people to report back from their interviews and observations. The data often comes back in the form of stories interviewees have told to illustrate a point. The leader invites responses from other co-investigators to the material presented, sometimes summarising and re-presenting what has been said to let people hear the evidence more clearly and begin to reflect on it. Towards the end of the session, the observer, who has been listening and taking notes, feeds back observations of the group process and the themes beginning to emerge. Co-investigators in their turn comment on these observations. Finally, the programme of interviews and observations to be carried out before the next meeting is agreed.

After the meeting the ALP workers, drawing on the notes and taperecordings, tentatively identify significant statements that have been made and themes that are emerging. This is typed up, given to co-investigators at the next meeting, and checked out with them. By the end of this stage, a number of themes have been named as they exist in the significant situations of people's experience.

Building codifications

The task now is to find a way of illustrating these themes in their social settings. The co-investigators are asked to describe the situations in which a theme first emerged. What was the setting? What was happening at the time? Who were the actors in the situation? How were they relating to one another? Out of this brainstorm, a series of briefs for codifications is prepared.

ALP has experimented with different media for codifying themes. At first, a local artist was asked to prepare drawings, schematic representations of a theme presented in several situations simultaneously. Later she was asked to make a more realistic representation of a situation, showing elements of the physical environment and the relationships of people to each other and to the situation itself. The advantage of a drawing is that it is a composition by the artist, who can include all the elements necessary for understanding the situation in one image. It was soon found, however, that drawings have their problems. People see them as art. They are distracted by the style and quality of the drawing, and whether or not it is an accurate representation. They also expect the artist to interpret reality for them.

Photography has proved to be a more suitable medium for ALP's purposes, though also not without problems. Most people take photographs for granted as mirroring reality. They know that the photographer has selected both image and viewpoint, but as a medium it does not intrude. People tend to read photographs the same way as they read reality. The main problem is that the photographer is limited by what the camera can include at any one moment and this may exclude some of the elements necessary for understanding the totality of a situation. The problem can be overcome by using several photographs. Good photographic codifications are really powerful tools enabling dialogue to take place.

A codification should not be too enigmatic, so that those responding to it in a group will be able to find themselves in it and interpret it in the light of their own experience; nor too explicit, otherwise the group is deprived of the task of interpretation. For the purposes of codification, the photographer, like the artist, is given a brief describing the situation, the elements to be contained in the image and the relationships of the elements to each other and to the whole. The photographer is asked to capture the significant moment, or peak of action, in the situation.

At later stages in the development of ALP, other media have been used for making codifications, including taperecorded interviews, articles from books and newspapers, videotapes, TV programmes and adverts, slides, poems and various combinations of these.

The next task is to make a selection of codifications and arrange them in a sequence which will allow participants involved in decoding to make connections between the themes and contradictions contained in each codification and in the sequence as a whole.

Decoding

Other residents are now invited to join in discussions around the codifications. The co-investigators invite people they have interviewed. Carefully designed publicity reaches out to those with first-hand experience of the situations to be explored, to members of community organisations, passers by, and anyone else who may be interested.

Several decoding groups of 10 or 12 are formed, meeting at different times of the day to allow a wide cross-section of residents to become involved. An ALP worker leads each group, with the help of another worker or a co-investigator whose role is to observe and record.

At the start of the first session the co-ordinator explains the purpose of decoding and the methods to be used. It is an opportunity to take a closer look at some familiar situations and say what you think. The success of the discussion depends on participants being prepared to share their experience of the situation with others in the group. The outcome of all these discussions will be the creation of learning and action programmes to tackle some of the issues raised.

The first codification is displayed on an easel. Participants sit round it in a semicircle. The co-ordinator asks a series of open questions designed to take people gradually into an analysis of the situation. A sequence of questions has been prepared in advance, but others are added as the dialogue in the group begins to take shape.

The first level of questions is simply descriptive. The group is invited to look at the picture and describe everything they see in it. They are encouraged to break the image down into its elements.

The next level of questions invites participants to identify with people in the situation. They are encouraged to read their expressions, postures and gestures, and suggest what their relationships to each other and to the situation might be. Since the situation is a familiar one, members are able to fill the picture out from their own experience.

The following levels are more challenging. Members are invited to relate the situation to their own lives, to place themselves in it. Then they are asked why the situation is as they have described it. This question encourages them to look beyond the particular and the personal to wider social, political, cultural and historical factors.

Themes and contradictions emerge throughout the session. Sometimes the co-ordinator intervenes to re-present what is beginning to emerge, choosing her moments carefully, so as not to interrupt the flow of discussion. She may draw together common threads in what people are saying, or move things on by posing further questions.

The process of communication in the group moves gradually from the responses of individuals, often directed at the co-ordinator, to dialogue in which members respond to each other's comments and begin to formulate their own questions.

One of the problems is keeping the group together, getting them to build on each other's contributions co-operatively. The codification helps by acting as a focus. The co-ordinator's skill in re-presenting what she hears and addressing questions to the whole group is also important. But the difficulty of keeping a balance between individual and group remains. The tension is particularly acute in this method, because the co-ordinator wants to encourage individuals to express themselves and value their experience, and at the same time to value the experience of others by listening and responding to their contributions.

At the end of each decoding session, the observer is invited to contribute. From his notes he outlines the key points of the discussion, quoting from what individuals have said. Key words and phrases may be written on the flip chart. He then offers to the group any themes or contradictions he has spotted which have been missed in the heat of discussion. The group responds, confirming or challenging the observer's comments and adding their own points. Finally, the co-ordinator checks out if it is possible to get agreement in the group about what has been the most important theme to emerge in the discussion.

A written record is made of each session and if possible posted out to members before the next meeting. It includes a distillation of the discussion, the themes and contradictions emerging, and the observer's comments on how the session went. At the end of the sequence of decoding discussions, the recordings are gathered together and used as the basis for a final workshop, where the task is to identify the most generative themes and to brief the ALP workers about the content of the curriculum.

Building the curriculum

The brief is the outcome of all the work done in co-investigation and decoding. People's concerns have been identified and their feelings about them explored. They have looked beneath the surface of taken-for-granted situations and begun to see them afresh, and in a wider context. They have identified themes requiring further action reflection.

The task now is to construct a thematic programme which will try to address different levels of reality simultaneously: personal, local, national, global. It will try to take account of the inner world of feelings and the outer world of facts, the influence of the past, the impact of the present and the potential for the future.

Such a programme can cut across the boundaries of subject disciplines. Appropriate experts are approached – for example, a psychologist, a historian, a political economist. They are given a detailed brief covering the exploration carried out so far and the questions which have arisen. They are asked how they would address these themes from the point of view of their own discipline. And the ALP process and their potential role in it is explained. The aim is to create a programme which will be a seamless garment. At early stages in the life of ALP the workers sometimes found it hard to give a clear enough brief, and some of the experts were unused to building interdisciplinary programmes and working dialogically. ALP is still struggling creatively with these challenges.

Learning programmes

Programmes usually run to 8 or 10 weekly sessions each lasting 1 1/2 to 2 hours. The importance of attending each meeting in the sequence is stressed, and participants are asked to make this commitment. For daytime sessions in which parents with small children are involved, a crèche is provided.

At each meeting group members have the first word. The ALP worker triggers the process by asking a key question arising out of decoding, which underlies the invitation to this particular expert. The expert then makes her presentation, based on the brief agreed beforehand with the worker, and adjusted to take into account what group members have just been saying.

Finally there is a dialogue, in which all take part in what Freire calls a mutual search for truth. The task here is to integrate the expert's knowledge and experience with the group's previous knowledge and experience. The ALP worker's role is to facilitate the dialogue. Problems can arise here from the compulsion of some experts to talk too much, and the tendency of some group members to become passive in the presence of experts. Much depends on the way the session has been set up, the facilitating role of the worker, and the experts' ability to respond quickly and sensitively.

Action outcomes

Participants know from the outset that some kind of action is a hoped-for outcome from the learning programmes. The action itself can be of different kinds. It may involve community action by the group in co-operation with other local people to tackle a specific problem, the creation of a new community organisation in the area, or action by individuals in their own lives. Changes in attitudes occurring during the learning programmes may result in people deciding to stay where they are in a positive sense. There may be gains in self-knowledge, self acceptance, personal effectiveness and social functioning. There is no way of predicting what the outcomes of learning programmes will be. Workers cannot- and should not- always know the personal outcomes for individuals. What we can say is that any action by the group in which the ALP worker is involved will always be characterised by prior investigation of the feasibility of the project, and continuing reflection on the process of action as it evolves.

The evolving process

Over the years the ALP process has become more flexible:
- the different stages can be of longer or shorter duration
- action can follow reflection or occur alongside it
- the process is often shortened and speeded up
- what is being investigated is clearly defined and can be limited in scope
- co-investigators are trained in the skills of interviewing and formulating questions
- each stage of the process has become more distinct – and more clearly linked to the following stage
- experts are integrated more fully into the learning process, often acting as resource persons or consultants to the group rather than as guest speakers
- group members themselves are asked to take on more responsibility for their own learning: building codifications, identifying key themes, recording the main points of the discussion, contributing ideas for the content of learning programmes, and leading their own action projects.

TED MILBURN
THE COMMUNITY EDUCATION SERVICE AND ITS ROLE IN DEVELOPING LEARNING OPPORTUNITIES FOR ADULTS

BRITISH COMPARATIVE AND INTERNATIONAL EDUCATION SOCIETY 1987

INTRODUCTION

This paper argues that the growth and development of the Community Education Service from its beginnings in youth work and community development have endowed it and its staff with philosophical pre-dispositions, group work, community work and informal educational skills for working in particular ways with community groups. The community development approach has taken a special kind of educational opportunity to those who have hitherto been unattracted by the style, content and mode of delivery of traditional adult education. It is argued that there are enormous gains in the harnessing of an educational dimension to the community development process both in human terms and in relation to the availability of educational opportunities to the whole population. The role of the Community Education Service in the post-compulsory education strategy is explored and the contribution of the community education worker as a 'network agent' in Lovett's terms is underlined. It is a role, which because of training and development, the community education worker is uniquely equipped to perform.

This paper will be concerned with underlining the role which the Community Education Service can and does play in the development of learning opportunities for adults. It will accept as its context the Strathclyde Region which has had a Community Education Service since 1975 and many of the examples of fieldwork practice which are highlighted are taken from work which has been developed in that Region. Exploring the topic of the paper I am intending to follow four main themes.

(a)   The growth of a Community Education Service in Strathclyde Region through developments in Youth and Community Service.

(b)   The theoretical and practical fieldwork implications of this process.

(c)   The application of a community development approach to the creation of learning opportunities for adults.

(d)   The role of a field based service in the Region's post compulsory educational strategy.

In all that follows I should make it quite clear that the views expressed are my own and not necessarily those of Strathclyde Regional Council.

The Growth of a Community Education Service in Strathclyde and some Theoretical and Practical Implications of the Process

In order to understand the development of the work of the Community Education Service in community based adult learning, it is important to trace its progress and growth through youth and community work. This section is concerned with this process.

Prior to the establishment of a Community Education Service in Strathclyde Region and other Scottish regions in the late 70's, a Youth and Community Service operated within the education department of the Regional Council. The growth of a youth service within statutory authorities had been relatively slow from the time of the Second World War until the publication of the *Albermarle Report*[1] in 1960 and the establishment of the Consultative Council for Youth Service in Scotland in the same year. The former recognised that, by this time, the work situations of youth workers in local authorities ranged from coffee bar management and 'detached' work in open play spaces, to the executive control of large youth centres[2]. Their work was seen in all cases, however, to contain elements of administration, planning and personal contact with young people – this latter dimension affording the opportunity for 'considerable social, educational and pastoral work'.

The *Albermarle Report* acted as an impetus to a speedy development of existing statutory Youth Service and provided the bases for the first full-time professional training course for youth workers. Before long, relatively large numbers of trained youth workers, many of whom had been mature college entrants from a range of industrial and commercial backgrounds, were being appointed to the Youth Services run by the County Councils in Scotland in the early 60's. The training, based broadly on the theme of the Report, which had emphasised 'training, association and challenge', was predominantly into roles as manager, counsellor, educator, group worker and social relations officer. Many of these graduates brought with them skills gained over years as voluntary workers in youth organisations.

The *Albermarle Report* had been inspired by the apparently increasing affluence and independence of the youth of the late 50's which was believed to have led to a breakdown of the 'traditional constraints of authority'[3]. Commitment to the idea of training and challenge was central to the report as was the concern to allow young people of both sexes to associate with each other within informal, relatively unstructured, learning experiences. A direct learning role was attributed to youth workers within the context of social education in the section of the report entitled "Preparation for Adult Life', indicating that youth club members should be encouraged to participate in discussions concerning religious, political and industrial relations issues. Above all there was an emphasis upon the need to reach the 'unattached' – the relatively large group of adolescents who had been alienated by the previous experiences of schooling, family and community life.

Because of these broad concerns, the value base of the developing Youth Service was the belief that programmes should begin with the needs of youth people and should 'start where they are'. It became important to know a great deal about the concerns of young people and their interests so that the programmes could appropriately reflect these. It was necessary for curricula to be flexible – to respond to changing need, to be available at times when young people preferred or were ready for it. Youth club programmes were to be developed as a means to an end and not necessarily an end in themselves. For example the 'shop window' attraction of the weekend camp was the means by which the worker was able to work positively with a group to develop new interests and create group learning situations. Every opportunity was to be taken to encourage young people to take leadership themselves and to undertake responsible roles in the organisation – so being allowed and encouraged to learn and grow from these experiences. These ideas provided a rich basis for the subsequent development of a community based model of adult learning.

During the late 50's and early 60's moves were already taking place in the development of a community dimension within statutory service provision. The Education (Scotland) Act of 1945 brought within the ambit of education a whole range of activities of numerous national and local adult organisations. The Act had opened up the way for authorities to assist these bodies, and in 1967 aid was given to some 2,750 local groups. The same Act enabled authorities to promote schemes of informal education for adults. In discharging their duties under the Act, authorities have given emphasis to establishing, maintaining and assisting organisations in the areas which are designed to service general community needs; in particular, community associations in centres.

The *Community of Interests Report*[4] gave an impetus to this development and the Youth Service Development Council in 1969 published a further report entitled *Youth and Community Work in the 70's* which effectively underlined the development of a Youth and Community Service[5]. Within the latter, the writers of the Report developed the theme of the social and political involvement of young people indicating 'we are not so much concerned today as in the past with basic education, with economic needs, or with the communication of an agreed value belief or system, but to help young people to create their place in the changing society and it is their critical involvement with the community which is the goal. We have in mind not that the young person would simply be practising democracy for future use in real life; but rather he would be living and contributing directly towards a democratic way of life'[6].

A central theme, therefore, was the emphasis upon the role of young people in community action and social change. Particularly significant for the subsequent development of a Community Education Service was the way in which the report and subsequent development in local authority's policies emphasised the community work dimension. The marriage of youth service and community work meant a commitment to all age groups, an extension of provision, and certain differences in approach in relation to working with people. In developing what it called the 'activity society', the Report called for the direct involvement of local people in their own affairs and for processes which would allow those most disadvantaged to gain the skills and to develop the abilities to improve the economic, social and cultural conditions of communities. The processes of community organisation, community development and community action encompassed a range of strategies which could encourage and support this process [7].

The Youth and Community Service, because of these changes in theory and practice, was now recruiting and training those who would work with adults as well as young people in a facilitating, non-directive and training role. Instead of 'leadership' provided from 'the front', so to speak, as in the early days of the Youth Service, the practitioner in the Youth and Community Service learned to work through a community development process. In this process the worker assists the community or group to identify its needs or objectives; to order these needs and objectives in terms of specific priorities; to build the skills and develop the confidence to work at the objectives; to find the resources both internal and external to deal with them; and finally to take action in respect of these objectives[8]. The group is encouraged by the worker to develop its own leadership resources.

In the community development approach there is the belief that control of key areas of community life can have beneficial repercussions for individuals in community groups and other aspects of living. it begins from the belief that individuals have the right to express individuality and it emphasises the value of self-induced change over induced change. There is also an intention to develop co-operation and integration amongst community groups. A central tenet of this approach is also the belief that process is all important, if not more important than content in educational programmed since the sensitive group worker would be attempting to use group experiences to develop skills and learning.

Throughout the period of the late 60's and early 70's, Youth and Community Services within statutory authorities in Scotland increasingly became involved with a wide range of community groups, tenants' associations, village hall committees and community councils. Programmes were for 'target' groups of all ages in the community. Work developed with play schemes, unattached young people, young mothers, the elderly, the unemployed and a range of other community groups with specific learning needs and interests. In 1975 the Alexander Report entitled *Adult Education: the Challenge of Change* recommended that adult education should be regarded as an aspect of community education and with the Youth and Community Service, should be incorporated into the Community Education Service[9]. Strathclyde Regional Council along with most of the other regional councils in Scotland, implemented this recommendation and the former Youth and Community Service became a Community Education Service.

Essentially the Alexander Report was not about community education *per se,* but concerned itself with the appropriate delivery of adult education in Scotland. At the heart of the Alexander Report was the concern to emphasise the belief that education should be a continuing experience spread over the whole of life. Secondly, the report stressed the belief that adult education was not concerned solely or primarily with the training of the intellect. 'The aim is to enable each person to develop his various capacities to the full and to become an informed and responsible citizen'[10]. It further emphasised that instead of the form and content of education being concentrated on subjects, it was necessary now to pay particular attention to the identification and satisfaction of needs. Even more significantly it emphasised the need to concentrate upon what educational programmes 'do' rather than on what educational programmes 'contain'.

The specific aims identified by the Alexander Report for adult education were:

a)   the reaffirmation of individuality

b)   the effective use of the resources of society

c)   to foster a pluralist society

d)   education for change.

Amongst other things, it highlighted specific areas of expansion relating to particular target groups; for example, young mothers, the elderly, those working unsocial hours, ethnic minority groups, the disadvantaged through educational or physical handicap, those living in areas of multiple deprivation and rural areas. In order to secure the proposed development, 200 additional full-time staff were considered to be required across Scotland. Unfortunately, the additional resources were not to be made available and the vision of the Alexander Report had to be approached from within the existing resources of the Community Education Service, voluntary organisations and the adult education departments of universities, with resulting restrictions upon the capacity to deliver a full service.

The Community Education Service had now, however, become established within Strathclyde, undertaking three principal functions:

(a)   services for young people

(b)   adult and continuing education

(c)   general services to the community.

In the late 70's, fieldwork community education staff, having been previously centre based, were re-organised into geographical area teams. Divisional adult basic education organisers were appointed and the education work which developed through area teams and from divisional units has been heavily reliant upon the part-time teachers, leaders and volunteer tutors. The Council's current policy for the role of community education and the delivery of adult and continuing education specifies its responsibility for the following:

(a)   participation in the planning and delivery of an integrated programme of post-16 learning opportunities across the Region, encompassing formal, informal and voluntary provision, including basic and compensatory education, residential courses and summer schools;

(b)   ensuring that adults have information/advice on and access to continuing educational opportunities;

(c)   the development and promotion of distance learning packages;

(d)   the development, in liaison with other appropriate Regional Council departments and other agencies, of adult education services for specific groups in need in the community, involving services for young mothers, the elderly, adults working unsocial hours, adult immigrants, the disadvantaged, inmates of penal establishments, the handicapped and one-parent families;

e) liaison with assistance and advisory services to voluntary groups involved in the field of services to adults and assisting communities in establishing voluntary groups and agencies where there is an expressed need;

f) collaboration with universities, colleges, the Workers' Educational Association and other voluntary agencies in respect of adult education provision;

g) provision of training for adult education tutors and specialists in various fields of adult education.

The Application of a Community Development Approach to the Creation of Learning Opportunities

From the section above it will be seen that the current Community Education Service consists of full-time, part-time and volunteer staff deployed in area and divisional teams across the breadth of Strathclyde. The council's social strategy for the 80's ensures that there is a clear emphasis in resource allocation to neighbourhoods which are designated areas of priority treatment. In practical terms this means that staffing and funding are proportionately allocated to give extra support to these areas. In addition, particular policy and practice emphases are given to key policy areas of strategic concern – notably youth services, single parents, adult education, pre-fives, the elderly and service to the unemployed. Community education workers are therefore continuously in contact with a wide range of target groups and are centrally placed to be involved in the kind of developmental role envisaged within a community based adult learning strategy. The natural relationship which exists between workers in the Service and a wide range of existing community groups, tenants' association and local structures makes this an excellent springboard for the field worker in the identification of realistic and expressed educational needs around which appropriate programmes can be developed.

Central to the whole concern for a community development approach to adult learning is the fear expressed by a number of commentators over the last few years that adult education services have served some publics far better than others because of the huge gap between public lifestyles and experience and the structure of provision[11]. Although informality has been seen to be the basis of the approach in traditional adult education, the rhetoric and the reality are a variance. As Lovett observes, 'the nature of the service is decided – with few exceptions – by those in control. The criterion for success is judged in terms of formal classes and the numbers attending. All the bureaucratic paraphernalia of register and forms are much in evidence. Students participate in an education process decided for them'[12]. This 'centre-periphery' model can be seen demonstrated in the way in which local authority adult education programmes have been advertised in the past (See Diagram I).

The criterion of success in this form of approach to the public is whether in fact classes receive sufficient applicants! It depended greatly upon the motivation of those who read the advertisements and whether they were already skilled or confident enough to become involved in formalised classes. It was not uncommon for a perverse judgement to be made on those from deprived communities who did not avail themselves of adult education classes and because of this were seen to be either too apathetic, intellectually limited, or only concerned to participate in more social past-times. The strength of recent research has, however, pointed to the fact that this is just not true and that the so-called lack of motivation or confidence has often been inspired by earlier unsatisfactory experiences of education which has damaged self-esteem[13]. Furthermore, when educational programmes are developed in accordance with the community development model, the results in this Region have been astounding and the personal gains for local people in terms of education development have exceeded even their own expectations!

This approach has the advantage of attempting to make adult learning relevant. Combining the value basis of youth work, community work and community education it attempts to start where people are; emphasises issues rather than subjects; concentrates on discovering local needs to examine them as local groups perceive them; it is flexible, open-ended and does not restrict itself to the periods during which education has traditionally been seen to be possible (e.g. between 7-9pm for 10 weeks per session and never during the summer holidays!).

The criticism that the Community Education Service, by espousing this model, has been unable to properly develop adult education which was sufficiently cognitive is open to debate. Such a view mistakenly overlooks the cognitive nature of issue based educational provision which is related to the examination of local problems; the introduction of new ideas and the creation of new experience; the development of skills; decision-making and practical implementation of programmes. Secondly, the viewpoint overlooks the fact that the good community education worker will seek for participants avenues out of initial experiences for adults into new and more challenging educational opportunities. It has not been uncommon for individuals from groups in deprived communities to demand further educational opportunities and to progress on through structured 'O' grade and Higher courses to further education college or university. Finally, the 'cognitive' argument seems always to argue for an elitist 'hierarchy' in education provision, relegating community based provision to the equivalent position of second best.

As Fordham et al. have indicated, the educational process of working with groups of people around topics or problems which are meaningful to them, and that they determine, is not easy[14]. The worker needs to spend time helping people to see what he or she is trying to achieve, and how that relates to the education service. When 'education' does not depend upon a central system of servicing or decision-making and becomes an activity directed by people themselves, it may seem to officials to be more difficult to separate it from other community activities. Clearly the rejection of the mystique of the expert and attachment to pre-packed curricula in favour of the positive commitment to provide educational opportunities which people in deprived communities really want, is close to the community development approach. With this approach it is more difficult to define 'success' and therefore to convince others in the educational world that what is going on is really educational! It is disappointing, but not surprising, that some educationalists need persuading that the work could not be better undertaken by 'teachers'! Those working face to face with groups in such a strategy as a network agent have special training and support needs which we have only just begun to be able to properly provide[15].

DIAGRAM 1

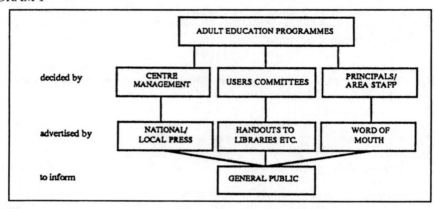

Problems

The programmes may not meet local needs. People are perhaps apprehensive about 'joining'. People are often put off by complicated enrolment procedures. There appears to be a general apathy and lack of motivation. The process reinforces the lack of confidence of local people by 'distancing' provision from their real needs. Classes are too expensive for many, despite concerns for the unemployed and disadvantaged.

DIAGRAM 2

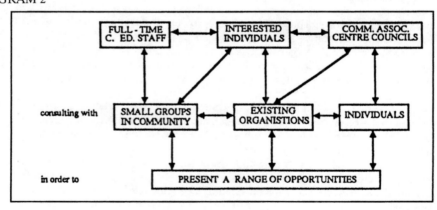

For adult learning which is then delivered in modes and settings which are appropriate to local people. The curriculum is negotiated, and further educational opportunities are built upon existing experiences.

KEY FEATURES: Real methods of consultation, utilisation of local skill, reliance upon local intuition and advice, de-formalisation of procedures, the engagement of local 'experts' as tutors

The approach which has been identified above (Diagram 2) refutes the pathological view towards people living in deprived communities. Encouraging examples of good practice are available right across the Region, such as the explosion in adult education opportunities which happened as a result of an adult education day conference held on a Sunday in a local primary school in the Strone/ Maukinhill area of Greenock. Over 100 local people attended, many of whom had never been to an educational conference before. The day included exhibitions, group discussions, seminars and work groups. An adult education advisory group of local people was established, from which has developed a whole string of educational opportunities relating to community studies, women's self-defence, budgeting on a low income, communication through drama, health issues, and businesses. The workers and local people operating together succeeded in providing adult education opportunities where previous traditional agencies and approaches had consistently failed.

The Role of a Field Based Service in the Region's Post-compulsory education survey

In the Autumn of 1982 the Regional Council agreed a policy for the development of post-compulsory education which was followed in January 1983 by the SED publication *16-18's in Scotland – an Action Plan*. This outlined the basis of a new system of education for the 16+ age group. The heart of the regional council's policy relating to post-compulsory education is as follows[16]:

a) the service provided by schools, colleges, the Community Education Service and the Careers Service should be developed to provide a coherent and comprehensive range of provision for the community as a whole within a locality;

b) the provision of post-compulsory education should be based on the concept of education as a continuing process in which the individual will be involved throughout life;

c) the arrangements for the provision of services and educational programmes should be sufficiently flexible to respond to change and changing needs; the planning of provision should be based on as local a framework as is compatible with efficient management and resourcing;

d) the arrangements should be designed to increase the level of participation in education beyond 16 years of age, and particularly in the 16-18 age group.

The intention has been to provide a widening choice to young people and adults over 16 years of age within the locality and to enable them to negotiate his or her programme of study and activity. New modular programmes of non-advanced vocational education are now provided by schools and colleges and provide means of rapidly updating the content of vocational education courses to meet changing needs in the course of work. Combined with a system of credits which lead to the new National Certificate, and their availability to adults throughout life, these courses provide the means of enabling adults to update and change occupational skills.

The secondary school is seen as an educational resource for the entire community and as a consequence becomes the stimulus for the expansion of educational opportunities for all members of the community. (Over 9,000 adults now participate in day-time courses within secondary schools in Strathclyde. Most of these involve mixed groups of day school students and adults).

In August 1983 a system of area curriculum planning groups (ACPGs) was introduced covering the Strathclyde area. The membership of area curriculum planning groups is made up of the local elected regional councillors, head teachers of secondary schools, college principals, the area careers officer, the area community education officer, a number of parents and a member of the divisional directorate.

Area curriculum planning groups are required to fulfil a strategic planning role in relation to the full range of post-16 educational opportunities for a given local area. This role includes:

(a)   the identification of the educational needs of the local population;

(b)   the planning of provision to meet these needs;

(c)   the advertising and marketing of the agreed programmes;

(d)   the monitoring of the implementation of the ACPG's plans;

(e)   the evaluation of the whole process.

In this exciting new development there is a key role for a field based service which has close contacts with community groups and which is involved in the development of adult basic and informal education.

The contribution of the Community Education Service within the post-compulsory educational strategy is as follows. It is delivered as part of the work of the area curriculum planning group.

(a)   a brokerage role in terms of having an overview of existing provision; identifying demand for existing provision; identifying unmet needs; matching demand to provision and negotiating or making alternative or additional provision, (taking into account the key client group identified in the social strategy for the 80's). This is a particularly important role in the light of the development of a vigorous outreach commitment by further education colleges. Already a number of successful collaborative ventures between community education staff and further education college colleagues have allowed key links to be made between the college and community groups with a resultant increase in their capacity to help local communities. Some of the success in bringing adults into schools is also due to the brokerage role which is being played by community education staff and the close relationships which have been developed by schools staff and the local community education team;

(b)   the marketing and publicising of existing provision to the general public, and the provision of information, advice and guidance in relation to the range and choice of educational opportunities. This is a role which the Community Education Service has shared in partnership with the careers service where more detailed expertise is available in relation to educational guidance.

(c)   organising and providing adult basic education, informal education, preparation for study courses, bridging courses and the interface with formal education and training. A great deal of the work which has been developed within and through the relationship of community education staff with existing community groups has been innovative and developmental. It has often served as a stepping stone for local people becoming involved in more formal education and training opportunities. The theory and practice of this innovative developmental work is still underdeveloped and further research and specific in-service training are necessary in order to allow it to flourish.

NOTES AND REFERENCES

1.   Ministry of Education *The Youth Service in England and Wales.* HMSO. The Albermarle Report, 1960.

2.   ibid p. 70.

3.   Abrams, M. *The Adolescent Consumer.* London Press Exchange 1959.

4.   Scottish Education Department *Community of Interests* (Schools, Youth Service, Community Service, Further Education Colleges, Evening Classes and Sports Organisations). HMSO. 1968.

5.   Department of Education & Science *Youth and Community Work in the 70's.* HMSO. 1969.

6.   ibid. p. 55.

7.   Jones, D. *'Community Work in the United Kingdom'* in Henderson, P. Thomas D.N., (1981). *Readings in Community Work* (p. 6.) George Allen & Unwin. London.

8.   Ross, M.G. *Community Organisation – Theory, Principles & Practice.* (pp. 7–9) Harper and Row, New York. 1967.

9.   Scottish Education, *Adult Education: The Challenge of Change.* Department HMSO. 1975.

10.   ibid. p. 23.

11.   Strathclyde Regional Council *Social Strategy for the Eighties* (SRC). 1984

12.   Jackson, K. *'Adult Education & Community Development'* in Studies in Adult Education. October 1970 p.156-79. Harrison, J. *'Community Work & Adult Education'* in Studies in Adult Education. Vol. 61974 pp.50-67. Fordham, P. et al. *Learning Networks in Adult Education.* Routledge & Keegan Paul. 1970.

13.   Lovett, T. *'Adult Education and Community Development – a Network Approach.'* Lecture at University of Liverpool, June 1973.

14.   Midwinter, E. *Priority Education:* An Account of the Liverpool Project. Penguin, London. 1972. Lovett, T. *Adult Education, Community Development and the Working Class.* Ward Lock. 1975.

15.   Fordham et al. op.cit., Chapter 8 *'Non-formal Work – a New Approach'.* 1979.

16.   Lovett identifies the network agent's role as follows:

    a)   making contact with the variety of informal groups and local activists operating in working class communities and establishing a close relationship with them, b) becoming aware of the problems, needs and interests in the community, c) identifying those that are explicitly educational recognising those that would benefit from some form of adult education and

    d)   translating these into acceptable educational forms (i.e. acceptable to those concerned). p.132.

17.   Strathclyde Regional Council Department of Education. *Post Compulsory Education – Current Position* (p.2 & 3). 1985.

Also consulted:

Newman M. *Adult Education and Community Action*, Writers and Reader's Co-operative, London. 1970.

Thompson, Jane L. *Adult Education for a Change*, Hutchinson and Co. London. 1980.

LEO HENDRY, IAN CRAIK, JOHN LOVE, and JOHN MACK
MEASURING THE BENEFITS OF YOUTH WORK

A REPORT TO THE SCOTTISH OFFICE EDUCATION DEPARTMENT pp 77-90 1991

Introduction

There are no symbolic 'rites of adulthood' in western society so any young person's route towards adulthood is not marked out by clearly defined signposts which indicate progress in a desired direction. Adolescence involves systematic changes in social development, in the nature of necessary social skills and in relationships. Family relations are altered and the adolescent begins to encounter many new demands and expectations within his/her social roles. Adolescents may begin dating, working with others in part-time jobs, spending time with peers without adult supervision, or being involved with peers and adults in youth work settings. In this process of socialisation various adults such as teachers, sports coaches and youth leaders with whom young people interact, are important as role models and social agents. When adults take on these more conscious educational goals and roles they are sometimes referred to as mentors. A mentor has been described[1] as an older more experienced person who seeks to further the development of character and competence in a younger person by guiding the latter in acquiring mastery of progressively more complex skills and tasks.

The role of youth groups can allow young people to interact with adult mentors outside their family. Nevertheless, for many young people in modern society there are limited opportunities and occasions to meet and socialise with mentors.[2] Hence the potential value of youth work settings.

The benefits of youth work?

Given the importance of both adults and peers in the development of adolescents, what basic interpretations can be made from the current findings?

We would suggest that there are six major themes underlying our results which will be discussed as follows:

(a) the value of youth work

(b) young people and types of youth work settings

(c) joining, staying with the organisation and leaving youth work

(d) youth work and youth leaders

(e) the benefits of youth work, and

(f) youth work and other professions.

The value of youth work

Given the fact that facilities varied among our five case study areas – creating their own constraints – the range of youth work settings means that there is a selection of activities to attract a broad spectrum of young people with varying interests. From our findings it is clear that the young people who participate in youth work settings value the opportunities and activities available to them. They particularly stressed the enjoyment of the activities, learning new skills, meeting friends, getting out into the community and making excursions and expeditions into the 'wider world'. From the young person's perspective this highlights the importance of experiential learning in adolescence. Further, since enjoyment in the process of learning is perceived as highly important learning may take place more readily, and perhaps less consciously for these adolescents.

From the youth worker's point of view the fact that young people apparently enjoy youth work settings creates the potential for them to provide learning contexts of a high order where young people develop appropriate learning styles. As one part-time youth leader suggested,

> "Youth workers complement what good school teachers should be doing and that is to instil an enquiring and discerning mind, encourage individuality, confidence and natural skills. Youth workers should also encourage social awareness and development in a friendly and relaxed manner which distinguishes them from the contribution associated with teachers".

This is in line with ideas of an enabling approach that aims to develop a young person's ability to think through, evaluate and make his or her own decisions and choices regarding social and leisure skills whilst understanding the impact of these choices upon their own life and upon others in society.[3] Such training of decision making and evaluative and social skills it has been argued would allow adolescents to develop an effective self-awareness and self-agency. It also raises questions about a broader based approach to youth work in later adolescence, away from membership towards a networking of skills learning (perhaps even linked to youth training schemes) with the inclusion of social skills. There is a need to consider the developmental sequencing of educational approaches in enabling young people to develop decision-making skills.

Drawing on complementary data from the Young People's Leisure & Lifestyles Project[4] there is strong evidence of an association between greater psychological well-being and membership of youth organisations. When coupled with evidence about the greater sociability of youth organisation participants (in terms of their free time associations), a picture begins to emerge of youth work drawing on a constituency of well-balanced and socially integrated young people. Although it would be inappropriate at this stage to posit any causal relationship between such benefits and youth work participation, there is a need to probe further – through longitudinal study – because the possibility of such an association is interesting indeed.

Young people and types of youth work settings

Youth clubs and youth organisations touch the majority of young people, however briefly and temporarily, and in this way do play a part in their social and leisure lives. Yet in a 1976 study of youth and community centres, one of the models found to be of major relevance was called the 'socialisation model' in which adolescents were seen to be socialised or made ready for adult society – learning and accepting approved patterns of social behaviour, knowledge and values. These views have been more recently extended and reconstructed to argue that this kind of 'conservative' youth work produces a compliant and unquestioning youth. Such studies consider young people to be capable of making sense of their situation in society but to be constrained by their position in the social structures of class, gender and race.

Whether or not youth work settings enable young people to understand better their developing roles in society, it is possible to claim from our study that youth clubs do attract a wide variety of young people cutting across class, gender and ethnic lines and this was true of all the areas we studied. There are differential attractions to membership of youth organisations however. Younger adolescents from the ages of twelve to fifteen are more likely to belong to youth clubs and also to uniformed groups. Further, youth club members are also highly likely to belong to sport and activity groups. As such, the findings demonstrate overlapping membership. Although no gender or class differences in membership of any youth organisations were found, there were nevertheless age and gender differences in the reasons given by young people for attending youth organisations. Males claimed that they were more likely to attend to take part in games and sports, while younger adolescents were more likely to attend because they had little else to do in their neighbourhood.

Notwithstanding the degree of overlapping membership (around 60% of the total sample) it is still possible to point towards certain differences in membership. In general it can be stated that young people attracted to uniformed organisations appeared to have more activities available to them and were afforded wider learning opportunities. Although this may suggest greater benefits from participation in uniformed organisations, it may be that possible benefits associated with more informal groups are simply more difficult to measure. Evidence from our case studies suggests that participants in every youth work setting derive benefits through involvement. Youth clubs appear to attract all types of young people and to be seen by adolescents mainly as venues in which to play sports and as a social context for meeting friends. Youth clubs also stand out as a setting in which young people can meet up with the opposite sex. Learning to relate to peers, the opposite sex and adults from the adolescents' perspective, is perhaps among the most important learning experiences gained at this stage of life. Sporting and activity groups were shown to attract both younger and older adolescents, males and females, and adolescents from both manual and non-manual social classes in equal proportions. From the one case study of ethnic groups, young Asian women appeared to derive personal and social benefits from single sex groupings. Thus, it would seem that the range of youth provision is attractive to a variety of young people, particularly in early adolescence, and provides opportunities for individual 'growth' in a variety of ways – physically, socially, in accepting challenge, in the acceptance of others and in the development of self-confidence. Developing self-confidence is essentially an educational experience for the individual, and learning about self, capabilities, being able to express views and challenge ideas should be measured in educational terms. Youth leaders stated that the process of helping youngsters to develop self-confidence was of high priority to them.

The current findings extend previous Scottish research[7] in showing that young people's attitudes to youth leaders are basically positive. Such positive attitudes, however, involved a variety of perceptions about the approved qualities of youth leaders. Thus friendliness, organising ability, trustworthiness and an ability to keep the peace were all descriptors readily applied to youth leaders by young people in the present study. Such favourable perceptions of youth leaders suggest that young people relate well with these adults and are willing to subscribe to an acceptance of rules and adult authority. Linked to this acceptance of leadership the case studies showed that young people's feelings of group solidarity were fairly clear. They were loyal to their own colleagues and youth leaders and indicated a strong need to identify and belong, and to support their own particular group, seeing it as a mirror image and a reinforcement of their own qualities and characteristics. By contrast their perceptions of young people of other groups contained certain negative views.

Joining, staying with the organisation and leaving youth work

Evidence from the Young People's Leisure & Lifestyles Project[8] suggests that there are differences among young people in terms of leisure behaviours and attitudes. Adolescents who are youth club members are less likely to spend leisure time alone and more likely to spend that time either with a boy or girl friend and likely to socialise in groups with other adolescent boys and girls. In terms of attitudes youth club members are more likely to want help in organising their leisure, to believe that leisure should teach them life skills and more likely to see links between the skills and attitudes of work and those of leisure time. The study showed that young people move on from adult-led youth organisations in mid-adolescence towards more casual peer-oriented activities and interests.

The turning point in membership of youth clubs seems to be around the age of 16/17 years. The drop-off is also associated with school attendance. Among those at school in the sample 36% were youth club members. Only 13% of those who had left school however were members. (All those aged 13 to 16 years were still at school). As such, leaving school goes along with leaving youth organisations. Further, it has been suggested that the reason for leaving youth work settings is partly due to the fact that young people on leaving school not only begin to seek greater control in decision-making but also because socially they are ready to experiment with adult-type roles without the ever presence of adults. The peer group – or a small network of close friends – is then used to reinforce and reaffirm developing social identities. This raises questions about the short-term and long-term benefits of youth work.

It can be argued that many young people grow through youth organisations towards more independent living in the adult world. Thus youth work can be seen as an important part of the developmental stage of early adolescence for many young people. Within the overall decline in youth membership noted from the Young People's Leisure & Lifestyles Project the fact that working class young people show a more marked drop out from youth club involvement merits further consideration. If many young people in early adolescence are disposed towards youth work settings as important learning contexts then should not youth work capitalise upon such positive attitudes and enable them to develop the social skills, self-agency and competencies necessary for later adolescence and adulthood.

The period of mid-adolescence is also important since it has been shown that the move towards casual peer-oriented activities around this time can be linked to delinquent behaviour. This is further compounded by various leisure provision which fails to address the needs of many adolescents at this critical developmental stage:

> 'Leisure provision tends to be structured in a manner that assumes potential users of facilities to have the characteristics of affluence, mobility and an ability to make rational selections among the leisure alternatives offered to them. There also appears to be an assumption on the part of leisure planners that social integration into the middle classes is the ultimate goal to which the working classes aspire. Social class appears to have been disregarded in planning for leisure.[9]

Whilst it is not suggested that youth work settings create such societal divisions it is important for youth workers to be aware of this crucial period in adolescence and to offer activities that are appropriate to young people's needs. It is also important to question how youth work values can be translated into the various sub-cultural needs of adolescents.

As the young person grows towards adulthood there is a desire for control to move from adults towards self-autonomy in planning and decision-making, thus rules begin to figure prominently in the young person's decisions about staying with youth organisations or moving on to other leisure pursuits. As the adolescent grows older he/she becomes more critical, questioning and sceptical of adult-oriented organisations and wishes to use young people of his/her own age to reinforce an emergent self-image. The need to feel independent of adult supervision may be a vital reason why many older adolescents move towards commercial leisure provision in pubs, clubs and discos in the pursuit of adult status.

Despite recent claims in national documents on aims and objectives for 'shared responsibility and decision-making' in youth work what evidence is there for opportunities to develop organisational and decision-making skills? With respect to 'shared responsibility' our findings show that 'decision-making' in youth groups is perceived by both the young people and youth workers as being mainly the prerogative of the leaders and only shared in the 'planning of events' and 'fund-raising'. There was limited evidence in the case studies, and no evidence from the survey of young people alone taking decisions (about anything). Such findings raise important questions about the perceptions of young people (and of those working with young people in early adolescence) concerning decision-making; about providing opportunities for young people to develop responsibility and decision-making skills; and about giving them opportunities to reflect on activities and having de-briefing sessions to raise awareness of decision-making processes. These procedures would also have implications for youth work training.

Youth work and youth leaders

Youth workers had a general acceptance of the official aims of youth work as stated by the various youth organisations. Overall they sought to instil confidence in young people, encourage decision-making and promote a variety of social skills. Such goals were variously expressed in response to a question about the qualities, skills, abilities and values young people gain specifically from youth work:

'.... self-confidence, the ability to talk to/form relations with others.'

[part-time worker, male, 26]

'.... (an) ability to test, build and sustain relationships ....'

[full-time worker, female, 26]

'.... taking responsibility, making choices, supporting group decisions ....'

[part-time worker, female, 36]

'.... confidence to speak out and be heard, patience, sharing, listening .... acceptance of others and the ability to make choices.'

[full-time worker, female, 37]

'.... ability to develop decision-making through informed choices.'

[full-time worker, male, 44]

'.... the ability to get on with others, particularly their peer group.... to learn .... to become confident, caring adults.'

[part-time worker, female, 38]

The question then becomes how these aims are interpreted into procedures in working with young people? Leadership in youth work settings has been questioned by several writers. The fundamental problem in successfully running a youth centre would seem to revolve around how authoritarian or democratic the youth workers should be. In some settings we saw a team of youth workers proceed in a most collaborative way taking on different roles so that there may be one who acted as the 'intuitive organiser', another as the more authoritarian 'rule-keeper', and yet another getting involved in helping young people to do things, overall creating a valuable integrated team. Nevertheless, in other settings a 'cognitive gap' seemed to appear where youth leaders were simply coping rather than working constructively and positively with young people in a planned way, perhaps because of the numbers involved. Indeed such functional involvement with young people was further evidenced in the responses of a number of youth leaders to a question about the major benefits of youth work to society:

'.... keeps them off the streets and allows them the chance to take part in activities and mix.'

[part-time worker, female, 27]

'.... keeping trouble off the streets – social control.'

[full-time worker, male, 44]

'.... keeps them off the streets, away from their parents, gives them the opportunities to enjoy themselves ....'

[full-time worker, male, 41]

'.... can be an agent of social control. It should allow young people to discuss issues affecting society and thus foster a better understanding.'

[fieldwork manager, male, 37]

In certain settings there were also differences in perceptions between full-time and part-time workers, with part-time workers considering the full-time leaders as not being sufficiently involved and caring about young people. This suggests a number of dilemmas and paradoxes that face youth leaders. These can be presented as a series of questions for youth leaders:

(a)   How much choice of activities to be offered to young people?

(b)   How much freedom to be allowed to the individual?

(c)   How to offer challenge with a long-term developmental goal?

(d)   How to provide for the short-term needs of young people?

(e)   How to provide appropriate facilities for young people given various resource constraints?

(f)   How to devise agreed rules for safety and security?

(g)   How to ensure enjoyment for young people?

(h)   How to convert aims into practices which can be understood by all concerned?

What this tends to suggest is that within some youth work settings youth leaders and adolescents may operate parallel agendas. It raises the question of whether or not youth work aims should remain implicit or be made more explicit and put 'up front' so that as young people grow older within youth organisations they are enabled to develop an understanding of the underlying objectives of the activities they engage in and are given greater awareness of the social control function of youth work described above as 'Keeping trouble off the streets'! This stresses the importance of 'reflection on learning processes' aimed at developing young people's strategies to discriminate, and assess values within youth work's hidden agenda: it enables choice rather than conformity.

It has been argued that there is a danger of a gap between what youth workers claim to be doing and the actual practices of youth work[10] and, in an English context, it has been suggested that youth workers are sometimes confused about their aims and objectives, that policies and priorities may be non-existent, unclear or confused, and that youth workers and officers are all well able to articulate a professional rhetoric but their notions of social education are extremely hazy.[11]

By comparison we would argue that youth workers present a fairly consensual view of aims and objectives commensurate with stated aims in national documents. Equally we would argue that the variety of approaches taken to youth work and the variety of styles employed suggest an expression of divergent ideologies and an emphasis on varying practices which reflect the wide range of youth work settings available to young people.

The benefits of youth work?

What our findings show is that over the year of fieldwork in the case study areas: young people who participate in youth work show a development of self-confidence, in their enjoyment of activities, in their participation, their improving sense of values, the development of their social skills and the widening of their horizons. Nevertheless, a year is an extremely short time to assess these developments accurately and whilst the Blantyre study gives some evidence of longer-term enhancement and empowerment of skills and social competences, it is recommended that a longer-term longitudinal study would be valuable in assessing the benefits of youth work to individuals by tracing them into adulthood and examining their socialisation over a period of time and assessing the perceptions of others about their attitudes, social skills, self-confidence and participation in their wider community. After all it was the perception of many youth leaders that youth work benefits society by preparing young people for their adult roles and responsibilities. Youth work was seen as:

> '.... encouraging young people to develop their full potential .... (in order to) make a more meaningful contribution to the society in which they live.'
> [part-time worker, female, 38]

> '.... an essential investment to produce responsible, participating citizens.'
> [part-time worker, male, 41]

> ... '(developing) young people who are well-balanced and have a stable outlook on society.'
> [part-time worker, male, 391]

> ... '(encouraging) young people to learn to live within a community and become a part of the community rather than against it.'
> [part-time worker, male, 31]

> '.... allowing young people to participate in projects in the community and giving them the skills to enter into life outside school .... as responsible adults'
> [fieldwork manager, female, 24]

It is also important to stress that there are benefits to youth leaders. Not only do they enjoy their professional roles, be it full-time or part-time but the challenges involved in working with young people develop their self-confidence. For instance, skills and competences gained through a variety of work roles can be usefully employed and developed in youth work situations.. Another important point to indicate is the way in which youth leaders are better able to see their own children in perspective through working with other adolescents.

Youth work and other professions

Youth work, unlike the teaching profession, has a curriculum that is focused largely on the affective domain – on the development of personal and interpersonal skills and cannot be measured in outcome terms of Standard Grades and Highers. This places the profession at somewhat of a disadvantage in arguing for resources to enhance its services for young people. Youth work, in outlining its needs in resource terms, has no formula to operate on like the 'Red Book' of the Scottish Office Education Department; thus youth work often operates with poor facilities and limited resources. The HMI Report 'Responsive Youth Work' (Department of Education and Science, 1990) might be a useful start to the debate as to how a resource formula for youth work is established.

Concluding Remarks

It has been suggested[12] that there is a substantial body of youth work which gains its identity and purpose from a wide range of institutions, groupings and organisations, and contains a variety of ideological differences built into its various traditions. Hence youth work does not coalesce into a cohesive whole but rather is manifested in forms that are independent and exist to be independent. We would contend from our study that this variety is indeed the strength whereby youth work flourishes in Scotland and fulfils adolescents' needs in a wide range of settings.

Despite these differences any study of young people reveals a complicated network of relationships among adolescents, their peers, adults and authority. This network is further complicated by the many and diverse situations in which young people find themselves. The key to success in youth work lies in this network of relationships and how it develops when young people and interested adults work together. Where this network does not develop positively, or breaks down, productive youth work is always at risk. The present report has attempted to outline the elements in various youth work settings which should be considered in trying to provide a framework within which this network of relationships is most likely to be positive and productive.

REFERENCES

1. Hamilton, S. & Darling, N., *'Mentors in Adolescents' lives'*, in Hurrelmann, K and Engel, V. (eds) *The Social World of Adolescents*. Berlin and New York: pp 121–139, 1989.

2. Hendry, L. *The Influence of Adults and Peers on Adolescents' Lifestyles and Leisure Styles*, in Harrelman and Engel ibid. pp 245–267, 1989.

3. Mundy, J. & Odum, L. *Leisure*. New York: Wiley 1979.

4. Hendry, L. et al *Young People's Leisure and Lifestyle Project Report*, Phase 1. Edinburgh Scottish Sports Council 1989.

5. Eggleston, J. *Adolescence and Community*. London Arnold, 1976.

6. Taylor, T. *Youth Workers as Character Builders*, In Jeffs, T. and Smith, M. *Youth Work*. London. MacMillan 1987.

7. Hendry, L. et al. *Adolescents in Community Centres: Some Urban and Rural Comparisons*, Scottish Journal of Physical Education 9, 28–40, 1981.

8. Hendry, L. et al op cit, 1989.

9. Hendry, L. *Growing Up and Going Out*. Aberdeen University Press. 1983(1983)

10. Taylor, op cit, 1987.

11. Jeffs, T & Smith, M, op cit, 1987

12. Jeffs, T & Smith, M, *Welfare and Youth Work Practice*. London MacMillan, 1988.

YOUTH WORK CURRICULUM

SCOTTISH STANDING CONFERENCE OF VOLUNTARY YOUTH ORGANISATIONS 1989 (REVISED 1994)

Youth work and youth provision

In developing guidelines for youth work, it is important to be clear what constitutes youth work and what does not. There is a difference between youth work and the provision of services and facilities for young people in their out of school or non-work time. Because the two often overlap, and good youth work also involves youth provision, the two are sometimes confused.

There are similarities and points of contact in that both are targeted at the same groups, and in both young people participate of their own free will. Youth work may happen within youth provision, e.g. the youth club meeting in the youth centre. This bridge between the two must be maintained as both youth work and youth provision are important to one another.

Youth work is distinguished by two main elements:

- youth work is always educational

- youth work involves constructive intervention

Youth work is always educational

The deliberate goal of youth work activities and programmes is the learning, growth and development of young people. The work of youth organisations encompasses young people from 5 to 25 years, but a focus on the transition from childhood to adulthood is a clear priority. It is about a conscious attempt to assist:

- their personal development and growth to maturity

- the development of participative and social skills that are transferable to enable involvement in society at large.

Youth work involves constructive intervention

Essential to youth work is the sensitive and skillful intervention of adults working alongside young people. Young people are not left totally on their own, with the adult simply making facilities available or stamping membership cards. The good youth worker is sensitive to the balance between the need for young people to be free to make their own decisions, and their need for assistance, advice and support. The youth worker's skill is in knowing how and when to intervene so enabling learning to take place.

Constructive intervention is not about controlling young people in such a way as to remove their freedom of choice. It is about facilitating their responsible decision making and action, with a view to the definite goals of youth work, i.e. learning, growth and development.

There is often confusion between the non-directive and 'laissez-faire' approaches to youth work. The 'laissez-faire' approach is at the opposite end of the spectrum from the authoritarian. It is an 'anything goes' approach, with few standards, and little or no effort by the adult to assist the learning process. It denies that there is any need for constructive intervention. The authoritarian by contrast seeks to impose adult standards, ideas and attitudes on young people. The non-directive approach involves adult intervention in a variety of supportive and constructive ways, e.g. with information that enables young people to make their own responsible decisions.

In practice youth workers often find that they are at different points on a continuum between directive and non directive. The actual point depends on a variety of factors, e.g. the age of the young people, the type of activity, or the situation in which they find themselves. The youth worker responsible for a group of young people on a mountain ridge will clearly need to be more directive than with the same group in the coffee bar. Constructive intervention is about the right approach at the right time.

Youth provision is about making facilities and resources available to young people, for example recreation facilities at an affordable price, a place to meet, or information about the where, how and when of meeting their varied needs. Youth provision is an important and still underdeveloped aspect of life in Scotland, and in its absence, e.g. if premises were unavailable, much youth work could not happen. It is essential to the development of youth work in Scotland that sufficient resources are made available to provide more and better facilities for young people.

What is youth work curriculum?

A certain mystique has been allowed to develop around youth work curriculum, yet there is no real mystery about it. Lack of clarity about its meaning has arisen because the important issues of objectives, method and ethos have become confused with content. Youth work curriculum is the programme content of a youth organisation or group, developed with the purpose of meeting its aims and objectives. Yet curriculum cannot be viewed in isolation from issues such as method, styles of leadership, or the ethos of an organisation or group. All of these, including an organisation's objectives, must be regularly informed and adapted to take account of the current needs and interests of young people, and the sort of society in which they live. While all these elements are distinct, they are also interdependent. One other element which must permeate all of these is evaluation. This is essential to all stages in the development and practice of youth work to ensure a curriculum that remains relevant. So while curriculum may be defined in simple terms as 'programme content', it is only part of a chain of interrelated and inter-dependent elements, the centre of which must be young people themselves.

Youth work and how it happens

Participation in youth work is voluntary

While young people have a variety of educational opportunities at home and in school, and will also experience adult intervention in both, youth work is different because of its voluntary nature. A young person cannot choose the family to which he or she belongs. Attendance at school is compulsory. In contrast the decision to be in a youth group is a voluntary one, although parental, peer and other pressures may be factors.

Members can choose to opt out of youth work, consequently in developing its curriculum, youth work must provide a wide range of stimuli relevant to young people in order to encourage them to opt in.

The role of the adult worker

The intervening adult's task is to ensure the availability of a range of information, skills, knowledge, attitudes, values and standards which may be accepted, challenged, modified or rejected by the young person. This role is highly significant in the development of the values of a young person. The worker's skill is in being available to assist in selecting and developing plans for action so that at the end of the process there is an identifiable change in the young people. Yet it is essential that the intervening adult, having offered such information and ideas, encourages the young person to make his or her own decision.

The importance of such intervention is clearly expressed in *"Education Observed – Effective Youth Work"*, an HMI Report from England: "... the youth workers' responses are carefully calculated. They use their knowledge of the young people with whom they work to gauge the extent of intervention appropriate to the situation. They make positive suggestions and lay down rational rules – guidelines of behaviour – but do so in a way which maximises the freedom of choice and autonomy of the young people."

The peer group and the adult worker

Nothing in this approach to youth work denies the importance of peer group learning among young people which is in itself one of the methods of youth work. The educational role of the adult in peer group learning is once again that of constructive intervention. For example, the adult is sometimes in a pro-active role, creating the conditions for peer group learning, and structuring the way youth work happens so that such learning can take place. As well as involvement with peer group learning, the adult may have to intervene in relation to peer group pressure. Sometimes the intervention is non-directive but at times it may have to be directive. For example, if a gang has formed within a club as a result of peer group pressure, and that gang is threatening to other young people in the club, a variety of directive interventionist approaches may be required by the worker. So the youth worker can be at various points on the continuum between directive and non-directive, depending on a variety of factors in the situation.

Youth provision, sport, information

The term youth work is often loosely used to cover a wide variety of activities. But some of these youth activities involve neither education nor constructive intervention. In the sense used in this paper, they are not youth work. Setting up a table tennis table in a hall, giving out bats and balls and leaving young people to do their own thing with no adult intervention either in terms of skills or personal development may meet a leisure and recreation need, but it is not youth work. Organising an aggressively competitive football match or boxing tournament with no personal growth and development goal may meet a 'sporting' need but is not youth work. Flooding young people with information without providing support and guidance in the selection of relevant information and its use is not youth work. Yet various activities have the potential to develop into positive youth work if the adults involved intervene to assist the learning process to take place.

Youth work – the social context

Youth work does not happen in a vacuum. When adults fail to take into account the changing social situation of young people, youth work can become irrelevant and ineffective. In the 1980s and early 1990s the transition from childhood to adult status has for many young people been extended due to a number of factors including unemployment and continuing economic dependence on parents yet this is set in the context of a society where many young people do not live in a family with both natural parents. There has been a delay for many young people in establishing their independence and reaching the point where they can exercise responsibilities commonly recognised as being adult, e.g. having disposable income and living in their own home. As a consequence the adoption of adult roles in society is for some occurring at an older age than was the case in the 1960s and 1970s. Yet by contrast, for some others increased wealth in the 1980s and 1990s has resulted in higher expectations and the demand for an earlier adoption of adult roles.

The 1990s have continued to bring further changes. There is already a falling youth population. With fewer young people seeking employment, there may be fewer unemployed, but possibly an even wider standard of living gap between those with and those without jobs.

The development of the European Union is bringing changes in the mobility of young people, jobs and workers. The importance of a second or third language has taken on new dimensions. Youth workers in the 1990s find that they are working in a different social environment from the 1980s. Youth work curriculum must be pro-active as it continues to anticipate and adapt to meet the challenge.

Youth work curriculum guidelines

Curricular guidelines

These guidelines provide a framework within which the curriculum of youth organisations and agencies at all levels should be set.

Regional or national headquarters activity, programme or training should have as its purpose the implementation and support of such a curriculum at local level.

Each youth organisation or group should draw up a curriculum which includes opportunities for young people to:

- Have a wide variety of physical, creative and aesthetic experiences which encourage their personal growth and development.
- Develop progressively towards full participation as partners with adults in the running of the youth organisation.
- Take decisions and accept responsibility for the consequences.
- Reflect on their experience as part of a learning process.
- Experience other environments and lifestyles outside their own immediate neighbourhood.
- Establish and sustain deep and satisfying interpersonal relationships.
- Test values and beliefs.
- Develop spiritual awareness.
- Develop awareness, knowledge and skills, both social and political, for involvement in society.
- Have access to counselling and guidance provision.

Developing curriculum within a youth organisation or group

Checking out the opportunities with members

It may be useful for organisations in planning their work to check out with individual young people who are members the availability of aspects of the curriculum using the chart.

Having identified the areas of curriculum to be developed there are essential and inter-related steps towards this development:

- Plan and negotiate with young people at a level and in a way appropriate to their needs
- Check that you are taking into account the needs of the young people
- Check the aims and objectives of the organisation or group. Ensure that they are related to the needs of young people and not just those of the organisation.
- Develop appropriate programmes. The development of curriculum at regional and national levels is about supporting work at local level, and about undertaking work which cannot be undertaken or is inappropriate at local level.
- Evaluate regularly. A relevant curriculum can never be static.

It is important that curriculum develops to meet changing needs. The youth organisation or group which repeats the same programme year after year will cease to be relevant.

Conclusions

Each group or organisation involved in youth work should be required to produce its own curriculum within these guidelines.

Youth work is always educational.

Youth work involves constructive intervention.

Constructive intervention is about the right approach at the right time.

Youth work curriculum is the programme content of a youth organisation or group, developed with the purpose of meeting its aims and objectives.

Members can choose to opt out of youth work, consequently in developing its curriculum, youth work must provide a wide range of stimuli relevant to young people in order to encourage them to opt in.

The educational role of the adult in peer group learning is once again that of constructive intervention.

Yet various activities have the potential to develop into positive youth work if the adults involved intervene to assist the learning process to take place.

Youth work curriculum must be pro-active as it continues to anticipate and adapts to meet the challenge.

> *"... an educational activity such as youth work, despite its informality and the voluntary nature of participation in it, does need to have clear objectives and to expose itself to the rigour of regular curricular analysis."*

> *"... given the needs of young people in modern society and the wide range of activities included in youth work, the curriculum devised should be characterised by breadth, progression and differentiation".* "Youth Work in Scotland",
>
> (HM Inspectors of Schools, SOED 1991).

COMMUNITY DEVELOPMENT IN THE COMMUNITY EDUCATION SERVICE

PRINCIPAL COMMUNITY EDUCATION OFFICERS GROUP 1992

Introduction

The Principal Community Education Officers in Scotland recently produced papers which considered youth work and adult education within the context of the context of the Community Education Service to assist in the development of comprehensive management plans for youth work and adult education in authorities throughout Scotland.

The intention of the paper is to illustrate how community development enhances the practice of community education by ensuring people of all ages have direct involvement in, and control provision in a way that is relevant to their needs. This is not a new approach but one that should be considered and implemented within the context of the work of the Community Education Service whenever it is relevant to do so.

Community development is not being considered here as a third strand of the Community Education Service to add to its practice in youth work and adult education. Rather it is being seen as an educational approach which builds on already well established good practice in youth work, adult education and community work.

It is not intended to suggest that community development is an approach that is necessarily applicable to all community education work ... it cannot be! However, it must be an important consideration when working with local people in youth work and adult education to develop strategies which address their ideas for development and their demands and problems.

Neither is it intended to suggest that community development is an approach which is the preserve only of the Community Education Service. Many other departments and agencies use this approach from their perspective although usually either to facilitate area based co-ordination of service delivery or to provide extensive consultation and participation before particular decisions are made. It is important to stress its validity within community education and more particularly when community education workers are involved in issues of inequality, disadvantage and marginalisation and are seeking to empower those groups who wish to improve their quality of life.

This Paper attempts to clarify the educational component of community development specifically through face to face development work with groups.

It is hoped that the Paper will provoke active consideration to be given to further growth of a community development approach within the Community Education Service in Scotland by:

- Community education workers

–   The groups with whom they work

–   Managers of the Community Education Service

–   Policy Makers

Historical Background

The Community Education Service and the community development process are inextricably linked and well documented. For example, the Alexander Report *(Adult Education, The Challenge of Change 1975)* stressed the educational character of community development. The Alexander Report defined community development as a process *'by which those who live in a community (defined in either geographical or social terms) are helped or encouraged to act together in tackling problems which affect their lives.'* The report concluded that *'adult education should participate increasingly in community development and much more experimentation is needed.'*

The place of community development within the Community Education Service has had an uncertain past. To some extent this uncertainty is bound up with the way in which the service was created as a result of the recommendations in the Alexander Report. The publication of the Alexander Report came at the time of the re-organisation of local government in Scotland 1975 when most of the Regional and Island Authorities implemented one of the Report's other recommendations which was to create a Community Education Service.

> *"Adult Education should be regarded as an aspect of community education and should, with the youth and community service be incorporated into a community education service".*

Part of the rationale behind this was the idea that education should be seen as a process of life-long learning and it was seen that this could be promoted in practice by integrating the existing services. It was therefore anticipated that community education workers would be able to support a wide range of developments in communities.

There is little doubt that this has been happening. Initiatives have included the Urban Aid programme of funded locally based projects, community self managed and community enterprise developments like co-operatives, tenants action groups, credit unions, many of which have been in partnership with the voluntary sector.

Considerable discussion has taken place since 1975 in reaching a clear view of what the Community Education Service is about in terms of its aims and objectives and how it should carry these out in its methods of work. Of particular interest has been the debate about community development – a term which has often become synonymous with community work. In the context of this report community work covers the wider range of support given to community centres, community groups and, local projects and the like and has been substituted by the Service in some Authorities as the 'third strand' of their main responsibilities i.e. youth work, adult education and community development.

The view is taken in this paper that community development is a process, or a way of working with communities and groups, through face to face developmental work which can be applied to all aspects of community education including youth work, adult education and community work. This view is based on the experience of using the community development approach within the Service (and the evidence from the work of other agencies) which has shown that it can be used with success in a variety of settings.

The Wider Context

During the past decade or so there have been immense social, political, economic and cultural changes in our communities – changes which, for many individuals and groups have engendered feelings of dislocation and loss. An important feature of these changes is the extent to which decision making has become centralised and local communities alienated from a range of decision making processes.

In response to these changes community development is increasingly advocated as a means on empowering local people to take more control of their own affairs and improve the quality of life in their communities. It is of interest to note, for example, that in recent years a number of Local Authorities in Scotland have undertaken a review of their Community Education Service. These reviews have led, amongst other things, to clearer statements about the aims, objectives and methods of community development and the particular educational role the Service can have in empowering people and supporting positive change in communities.

It is important to note that this interest in community development is not confined to the Community Education Service. It can also be seen in the policy statements and activities of other Local Authority departments such as Social Work and Planning or sections of departments specifically charged with developing social/community regeneration strategies. The interest is also evident in the policies of District Councils, Voluntary Organisations and Central Government departments and agencies.

Many of the policies include statements about area based co-ordination of service delivery through inter-department/agency co-operation and partnership and the need to consider integrated strategies for community development which allow a degree of customer participation. This can only be brought about through concerted effort and the sharing of knowledge, skills and resources.

However, it should not be assumed without question that the aims, objectives and methods of one organisation, department or agency are the same as another. Because of this, it is extremely important that the Community Education Service at all levels is clear about what it means by community development both as an idea and also in terms of practice. This is especially the case when co-operative projects and partnerships are being considered, since clarity and understanding of the community education worker's role provides a sound basis for effective collaboration.

One of the few areas of professional training to have developed and concentrated on community development skills as part of its critical qualifying requirements is community education. Many practitioners and trainers are recognised as holding a high level of professional expertise in the theory and practice of community development.

The Community Development Process

The community development process is perhaps best understood as an approach which enables individuals, groups and organisations to come together to identify the things which they think should be improved or changed in their communities and assists them in brining about the actual improvements or changes needed. At its heart, the process is about ordinary people shaping the future of their communities.

From the point of view of the Community Education Service, the process is educational. It is about people in communities creating opportunities for growth and change and deliberate movement towards the ends which they determine and in the process of doing so increase their actual awareness, knowledge, skills and abilities.

As already indicated, the experience of using the community development approach within the Service has shown that it can be used with success in different areas of work. Experience has also demonstrated that successful change is likely to take time to achieve and requires a disciplined and systematic approach by those involved.

An analysis of successful community development initiatives suggests that the process usually involves people in a number of key stages or phases of development. Furthermore, the various stages of development can be made apparent to all those involved and understood by them as a means of planning progress and achieving short and long term goals.

However, it would be a mistake to see or apply these stages of development in a mechanical way. The reality of work is much more fluid; the significance of any stage, the degree to which one stage overlaps with another, the amount and detail of the work involved and the time it will take etc., will vary from one situation to another.

The following exploration of the detailed stages of development is based on a model constructed by the Community Education Service in Lothian Region.

The key stages of the process are:

* **Making contact with the community**

The importance of initial contacts with individuals, groups and organisations, is often underestimated. The way in which it is done and who is contacted will determine a great deal about the future direction of developments and, in particular, whether the ownership of these will be with local people and will be seen to be with local people. Thus workers need to be clear at the outset about the purposes of their contacts, the methods to be used and how the information gathered will be recorded and fed into the next stages of the process.

* **The identification of ideas for development**

It is important to recognise the different sources of ideas e.g. those from individuals, groups or organisations in the community – and those from the worker(s). It is very difficult for the meaningful change to take place unless there is a positive vision of the future. Thus the identification of ideas which present hope, expectations and widen horizons is essential.

Initial ideas need to be examined in terms of their potential for change and whether or not they are attainable. Other factors involved at this stage are the worker's judgement of the ideas, whether they can be taken on by the funding agency, or whether there may be a conflict of ideas. The latter point needs careful consideration since action around a particular objective may bring the group/organisation/worker into conflict with each other or the funding agency or another organisation or agency in the area.

* **Establishing the contact**

This stage involves detailed discussion of the expectations held by the group(s)/organisation(s)/worker(s) concerned, and negotiating common objectives and decisions about how responsibilities should be shared out.

* **Clarifying and researching the issues**

This stage involves establishing the exact nature of the issues and problems which need to be tackled, including the extent and complexity of the issue and whether its source lies inside or outside the community. It also involves thinking about the demands to be made and the range of options which might exist, and evaluating the possible courses of action around these – distinguishing between the action of the worker(s) and that of the group(s) or organisation(s) concerned. It is also important at this stage to examine the levels of support within the local community, whether there is scope for widening the action and creating alliances, and if there is any opposition.

* **Representing the issues**

Essentially this is about deciding on the issues which are to be tackled and the demands to be made, and making the actual case for change and widening support for it. It is also about preparing for action and identifying the particular skill or training needs of local people, and about understanding and development of democratic processes and accountability.

* **Carrying out the action**

This stage is about putting ideas into action and involves the organisation of learning and change, It is important to recognise the potential for learning and change in terms of

- individuals;

- groups;

- communities.

The process of learning and change must be open and flexible; relate to meaningful tasks; use the skills and abilities of the group/organisation members: be built on a mutual trust and respect and shared commitment to the task in hand. This stage is also concerned with on-going monitoring of the action and the possible need to re-define objectives.

*   **Evaluation**

Evaluation is concerned with making judgements about the development work which has been undertaken including its successes and failures. Evaluation is not a task which is considered towards the end of a project – it must be thought about at the beginning in terms of the purpose of the task, who will be involved in doing it and the methods to be used. Participative evaluation techniques are most appropriate. The importance of evaluating what is done lies in the lessons that can be learnt about how effective change can be brought about in local communities and how that knowledge can be shared as widely as possible. Community education workers in evaluating their own role in the process must also consider their disengagement from the group as the project develops.

Practical Considerations and Dilemmas

Using a community development approach within the Community Education Service produces a number of challenges which can be far from straightforward for those involved, whether they are local people, community education workers, community education managers or policy makers/elected members.

But community development in any case is about challenge and therefore it is important to see such issues in a positive way when they arise. The various groups involved come at it from different experience, knowledge, skills and viewpoints, which all merit serious consideration and harnessing by the Community Education Worker as a natural part of the overall process. Therefore, such challenges should not be used as reasons for not adopting a community development approach no matter the risks involved, the problems that arise or the dilemmas that ensure!

By building on good practice derived from looking at and learning from case study material available from other areas, and by simply working together, clear solutions will emerge. Certainly the staged process as described earlier in this paper must assist. In addition, using performance indicators, relevant staff development and training opportunities, plus good resource back up will also be important. It may be useful to clarify some of the blocks that prevent such an approach being adopted or that undermine its effectiveness.

Consultation

For consultation to be effective and relevant each participant group in the consultative process must be able to influence the outcome. Lack of consultation or an exercise with a rigid agenda within time limits set by the needs of the agency will block or stifle local participation. If the development of communities is a desired objective, consultation should be a shared exercise, with negotiation preceding the agenda; timescale; venue etc.

Power Cliques

Community development will shift power and decision-making towards the wider community. This will be perceived as a threat by individuals or groups who control information or resources and who may have grown used to exercising control within an agency or community. There will always be a risk of the process being blocked by established interest groups. However, the democratic nature of the community development process and the momentum built up through wider participation will assist in moving beyond entrenched positions.

Role-Conflict

This is probably the most apparent in the "exposed" role of the worker engaged in a community development project. When a shift in power arises, complaints may be made and workers can be warned off further involvement. Therefore, for workers to be effective they must be trusted and respected by community groups, by management and by elected members. There should be few difficulties when the worker adopts such a pro-active role, as long as this is based on community development principles and not on the workers' personal interests or aspirations. However, elected members may perceive a community development approach affecting their own position since it can encourage a conflicting system of representation managed by community activists. While there is no easy solution to these issues, all concerned should strive for a sharing of information and 'openness' coupled with the adoption of clear policies for that balance the claims and aspirations of the community with the obligations and duties of the Local Authority.

Collaborative Partnerships

For partnerships between Local Authorities, their departments and community groups to be meaningful and fruitful, each member must be able to initiate and veto ideas and projects. Change therefore is not simply something which happens at community level. It must be encouraged throughout the Local Authority and this could require the need to modify structures that otherwise would create divisions between Departments and between the Local Authority and the community. Job remits may themselves limit and stifle community development. Training should be available on an inter-departmental basis since this will ensure that there is a common understanding of the community development strategy and assist with inter-departmental co-ordination and collaboration.

Evaluation

As with consultation, an evaluation exercise which is based solely on the views of the funding agency will effectively block the process of community development. As already indicated evaluation of community development projects requires a collaborative approach. Joint evaluation by community activists and workers should be organised and conducted at all stages of the process. As community development is a dynamic process any evaluation exercise must build in the changing aspirations and views of all participants.

Funding – Control of Resources

Lack of funding and budgetary controls are real limitations to the implementation of a community development strategy They are also used as a barrier to fend off the threat of change. Decentralisation may cost more than retaining a relatively centralised structure: but by adopting a community development strategy this should become more cost effective than a strategy which may lead to piece-meal inappropriate solutions to an ill-defined "problem". Access to funding should be clear and comprehensible to all participants in the community development process, and use of resources should be made as flexible as possible in order to facilitate community development strategies.

Training Implications

A number of authorities and individual projects have recognised the need for training in community development processes for full-time and part-time staff, volunteers and community activists. Some courses have focused on conceptual theories of participation and empowerment; others have provided a more nut and bolt approach – providing practical skills training in identifying issues, planning actions, maximising local involvement, examining survey methods and developing committee skills.

The recent competency based submissions to the CNNA and CeVe Scotland for accreditation of the Batchelor of Arts in Community Education courses provided by Colleges of Education in Scotland emphasised the importance of training in the community development process and although designed to meet the needs of potential full-time staff also provide a useful curriculum for courses for both existing staff, volunteers and activists. Quality training requires the involvement and commitment of policy makers, line managers and participants. It also requires the commitment of resources. It is essential that the commitment is made at the planning stage of the process. Recent training initiatives have clearly demonstrated the benefits of an inter agency basis for training.

Monitoring and Evaluation

In the current financial climate it is essential that when allocating resources to the process of community development, criteria are developed which enable the effect and effectiveness of these resources to be evaluated. A number of organisations are currently developing systems which can be applied for evaluating the process of community development. For some organisations this has been applied internally by examining the aims and objectives of their own particular project and identifying evaluation processes which will asses the quality of the outcome. Other organisations have been operating at regional and national levels developing criteria which can be used to assess the quality of the process and whether or not they can be applied across a number of different types of community development projects.

Although the community development process is complex, the evaluation process should address the following key indicators:

- engages with the community;
- empowers the participant;
- develops awareness of the participant's potential;
- develops ownership of outcomes;
- demonstrates sensitivities to participant's needs, aspirations and feelings;
- and demonstrates active support for community development.

Resource Implications

Within the field of Community Education, managers have a particular responsibility for ensuring that adequate resources are provided to enable the promotion of community development. Although it could be argued that promoting community development is about the philosophy and approach to work, there is little doubt that policies designed to encourage community development have resource implications attached to them – the community development process is time intensive.

It should also be recognised that in a community development context, the major resource which exists is local people themselves who should be encouraged to develop their skills and participate in the community development process. It must be appreciated, however, that whilst additional resources would be helpful, a great deal of resources presently exist which could be used more effectively to promote a community development approach.

Local Authorities and the Community Education Service can tackle the issue of resources by adopting the following strategy:

- Identify the range of resources presently available within the Local Authority which could be used to promote community development.
- Promote changes in the method of allocating resources. for example, decentralise decision making to those most directly involved.
- Encourage the creative and flexible use of existing budgets.
- Encourage principles of empowerment and community self-management in the allocation of resources.
- Target resources to areas of greatest need.
- Ensure that there is an understanding and commitment to the need to promote a community development approach in the delivery of local services.
- Actively support policy and practice through the encouragement of collaboration so that resources are used more effectively.
- Finally, develop short, medium and long term strategies for securing additional resources aimed at promoting community development.

Conclusions and Recommendations

- Community development is an approach which should be applied more widely in adult education, youth work and community work.

- The application of community development in the Community Education Service should normally follow a process of staged development as a means of planning progress and of achieving short and long term goals.

- Participants (e.g. local people) must be fully involved from the start and throughout the process.

- Community education workers must always consider the appropriate time when they should disengage from the project to allow the participants to continue the ongoing development.

- The risks involved in adopting a community development approach within the Community Education Service should not be used as a reason for not operating in this way.

- Managers and elected members must be aware of the inevitable risks and dilemmas which can arise when adopting a community development approach and therefore should provide adequate support to the community education workers involved.

- Wide ranging opportunities should be made available for training as part of this process of support to ensure that the community education workers involved have an adequate conceptual understanding as well as the practical skills required.

- Such training should be made available to part-time staff, volunteer, community activists as well as to managers and elected members. On occasion it will be beneficial to offer such training on a collaborative basis.

- Flexible strategies should be devised to ensure that adequate resources are made available to enable the active promotion of community development including the involvement of local people in decision making.

- Criteria should be developed along with the participants to enable the effect and effectiveness of adopting a community development approach to be evaluated.

GUIDELINES FOR QUALIFYING COMMUNITIY EDUCATION TRAINING

COMMUNTIY EDUCATION VALIDATION AND ENDORSEMENT 1990 (REVISED 1995)

THE ORIGINS OF THE COMMUNITY EDUCATION PROFESSION

It was the Government's Report *The Challenge of Change* chaired by Kenneth Alexander that recommended the setting up of the Community Education Services in Scotland in 1975. Whilst community education has its origins prior to 1975, the Alexander Report gave public policy recognition to the term, through recommending to Government the merging of the former adult education, youth and community work services under a new title – community education. Alexander drew upon the three traditions, placing community education within a lifelong education framework.

The Alexander Report recognised the need to train community educators to the highest quality to take on this challenge. A further working party was established by the Government, chaired by Elizabeth Carnegy, to make detailed recommendations on professional training. The Carnegy Report, published in 1977, reviewed existing professional training provision in Scotland through the still somewhat separate traditions of adult education, youth and community work provided by several Colleges of Education and Universities.

The Carnegy Report focused primarily upon the content of training, recommending a social and political science base and taught and practical elements in adult education, community work and youth work. By the end of the 1970s and early 1980s integrated professional community education courses at diploma and post-graduate certificate level were available in Scotland. There did not exist at this time, however, a central validation and endorsement process or national body to oversee training.

A desire by practitioners, employers and trainers to raise the status of the profession developed, paralleled by a growing interest in opening up new forms of flexible access to training and accreditation. In 1982 the national agency for community education, the Scottish Community Education Council, recommended by the Alexander Report, was established by the Scottish Office. As one of its first tasks the Scottish Community Education Council established a second working party on training chaired by Geoffrey Drought. This committee reported in 1984 under the title *"Training for Change"*. It examined in detail issues of flexibility and accessibility to training, the need to enhance the quality of training, and the need to establish a Training Council to oversee the training system. Whilst the Carnegy Working Party had set out a common core content of knowledge and skills, generally accepted by the Drought Working Party, *Training for Change* focused upon establishing a flexible community education training system through which there should be a variety of routes, recommending the introduction of a modular approach to training. The Report also called for improvements in the quality of fieldwork practice and supervision and for employers to be given greater recognition in the planning of training.

Modularisation of training and tentative experimentation with innovative access routes continued through the 1980s. There was a greater clarity in terms of the focus upon learning outcomes through both college and practice elements of training.

In 1990 the "National Council" function was finally established by the Minister of Education as CeVe (Community Education Validation and Endorsement), a committee serviced and supported by SCEC.

CeVe has the following delegated powers approved by the Minister for Education:

- to maintain and implement methods leading to the endorsement of qualifying training for professional staff in community education
- to maintain and implement methods leading to mutual recognition of community education qualifications within the European Union and internationally
- to maintain and implement methods leading to the endorsement of training for part-time and voluntary workers and for pre-qualifying training
- to maintain and implement methods leading to the endorsement of in-service courses and staff development programmes
- to provide such advice as may from time to time be required
- to establish sub-committees

The CeVe Committee has members appointed by SCEC, representative of the principal local government and voluntary sector employers, the professional associations and trade unions, and the main training providers.

CeVe established a number of standing sub-committees in December 1991, one of which was the Qualifying Training Sub-Committee. The aim of this sub-committee is to "ensure that professional standards are enhanced through the endorsement of courses leading to a professional qualification in Community Education". It has the following remit:

- to examine all courses which training providers submit for endorsement and, if appropriate, endorse
- to develop and monitor the guidelines to training providers of under-graduate courses
- to develop and monitor guidelines to training providers of post-graduate courses
- to review the endorsement of existing courses
- to encourage the development of innovative ways of delivering qualifying training

The central concern of CeVe in devising the guidelines for the endorsement of training is to ensure the preparation of the highest quality community educators at all levels. The first point of entry for professional posts is the degree level qualification which these guidelines address.

VALUE BASE AND PRINCIPLES

Defining Community Education

In 1990 the Minister of Education approved the following definition of community education against which a functional analysis for community educators was carried out:

> *"Community education is a process designed to enrich the lives of individuals and groups by engaging with people living within a geographical area, or sharing a common interest, to develop voluntarily a range of learning, action, and reflection opportunities determined by their personal, social, economic and political needs".*

The function or role of the community educator in society, therefore, is that of an animateur, positively intervening and engaging with people within their community, motivating, organising and enthusing them to acquire new knowledge, skills and confidence. In Scotland this has been closely linked to community development strategies for tackling social exclusion, for supporting individual and community enterprise and self help and for encouraging public participation in determining change.

The Value Base

At the core of the training and practice of community education is an active concern to promote certain professional values which underpin and give coherence to its operation. The Report on community education training *Training for Change* published by the Scottish Community Education Council in 1984, noted that:

> *"despite the differing traditions of adult education, youth and community work, there is common ground. They have, as a common aim, the building of a healthy democracy in a pluralist society . . . founded . . . on a belief in the individual as an active participant in a shared process of personal and group development through education"*

This value base has since been reinforced and developed in the first published CeVe Guidelines (1991), the Principal Community Education Officers' Report "Value for People" (1993) and the Convention of Scottish Local Authorities Report on Community Education (1995).

The underlying values at the heart of community education are that education :

* Respects the individual and the right to self-determination;
* Respects and values pluralism;
* Values equality and develops anti-discriminatory practice
* Encourages collective action and collaborative working relationships;
* Promotes learning as a lifelong process;
* Encourages a participating democracy.

Principles of community education practice

In its first published guidelines, CeVe noted that these values should themselves be reflected "at the level of the operating principles" of community education practice. Community education providers should encourage:

*   equality of opportunity, positive action and open access particularly for disadvantaged learners;

*   active participation of learners in the process of identifying learning needs, planning a learning programme and monitoring it;

*   flexibility of approach, covering content, location and style;

*   recognition that learning can relate to personal, social, economic and political experiences as well as more academic and vocational subjects;

*   an emphasis upon learning as well as teaching, and on matching the content and manner of delivery to the needs of the people concerned;

*   a positive response by participants to change and to the demands made on them in the present and the future.

COMPETENCE IN COMMUNITY EDUCATION

In the guidelines for qualifying training CeVe has taken account of the national trend towards a competence based approach to training. In adopting this approach, CeVe has not simply adopted a "mechanistic" model of training, but sought to develop a broader application and understanding of competence defined in terms of the values and principles outlined. Competence in community education practice is the product of an integration of knowledge, skills and values, with the competent community educator being able to think, to act and to critically reflect on practice.

CeVe, the training providers, and the community education profession have been at the forefront in developing a competence based approach rooted in the ability of the community educator to "do" but also to have the capacity to reflect critically upon contexts, processes and change. Qualifying community educators will, therefore, need to demonstrate their understanding of the value base and principles, to demonstrate that they are able to conceptualise, reflect and analyse competing theories, ideologies and models of practice, and to demonstrate these in fieldwork practice as educators.

Functional Analysis

In order to describe the competences necessary to be a community educator, ie. an educator engaging within the community around people's personal, social, economic and political needs, CeVe undertook a "functional analysis" of community education. This involved identifying the key purpose of the occupational area, the key purpose being broken down into key roles which themselves are broken down into elements of competence. These elements were revised in 1994.

CeVe has determined six key elements. These are:

(a) **to engage with the community.**
The community educator requires to be able to intervene within a given community; establish and sustain contact with local adult, youth and community organisations; identify needs; reach and engage with traditional non-participants; establish inter-agency links with other professionals working in the area; begin to identify from the assessed needs of the community, the concerns and aspirations of the people in the area and relevant opportunities for community action and learning.

(b) **to develop relevant learning and educational opportunities.**
The community educator requires to be able to target individuals and groups within a community; provide potential participants with appropriate guidance; take advantage of spontaneous learning and development opportunities in everyday situations; design with the participants relevant learning programmes and curricula content; identify any special learning needs; promote and market learning opportunities eg. through use of the media; organise appropriate structures for learning and community action; implement the learning and teaching programme; and use a range of formal and informal educational methods and techniques.

(c) **to empower the participants.**
The community educator requires to be able to empower the participants through developing collective action and learning; involve participants in planning, delivery and evaluation; enable participants to work towards their goals; encourage community-led development; develop the confidence, knowledge, skills and understanding of the participants; and widen participants' awareness of the concepts of power and change.

(d) **to organise and manage resources.**
The community educator requires to be able to develop and plan a work programme; organise and deliver quality activities and projects; recruit and manage human resources such as part-time staff and volunteers; identify funding and resources; apply relevant legislation and policy; demonstrate skills in self-management; manage financial resources; and manage equipment and physical resources.

(e) **to practise community education within different settings.**
The community educator requires to be able to express the values underlying community education through practice; apply the principles underlying community education in practice; apply the community development approach; practice across a range of age groups and within a range of settings; identify the external influences on the development of practice; demonstrate skills in working as part of a local multi-agency team; and be able to implement appropriate exit strategies from the community and learning groups.

(f) **to use evaluative practice to assess and implement appropriate changes.**
The community educator requires to be able to use appropriate quality assurance and performance measurement techniques; plan and apply a range of participative methods of evaluation; use information technology; demonstrate skills in report writing and presentation for a variety of audiences; and use findings to influence practice.

These key elements of community education are further broken down into key competences.

It is important to stress that whilst disaggregated for the purpose of clarity, these elements form part of an integrated process. In endorsing training programmes, CeVe will be concerned to ensure the coherence of the programme. This is a key issue of design which needs to be addressed by training providers in partnership with fieldwork placement agencies to combine a holistic approach to practice without omitting aspects of that practice. This requires that curriculum design and assessment strategy provides an integrated process in practice. Various areas of performance will be assessed concurrently from the different key elements and performance criteria which can be used to assess aspects of more than one competence

SETTINGS IN COMMUNITY EDUCATION

In analysing the competences necessary to be a community educator, CeVe is aware that the practice of community education takes place in a wide variety of settings.

With local government re-organisation local authority education departments remain the main employers of community educators in Scotland, however a significant number of community educators are also employed within other local authority departments such as community and neighbourhood services, social work, community leisure services, by the voluntary sector and by F.E. Colleges.

The rich variety of posts, settings, contexts and organisations reflects the growing influence that community education has had in recent years but also poses a challenge to CeVe and all training providers. Whilst the key purpose of some of these employing organisations may be only in part educational, the professional community educator, is trained to operate primarily in an educative way. Increasingly community educators are being employed in inter-disciplinary and inter-agency teams. With changes in the role of local government, trends in decentralisation of service provision and area management, it is important that barriers and negative perceptions are broken down between different professions. As community educators are increasingly required to work alongside eg. teachers, social workers, planners, health professionals, so too there is a need at pre- and in-service level for inter-professional training. CeVe actively encourages this trend. Training providers should demonstrate opportunities for training in inter-professional working.

Compared with other parts of the U.K. the strength of community education in Scotland has emerged from the integration of adult education, community work and youth work practice/theory since 1975. A new occupation and profession has emerged that has also been able to synthesise and build upon these three traditions. The **community** educator is now recognised alongside the **school** teacher and the **college** lecturer as an educational professional. Whilst recognising that specialisation may be demanded of community educators, training providers should reinforce integration and synthesis through both institution and practice elements of the training programme.

CeVe recognises that some employers, largely outwith the local authority education services do, for example, focus primarily upon education work with adults, or upon work with young people, or in supporting community action. The Scottish experience suggests that integrated community education practice has significantly strengthened the quality of the education intervention and the ability through its community-based emphasis to reach new target groups. Local authorities require community educators with an ability to transfer across age groups and socio-economic contexts. Continued political, social and economic change and the trends towards pluralism of service provision have created new opportunities for employment settings in other agencies for people entering into their first professional post. This trend is likely to continue. As the employment settings for community educators and the needs of individuals and communities change so too does the need for community educators to acquire an ability to work in different settings. This should not lead to a fragmentation of the community educators approach but rather a transferability of skills.

It would be unrealistic to expect qualifying community educators to be competent in every context and with all groups. By the nature of the world we live in, the settings and an understanding of them is in any event constantly changing. Community educators require opportunities for continuing professional development through in-service training.

Initial training at qualifying level for entry into their first professional post, requires that all qualifying community educators, in addition to satisfying the competences outlined within the three primary practice contexts of adult education, community work and youth work, are encouraged to pursue one or more areas of professional interest in some depth selected from:

* a range of target groups

* a range of geographic settings

* a range of appropriate specialist fields

(See Appendix 2 for examples of the above)

All qualifying community educators should be able to work with more than one target group, and in more than one setting and specialist field.

Membership of the European Union (E.U.) and Directives from the Commission provide wider opportunities for employment of community educators in other member countries. Whilst there are considerable differences between the contexts, organisations, policy and administrative structures, training providers through such schemes as ERASMUS and SOCRATES are encouraged to provide opportunities for trainees to understand about E.U. policy and to undertake exchanges and practice placements in E.U. countries.

CONTENT AND FORM OF TRAINING

As the context and settings for community education practice is changing, so too does the content of training require to be updated. Whilst CeVe offers guidelines and not tight prescriptions to the training providers as to content and form of training it accepts the broad recommendations outlined in the Carnegy and in the *"Training for Change"* Reports i.e. programmes should be underpinned by a social and political science conceptual framework; programmes should be fully up-to-date in terms of community education practice/theory in Scotland, the UK. and internationally; programmes should cover changes in education and social policy and public administration; programmes should address the three traditions of community education – adult education, community work and youth work and their integration; and programmes should introduce students to a range of target groups, geographic settings and specialist fields. Training providers should update all theory and practice-based content on a regular basis, utilising appropriate training materials relating to the key elements.

The challenge facing CeVe as the national training standards committee, is to ensure national coherence in the content and form of qualifying training provision without being over-prescriptive. The content of programmes drawn from the key elements of community education, are unlikely to differ greatly between training providers. It is not the intention of CeVe to prescribe in detail the curriculum or teaching methodology used in training programmes, although an outline of the curriculum and teaching methodology would be required as part of the submission.

Training providers must equip the qualifying community educator to be able to practise across Scotland (and increasingly other parts of the E.U.). CeVe recognises that encouraging principles of both flexibility and a system of articulation and accreditation can be contradictory. Comparability between training providers, and encouragement to innovate are both necessary.

The CeVe Committee remains concerned about the need to promote various pathways into training and to encourage articulation between training providers. This is particularly relevant in relation to such issues as APL and APEL (Accreditation of Prior Learning and Prior Experiential Learning), credit accumulation, and the ability of a student to transfer between courses or to complete qualifying training through more open learning routes.

CeVe has identified three concerns in this respect, which training providers should address in submissions. These relate to:

*   Assesment and accreditation of the individual learner for APL and APEL

*   Articulation of programmes with other endorsed qualifying and pre-qualifying programmes

*   Recognition for the participant who leaves at the end of a given period, prior to completion of the programme, of the training undertaken, so that they might continue training at a later date or with another training provider

    Guidance for training providers with respect to articulation and pathways is outlined in the CeVe guidance notes – *Articulation and Pathways to Training*.

CeVe expects training providers offering Degree level community education training to give recognition to applicants having completed pre-qualifying endorsed training programmes, helping them enhance their practice by accrediting previous training either as access to the Degree or, if appropriate, exemption from certain elements of the programme. A modular structure to degree design and APL procedures should provide flexibility to allow applicants to obtain credit for appropriate pre-Degree training programmes. The credit accumulation and transfer scheme (ScotCat) provides a recognised national system between training institutions.

APPENDIX 1

Glossary of Definitions

Competence embraces the specific skills, understanding, knowledge, values, attitudes and personal attributes required to undertake tasks effectively and to an appropriate standard. In the training of community educators it embodies the inter-relationship between values, ideologies and reflective action. The emphasis within training is on what students are able to do. Through identifying key elements of competence and appropriate learning outcomes, a competence-based training should ensure that students can conceptualise, analyse competing theories, ideologies and models of practice, and reflect critically on their actions which are informed by a strong ethical framework.

Performance Criteria are defined as statements by which an assessor judges the evidence that an individual can perform the activity specified in a competence, to a level acceptable in employment.

Teaching Staff are those who are employed by training providers for the prime purpose of delivering community education training.

Fieldwork Practice Supervisors are those who carry responsibility for the supervision and assessment of fieldwork placements.

Accreditation of Prior Learning (APL) and **Accreditation of Prior Experiencial Learning (APEL)** is defined as a process which enables people to gain certification for their past achievements. The emphasis is on what the individual can do or knows – the outcomes or achievements of previous learning and experience. The learning may have been achieved in different ways – through work experience, leisure pursuits or through training. The person seeking accreditation will be assessed on a portfolio of evidence which proves their claim to prior learning and experience, together with any other assessment required such as interview or observation.

Critical Friend is the person nominated by the training provider to the CeVe endorsement panel. This person would normally be an experienced practitioner, trainer or of equivalent standing, knowledgeable of the training programme, yet independent of the provider.

APPENDIX 2

Examples of target groups:

* Children
* Teenagers
* Young Adults
* Adults
* Older people
* Special needs
* Unemployed
* Women
* Ethnic minorities
* Disabled
* Travelling people

Examples of geographic settings:

* Urban/rural
* Village
* Peripheral estates
* Islands
* Inner City
* Semi-rural
* Isolated communities
* New towns
* Designated areas of deprivation

Examples of specialist fields:

* Community arts
* Environmental education
* Urban and rural regeneration
* Community planning
* Community economic development
* Community safety
* Health education
* Community care
* Home-school-community links
* Adult basic education/essential skills
* Outdoor education

This list can only illustrate the range of areas in which community education can be practised and the wide potential curriculum content for community education programmes.

HM INSPECTOR OF SCHOOLS
PERFORMANCE INDICATORS FOR COMMUNITY EDUCATION SERVICES

SCOTTISH OFFICE EDUCATION DEPARTMENT, 1993

FOREWORD

The importance of promoting good management in education was recognised in the establishment of the Management of Educational Resources Unit (MERU) and later the Audit Unit within HM Inspectorate. One of the tasks addressed by both Units has been the development of educational indicators to focus attention on, and to encourage a more informed debate about, the performance of all aspects of the education system.

In 1989 it was agreed with the Association of Directors of Education in Scotland (ADES) and the Principal Community Education Officers Group for Scotland (PCEOGS) that a scheme of performance indicators should be developed for the Community Education Services of the education authorities. This package is the result of that agreement. It is part of the series of publications by HM Inspectors of Schools on performance indicators but it builds on the extensive commitment of large numbers of staff at all levels in the education authorities. It was recognised from the outset that the development should be collaborative, between HM Inspectorate and the education authorities, and between management and staff. This shared commitment augurs well for the future development of evaluation and planning in community education. The package includes a set of performance indicators covering learning and management, together with staff development materials designed to assist in their introduction.

Definition

'Community education is a process designed to enrich the lives of individuals and groups by engaging with people living within a geographical area, or sharing a common interest, to develop voluntarily a range of learning, action and reflection opportunities determined by their personal, social, economic and political needs.' (Pre-service Training for Community Education Work, Community Education Validation and Endorsement [CEVE] - Scotland, Scottish Community Education Council, 1990)

The aim of this document is to provide a practical way of evaluating the benefits which involvement in the work of Community Education Services brings to children, young people and adults. Its basic assumption is that clear evaluation leads to improvement and development. The main focus is on quality but, by considering efficiency as well, its intention is to help spread quality education to as many people as possible. It proposes an overall scheme of performance indicators as a means of undertaking the necessary evaluations....

Background

The twin aims of continually improving the quality of services and making the best use of available resources have increasingly led Community Education Services (CES's) to emphasise careful planning. Effective evaluation is a crucial element as decisions about what to do in the future will be flawed if they are not based on good information about what is being done now: this is why there has recently been extensive interest in performance indicators (Pls) throughout the education service.

Performance indicators are one approach to evaluation. They will not meet all the evaluation needs of the CES's but they can give a particular type of information that is essential to good planning. They offer a fairly quick and standardised indication of how the organisation is performing in practice. They provide detailed feedback to the teams which are responsible for delivery as well as local planning, and give an overall profile of organisational performance for those responsible for strategic decisions. They are not designed to assess the performance of any individual member of staff.

The ways that the PI Scheme is used, and the ways in which it relates to other CES review procedures, should be monitored by the education authorities. A healthy variety of use is likely. In its own use of indicators, the Inspectorate will want to keep close contact with developments in the authorities.

The Package

The indicators presented here represent a 'core' set which will need to be supplemented and modified by CES's to meet their own particular needs. The format of the package, and the numbering system used for the indicators, should make it easy to include others as required.

A considerable volume of evidence, on which the package is based, derived from the work of CES staff. It should be stressed that the origins of the material lie in this evidence and that the processes by which it was obtained have themselves contributed to local development in advance of the publication of this document.

The Readers and Users of the Scheme

The general approach taken throughout this PI Scheme is to promote self assessment by teams of workers. The material is written, therefore, with the primary aim that it will be used by team leaders and the members of their teams.

Throughout the document there is reference to teams and field work teams as this is the way that most CES's are organised. In some education authorities, however, the approach to organisation is different, and there are also variations in the range of services included within community education. The references to teams and field work teams in the package are a matter of convention, and there is no reason why the PI Scheme should not be used throughout all CES's.

The Coverage of PIs

Teams usually, but not always, cover a geographical area and consist of from two or three to, perhaps, a dozen community education workers, supplemented by larger numbers of part time paid staff and volunteers Such teams are taken as the basic units for the PI Scheme although a group of staff responsible for a major facility could equally well be considered as the focus. In many areas there is direct contact between the community and specialist services of the CES or senior staff holding particular responsibilities, for example, for capital projects. It nevertheless remains clear that the main responsibilities for educational programmes lie with the teams. As the critical focus of evaluation should be the quality of education experienced by the participants and the fieldwork teams are the parts of the organisation that have the key responsibility for making community education a reality, it is logical to start with them when evaluating what the organisation is providing. 'Start', however, is a word that requires some emphasis, as it is hoped that the full development of performance indicators will, in due course, cover all levels of the CES's......

Applications of the PI Scheme

Definition

This PI Scheme should be considered as a standardised approach to the professional assessment of the effectiveness and efficiency of a community education organisation. In this definition it is important to stress that:

- it is the overall educational performance of the organisation which is being evaluated, not any individual;

- quality and efficiency both matter;

- standardisation is explicit; this brings some problems, but these are outweighed by the benefits.

Purpose

The Scheme is designed to promote evaluation and development in the CES's. It should be used as part of development planning and should be accompanied by staff development programmes.

The PI Scheme could be used as an audit in advance of preparing a development plan or as the evaluation element of such a plan. In the latter case, its core indicators would probably be used in association with others devised specifically for the purpose. In either case, the broad purposes of the PI Scheme will include the following:

- to allow the CES and the education authority to find out how well they are performing in relation to stated aims and objectives;

- to extend the ability of teams to communicate the results of their work and to comment on issues affecting it;

- to help to identify strengths to build on and areas requiring support;

- to provide an overall profile of fieldwork which will grow over the years;

- to provide the education authority with valuable information on which to base strategic decisions;

- to contribute information which may be of value when considering the range of skills and abilities which the team needs.

Consideration of the skills and abilities available to a team and of the strengths and weaknesses of organisational performance provides a useful and acceptable link between the PI scheme and staff development.

Categories of Work

Whether the aim is to evaluate some or all of a team's activity, the work will have to be divided up into manageable elements. Although many authorities follow the three-way division of community education into adult education, community development and youth work, smaller sub-divisions are needed for the PI Scheme. No single set of sub-divisions or categories of work can be used across the country, as local variations are too great.

It follows that the categorisation of CES work for the purposes of evaluation must be the responsibility of the CES within each education authority.

There are two main factors to be kept in mind when deciding on these categories. The first relates to statistics. One of the aims of the PI Scheme is to make it possible to collate education authority statistics nationally to give a much needed Scottish picture of community education. If this aim is to be achieved all authorities will have to use the same broad categories of work agreed nationally - within which they can create sub-divisions to meet their own needs.

The second issue concerns the observation of enough representative work to justify the generalisation simplified by the use of PIs. The narrower the category of work selected, the easier it will be to secure reasonable coverage. Taken too far, this approach would make it impossible to get round all aspects of CES work, so compromise will be needed. It will be best to start from the position that using narrower categories, such as work with adults with special educational needs, makes for easier and probably better evaluation than broad categories, such as all adult education.

When deciding how to categorise the work it will be useful to consider the following:

- CES practice and the familiarity of staff and participants with current categories of work;

- the use of common definitions across the authority;

- the need to see enough of the category of work in question;

- the need to operate within the broad categories used in the statistical forms.

Evaluation and Development Planning

A close relationship between the Pl Scheme and development planning is essential. There is little point in evaluating anything if the aim is not to improve what happens in the future.

The PI Scheme can be used either to evaluate how well a development plan is being implemented at a particular time or to audit basic educational objectives. In the first case the PIs have to relate to the stated objectives of the plan; in the second they must address the overall quality of education provided rather than these particular objectives.

In either case, the Scheme can be used in whole or in part and with or without additional indicators designed to meet particular needs. The approach is flexible enough to adapt to most circumstances but provides sufficient standardisation to give firm underpinning to the whole process of development planning.

This relationship between the Scheme of PIs and development planning places an onus on education authorities to establish clear strategies for the use of PIs. Teams will use them for self-evaluation but they will also need to work within an agreed set of parameters which ensures that the whole process contributes fully to regional decision making. It is for the education authorities to establish these parameters.

The evaluation procedures in the PI Scheme will not be implemented quickly. The process of establishing the use of PIs should be seen as a development exercise in its own right. In some authorities, where development planning has already involved staff in audit procedures, it might be possible to identify immediately a set of indicators to accompany the current development plan, and to start the evaluation cycle right away. Elsewhere, rather more time will be needed to introduce staff to ways of working that involve this approach to evaluation as a normal part of work patterns.

Elements of the Scheme

The PI Scheme comprises the following sets of indicators or data:

Quality Indicators (QIs) assess the quality of service to participants. Back ground Indicators (BIs) assess the quality of resources or 'tools' available to staff. Statistics show the amount of resource being funded and the numbers benefiting from the service: these are not yet in the form of quantitative indicators but should lead to their development.

SCHEME OF PERFORMANCE INDICATORS

Quality Indicators QIs	Background Indicators BIs	Statistics

Quality Indicators (QIs)

The QIs in this package should be regarded as a core set, not a fully comprehensive one. They cover Key Issues of concern to any CES activity, namely:

- the benefits to the participants in the learning activity;
- the nature of the learning context;
- the management which planned and supports the activity.

The first Key Issue highlights the educational benefits which people gain by taking part in community education. There are no hidden messages in the use of the words 'participant/learner' which appear in all the indicators. While it is usual in adult education to refer to participants as learners, this is less common in youth work and community development, so the PIs as presented cover both options.

The second Key Issue concentrates on the specific circumstances in which the activity and learning take place. This includes the management of that activity and the curriculum on offer but not the wider aspects of local management such as deployment of staff which are taken in the third group of indicators. The essential purpose of this group of indicators is to evaluate the context that has been created for learning.

The third Key Issue deals with everything that has been done to bring the activity into being, i.e. management of resources, including staff. Attention is clearly focused on the purpose of the whole enterprise - learning in the community. The Key Issue is concerned only with those aspects of management that are within the control of the field work team. Issues that are relevant to management but outwith the team's control, such as the size of its budget, are dealt with as Background Indicators. (The full list of the QIs covering these three Key Issues appears see Diagram 1) (ed).

It is important to recognise that these Key Issues are not the only ones that might have been identified, and that different QIs might have been found for each heading. They are neither perfect nor unchangeable. They are, however, the product of extensive consultation with community education workers throughout the country and they therefore represent a particularly important statement of key concerns in community education.

Because of the diversity of CES activity, and the different ways in which indicators can be used, CESs may need to design their own QIs to be used with the core set. For example, a CES might want its development plan to include a set of QIs to assess its implementation but find that the core set here did not cover all of the details.

The core set of QIs provides a satisfactory basis for an audit of CES activities but using all of them at the same time, for all aspects of CES work, would be ambitious. In most cases it will be more realistic to evaluate one aspect at a time, thus initiating a cumulative process. This has the following benefits:

- evaluation, including local consultation, is confirmed as a regular part of team activity;
- priorities for evaluation can be identified early, but all aspects of CES work will reappear regularly in the evaluation programme;
- the problems of generalising from a small number of examples can be minimised by restricting evaluation to appropriately sized fields;
- it is feasible to use the full set of QIs in relation to a limited field;
- packages of QIs can be selected which are particularly appropriate in a given set of circumstances.

Background Indicators

Contexts in which community education takes place vary much more than in other education sectors. The context can affect quality yet, to a large extent, is usually outwith the control of the field work staff. Given the great variety of circumstances in which fieldwork teams operate, it is essential that BIs are an explicit part of the PI Scheme. They cover five topics

- policy;
- accommodation;
- equipment and materials;
- staffing levels;
- budgets.

Like the QIs, BIs are concerned with quality (numerical information concerning some of these topics appears as statistics). The information they provide will probably change little from year to year so, after the first evaluation, the process of updating them should not be time-consuming. (A summary of the BIs is given - see Diagram 2) (ed).

The defining attribute of BI issues is that the field work team cannot change them. They comprise, for example, the size of their budgets, the range of decision-making powers which is devolved to them, and the policies of the education authority. The team's interpretation of policy, however, or their use of budgets can be evaluated.

The inclusion of BIs in the Scheme does not imply that there is a simple relationship between background factors and the quality of educational experience. The best policies in the world will not automatically produce a high quality of experience and learners can benefit from highly effective programmes in the face of poor physical resources. Their inclusion, however, provides additional information which is relevant to performance and is an essential complement to the QIs and statistics.

Statistics

Good numerical information is essential to any assessment of efficiency. To give a simplistic example, if it is possible to achieve the same quality of learning for ten people using one approach, but for only five using another which costs the same, then, other things being equal, the method which benefits more people is more efficient. Judgments about efficiency must bebased on good information about both quality and quantity.

For many years CESs have been seriously concerned about efficiency as they have tried to cover growing fields of work with limited resources. Their assessment of efficiency has, at best, not been helped by the variability and, in some cases, the lack of good quantitative data. For this PI Scheme, it is essential to develop a systematic collection of statistics. It will take a good deal of sensitive experimentation to produce valid and reliable quantitative indicators from the statistics but it is important that the process should be started.

Many statistics are already collected and have value in their own right. They are not, however, collected in a uniform way by the education authorities and so it is not always possible to study a number of important relationships. The proposals made here will provide insight into such relationships, for example:

- between resources and benefits;
- between different aspects of resources, such as full-time and part-time staff;
- between different aspects of the use of resources, such as numbers of individuals and numbers of groups.

The statistics in this package are concerned with four main issues:

- staff;
- participants;
- budgets;
- urban aid projects.

Such statistics will normally relate to Key Issues rather than to individual QIs and BIs, with their precise use depending on the nature of the evaluation. On their own they will help to fill out the overall picture, but their full value will come from setting them alongside information about quality. The pilot work for the PI Scheme provided guidance on the types of statistical collection that are needed but less on how to use statistics and QIs in combination. This needs to be kept under continuing review.

Reliable recording of information at grass-roots level, for example on enrolments, attendance or funding, will be needed if statistical forms are to be properly completed. The importance of such information for monitoring, evaluating and prioritising work should be recognised, perhaps by giving one member of the team a clear responsibility for all statistical work.

One of the problems regarding the use of statistics in the PI Scheme is how to record the deployment of the team's time in relation to agreed categories of work. The staff of the Community Education Service are its most valuable resource and the way that their time is used, particularly in relation to priorities, is crucial. The information is needed to show:

- whether teams are able to commit the necessary time to priority issues;

- whether they are able to allocate time across their full range of concerns;

- whether they are able to keep a reasonable time balance between fieldwork and, for example, organisational tasks.

The lack of good, comprehensive statistics is not just a matter of concern in relation to the PI Scheme. At present there are few national statistics on such matters as total CES staff or numbers of people benefiting from Community Education Services. This is a major deficiency. Although diversity of provi-sion makes the collection of statistics difficult, they are vital for planning purposes. They should improve the effectiveness of communication about the services being provided, help teams to identify strengths and weaknesses and enable trends to be identified.

Statistics are renowned for the use and abuse that can be made of them. Because of the complexity of recording statistics in community education, it is important that hasty conclusions are not drawn from bare figures. Careful examination of the context, including both the QIs and BIs, should be made as part of their interpretation.

The Key Decisions

In a team of average size with, say, five full-time workers and the normal range of responsibilities, it is unlikely that a review of all of its work, using the full PI Scheme, could be completed in under 30 worker-days. Although that is a large amount of staff time, it is worth remembering that five full-time workers provide about 1,100 working days per year. When the contributions of the part-time paid and voluntary staff are added, 30 days does not seem so excessive.

Whether a full review of all categories of work at one time or a rolling programme of reviews is implemented, all three elements of the PI Scheme - QIs, BIs and statistics - should be included. The key decisions are as follows:

- First decision: Is itbetter to conduct a full review or begin a rolling programme? This decision will probably be taken at authority rather than team level.

- Second decision: If a rolling programme is to be implemented, which categories of work are to be reviewed, and when? This decision will probably be negotiated between the CES and the team.

- Third decision: Should all the QIs be used or is there good reason to use only some of them? Are any new ones needed?

- Subsequent decisions relate to the procedures for implementing the Scheme, all three parts of which together produce a profile of the work under review.

- Final decisions concern the action to be taken as a result of the evaluations.

A rolling programme of reviews will lead to a regular cycle of evaluation.

DIAGRAM 1

THE QUALITY INDICATORS ... AND THEIR THEMES

Key Issue - Benefit to Participants/Learners

Q1 Benefits 1: Assessment of Learning Needs
- strategies for making contact with potential participants
- procedures for identifying learning needs
- participant awareness

Q1 Benefits 2: Negotiation of the Learning Programme
- quality of negotiation
- content of negotiation
- learning contract

Q1 Benefits 3: Group Development
- groups provide support to learning
- participants value working in a group

Q1 Benefits 4: Progress, Including Continuous Assessment
- progress towards identified objectives
- continuous assessment
- the results of assessment influence the learning programme

Q1 Benefits 5: Empowerment
- awareness of potential
- activity beyond the group
- ownership

Q1 Benefit 6: Participant Satisfaction
- arrangements for feedback
- levels of satisfaction

Key Issues - The Learning Context

Q1 Context 1: Curriculum
- range of available opportunities
- internal coherence
- relevance

Q1 Context 2: Activity
- interaction among participants and staff
- stimulation of the activity
- thoroughness of the activity

Q1 Context 3: Staff Input and Methods
- design of the activity
- selection of methods
- quality of practice

Q1 Context 4: Use of Resources
- planning the use of resources
- use of physical resources
- use of human resources

Q1 Context 5: Guidance
- initial contact and guidance
- continuing guidance
- quality of information

Q1 Context 6: Programme Evaluation
- evaluation methods suit the circumstances
- evaluation involves appropriate people
- the results of evaluation are used

Key Issue - Management of Resources

Q1 Management 1: Area Needs Assessment
- assessment procedures
- quality and range of information
- local consultations

Q1 Management 2: Establishment of Priorities
- decisions are guided by area needs
- decisions are guided by policy statements
- decisions are guided by resource availability

Q1 Management 3: Planning the Work of the Team
- consistency of approach
- involvement of team members
- time allocations

Q1 Management 4: Development of the Community as a Resource
- support for community development
- local influence on team activities
- volunteers

Q1 Management 5: Liaison with Other Organisations
- links and work with local groups
- links and work with relevant agencies
- collaboration in education

Q1 Management 6: Deployment of Resources
- deployment of staff time
- deployment of other resources
- monitoring and renegotiation of resource commitments (including staff time)

Q1 Management 7: Staff Management Systems
- staff development
- staff support and supervision
- in-service training

Q1 Management 8: Monitoring and Evaluation
- monitoring
- evaluation
- use of results

DIAGRAM 2

THE BACKGROUND INDICATORS ...
AND THEIR THEMES

B1 **1 Policy**
- clarity
- extent
- openness to influence

B1 **2 Accommodation**
- availability
- suitability
- costs
- access for people with physical disabilities

B1 **3 Equipment and Materials**
- availability
- suitability
- provision for people with particular needs

B1 **4 Staff in Post**
- availability of staff time
- professional skills
- clerical and ancillary staff

B1 **5 Budgets**
- amounts in the budgets
- organisation of budgets
- charging policies

JOHN NISBET AND JOYCE WATT
EDUCATIONAL DISADVANTAGE IN SCOTLAND
– A 1990s PERSPECTIVE

SCOTTISH COMMUNITY EDUCATION COUNCIL, 1994 pp76–83, 87–94

THE COMMUNITY

Tackling educational disadvantage through [schools], faces a serious obstacle in the antagonism felt by many adults and pupils to schools and to the authority which they represent. Our 1984 report, reviewing the Glasgow Eastern Area Renewal Project (GEAR), noted this attitude in relation to the provision of adult education in local schools. 'There is a psychological barrier at the gate of a school (especially a secondary school)' *(page 37)*.

In the same area ten years later in one of the women's groups which we visited, a similar attitude was expressed – not just to schools but to anything run by 'authority'. The nursery school wasn't for them; the mother and toddler group was no good; the community centre was a waste of time. The heart of the matter is the perception of 'authority', and the formal procedures and barriers which authority sets up between 'managers' and the public. The women had ownership of their own group: formal organisations denied them that sense of belonging.

Add to this the experience which many of those who live in depressed areas have had of schools: failing in school work and being made to feel a failure, undermining confidence and lowering self-image, accentuating social differences, reinforcing inequality, being treated as second-rate, in an alien life-style where even the language of the home is regarded as an inferior dialect which has to be eradicated. The realisation (or the dawning awareness) that school is a powerful factor in determining life chances, and that the chances are not evenly loaded, leads to feelings of alienation and powerlessness.

There is some evidence that attitudes are changing. Adults are returning to continuing education – and even to classes in school – in large numbers; many more pupils are staying on beyond age 16 (though this trend is affected by unemployment and changes in benefit regulations). But changing the norms of a community is not something which happens quickly – if only it could be done so simply!

The community is a powerful educative influence on our lives. If we include the family in the concept of community, then it is the most powerful influence. It stamps its pattern on our speech, our behaviour and our thinking; we absorb its values through the models which it gives us and only with a struggle can we escape their power. As Smith (1992) puts it vividly, we learn 'from the company we keep'. The influence of the community is powerful because it is informal and not explicit, and therefore not easy to control or manage.

We need to beware of thinking of the influence of the community in disadvantaged areas as something that needs to be changed. It is better viewed as a potential strength to build on. Coleman (1991) uses the concept of 'social capital' (in the currently acceptable language of the market) to express this point:

> *Social capital held by a person lies in the strength of social relations that make available to the person the resources of others . . . Traditional discussions of capital have focused on its tangible form, whether financial capital or productive equipment. Building on this concept, economists have developed over the past 30 years the idea of human capital, that is, the assets embodied in the knowledge and skill that a person has . . . (But) the social relations that exist in the family or in the community outside the family also constitute a form of capital. While physical or financial capital exists wholly in tangible resources, and human capital is a property of individual persons, social capital exists in the relations between persons. (pages 6-7)*

In this century, Coleman argues, the available financial and human capital has increased, whereas social capital has decreased with new work patterns and smaller families. Rebuilding social capital, he says, is the new role for the school. Clearly, it is not a task for the school alone. This could be expressed as a re-expression of the aims of community education in disadvantaged areas. Other agencies also in the voluntary sector have a part to play, and current policies aim to enlist the private sector.

Community education has made a substantial contribution to tackling disadvantage and deprivation. Community education workers have been to the fore in projects in the Urban Programme, in working with disadvantaged and alienated young people and in community centres and community schools. Community education has helped to promote continuing education by initiating self-help groups and providing guidance and support leading on from informal education to enrolment in more formal courses. It also has kept alive the development of pre-school provision, supporting play groups and mother-and-toddler groups in the poorest areas. There has been a great variety of action across the country, some formalised as projects, others resulting from informal groups and the routine work of the Community Education Services, almost all unreported (possibly because of reluctance to make 'capital' out of one's clients).

An important achievement of community education is that it has established a principle and a style of working, in helping individuals and groups to take responsibility in issues which affect their lives – especially important for the disadvantaged. This Freirean concept of 'empowerment' of the underprivileged runs through much of the philosophy of community education. Paradoxically, a parallel theme appears in the rhetoric of contemporary conservative thinking: shifting power to the lay person, customer, client or citizen, in order to make bureaucratic institutions more answerable. In the philosophy of enterprise, the involvement of local people is a key principle in any programme of regeneration.

In one of our interviews, the suggestion was made that perhaps in the past community education had become too closely identified with disadvantage, in the sense that some politicians saw it as in danger of becoming 'a strategy to support working class actions in defence of their class interests and to develop effective challenges to the operation of private capital.'

Instead, they wished the techniques associated with community education used to promote economic and social regeneration of a rather different kind. 'Community education . . . was oft-times regarded as a plaything of the political Left . . . (But now) empowerment has been captured by the Right, with community education as its handmaiden.'

A new agenda

The two contrasting approaches are not wholly irreconcilable, though a conflict of values seems inevitable. Industry and commerce are part of the 'community' though their values are not readily accepted by the disadvantaged. The various Regions' policies for community education recognise the need for collaboration in Partnership and Enterprise programmes, while retaining the well-established primary concerns of the community education service. In 1989, the Chief Inspector for community education had anticipated this pressure to bring the development of community education into line with other government policies. In an article in *SCAN* (the newsletter of community education in Scotland), he wrote: 'Urban regeneration, basic education, law and order, enterprise . . . occupy the 'high ground' in public perception . . . It will not compromise purity to relate openly to such issues.'

In a speech in Glasgow in March 1992, the Minister, Lord James Douglas-Hamilton, expressed a similar broad view in outlining the Government's aims for community education as a whole:

> to make life-long education a reality for the whole community . . .; to develop collaborative initiatives amongst agencies to suit the needs of local communities; and to support various government policies, such as rural and urban development, community care and the Citizen's Charter, through appropriate informal education .
> . . The major objectives which the Government would wish to pursue in this area (community development) are: the promotion of a sense of responsibility; the furtherance of initiatives designed to counter deprivation or health threatening practices; and the stimulation of local enterprise. (Scottish Journal of Adult Education, 1 (4), 52-59)

The pressures to adapt to a new style of working are particularly evident in recent changes in the mode of working of the Scottish Community Education Council (SCEC). An article in the Times Educational Supplement Scotland (headlined 'How the SCEC has found a niche in the market-place') begins: 'Anybody looking for a classic example of how Government policy has changed the educational agenda need look no further than the Scottish Community Education Council.'

The new Executive Director of the Council, the article goes on,

> *'takes a robust view of the SCEC's role. The reality is that we are in the market-place and we have got to get on with it, he says. Although he stresses his strong belief in the Council continuing to be a public service, the fact is that SCEC has to bring in £500, 000 of business each year and must therefore contract with education authorities, the voluntary sector, local enterprise companies and private organisations.'*

The article concludes:

> *'If community education is now as much about stimulating local business enterprise as about assisting tenants' associations through informal education – no longer about revolutionising communities but empowering individuals – then it has indeed come of age. In an age of scarce resources, it has found a niche.'*

In a personal statement subsequently, the Director challenges the article's somewhat contentious claim that community education has been captured by the 'right'. His position, he asserts, is that *"community education must remain a public service, provided both by local government and through public investment support for the voluntary sector. Community educators require to understand and address the agendas of local and central government, whether of left, centre or right, and to secure cross party support. That said, the concern of community education to tackle disadvantage and to promote community as well as individual empowerment clearly places it within a progressive education tradition."*

There remains, however, a conflict of values for community education workers in having to fit in with the very structures which 'empowered' groups might have set out to challenge. This new role and the push for a management style of working, it was said in one interview, have combined to remove professional workers from the field into clerking and running committees.

In the context of social policies in the 1990s, community education must collaborate with other agencies if it is to be effective in reducing the barriers of educational disadvantage. The ideal of cooperative working is readily compatible with the principles of community education, but is not so easy to achieve in practice. In his 1992 speech, the Minister recognised this: 'I am asking for a willingness to be imaginative in working with new partners in contexts and places well beyond the conventional educational environment.'

In fact there has been successful cooperation with the many partners with which community education has to work: the schools, further education colleges and universities, social work departments, planning authorities, the voluntary sector, health boards and social security services, the local enterprise companies and the new initiatives in urban regeneration. But there remains the danger of conflicting values: for each of these many partners, the modes of working are different – differences which are not to be overcome simply by an expression of intent. Community education has to work differently if the cooperation is to be a partnership and not a battle-ground. The Minister's willingness to be imaginative in working with new partners will certainly be required if community education is to work effectively to its new agenda.

Rural disadvantage

This review has been limited to educational disadvantage linked to poverty in urban areas. Discrimination on the basis of handicap, gender or race often interacts with poverty to result in serious disadvantage. But each of these aspects raises distinctive issues, and each has a literature of its own. Rural disadvantage is a topic which deserves a report of its own: it is different from the urban situation in distinctive ways, it raises different issues, and requires different action.

In recent years there has been a growing awareness of disadvantage in rural areas, and of the need to introduce appropriate action. In particular, rural deprivation often is to be found in small pockets widely dispersed, and consequently poverty is not so readily identifiable:

> *'Rural deprivation tends not to be concentrated, in the manner of urban deprivation, but dispersed . . . This makes rural deprivation less visible and less obviously tractable.'* (Shucksmith, 1990, page iii)

> *'Because these conditions are to be found in small pockets dispersed over rural areas as a whole . . . they tend to be ignored.'* (Midwinter et al, 1988, page 8)

At a conference organised in 1992 by the Scottish Children and Families Alliance (SCAFA), the coordinator of the European Community Childcare Network said that 'There is increasing recognition that attention has got to be given to rural areas, which have had rather a bad deal in the past.'

In 1985 the Convention of Scottish Local Authorities had pressed the Scottish Office to set up a Rural Aid Fund with aims and format similar to Urban Aid. The Government, however, rejected the proposal, on the grounds that it was already allocating considerable resources to rural areas.

In current policy and research, the problem is regarded as primarily economic. Changes in the basic rural industries of agriculture and fishing have had a devastating effect on some sections of the community. In other areas, the collapse of small local industries has destroyed the livelihood of an entire community, as in the case of the mining villages in rural Central Scotland. These pockets of deprivation do not fit the criteria for aid under the Urban Programme, but some have recently become eligible for support from EC funding. As with inner city areas, regeneration of the rural economy is at the heart of the strategy to counter disadvantage, but the economic methods of achieving this are different from those in inner cities; and the issues lie outside the scope of this review of educational disadvantage. [For discussion of economic issues, see Midwinter, A, Mair, C and Moxen, J (1988); *Rural Deprivation in Scotland*, University of Strathclyde; Highland Regional Council (1988) *Rural Aid Fund for Scotland*, Seminar at Inverness; Shucksmith, M (1990) *The Definition of Rural Areas and Rural Deprivation*, Report to Scottish Homes].

The fact of living in the country is not itself a major factor in educational disadvantage for children at the primary school stage, except possibly in extremely remote areas. The educational attainment of children in small rural schools is generally as good as that of their counterparts in towns. There is even evidence to suggest that, at the stage of transfer from primary to secondary school, those from very small schools adjust more readily to the change than children from small town schools (Shanks and Welsh, 1985). At the secondary school stage, the burden of travel and an extended day is likely to be greater for many rural pupils. As the costs of public services are higher in rural areas, the availability of services is more limited when their provision by local authorities is on a discretionary basis and not obligatory. Consequently, outside the years of compulsory schooling, the factors of distance and isolation begin to have a more serious effect. Providing pre-school facilities presents special problems. Opportunities for continuing education and training for adults are quite seriously limited; for those school pupils who consider staying on to further and higher education distance is a deterrent to recruitment; and links with business and industry can only be made on a small scale; (though this may change in time with proposals for computer networks to link remote areas to urban centres).

Adult education and child care are the two educational aspects which have received most attention in recent years. The Scottish Community Education Council held a conference in Inverness in 1990 reviewing informal adult education in rural areas, and in the same year it published *Good Practice Guidelines on Adult Basic Education in Rural Areas, and Working with Travelling People*. For child care, voluntary groups have taken most of the responsibility; but the report by SCAFA, Child Care in Rural Communities (Palmer, 1991) describes a number of joint initiatives in the areas surveyed: for example, the Upper Deeside Project, where two nursery teams work their way round six nursery bases each week in local schools; and the Play and Learning Sessions (PALS) in Highland Region for pre-school children in primary schools. In the Borders Region in 1992, SCAFA held a conference on 'Children and families in rural areas', and the Pre-Five Development Project there is a collaborative venture between the Region and SCAFA.

Scottish Environment now has a rural officer; in some Regions there is now a designated official for rural development; and Scottish Homes have funded research on the topic of rural deprivation. Though their main concern is economic regeneration, it is recognised that education has a contribution to make in an integrated rural development policy. . .

Continuing education

A major change in the past decade has been the focus on adult and continuing education. This is not altogether a new development: the community education programmes of the late 1970s aimed to involve adults in the regeneration of disadvantaged communities through self-help and education, and the writings of Paolo Friere introduced the concept of 'empowerment'. In the past, however, much of the provision of adult education was directed towards liberal and humane studies: this older 'liberal education' style of adult education has been supplemented by community education, by 'outreach' programmes and by a blurring of the former distinction between further education and adult education, drawing from new sectors of the population and since the most rapid growth has been in courses leading to qualifications or access to such courses opening up new opportunities for those whose school experience was unsuccessful and unhappy. Adult education has really taken root, as one of those interviewed said.

As an approach to tackling educational disadvantage, this represents a significant change of focus. The rationale of the 1970s in directing resources towards the under-fives and to schools and young people was that better educational provision for the young would save them from the educational disadvantage experienced by their parents. The current expansion of continuing education faces disadvantage more directly and more immediately – not ignoring the preventative strategy but providing avenues of opportunity for adults as a 'second chance'. This is a 'two generation' policy – providing for two generations at the same time.

It is arguable whether this shift of emphasis has occurred as a result of planned policy, or from changing attitudes, new awareness and new aspirations: most likely it has been a combination of all these factors. In Tayside Region, for example, there was a planned development from 1984 to the present, covering different lines of provision, coordinated within a 'Continuing Education Initiative':

a liberal education network, decentralised to 20 associations across the region, mainly recruiting the traditional adult education participants;

locally-based issue-oriented groups, organised with the help of community education workers;

adult learning linked with community enterprise, and business plans (eg Tayside Community Business, WABET);

guidance, using school resources for vocational guidance (TAGS – Tayside Adult Guidance Service).

Whether planned in this systematic way or not, the expansion of recruitment was the result of changing public attitudes – a growing recognition of education as an avenue to worthwhile qualifications and job opportunities, especially in a period of recession, together with other more fundamental changes involving awareness of women's rights and equality of opportunity. Adult education itself changed to meet the demand, and people have felt less inhibited by the psychological barriers which had discouraged them formerly.

The drive to extend continuing education has taken a variety of forms: new patterns of adult basic education; the Local Collaborative Programme in Strathclyde; adult enrolment in secondary schools; and access to higher and further education.

Adult basic education

The title 'Adult basic education' carries a stigma. (The original, 'Adult illiteracy', was even worse.) Even the word 'education' may give the impression to potential students that if they need education they are 'uneducated'. Also the word may create difficulties for some whose previous experience of education is only of failure. The provision itself (classroom, institutional building), inconvenient hours and lack of creche facilities, may not help. How then do we interest those whose lack of basic educational skills prevents them from using opportunities in continuing education? Commonly, and increasingly over the period of our review, basic courses have been provided along with other courses in further education colleges or schools, not labelled as such but as training in skills (eg word processing) or for gaining qualifications (eg driving licence), or as a package of skills to help get a job. Consequently there are no reliable statistics of those enrolled in adult basic education. It is clearly a growing provision, going well beyond literacy and numeracy to other social competencies, including health.

Appendix 2 of the Scottish Office publication, *The Education of Adults in Scotland* (HMSO, 1992), illustrates the range of provision. The Focus Learning Centre at Saltcoats, for example, was established in 1988 in a primary school in a disadvantaged area, to provide 'taster' or 'First Step' courses and 'follow on' 'Progressive' courses. The facilities include typing and word-processing rooms and a workshop with graphics equipment as well as a coffee bar, lounge and creche. Eighty-one per cent of the users are unemployed and at the time of the report, 687 had successfully completed 'First Step' courses and 472 'Progressive' courses (including SCOTVEC modules). In the Dundee Partnership project at Whitfield, WABET (Whitfield Adult Basic Education Trust) started in 1989 teaches adult basic education through computers. In the Edinburgh Partnership at Wester Hailes, the courses run by WHOT (Wester Hailes Opportunities Trust) have a stronger vocational emphasis. Every area makes provision for adult basic education, either through community education or separately.

The local collaborative programme in Strathclyde

Strathclyde's Local Collaborative Programme (LCP) was initiated in 1987 from unused bursary funds 'to establish progression routes between informal and formal education, to stimulate social and economic regeneration . . . and to build bridges between separate elements of the education service.' *(SOED, 1991, 2.1.3)*.

The Community Education Service, identifying groups or needs, collaborates with the further education colleges, which provide courses. Between 500 and 600 courses are provided each term (three terms per year) in many centres across the Region, both vocational and non-vocational (the distinction is not made): typing, computing, book-keeping, machine-knitting, photography, drama, basic literacy, committee skills, caring, first aid, sewing, dress-making and so on. In more than half of these courses, there are links to further courses. The LCPs attracted 15,000 adults in session 1992-93 *(Adult Education Conference, Glasgow, March 1993, Report,* page 4).

Although there is no specific reference to disadvantage, the provision of further education free of charge to those in need, near to where they live, is directed primarily at those who would not normally enrol in further education. Most of the students in these courses left school at the minimum leaving age. The 1991 Inspectors' report describes the programme as 'a valuable experiment which has brought educational opportunities to adults who, for the most part, have had little involvement in education since leaving school.'

Enrolment in these courses and similar provision in other Regions illustrate a growing awareness in the adult population of the need for training in skills. With limited job opportunities in every part of the country, the usefulness of further education has come to be recognised more and more widely. As a result, the demand is for vocational (or 'useful') courses, and for courses which lead to a certificate or qualification and which lead on to more advanced study. What is happening is the opening of alternative routes, especially for those who have dropped out at an early age from the standard progression from school to college.

Adult enrolment in secondary schools

The growing number of adults enrolling in secondary schools is one of the most striking developments of the past decade. In session 1990-91, according to *A Survey of the Provision for Adults in Schools: Strathclyde Region* (SOED, 1992, p.1), 14000 adults enrolled in secondary schools in Scotland as a whole, 9000 in the Strathclyde Region. Most of these attended part-time, and so the figures may give an over-optimistic impression. (Though the figure of 14000 is given in two HMI reports, it seems questionable, since, for example, the Fife figure for 1990 is 275, and the Grampian figure is 345.) In some schools, adults constitute 25 per cent of the role.

A main target of adults attending school classes is to obtain a qualification in the Scottish Certificate of Education or through SCOTVEC modules. Formerly this was possible only through attendance at evening classes run by the local authority or at courses in further education colleges. The idea of adults attending a local secondary school alongside school pupils to study for SCE examinations was promoted by the community school movement of the 1970s. It was linked in some inner city areas with a decline in school rolls, which made adult recruitment attractive to maintain numbers above the survival limit. Starting as an initiative by a few schools, it rapidly gained popularity in some disadvantaged areas where school staffs were highly successful in overcoming some of the traditional barriers to adult participation.

These barriers are familiar enough, and at one time seemed insurmountable: hostility to schools because of their childhood experience of failure, the pressure of peer groups, lack of confidence and belief that one is too old to learn, the forbidding institutional atmosphere, inconvenient hours and lack of time, money, transport and child care facilities. Yet schools are often conveniently within reach; staff make special efforts to create a welcoming atmosphere; and the support of peers and (perhaps most important) changing attitudes have promoted a movement which has opened up another avenue for the educationally disadvantaged.'The schools . . . had attracted a clientele for whom traditional modes of continuing education had not been considered an option.' *(SOED, 1992c, page 5)*.

The presence of adults in school classrooms, though not without problems, has contributed indirectly to changing attitudes in the regular school population:

'By their presence in the classroom, adult students were making an overt statement to school age pupils that education is not a stage to be passed through, outgrown and discarded at the first opportunity, but is an enjoyable, rewarding and life-long process.' (page 22)

Meanwhile, a similar development was taking place in the admission of mature students to higher education courses in universities and colleges. Previously, mature students were admitted to university only after they had qualified for entrance by passing the same examinations as were required of direct entrants from school. In the 1980s, there was a remarkable development of 'access courses' – courses for adults which are accepted as the equivalent of the normal entrance requirements. At first sight this may not appear to contribute greatly to remedying educational disadvantage; but it has opened the door to many whose limited previous education had barred them from entry to higher education.

Access courses

The Open University throughout the 1970s and 80s had demonstrated that older students, without the conventional entrance requirements, could make a success of higher education courses, and in this way it contributed to creating a demand for access. The introduction, nationwide, of comprehensive secondary schools in the 1970s was also part of a trend to question the validity of early selection by examinations, and an awareness of an 'untapped reservoir of talent' (a common metaphor at that time). At a more mundane level (as with the secondary schools), increasing adult admissions was also seen as a way to overcome the approaching decline in numbers in the 18-year-old population.

In 1979, Glasgow University Extra-Mural Department introduced a course, 'A University introduction to study for mature students', as an alternative route to entry. Dundee followed in 1980 ('New opportunities . . .'), Aberdeen in 1984 ('Access to degree studies') and Strathclyde in 1985 ('Pre-entry certificate'), holding out the possibility of entry – in some cases guaranteeing a place – for those completing successfully. By the mid 1980s, a variety of routes to higher education were available to those who had left school at the minimum leaving age or before gaining the required entrance qualifications. By 1992, 43 such courses were listed in nine universities, some of these in collaboration with further education colleges (SUCE Access Database 1992).

At first there was no coordination of these courses and no system of guidance for would-be entrants. In April 1988, the Scottish Education Department introduced the Scottish Wider Access Programme (SWAP), 'designed to extend access to further and higher education to adults who lack traditional entry requirements.' *(SOED, 1992b, page 25)*.

The scheme coordinated arrangements, providing funding for consortia of local authorities, colleges and universities across Scotland. Enrolments rose from 750 in 1989-90 to 1588 in 1991-92, with a success rate of 70 per cent. A substantial proportion of these are 'new client groups from a wide variety of backgrounds' (SOED, 1992d). The Education of Adults in Scotland(SOED, 1992b) makes the point more directly:

> *The success of SWAP's efforts to attract non-traditional students to higher education is testified by the fact that 39 per cent of enrolments for 1990-91 came from special areas of economic and social deprivation. (page 25)*

The percentage in 1993 had risen to 41 per cent (Report of Adult Education Conference, Glasgow, March 1993, page 4).

Provision for disadvantaged groups has recently been extended by the introduction of a Summer School for Access. The Aberdeen University Summer School, which began in 1991 targets two groups: adults who had experienced 'academic disruption' (a euphemism which means, in most cases, leaving school before gaining university entrance requirements), and senior pupils from schools in deprived areas:

> *A particular emphasis is the admission of pupils from schools serving designated areas of social and economic deprivation . . . There are special partnership arrangements with schools and the further education sector in Orkney, Shetland, Western Isles, Grampian and Highland regions, to identify and admit appropriate candidates.(SUCE Access Course Database, Section 3)*

Other regions (Lothian in partnership with the University of Edinburgh, Strathclyde with Glasgow) have similar provision. In Aberdeen, the Summer School is an intensive ten-week course, including study skills, which is seen as equivalent to one term of undergraduate study (and consequently is called 'Term Zero'). Over 90 per cent of the students continue in higher education after the Summer School. Enrolments in Aberdeen have grown from 50 in 1991 to 130 in 1992 and 160 in 1993, with twice as many applicants as places. There are no fees, and senior school pupils make up almost one quarter of the total.

Thus, through Access courses, higher education is beginning to recruit successfully people with no post-16 education and with no previous links with higher education: 'Of the 1200 students enrolled (in SWAP Access courses) in session 1990-91, 66 per cent reported that no member of their immediate family had ever attended a higher education course.' *(SOED, 1992b, page 25)*. The provision, however, is vulnerable in these times of financial constraint: 'Policies for equality of opportunity . . . (are) justifiable in the cause of improving the utilization of scarce talent, but they are investments for the medium term which may conflict with short-run economy.' *(Fulton, 1992, page 916)*. The government is putting brakes on expansion in post-secondary education, particularly in Arts and Social Sciences, the faculties which most Access students aim to enter.

As a means of tackling educational disadvantage, adult education has commonly been criticised in that: 'the main beneficiaries . . . are those who have had the largest initial educational experience.' *(SOED, 1992b, page 7)*. Or, to quote from one of those we interviewed, 'Those who come are well on the road already'. This has been described as the 'iron law of education': 'The more education people have had, the more likely they are to want more and the more competent they will be at getting it.' *(SOED, 1992b, page 7)*.

Possibly we may now be finding a way to circumvent, if not to break, that 'iron law. In the past we tended to think of 'barriers' to continuing education as residing in the *individual*, such as lack of confidence or hostility to schools. But barriers exist not only in individuals: they come also from the *system*. Because of the structure of the educational system – procedures for getting information, requirements for entry, and the widespread (hidden) assumption that higher education was not for those unsuccessful in school – access to higher education was almost irretrievably lost for those who left school at 14, 15 or 16. With Access programmes and new modular courses in secondary schools open to adults, this barrier has now certainly been breached, though it is far from being removed.

Developments in adult and continuing education in the past decade demonstrate a change in priorities. The expansion illustrates the powerful attraction of certificates and qualifications: is this what people look for primarily from education? It is a dramatic shift from the Frierean view of continuing education as empowerment for the underprivileged, and from the older view of adult education as having a humane, liberal aim. Whereas formerly education for the socially disadvantaged was envisaged as a force for radical change, it may now be seen by some as aiming to fit students for the competitive society of the 1990s. The question is whether 'adult education (and indeed all forms of formal education) seeks to perpetuate social norms rather than transform them'. *(Blair et al, 1993).*

References

Blair, A, McPake, J & Munn, P (1993)
Facing Goliath: Adults' Experiences of Participation, Guidance and Progression in Education.
Edinburgh: SCRE.

Fulton, O (1992)
Equality and higher education, in
Clark, B R & Neave, G R (eds)
Encyclopaedia of Higher Education.
Oxford: Pergamon Press.

Midwinter, A, Mair, C & Moxen, J (1988)
Rural Deprivation in Scotland. Glasgow: University of Strathclyde.

Nisbet, J & Watt, J (1984)
Educational Disadvantage: Ten Years On.
Edinburgh: HMSO.

Palmer, J (1991)
Child Care in Rural Communities: Scotland in Europe.
Edinburgh: HMSO.

Scottish Office Education Department (1992b)
The Education of Adults in Scotland.
Edinburgh: HMSO.

Scottish Office Education Department (1992c)
A Survey of the Provision for Adults in Schools: Strathclyde Region.
Edinburgh: HMSO.

Scottish Office Education Department (1992d)
The Scottish Wider Access Programme.
Edinburgh: HMSO.

Scottish Office Education Department (1991)
Local Collaborative Programme: Strathclyde Region.
Edinburgh: HMSO.

Shucksmith, M (1990)
The Definition of Rural Areas and Rural Deprivation.
Edinburgh: Scottish Homes.

StrathclydeRegional Council (1993)
The Social Strategy – Reducing disadvantage – building better communities.
Glasgow: Strathclyde Regional Council.

DOUGLAS SINCLAIR
COMMUNITY EDUCATION AND THE NEW COUNCILS
CENTRAL REGIONAL COUNCIL 1994

COMMUNITY EDUCATION

I want to try and stimulate discussion by asking two questions. Firstly, – where is community education going to be in the structure of the new Councils? Secondly, – what kind of service might be in operation?

Let's look at the first question first. We don't get any guidance in the Government's Consultation Paper, or indeed the White Paper. You look in vain for any mention of community education. There is an oblique reference that a single tier local authority structure would improve the co-ordination of service delivery by bringing sport, leisure and recreation, more closely to the Education Service with which it is clearly linked but how it is linked is not spelt out. I am less concerned about the new structures a council puts in place as opposed to the process which the new Councils go through in coming to the conclusions about structures. I have a real worry that the focus of the new Councils when they are elected in 1995 will be in many cases exclusively about structure and I suspect also that there will be collusion by at least some of the new Chief Executives with this approach! The starting point for any council must be to say – what are the needs of our communities? What are the objectives that we want to set for meeting those needs? What are the structures that can help us fulfil those objectives? Structure must follow strategy, not vice versa.

The worry that I have is that the bias in thinking in local government, dating from *The Paterson Report* in 1974, is still about prescriptive structures rather than a concern about the processes and culture of a local authority. I also have a real worry that the interests of communities will be lost or will take second place in a battleground between professionals as to who runs departments, brought together, such as Community Education and Leisure and Recreation, or in a debate which does not have as its starting point the shape of services to meet community needs, but a debate about safeguarding professional interests in the management of services, such as Social Work and Education. Just take the example of Housing and Social Work. One of the great arguments against the present two tier system is the division between the two services. As we move to single tier local government, try and find a Director of Housing who believes that he or she should be part of a Social Work Department!

There is a real danger in professional self-interest dominating the agenda to the exclusion of community interests. My other worry is not just that the interests of communities may become marginalised in this process, but the interests of voluntary groups will also become marginalised in the immediate priorities of the new councils and in the general disruption we are going to face at least one year either side of reorganisation. There must be a particular concern about voluntary organisations which currently have a regional wide remit (- there are 60 in Central Region) – who will have to secure a whole set of new relationships in many cases with more than one new council. It is critically important that they do that as early as possible in 1995 when the new Councils are elected.

Having made the point about the primary community needs determining organisational structure, let me now just touch on the issue of what kind of organisational structure. Duncan Kirkpatrick HMI in his letter to me outlined two possible approaches –

> *One – where you link Community Education to the Community Development aspects of Social Work and Community Economic Development together in a Community Services Department. The other – the concept of the Enabling Council of placing more responsibility with voluntary organisations to meet community needs.*

Firstly, I am not sure that the two models are necessarily contradictory. I say this because community education should be less about direct service provision as opposed to enabling and supporting the community to help itself. I may say that I have a reservation about the application of the true enabling model in this field – that is – where service delivery by a wide variety of bodies is separated from service specification by the local authority. It is that I do not believe that voluntary organisations, however capable, however able, can enjoy the legitimacy which local government has by virtue of its democratic nature, to act on behalf of the community in co-ordinating the work of other agencies. (Non-elected bodies do not have that legitimacy). I think that is a key feature of local government which we forget too easily.

Having made that comment about the true enabling vision of community education, I am not sure that the concept of yet another department being created, such as a Community Services Department, is any better a solution. I say this because by creating it, it seems to me you are simply creating another set of institutional arrangements which need to be crossed if community needs are to be corporately addressed. Community needs do not fit easily within the structure of any single department and the more you divide community needs into separate professional departments, the harder the task of securing cross-boundary co-operation, the harder the task of seeing community needs in the whole and in the round. My starting point would be to ask the question – Where is the greatest degree of overlap between Community Education and any other local government service? I would argue that the greatest degree of overlap is with Leisure and Recreation in for example, youth work, sports work, the arts. It's also clear that the present two tier system which splits these two services, has led to ineffective planning and duplication of effort as well as a waste of resources. The school is the key community facility and yet because many schools have not been made as available as possible by Education Departments for use as community facilities, the response by some Leisure and Recreation Services has been to build duplicate community facilities.

I think they do need to be brought together within an Education Service – not an Education Service of the past, but a new Education Service which recognises the impact that devolved management will have on the operation of the Directorate. We will I hope, move from the model of a traditional Directorate with a focus on controlling schools, to one which is about supporting schools – to one which sees education, not simply as schools education but education on a much broader basis. I think that the management of schools will go down the agenda in importance, – if this happens – other issues like pre-school provision and community education or community services will have the space to come much higher up the agenda in terms of importance.

Let me just touch on the community aspects of Social Work and of Economic Development. It does seem to me that in Social Work we are facing an increasing specialisation of the profession – the development of community care, the development of separate Children's and Families' Teams, – and whilst there is a rhetoric about the community dimension, I suspect that the increased client focus of professionalism is forcing Social Work away from that agenda. In any event I am not sure that there is a need to duplicate in Social Work the skills that exist in Community Education as opposed to a model of Social Work buying in the necessary community skills from Community Education. For example, in Central, our Social Work Service has contracted with our Community Education Service to provide a specialist worker dealing with a group of clients with mental health problems in the community. I think that makes a great deal of sense. It is recognising that you don't need to have all the skills within your service – you can buy them in from another service and the other benefit of this kind of arrangement is that it breaks down the professional barriers between councils and helps the development of networks across services. In terms of Economic Development whilst issues like community development and credit unions are important, they tend to get lost in the bigger priorities such as factories, estates and inward investment of many Economic Development Departments. I think it is better that community economic development or credit unions are located within Community Education and that any necessary professional back up is provided as a resource of expertise from the Economic Development Department.

Again in Central the responsibility for community economic development and credit unions is now with the Community Education Service, but there is a form of matrix management in place – the line management is with Community Education, but management on professional issues – to make sure that the business development expertise is not lost – is provided from the Economic Development Department.

In summary, it might be argued the perspective of Community Education has been traditionally rooted in Education – in the mind and Leisure and Recreation one might say, – in the body. What we need is to put the body and the mind together to create the whole being and relate that whole being to the community. My vision of a Community Services Section within Education headed by a manager at Directorate level would I suggest be a powerful force for community development within a local authority. I think that's all I want to say about organisational structure. Let me touch on the issue of – What kind of service?

Jim Findlay our Principal Community Education Officer talks about the "bagpipe" syndrome where a Community Education Officer says to the local community – what you need is bagpipe tuition – not because the community want it, but because that's his or her pet interest. There are still too many examples in local government of professionals who say – the customer may know what he wants, but I know what he needs and he will get what he deserves!

What we need is a Community Education Service with a clear plan of where it wants to go based on the needs of the community; a plan linked to the overall goals of the council, with clear objectives and clear performance indicators for measuring whether those objectives have been achieved or not. We do need to move away from a focus on inputs of resource to ask the question – What are we getting from that resource? What are the outputs and outcomes that have actually been achieved?

These overall service plans for the Community Education Service have to be translated into local area plans. A failure of the two tier system has been the difficulty in securing the development of effective local plans which embrace all local government services. Far too often we have seen alleged strategies for local community development which are little more than the professional priorities of one service where for example the housing issues in a community have been tackled, but the issues of unemployment, inadequate health services, poor education services have simply not been tackled. We do need to get integrated local plans which engage all local government services. One might think that single tier local government will guarantee the development of an integrated local plan for particular communities. But we should not under-estimate professional boundaries, professional jealousies and the narrowness of professional focus. Unless there is a common and shared culture amongst the key managers in the local authority about the agreed objectives of the local authority and the values and style of management for achieving those objectives, then we will get bogged down in separate professional cultures and professional rivalries.

Local government is never more innovative than when it is working across professional boundaries. I remember Anne Wallace, the Convenor, saying to me when I talked to her about what was the thing that she wanted to see most of all in local government and she said, "it was to get the local housing manager, the local headteacher, the local social work manager, the local policeman to work across the professional boundaries, to work together for the community."

I think an essential ingredient for this to happen is the need for Councils to recognise the importance of service decentralisation, to make sure that the focus of the Council headquarters is on strategic decisions and that issues about local service delivery, for the development of local strategies, should be locked into local communities. My model of ideal local government is a Council which is large enough to achieve the economies of scale with the capacity to deliver all local government services without getting into the need for joint arrangements, but at the same time recognises the need to put 'local' back into local government through an extensive scheme of decentralisation. This is something that we are developing in Central through the concept of Area Committees. These are not unique. There are other examples in Scotland. We have developed these to reflect former Burgh areas where there is still a strong sense of identity. The essential aim of these 13 Area Committees, at least in the initial phase, will be to do three things:

One – secure the accountability of local service managers.

Two – to give them delegated authority to make decisions on essentially local issues.

Third – to give expression to civic pride and identity.

I could easily see as a fourth role the development of local strategies or plans which meet community needs which go across community boundaries. I think that community education or community development, has a key role in the co-ordination and facilitation of these local strategies in helping meet the needs of communities. The links need to be made – the professional boundaries negotiated – the networking achieved – community education has the potential to deliver!

COMMUNITY EDUCATION – ITS PLACE IN LOCAL GOVERNMENT

CONVENTION OF SCOTTISH LOCAL AUTHORITIES (1995)

THE NEW UNITARY AUTHORITIES – MEETING THE CHALLENGE

The challenge which will face the new Councils in catering for the wide range of needs and services for which they are to be responsible is immense. The aspirations of the Government as expressed in the document *"The Structure of Local Government in Scotland: Shaping the New Councils"* H.M.S.O. Dd 4563 10/92, were:

> " ... *to have strong, effective and democratic local government which represents and responds, to the wishes of those it serves ... By definition, local government is intended to be responsible for issues best dealt with at local level and one of the principal aims of this re-organisation is to ensure that the new authorities are structured in a way which allows them most effectively to fulfil that role.* "

In response to concerns about the functions and viability of the new Councils, the document focused upon the accountability of local Councils, increasing emphasis on their enabling role, the scope for decentralisation, and the improvements to be gained in the delivery of several key services by bringing them together under a single authority. It was argued that the differing needs of local populations meant that the new Councils should be left to consider the forms of organisation and structure which could best meet these needs. It was also stated that:

> *"Irrespective of the structure chosen for the unitary authorities, the Government will expect all the new Councils to explore ways in which greater accountability and stronger community links can be forged with their electorates. They recognise, however, that there must be limits to how far this type of decentralisation can usefully go. After a certain level, the practical and cost implications will be unreasonable. "*

All Local Authorities would accept the principle that individuals should be educated to the limit of their abilities and in accordance with their aspirations and needs. To this end, Education Authorities have established provision for life-long education which is comprehensive in length and breadth and which is reflected in terms of structure, by undertaking the following essential roles:

(a) **Planning** – determining the pattern of educational provision in terms of demography, local views, and the criteria of educational quality and cost effectiveness;

(b) **Funding** – setting the level of revenue funding for the sectors of the Service, equitable distribution of resources, and financing of locally determined services which add value to basic educational provision;

(c)   **Statutory Duties** – fulfilling the requirements of educational legislation;

(d)   **Support Services** – providing support services to management, professional development, curriculum, finance and personnel;

(e)   **Quality Assurance** – securing high standards of provision through local professional monitoring and support, and managerial effectiveness;

(f)   **Co-ordination** – ensuring that the individual components interact to provide a coherent and comprehensive service.

In the re-organisation consultation process, although there was little support for the Government's proposals, it was reported that the principles set out in the initial consultation were widely supported. Among those principles were:

–   that the new system should be firmly rooted in the democratic tradition, and the new Councils clearly accountable to their electorates;

that the new units:

–   need not be of uniform size;

–   should reflect local loyalties and allegiances and be truly representative of them;

–   should be strong, cost-effective, resourced and capable of discharging their statutory functions effectively and efficiently;

–   should be capable of effective management of services and resources and of seeking better and more cost-effective methods of service delivery which reflect local needs, wishes and circumstances;

–   should demonstrably provide value for money across the range of statutory functions;

–   should be able to recruit sufficient staff of appropriate calibre and to train and manage them effectively.

The final map of the new Council boundaries has produced wide disparities between authorities in terms of size, geographical and social features. All will have the statutory duty to secure adequate and efficient education but they will be operating from differing economic, financial and functional experience. For all authorities, both aggregating and disaggregating, the process of formulating a clear identity and merging functions into a coherent whole will be a major challenge. The Government has stressed the advantage of bringing together a number of key services under a single authority as a means of improving delivery. In the present financial climate the ability to deliver services in the most cost-effective and economical manner possible must rank high among the priorities of the new Councils. In their role as Education Authorities, the new Councils will require time to consider the most appropriate structures to deliver their responsibilities and aspirations. Irrespective of how narrowly one defines the scope of education, it must still rate as a major area of investment by any authority. Education accounts for over a third of total Local

Authority expenditure and twice as much as the next largest service provision (1992/93 Total Expenditure £7517m – Education £2563m – Housing £1202m).

The Working Party regard community education as an integral part of educational provision and see clear advantages to be gained by considering the formal linkage of related services to education departments. The issues which authorities will need to address in arriving at their final organisational structures and delivery mechanisms will be influenced by current expertise and resources and the identified needs of the local area. It is worth stressing that many of the factors which will assist Councils in devising appropriate methods of working are currently embodied in the strategies and practices of Community Education Services throughout the country.

Three main challenges face the new unitary authorities in relation to Community Education Services:-

To Secure the Gains made since 1975 in the Community Education Service

* *Building upon best practice*
  While recognising that the new Councils will wish to forge their own identities and policies it would be unwise for them to ignore the lessons of the past. The development of Community Education Services over the past two decades has been an object lesson in bringing together apparently disparate elements of educational provision into a cost effective and efficient resource. In both philosophical and practical terms, there is much to be gained by examining current practice in the identified priorities of the authorities.

  The responsiveness and relevance of Council services will be judged at local level, by the extent to which they are seen to meet perceived needs. Community education workers are trained in the techniques of supporting communities in articulating their needs and in the presentation of these needs in a format which illustrates practical ways of meeting them. In most Regions, this type of exercise has also informed the strategic planning of the Education Department and could be applied to all local authority services.

* *Training in the Community*
  There will be a need to provide training for people at all levels within the community, a role which has been undertaken by community education workers both as direct providers and as organisers. These skills will require to be used to their maximum to secure the commitment and participation of individuals and groups. A series of national training targets have been established and it would be appropriate for community education workers, in collaboration with schools and colleges of further education, to assess the relevance of these targets to their localities and to develop strategies to meet the agreed levels of attainment.

* *Quality Assurance*
  The public focus upon performance indicators and statistics and the debates surrounding the fallibility of such figures have to some extent clouded the very real

benefits that regular review and monitoring of progress can bring. Community Education Services nationally have been involved in the establishment of appropriate performance indicators for the operations they undertake. These schemes have been defined as a standardised approach to the professional assessment of the effectiveness and efficiency of Community Education Services performance with the following main purposes:

–   to find out how well Community Education Services are performing in relation to stated aims and objectives;

–   to extend the ability of individual sectors and units of Community Education Services to communicate the results of their work and issues affecting it;

–   to help identify strengths and develop areas requiring support;

–   to provide an overall profile of Community Education Services;

–   to provide the Authority with valuable information which will facilitate decision-making including the allocation of resources;

–   to contribute information which will help consider the range of skills and abilities required in any one sector/unit.

This process is not only valuable in its own right but can be used to assist groups within a community to provide a programme for progression, evaluation, and amendment, as appropriate of their own activities and goals. It can also be seen to lend a rigour and objectiveness to the provision of Community Education Services and dispel the myth that informal work is directionless and inefficient.

To Secure the Benefits of Collaboration with other Services in the Unitary Authority

*   *Co-operation and Collaboration*
     The success of a Council in meeting the educational demands of the population will necessitate making the best use of existing resources and expertise, both within and outwith Council Departments. Community Education Services have actively pursued the practice of creating partnerships and collaborative strategies that are positively inclusive in their nature. The essence of a community education worker's professionalism is facilitation and empowerment: they will thus be well placed to support others in their efforts to develop partnership practices.

*   *Enhancement of the Quality of Life*
     The diverse needs of people cannot be met by a narrowly focused curriculum or programme. Ease of access to areas of experience within the arts, leisure and cultural fields can best be achieved through a strategic framework and a linking of participation to progress. The organisation of these services, the centrality of Community Education Services as a linchpin, and the procedures whereby policies are developed to meet a broad range of needs and aspirations demand a strong operational framework.

* *Issue-based Education*
In the complex and demanding society in which we live and work, issues relating to nationality, health, or modes of behaviour constantly arise. The difficulties of dealing with these within a formal framework is well documented but also there is clear evidence of success in achieving consensus through programmes operated by Community Education Services. The techniques, skills, and attitudes which community education workers bring to this process have much to commend them and in developing strategies for tackling these concerns, Councils will require to look at both the mandatory education system and that provided through Community Education Services.

* *Social Exclusion*
Social exclusion can be seen to indicate the position of those individuals or groups who are unable to participate and contribute fully in the society in which they live. The concept and reality of social exclusion cannot have escaped persons with responsibilities for organising or providing services to communities. The development of procedures and practices to eliminate this must on one hand be based in the educational process in schools, but there is a need to educate communities on the needs, expectations, and attitudes of young people. Community Education Services can act as a bridge between these two levels of environment both of which are of major relevance to the self-esteem and attitudes of young people. Local authorities would do well to recognise this and utilise the expertise and co-operation presently exhibited.

To Secure Wider Goals of the Council by using the Community Education Services' skills and expertise

* *Initial Audit*
As well as the necessary audit of physical assets and resources, there will be a need to examine linkages and communications at local level. Community education staff are well placed to assist in this process, since some of their skills relate to the identification of local resources and sources of support.

* *Decentralisation*
The theme of decentralisation has been to the fore in both Government and local authority pronouncements on strategies. Although the precise nature of the process has never been adequately defined, it must involve a degree of autonomy at local level to determine priorities and to finance developments. This will require to be undertaken within a strong strategic and policy framework and should not be seen as an abdication of responsibilities by Councils. Both the current practice of Devolved School Management and the provision of Community Education Services in many of the Regional Councils have this concept as a focal point. The new Councils should consider the advantages of models currently being used. Community education staff, in any consultation process have a broader role to play here, across local authority services, enhancing links between service providers and local community organisations.

* *Identifying Needs*
The responsiveness and relevance of Council services will be judged at local level, by the extent to which they are seen to meet perceived needs. Community education workers are trained in the techniques of supporting communities in articulating their needs and in the presentation of these needs in a format which illustrates practical ways of meeting them. In most Regions, this type of exercise has also informed the strategic planning of the Education Department and could be applied to all local authority services.

* *Multiple Deprivation*
The development of cross department strategies and practices to tackle disadvantage must be established. Educational disadvantage is a key feature of social exclusion. The Community Education Services have a major role to play in enabling disadvantaged young people and adults to return to learning and to assist local communities to tackle local deprivation.

The Working Party were firmly and unanimously of the view that Community Education Services could play an invaluable part in bridging the gap between the schools sector and the wider community issues which face young people in their everyday life. The concept of a continuum of educational opportunities relating to life-long learning required a firm relationship between education through the identification of community, group and individual needs and providers through schools and colleges of further education. The Community education sector was viewed by the Working Party as being best placed to provide the necessary cohesive force between these distinct and often separate elements of the educational process.

Conclusion and Recommendations

In discussing the role of Community Education Services in the framework of re-organisation of local government in Scotland, the Working Party were mindful of the legal obligations of the new councils to secure adequate and efficient education. The Working Party considered that the overwhelming demand for education and the necessity to facilitate access to opportunities had major implications for the new councils in Scotland. The translation of rhetoric into practice and the organisation of opportunities for life-long learning in a period of scarce resources would require collaborative approaches between all relevant organisations, both at strategic and operational level. The contribution of community education to the furtherance of ideals should not be undervalued and the experience of Regional Councils in welding what had been viewed as three separate elements into a coherent force should not be ignored. The expertise and experience of community education workers in facilitating developments at local level could be a crucial element in supporting the new councils in gaining acceptance and credibility with communities.

With these points in mind, the Working Party would advocate the following:

* The experience of Regional Councils has demonstrated the benefits and efficiency gained by combining the three functions – youth work, community work and adult education.

* Community Education Services should be retained as an integral part of the Education Service.

* The expertise of Community education workers in dealing with issue-based learning has much to offer the wider-Council strategies and services as well as those pertaining to the formal education services.

* The role of voluntary organisations is of major importance in delivering educational objectives and this shall be maximised by the provision of support from Community Education Services.

* Collaborative and co-operative working is an essential component in any future strategy for meeting the educational aspirations of communities. Community Education Services are well placed in terms of philosophy and training to contribute to this strategy and act as a linchpin at local level.

* There is an immediate need for an infrastructure of adult educational guidance and support at local level if people are to be encouraged to develop in the context of our complex and ever changing society. Community Education Services are an essential component of this infrastructure.

* Leisure and recreational facilities are an important resource in supporting individual and group development. There is a need to examine the relationship between Community Education Services and leisure, recreation and cultural facilities to maximise benefits of effective use of resources and support the concept of life-long learning.

* Multi-disciplinary and specialised training at all levels is of immediate urgency in terms of shared understanding of aims and philosophy and progression of common principles in addressing community needs and corporate strategies.

GUIDANCE TO NEW AUTHORITIES ON THEIR RESPONSIBILITIES FOR COMMUNITY EDUCATION

SCOTTISH OFFICE EDUCATION DEPARTMENT CIRCULAR NO 6/95

INTRODUCTION

This circular offers guidance to the unitary authorities on the discharge of their responsibilities for community education. As foreshadowed in paragraph 111 of Circular No 5/95, it supplements and complements the guidance contained in that circular on authorities' responsibilities for education more generally.

Statutory Position

Education authorities provide community education as part of the exercise of their duty under section 1 of the Education (Scotland) Act 1980 to secure the adequate and efficient provision of further education. The relevant sections of the Act, and of the Further and Higher Education (Scotland) Act 1992, which amended it, are set out in the legislative background at Appendix A.

There is no statutory definition of community education. Nor have the courts been called upon to interpret the term or to define education authorities' statutory responsibilities in relation to the provision of community education. Appendix B, however, sets out the key elements of community education provision which have been identified by HM Inspectors in the course of inspection of community education provision by existing education authorities. These key elements will continue to be the focus for future inspections of the community education provision of the new authorities.

Government Objectives

The Minister for Education at The Scottish Office has made the following statement of the Government's three main aims for community education:-

– to make life-long education a reality for the whole community, especially for those who are not yet associated with formal education and training;

– to develop collaborative initiatives amongst agencies to suit the needs of local communities;

– to support various government policies, such as rural and urban development, community care and the Citizen's Charter, through appropriate informal education.

Current Practice

With one exception, the existing regional and islands councils have integrated community education services within their Education Departments, in some cases alongside other services. The exception is Shetland Islands Council, which fulfils the requirements of the 1980 Act through a Community Work Division within its Department of Leisure and Recreation and adult education staff in its Education Department.

Regardless of organisational arrangements, the functions of community education which the SOED regards as essential and which all education authorities provide at present are:-

adult education;

educational support for community development;

work with children and young people.

These are the main functions identified at Appendix B.

There are wide and quite appropriate variations in the approaches currently taken by education authorities to their provision of community education and it is not the purpose of this circular to limit the responsiveness of the new councils to their own circumstances. The legislation does, however, place a duty on the new councils to secure "adequate and efficient provision" and attention must be given to both adequacy and efficiency.

Differing structures of internal organisation and variations in service delivery patterns mean that community education does not lend itself easily to exhaustive guidance on all aspects of provision. New councils may wish, therefore, to consider drawing up policy and operational descriptions of community education provision. There is, of course, no obligation upon new councils to do so but if they decided that such an approach might be appropriate the following general format may be useful in the preparation of descriptive schemes.

Possible Schemes of Provision

It will be for councils to determine the content of schemes but the following outline is provided simply to illustrate basic elements that might be common to all schemes:

a general description of the council's geographical areas in terms which are relevant to community education;

a description of existing community education provision;

an analysis of community education needs, showing priorities;

a set of proposals, with timescales, for any developments in community education that are seen as (a) essential and (b) desirable in relation to these needs;

a commentary on present and future organisational structures;

a commentary on resources;

a description of quality assurance procedures;

the council's objectives to secure "adequate provision";

proposals for support for, and collaboration with, the voluntary sector.

Where a council intends to secure provision through agencies other than its own department(s), it should show the principles to be used to determine when to do so, the levels and standards of provision expected and the main procedures to be used when delegating and monitoring such provision.

SOED will be glad to discuss, on an informal basis, schemes of provision as they are established. A copy of each scheme might be sent to the Department and updated as and when amendments are made. HM Inspectors of Schools would find it helpful to have the latest version available when inspecting community education provision in a council area.

SOED Guidance

SOED will make every effort to respond positively to requests from authorities for guidance on their responsibilities in the field of community education and on their ways of addressing these, whether in relation to their schemes of provision or more generally. The Department recognises that community education is an evolving field and is interested to hear from the new authorities of any plans for innovation or change that may be of benefit to other authorities.

APPENDIX A

Community Education: The Legislative Background Statutory Position

1.   Section 1 of the Education (Scotland) Act 1980, as amended, includes these relevant provisions:-

"(1)   It shall be the duty of every education authority to secure that there is made for their area adequate and efficient provision of school education and further education.

(2A)   The duty imposed on an education authority by subsection (1) above shall not include the provision of further education within the meaning of Part I of the Further and Higher Education (Scotland) Act 1992, but an education authority shall have power to provide such further education for their area.

(3)   Every education authority shall for the purposes of their duty under subsection (1) above

(a)   have power to secure for their area ...
        the provision of adequate facilities for social, cultural and recreative activities and for physical education and training.

(5)   In this Act

    (b)   further education includes ...

        (i)   [Provision revoked by the Self-Governing Schools etc. (Scotland) Act 1989, Schedule 11]

        (ii)   voluntary part-time and full-time courses of instruction for persons over school age;

        (iii)   social, cultural and recreative activities and physical education and training, either as voluntary organised activities designed to promote the educational development of persons taking part therein or as part of a course of instruction;

        (iv)   the teaching of Gaelic in Gaelic-speaking areas.
[Section 1(3) and section 1(5)(b) were amended by the Local Government and Planning (Scotland) Act 1982, Sch. 3 para. 37.]

2.   Education authorities' duty to provide further education was modified by section 2(b) of the Further and Higher Education (Scotland) Act 1992, which inserted the new subsection (2A) in Section 1 of the 1980 Act. For the purpose of subsection (2A), further education within the meaning of Part 1 of the 1992 Act (i.e. that which the education authority has a power, but no duty, to provide) comprises, in terms of section 1(3) of the 1992 Act:-

"any programme of learning, not being school education, provided for persons over school age, being a programme falling, for the time being, within section 6 of this Act."

3.   Section 6 of the 1992 Act provides:

"(1)   A programme of learning falls within this section if it -

    (a)   prepares a person for a vocational qualification;

    (b)   prepares a person for -

        (i)   a Scottish Examination Board qualification; or

        (ii)   a General Certificate of Education qualification of England and Wales or Northern Ireland;

    (c)   provides instruction for persons who are participating in a programme of learning which falls within this section and who have a learning difficulty within the meaning of section 1 of this Act;

    (d)   prepares a person for access to higher education;

(e)   is designed to assist persons whose first language is not English to achieve any level of competence in English Language;

(f)   is designed predominantly to prepare a person for participation in any programme of learning which falls within this section."

[Sections 6(2) and (3) provide for amendment of the list, after consultation, by order of the Secretary of State.]

4.   Section 6 of the 1980 Act provides:-

"(1)   For the purposes of securing, under section 1(3) of this Act, the provision of facilities for social, cultural and recreative activities and physical education and training, an education authority may -

(a)   establish, maintain and manage -

(i)   camps, outdoor centres, playing fields and swimming pools;

(ii)   play areas and centres;

(iii) sports halls, centres and clubs;

(iv)   youth, community and cultural centres and clubs,

and other places at which any such facilities as aforesaid are available;

(b)   organise holiday classes, games, expeditions and other activities.

(2)   In the exercise of their powers under subsection (1) above an education authority

[(a)]   may assist any body whose objects include

[(b)   shall, so far as practicable, co-operate with local authorities and with voluntary societies or bodies whose objects include,]

the provision or promotion of social, cultural and recreative activities and physical education and training or the facilities for such activities, education and training."

Note

Section 6(1) was amended by the Local Government and Planning (Scotland) Act 1982, Schedule 2, paragraph 28.

Section 6(2) is amended by the Local Government Etc (Scotland) Act 1994, Schedule 13, paragraph 118(3) and Schedule 14.

(The amendments will delete the square-bracketed words and are intended to take effect on 1 April 1996.)

APPENDIX B
Key Elements of Community Education Provision

1.   Adult Education

Community education plays a major role in providing adult learning opportunities, primarily offered in community settings. While the main focus of this work may be described as community-based adult learning, provision is also available within institutions, often in collaboration with further education colleges and schools. Such joint initiatives enable adults to return to learning, to acquire certification within community sites and to progress, if desired, to more formal programmes. The general term adult education is, therefore, used in this circular in the interests of simplicity.

Local provision includes:

> independent educational guidance for adults linked to cross-sectoral regional guidance networks;

> courses and other educational activities which enable people to develop their confidence, knowledge, understanding and skills, thereby enabling them to progress to more formal education and training, if desired;

> courses and other educational activities which are negotiated with individuals and groups in order to address such issues as social, environmental, economic and health needs, particularly in relation to government programmes and community needs, and to enhance employment prospects;

> courses, offered in community and work based settings, to develop basic skills and offer certificated options, thus extending access to lifelong learning;

> educational opportunities for people (both users and carers) with needs in relation to community care. These may take the form of courses (both specialist and mainstream) providing an education component to community care programmes (for example, developing skills for independent living, participation in education, training, sheltered employment and in social and recreational situations).

2.   Educational support for community development

Aspects of community development, such as participation or learning based on a group's own activities, are characteristic of much community education but are also found in other fields of work. Its qualities concern the methods of work employed, the processes that take place in communities and the achievement of improvements in quality of life. Although it is of particular concern to areas with major social, economic and environmental disadvantages or needs, community development can be relevant to all local areas.

Educational support for community development includes activities which, taken together, are generally referred to as community work. This includes providing community groups and organisations with educative, organising and, where appropriate, technical support. Educational support also extends to other activities that would not always sit easily under the heading of community work. Educational support for community development includes:

supporting local involvement in democratic processes, as in the decentralisation arrangements for local government;

maintaining and developing access to educational expertise, advice and facilities for individuals, community groups and organisations;

supporting the establishment of, working with or for local, ethnic, minority and interest groups or organisations, using methods that emphasise working and learning together, that help them to be effective, to take responsibility and to tackle disadvantage;

promotion of, and support for, volunteering and for voluntary organisations;

educational support for communities engaged in community regeneration and community enterprise;

informal educational support to communities in relation to government programmes and priorities;

devolution of responsibility for community education operations in ways that strengthen the local capacity for decision-making.

promotion of such interests as sports and the arts in ways which support community development

## 3.	Work with children and young people

Such work is designed to foster the personal and social development of children and young people. It is clearly educational, has a measure of adult intervention and young people participate in a voluntary capacity. It includes:

informal youth club provision and the programmes of voluntary youth organisations;

after-school care and holiday playscheme provision;

detached youth work;

health education programmes, particularly in relation to alcohol, tobacco, drugs, HIV and AIDS;

residential , outdoor and environmental education programmes;

youth information services;

crime prevention;

issue-based work;

sport and the arts.

4.　　Common to all functions

Effective collaboration with other providers of education including the voluntary sector, to help ensure that communities are served by the education system in the most effective and efficient ways possible.

Effective collaboration with other organisations and others in the new councils to promote good communication, effective strategies and cohesive responses by statutory bodies to the needs of communities.

Assessment of community needs and development of appropriate strategies for intervention.

Effective collaboration with members of communities to secure the development of community education.

Provision of grant-aid to the voluntary sector, where appropriate.

SCOTLAND AS A LEARNING SOCIETY: MYTH, REALITY AND CHALLENGE

SCOTTISH COMMUNITY EDUCATION COUNCIL, 1995

INTRODUCTION

People learn in many different contexts, and they learn better and more effectively if the whole society in which they live regards learning as a natural activity for people of all ages. In such a society:

* it would be taken for granted that virtually everyone would wish to engage in some form of learning at different stages of their lives;

* education would no longer be regarded as an activity largely confined to schools and colleges and appropriate only for children and young people;

* structures, working hours and other aspects of employment, and social life, both nationally and within local communities, would be adapted to encourage learning and provide everyone with ready access to the facilities they require to pursue the kind of learning they need or want.

Knowledge, skills, understanding, curiosity and wisdom cannot be kept in separate boxes, depending simply on who is paying for or providing them. Neither training systems nor educational institutions, nor informal learning opportunities – no matter how high the quality – will be enough on their own to meet the learning needs of society. This report uses the term "learning", in preference to "education" in many instances, in order to emphasise the natural and lifelong nature of learning and to avoid the widespread tendency to equate education with only the work done in schools and colleges.

It may have been this kind of realisation that led Robert Hutchins, writing in 1968, to define a Learning Society as *"one that, in addition to offering part-time adult education to every man and woman at every stage of grown-up life, (has) succeeded in transforming its values in such a way that learning, fulfilment (and) becoming human (have) become its aims, and all its institutions (are) directed to this end"*. An updated version might read: *"A society whose citizens value, support and engage in learning, as a matter of course, in all areas of activity"*. It is a vision of Scotland as that kind of society which forms the basis of this report.

Contrary to much popular belief, there is no single set of "roots, values and traditions" at the heart of education in Scotland. Enthusiasts for the Scottish tradition have made much of the poor but talented "lad o' pairts" whose eventual success in our education system is presented as the proof of its openness and essential fairness. In practice, the picture is less impressive. The present system:

* is arguably less "democratic" than is often claimed;

* is individualistic in emphasis and tends to reinforce gender stereotypes in its treatment of young people;

* creates a sense of failure in many young people who do not succeed in climbing the competitive ladder it provides;

* fails to sustain beyond school the relatively high levels of academic achievement attained in comparison with England;

* results in relatively high levels of employee related training offered to young people in comparison with England, but low levels of workplace training offered to adults over the age of 20 in comparison with England;

* results in only 20% of the adult population in Scotland engaging in organised learning, compared with 24% for Britain as a whole (NIACE, 1994).

Any attempt to reform Scottish education has to contend with the contrast between the high value which Scottish people often place on education, and the mixed feelings and reactions which many of them display towards it in practice.

Nevertheless the current education scene in Scotland is characterised by good community-based adult learning initiatives, which succeed in engaging adults who do not normally seek out learning opportunities. A further strength of the present system in recent years has been the growth of cross sectoral adult educational guidance networks. *Adult Learners' Week* has played an important part in their development. Both these features, however, are highly vulnerable to ad hoc and short-term present funding arrangements and to the imminent changes in the structure and organisation of the education system.

This report reaffirms the existing good practice and the reputed value of education held within Scottish society, but challenges individuals and organisations to give greater substance to the valuing of learning.

The main reasons are:

* because knowledge and skills inevitably go out-of-date and are currently doing so at an increasing rate. This is true not only in economic and work areas but also in the social arena. Much attention is rightly focused on how employees are to keep up with technical change in their work situations: it is no less important, however, to equip parents to keep in touch with their children and young people, and to enable citizens in general to cope with political and cultural change.

* because a great deal of human potential is being neglected by the present system. This neglect affects people as learners and, less obviously, as learning resources for each other. The wasted potential is of many kinds, not just intellectual. It restricts and reduces individuals' economic performance, as well as their contribution to the social and cultural life of their communities and the country as a whole.

* because a healthy modern society needs its people to possess a high degree of critical awareness. Unless they acquire the critical skills to cope with the power of advertising, media manipulation, and floods of information and disinformation, and to interpret and respond to social, political and economic trends, society and the individuals within it will suffer. The damage will be of many kinds, ranging from financial fraud to impoverishment of the whole culture.

* because learning is a profoundly social activity, as well as an individual one, and our social relations need strengthening. Learning alongside other people assists social communication and promotes collective understanding: it is especially vital in the present era of increasing privatisation of what have hitherto been public services.

* because the protection of the environment depends on people acquiring levels of knowledge and understanding of our world well beyond their current levels. What is more, learning itself can lead to active ways of living in a society which make more modest demands on the world's natural resources than the high-consumption, mainly passive, lifestyles of many people today.

* because even the most progressive schools are not able to meet all the learning needs of our young people and communities. In our vision of a Learning Society effective schools would be a vital element in the life long educational process.

* because we need to build capacity. People need support to develop their potential to contribute to the economic growth of their society.

How would we recognise a Learning Society if we saw one, or more to the point, if we found ourselves part of one? It would be relatively easy to describe it in material terms alone, by referring to levels of financial and physical resources and other easily measured features. A full description, however, must also include less tangible factors, such as prevailing attitudes and values, levels of participation, etc. We believe that a Learning Society would have the following essential characteristics:

* Learning would be a crucial element in people's sense of personal and community identity, encouraging positive attitudes to their communities and to society as a whole, a willingness to accept their responsibilities for determining its future, and a dynamic understanding of tradition;

* Levels of resourcing would match and confirm the importance given to learning. A society's commitment to learning is not measured by rhetoric but by the priority it receives in the allocation of limited resources. This applies at all levels of society – national, local and domestic. It applies to the distribution of resources among different areas of need, including geographical areas, as well as their overall volume;

* There would be a high quality infrastructure – buildings, and communication systems – capable of supporting and encouraging the pursuit of learning, by providing real access for all citizens, and the best achievable physical environment and facilities for the purpose;

* A supportive legal and administrative framework would be designed to encourage learning and to remove barriers and disincentives to would-be learners. This would involve not only establishing individual rights and entitlements, but also framing obligations on employers and other organisations to ensure minimum standards of provision and/or financial commitment;

* Good industrial practice would be encouraged and supported, including formal commitments by employers, of the kind encouraged by *"Investors in People"*. Human resource development would be positively valued and explicitly included in a company's statement of accounts;

*   People would find it easy to move through successive stages of a learning process and from one learning opportunity to another. They would receive appropriate incentives and rewards for learning achievements, which need not be material;

*   A place would be found for a positive valuation of human growth through learning in the assessment of the society's economic and financial progress;

*   The whole society would be notable for the high degree of participation of its citizens in all areas of activity. Measures of this kind would include the uptake of existing learning opportunities in different geographical areas and among all sections of the population.

We believe it important, as well as articulating the main features of the vision of Scotland as a Learning Society, to offer some specific targets, which we see as practical goals to work towards within an identified timescale. Progress can be assessed in a number of ways, by comparing present with past performance within our own society and by looking at the levels of success achieved in comparable societies, in Western Europe and elsewhere.

We present here a list of target arenas and, within each, a number of national targets in pursuit of the long-term goal of establishing Scotland as a Learning Society. We wish to avoid painting an idealised picture and consider these targets to be realistic and achievable, although we acknowledge that their attainment will present a serious challenge to many established priorities and assumptions in Scottish education and in the wider society. Within the proposed framework, councils, companies and local organisations are invited to adapt and adjust the targets to take account of their own priorities.

Participation

One of our main aims is to increase the total number of people taking part in adult education in Scotland and to attract them from a wider cross-section of the population and, in particular, from groups who have traditionally been under-represented among adult learners.

In order to do this we need a broader debate on the meaning of learning and its place in society. A comprehensive study of people's attitudes to learning, with the findings regularly monitored and updated, would be a major step towards both stimulating and informing such a debate. The material produced would be useful both for promoting learning opportunities and for planning programmes and activities. Specifically we propose that:

a)   the percentage of all adults taking part in education should be increased by at least 3% in each of the next five years;

b)   the number of students in adult education drawn from hitherto under-represented groups – including the long-term unemployed, unskilled and semi-skilled men, the over 50s, the unskilled employed, members of ethnic minority communities and disabled people – should be increased disproportionately to the total;

c)   the number of adults engaged in part-time further and higher education should be increased in absolute terms and as a proportion of the total number engaged in education;

d) the support and guidance infrastructure in further and higher education institutions should be expanded and strengthened to assist student retention rates.

Investment in Employees

The need for employers – in the public, private and voluntary sectors – to see their employees as their most important assets and to invest resources in their development is, we believe, central to the creation of a Learning Society. Personal development combines employment-related skills with learning based on individuals' own interests, to the mutual benefit of employers and employees. To this end, we propose that:

a) every working adult should be guaranteed a small group guidance meeting in the workplace, at least once every two years;

b) the proportion of corporate budgets spent on employee development schemes, staff development and paid leave for educational purposes should be increased.

c) a sponsored consultancy service should be set up to support the expansion of employee development schemes, especially among small and medium-sized employers.

Government Investment

Central government will have a key supportive role in the creation of a Learning Society, in enacting appropriate legislation and increasing the level of investment necessary to make the concept of lifelong learning a reality. In particular, we propose that:

a) the percentage of the Gross Domestic Product (GDP) spent on education should be increased and a greater proportion of the total allocated to broadening the base of participation in learning by hitherto under-represented groups;

b) the number of nursery school places should be increased so as to achieve the target of places for all 3 and 4 year olds by the year 1999;

c) there should be equity of funding for full-time and part-time students in post-school education.

d) the allocation of additional resources should be aimed at increasing participation in education in areas/among groups where uptake of learning provision is low.

National Initiatives

We recognise the need for certain steps to be taken at national level, in order to bring about some of the key changes in the political and economic climate that are required for the creation of a Learning Society. Specifically, we propose that:

a) every long-term unemployed person should be guaranteed a free, 2-hour impartial guidance interview annually;

b) the percentage of adults lacking essential skills, such as literacy, numeracy, communication skills and basic familiarity with information technology should be halved over the next 10 years;

c) a National Human Resources Audit should be undertaken by the Advisory Scottish Council for Education and Training Targets and conducted at regular intervals;

d) the Advisory Scottish Council for Education and Training Targets should develop a target for general vocational training and non-vocational programmes which are designed, as a first step, to rekindle the desire and ability to participate in post-school education and training.

The Active Society

Targets for society as a whole are more difficult to formulate, but they are crucial to the creation of a Learning Society. Responsibility for the building of a Learning Society lies not only with the education providers but with the whole range of organisations and institutions in Scotland. We propose that:

a) parental involvement in schools, measured by the number and quality (in terms of levels of participation in decision-making, etc.) of Parent-Teacher Associations, Parents' Associations and School Boards, should be increased;

b) educational broadcasting to encourage and support learning should be increased;

c) increased use of libraries, theatres, museums, cinemas, leisure and sports centres should be actively promoted amongst hitherto under-represented groups;

d) the growth of self-help groups eg study circles and community-based learning groups providing networking, mutual support and learning should be encouraged;

e) new communications technology should be put at the service of adult learners and teachers;

f) the level of involvement in voluntary service and community work should be increased;

g) all local authority departments (not just education departments) should be encouraged to recognise their role in stimulating and supporting learning;

(h) the proportion of the population voting in local, national and European elections should increase.

We have the real possibility of creating, in Scotland, a Learning Society. Many of the constituent elements are already in place - an increasingly effective primary and secondary schools sector; a revamped further education college structure, a Community Education Service that uniquely in Europe offers an integrated structure for the promotion of lifelong learning; a progressive library and information service; and a small but significant voluntary sector. There is growing evidence of increasing business and education partnerships. There is, however, much still to be done if the vision of Scotland as a Learning Society is to be realised.

We hope this paper will stimulate a debate and subsequent action. The targets that we have identified are an initial list and we would fully expect these to be re-worked, expanded and made more specific by each company, organisation or authority.

We also hope that the sense of urgency expressed by many in the group may be shared by those who receive this document. We believe that the forthcoming *European Year of Lifelong Learning* in 1996 will be a further stimulus to future action.

The challenge confronting us is to recapture the positive and enthusiastic belief in the power of learning and in the worth and potential of all our people. The practical promotion of Scotland as a Learning Society would be a significant step towards releasing the creative capacities of this nation.